The History Of Scottish Pop & Rock:
All That Ever Mattered

for Joe

The History of Scottish Rock and Pop
all that ever mattered

Brian Hogg

GUINNESS PUBLISHING

First published in 1993 by
GUINNESS PUBLISHING LTD
33 London Road, Enfield, Middlesex EN2 6DJ, England

Guinness is a registered trademark of Guinness Publishing Ltd

This work is Copyright © Brian Hogg 1993

All rights reserved.
No part of this publication may be reproduced, stored in a retrieval system,
or transmitted in any form or by any means, electronic, mechanical,
photocopying, recording or otherwise, without the prior permission of both of
the copyright owners.

British Library Cataloguing-in-Publication data
A catalogue record for this book is available from the British Library

ISBN 0-85112-723-1

Library of Congress Cataloging-in-Publication Data
A catalog record for this book is available from the Library of Congress

Produced by
SQUARE ONE BOOKS LTD
Iron Bridge House, 3 Bridge Approach, Chalk Farm, London NW1 8BD
Edited and Designed by Colin Larkin
Editorial and production: Susan Pipe and John Martland
Additional production assistance: Alex Ogg, Fran Lass, Marina Arnold,
Ben Larkin, Guy at L & S and Ian Slater
Special thanks to Mark Cohen, David Roberts and Simon Duncan
of Guinness Publishing

Image set by L & S Communications Ltd

Printed and bound in Great Britain by The Bath Press

Contents

Introduction *page 7*
Prologue *page 11*
Part One: *Beatstalking*
Chapter 1: Jump Jive And Wail *page 13*
Chapter 2: Beat City *page 26*
Chapter 3: Something To Shout About *page 39*
Chapter 4: 'I was fired four times.
I left on the fifth occasion' *page 49*
Chapter 5: The Invisible Insurrection *page 62*
Chapter 6: It's All Leading Up To Saturday Night *page 74*
Chapter 7: '…wearing black cherries for rings…' *page 91*
Chapter 8: In The Land Of Dreams *page 102*
Chapter 9: Pick Up The Pieces *page 113*
Chapter 10: Please Sing A Song For Us *page 124*
Chapter 11: Keep On Dancing *page 131*
Chapter 12: Tomorrow Belongs To Me *page 137*

Part Two: *New Thing In Cartons*
Chapter 13: Deranged, Demented And Free *page 155*
Chapter 14: Goodbye 1970s *page 199*
Chapter 15: 'Get on with your life or you'll end up like
Meaulines' *page 209*
Chapter 16: 'The commodity itself made the laws.' *page 218*
Chapter 17: Electric Heat *page 232*
Chapter 18: 'One day I'm listening to Wes Montgomery,
the next it's Johnny Thunders.' *page 243*
Chapter 19: Wishing I Was Lucky *page 256*
Chapter 20: Truckload Of Trouble *page 268*
Chapter 21: 'We didn't have any scheme
to be bigger than Elvis.' *page 283*

CHAPTER 22: HAMISH MACALPINE *page 295*
CHAPTER 23: YOU'LL NEVER BE THAT YOUNG AGAIN *page 303*
CHAPTER 24: A TASTY HEIDFU *page 319*
CHAPTER 25: 'I MET ALL THE P-FUNK PEOPLE AND BECAME A SPACE CADET.' *page 329*
CHAPTER 26: 'I AM THE LONE RANGER'S ONLY FRIEND. THE MARTIANS HAVE LANDED' *page 343*
CHAPTER 27: RIMBAUD AND ME *page 356*
EPILOGUE *page 369*
DISCOGRAPHY *page 371*
BIBLIOGRAPHY *page 401*
INDEX *page 405*
PHOTOGRAPHIC ACKNOWLEDGEMENTS *page 415*

INTRODUCTION

What is a Scot?

Should we cheer when Glasgow-born Ray Houghton, playing for the Republic of Ireland, puts the ball past the Oldham-born Andy Goram, in goal for Scotland?

This conundrum was the subject of a BBC radio 'phone-in, and a similar quandary was posed preparing this book. The qualification 'Scottish Rock and Pop' is partially useful, as is 'Rock and Pop in Scotland', but it's clear such parameters requires a lengthier explanation. It's convenient to begin by listing names not discussed herein, for instance; Annie Lennox, Jack Bruce, Jimmy Somerville, Ian Anderson, Bill Drummond, Robin Guthrie and Elizabeth Fraser. Their absence is due to the fact that such individuals found fame as exiles, and their careers have progressed without apparent reference to Scotland. Success followed irrespective of birthplace, and for those who, by the same token, query the presence of Alan McGee, I can only counter that the face of Scottish music would have been much poorer, and distinctly different, without the existence of Creation Records, despite its London base.

Lonnie Donegan is also featured, despite an early exit from Glasgow. His pioneering role in British pop, particularly at a time when little heed was paid to performers north of the border, demands an acknowledgement. Scottish music prospered by his influence in a way it has not done under Annie Lennox, irrespective of whatever talent she may have. Folk singer Donovan is another artist who won attention outside of Scotland, but his work would be considerably diminished without the influence of his homeland.

What is Scottish pop and rock? The answer is two-fold. It begins in 1955, when the rock 'n' roll of Bill Haley and Elvis Presley exploded in Glasgow and Edinburgh; it describes acts and entrepreneurs who began a career in Scotland, or moved elsewhere, and how this affected their successors. As well as Alex Harvey, Alan Gorrie, Alan Horne, Jim Kerr and Jim and William Reid, such figures also include Stuart Adamson, Bob Last, Eugene Reynolds and Lloyd Cole, none of whom was born in Scotland, yet whose work places them in its cultural context. In short, this is not a Scottish Nationalist diatribe, a 'wha's like us' of pop. If so, then I could logistically argue for the inclusion of Talking

Heads, whose co-founder, David Byrne, was born in Dumbarton. Again, the nascent Beatles and Rolling Stones are unthinkable without Stuart Sutcliffe and Ian Stewart, respectively sons of Edinburgh and Pittenweem. That both were axed from early line-ups produces a convenient conspiracy theory, which I'll leave to that tartan warrior in the corner.

Nationalism is not on offer here, but a certain pride is, and if asked to précis my reasons for writing this book, it is because Scotland has produced some excellent music and the mercurial characters to match it. It's a story that needs telling.

I started this book in 1985, inspired by the BBC Radio series, *Beatstalking*. Its early draft closed with the death of Alex Harvey, but reactions from publishers generally fell into two camps. Scottish publishers were, at that time, wary of pop, while others were equally shy of anything Scottish. So it goes.

Work continued, not apace, but with considerable enthusiasm. More material was gathered, the subject was brought up to date, and a second period of feverish activity began late in 1991 when the title was commissioned by Colin Larkin at Square One Books who involved Donald McFarlan who was at Guinness Publishing at the time. I'd like to thank them both for showing faith in the title and author.

This book would not have happened without the unflinching support of Stewart Cruickshank. His advice, suggestions, and assistance were invaluable and I'm deeply grateful for it. Access to his cache of interviews, particularly those of the 'pre-punk' era, was crucial to the project's development. Puzzled musicians who can't quite recall our meeting are correct; they spoke to Stewart. He gave me records, contact numbers, and a floor to sleep on, and although we've been friends for more years than we care to mention, I still can't say 'thank you' enough.

I'd like to acknowledge all those who consented to answer questions, some of whom did so at considerable inconvenience. Meeting old acquaintances and making new ones was one of the book's unexpected bonuses. Deacon Blue, being 'too busy to be interviewed', was the only refusal I had, and although I enjoyed a stimulating 'phone call with Wet Wet Wet manager Elliot Davies, I could not agree to the pre-conditions set in order to interview his charges. Their uncredited statements herein are derived from the BBC Radio documentary *Glasgow A Go-Go*.

Where conflicting schedules prevented a 'one-to-one' with an individual, I have referred to other sources. I'm indebted to the pages of *Cut* and *TLN* from whom I've drawn occasional quotes; thanks too to the late, lamented *ZigZag*, whose interviews with Gerry Rafferty, Bert Jansch and John Martyn were particularly illuminating. Non-original statements are, as far as possible, acknowledged in the text, but I apologise for any error or omission which may have occurred.

On a sadder note, one of the book's contributors, Linnie Patterson, vocalist with Writing On The Wall, has since died. I retained his observations intact as a tribute to one of Scotland's under-rated talents. Phil Smee was a staunch fan of Linnie's group, following them across the home counties during the late 60s. This devotion is now recognised in print. Both he and Peter Doggett were sounding boards during the book's long gestation and I appreciate their counsel. Peter Rimmer and Cara Stewart have brought new meaning to 'Friday Nights', and our lengthy discussions on almost every topic helped refocus work-in-progress and provide a much needed sense of perspective.

Last, but not least, I want to thank my partner Jacki, who has survived hours of dodgy b-sides and withstood the full tantrum when the words 'fatal error' replaced a chapter following the unseen intervention of small fingers. She knows how much this book means to me and, in doing everything possible to help, has remained an unflinching source of strength.

Brian Hogg
July 1993

PART ONE
Beatstalking

PROLOGUE

Albert Bonici was the entrepreneur who, in 1960, booked the Beatles for their first appearance on the Moray Firth circuit. Be it luck or shrewdness, he later became the group's Scottish agent, a post he retained throughout the Beatlemania era.

In 1967 the Alan Price Set was following a similar path along the northeast coast. They came offstage following one engagement and, in the dressing room, Bonici pulled aside the group's trumpeter, John Walters. 'At least you lot know how to behave,' the promoter confided. 'See those we had last week, the Cream?' He shook his head. 'I'll tell you this. They'll never play Elgin again.'

Hindsight allows us a smile. By that point Bonici was slipping into the past while Cream represented the future, three superb musicians bonded by mutual respect. Their's was a brave new sound; improvisational, radical, and unfettered by commercial considerations. They were anti-pop, and where the norm was a flash of success followed by obscurity, Cream demanded permanence. To the promoter, however, it was just another group, one-hit wonders who would pass and be replaced, their individual reputations meaningless.

Cream, of course, had no further use for Elgin. They, and others, turned pop into rock, a move which, within a handful of years, would change the face of Scotland's music. Bonici's words represented a last act of defiance by an old guard about to be eclipsed.

Chapter 1
Jump Jive And Wail

No matter how hard the diligent reader scans their entertainment pages, newspapers from the early 50s show little sign of the impending rock 'n' roll rumble. Dancehall programmes reflected the pattern of the previous two decades, when big bands offered standard routines, and weekends were passed in the archaic splendour of local ballrooms. Each of Scotland's major cities boasted a succession of venues. Although fewer than in pre-war years, they nonetheless supplied an intoxicating mixture of dance styles, such as old-time, Latin American, Scottish Country as well as modern. To those born since those days it has the feel of Ealing cinema, of a generation lost in time, queuing for the advertised late-night buses, 'specials' laid on to return them to housing schemes sited on the outskirts, the answer to overspill and slum clearances.

The bands modelled themselves on those they heard on the wireless; the Ted Heath Band, Henry Hall or Ambrose And His Orchestra. Generally they were large, in-residence aggregations in which the musicians followed set arrangements of standards and sweet current favourites, performed with taste and strict tempo according to their adopted style. Edinburgh, for example, boasted the Palais de Danse in Home Street, the Locarno, McDonald's, the Excelsior, the Plaza, the New Cavendish (with two halls) and the Victoria. Such establishments featured, among others, George Sumner And His Orchestra, the Bill Shearer Quartet and John Baxter's Orchestra, the last of which was billed as being of 'rare ability'. However, when Baxter took his musicians from the Assembly Rooms to the Locarno, their replacement, Alexander And His Band, assumed the same billing. Perhaps such ability was not so rare.

The image of propriety was, however, misleading. Some halls had notorious problems with sporadic gang fights erupting in the rush for territorial claims and shattering the evening's entertainment. But, whatever their individual variations, the ballrooms were bound by one common factor. They remained, inflexibly, adult domains.

The early 50s saw the dawn of a defined youth culture, one independent of, and often at odds with, its parent. In a move curiously echoed some 10 years later, certain Savile Row tailors enlivened drab male fashion by introducing lines recalling the classic Edwardian suit; a long jacket with narrow lapels, bright waistcoat and close-fitting trousers. This flamboyance had been intended for the dandies of Mayfair but, in a perverse twist, it was snapped up by a completely different group, stuck in south London slums. Disaffected by poverty and post-war austerity, many of the locality's teenagers took to such finery as a means of proclaiming their individuality. Their clothing was quickly exaggerated; velvet was pressed on to the collars, trousers (or jeans) became drainpipe tight, while bootlace ties and thick, suede shoes proved similarly essential. Hair was long and greased, swept back into a 'duck's arse' quiff known as a D.A. As the Edwardian style became extreme, so the name was bastardised into Teddy Boy.

The new sub-culture lay dormant until 1953 when the 'Teddy Boy' murder on Clapham Common propelled it to national prominence and fired the indignation of the press. The image of snarl was born; of idle youth bent on mayhem, flick-knives, razors, and senseless violence, lurking on street-corners at the edge of suburbia. Pockets of Teds began appearing in many deprived areas as the focus for a malcontent generation. Money was tight and entertainment dull, while a desire for self-expression was doubly fuelled by the barrage of excitement coming from the USA. Films, notably *Rebel Without A Cause*, encapsulated their 'outcast' image, and the new generation empathised with James Dean's starring role. Few teenagers embraced the new creed wholeheartedly, but many were thankful for the opportunities now offered.

To the adult world this was another erosion, the same challenge to values posed in the play *Look Back In Anger*. Its author, John Osborne, was even dubbed an 'intellectual Teddy Boy' by the generation who'd fought for clear-cut standards and resented these questions from within. Youth naturally scorned the sociologist and merely looked for fun. Too young to drink legally, they took instead to coffee bars where Gaggia machines spurted expressos and jukeboxes blasted out rock 'n' roll.

Pin-pointing the origins of rock 'n' roll is problematic. The music is merely part of an evolution, pitched somewhere between jump blues and boogie woogie. At first the style was exclusively Black American, but when stirred with a dash of rebel C&W, it broke free of a 'race music' tag to become something more cosmopolitan. The new exponents were white enthusiasts of R&B - Bill Haley And His Saddlemen based themselves on the joyful rock of the Treniers - while early Elvis Presley releases were drawn from songs by Arthur Crudup, Junior Parker and Roy Brown. White faces made these songs acceptable to mainstream pop, but while remaining controversial, the success they enjoyed was seen in national terms, and not that of a specialist fringe.

Lonnie Donegan

Bill Haley's 'Rock Around The Clock' passed by almost unnoticed on its first British release in September 1954. The track later became the aural backdrop to *The Blackboard Jungle*, a menacing Hollywood flick chronicling a teacher's struggle against surly hoodlums in a collapsing New York school. The brazen beat which accompanied the opening credits was aligned with the malevolent fights peppering the plot. Music and violence had already become intertwined in the minds of an uneasy older generation. Riots on screen inspired riots in cinemas, riots in cinemas inspired riots outside; Teddy Boys, trouble and rock 'n' roll forged a triumvirate perceived as unbreakable. Pressure from outside naturally increased loyalty within. 'Rock Around The Clock' reached number 1 in October 1955; it was, by then, too late to stop.

The new order was not lost in Scotland, merely obscured. Rock 'n' roll was seen as another passing fad, a momentary madness which did not require consideration. Little of it would touch the ballroom world of cosy consistency and most of the danceband musicians poured scorn on this vulgar pop. A few, however, not only listened, but were genuinely excited. These included Ricky Barnes, George McGowan and Bill Patrick.

'Big bands dominated the early to mid-50s,' recalls Patrick. 'They were there when you turned on your radio or went dancing. One or two smaller groups existed to let the others go to the bar, but running parallel with waltzes, tangos, quicksteps and foxtrots was the dixieland revival.'

Dixieland - traditional or trad jazz - had gradually become more prevalent in Scotland. It seemed more rootsy than the conservative dancehalls, and several specialist clubs, including the Stud Jazz and the 88, were already in operation. The ballrooms were not entirely blind to this shift; the Edinburgh Palais ran a lunchtime jazz session - records only - while Alex Welsh And The Clyde Valley Stompers began attracting a new audience. Meanwhile modern jazz was also an important influence, though it was heard less than its dixieland counterpart. Saxophonist Ricky Barnes featured in several of Glasgow's dancebands.

'The cool era was in and Stan Getz was the big thing on tenor; everyone tried to play like him. I was fortunate to be in the Beavers, who won an all-Britain contest run in *Melody Maker*. They were big; five saxes and an eight-piece brass section, but as everyone played in other bands they only gigged about once a month.'

Barnes subsequently joined the resident ensemble at London's Streatham Locarno, before enjoying spells in the Palais de Danse in Nottingham, Manchester and Belfast. He returned to Glasgow in 1955 where he founded the 'wee band', with Stevie O'Neill (vocals), George Scott Henderson (piano), Jimmy Bell (bass) and Jackie Holden (drums).

'We played a lot of Louis Prima stuff and a rhythmic, 'shuffle' music very like early rock 'n' roll. None of us could live on the money we earned, so that band led on to the Ricky Barnes All-Stars.'

Over the next few years the saxophonist led what could arguably be described as Britain's first rock 'n' roll combo, pre-dating London-based pioneers Rory Blackwell's Rock 'n' Rollers and Tony Crombie And His Rockets. Indeed, Barnes' passions mirrored English-based contemporaries also flirting with alternative sounds and styles. Both the Five Smith Brothers and the Kirchins introduced the occasional R&B tune to their accustomed Afro-Cuban preferences. Others drifted from New Orleans jazz to Crescent City beat, on the way discovering Smiley Lewis and Fats Domino. Such bands were rare however, and what separated Barnes was his foresight and commitment. Fellow musicians took a dim view of the saxophonist's ambition, as George McGowan, later a drummer in the All-Stars, freely admits. 'I was a jazz man. I didn't want to play on the off-beat all the time, but to do it properly, of course, took a great deal of effort.'

The original line-up featured Barnes, Holden and O'Neill from the R&B band, adding Bernie O'Connor (double bass) and a now-forgotten guitarist. O'Connor bought an electric bass when his old instrument was smashed in a car-crash. In fact, the All-Stars' rigorous schedule was regularly plagued by problems in the pre-motorway UK. The engine of their first car blew up en route to Hexham, while a replacement Dormobile struck a dry-stone dyke and turned over. 'There were no windows left in the van. We put it back on its wheels and drove back to Glasgow – and it was snowing.'

While Barnes endured the perils of one-night stands, another Scot grabbed national prominence. Anthony 'Lonnie' Donegan was born in Glasgow of Irish ancestry in 1931, but his family later moved to London's East End. Although never an integral part of Scottish beat, his influence was vitally important. Demobbed in 1951, Donegan took up the banjo and, having joined the trad jazz circuit, was a member of the band supporting Lonnie Johnson at the Royal Festival Hall. It is from this stellar bluesman that the young musician took his stage name.

Donegan steeped himself in the American folk tradition, learning Leadbelly songs from Library Of Congress records borrowed from the American Embassy. He later surfaced in the 'skiffle' group that Ken Colyer's Jazzmen featured during intermissions. The term skiffle originally referred to music heard at Chicago rent parties or 'shebeens', but it was popularised by black journalist and pianist Dan Burley. Colyer's skiffle interlude, which began in 1949, offered material drawn from country blues and work songs, a repertoire which coincided with Donegan's own infatuations. His performances steadily grew in popularity, particularly when trombonist Chris Barber took control of the group.

In 1954 the renamed Chris Barber Jazzband recorded a 10-inch album, *New Orleans Joys*. Its content included two Leadbelly songs, 'Rock Island Line' and 'John Henry', credited to the Lonnie Donegan Skiffle Group, which were coupled as a single the following year. Donegan left for a solo career when the new release charted and, dubbed 'the Irish hillbilly', became the mouthpiece for the skiffle trend. Sung in an adenoidal whine, the material he subsequently recorded brought many their first glimpse of traditional music. 'Alabama Bound', 'Stack O Lee', 'Midnight Special' and 'Stewball' were featured on Donegan's early recordings and displayed his remarkable range of taste.

But if Donegan was the 'King of Skiffle' he was not its sole proponent. The Original London Blue Flowers pre-dated even Colyer's first experiments. Soho's coffee-bars; the Gyre and Gimble, the Nucleus, the Breadbasket and 2 I's, boasted hopefuls thrashing on washboards, guitars and a tea-chest bass, singing songs about railroads, lust and murder. The music's home-made quality was its main attraction, a factor not lost on Scotland.

'The campers and hitchhikers appeared about the same time as the dixieland revival,' says Bill Patrick. 'They would go away on a Friday night, pitch a tent up Balloch or at Loch Lomond, and come back on Sunday. Everybody seemed to have a guitar, and they played what we now call country and western, stuff like Jimmie Rodgers or Hank Williams.'

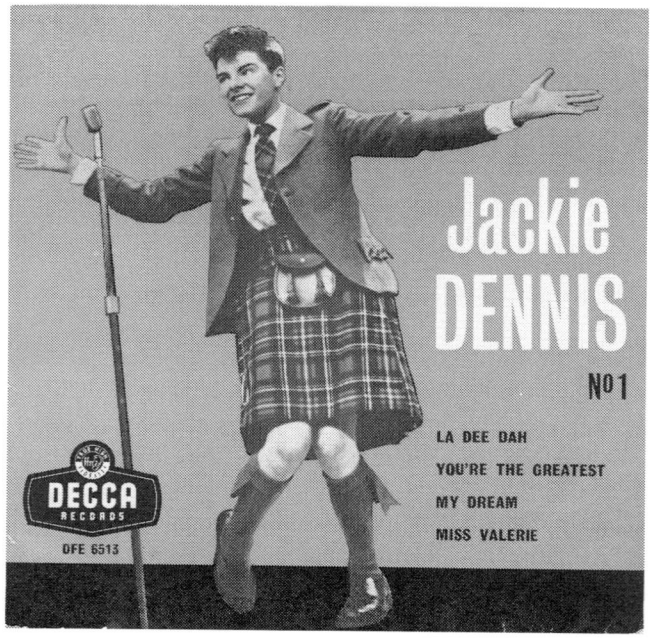

Jackie Dennis' first EP for Decca

A surfeit of war-surplus equipment provided the impetus for this piquant pastime, which was also inspired, in part, by gatherings of the Young Communist League and a nascent CND. These weekend hobos sought temporary relief from urban miseries, and the evenings' campfire entertainment provided a valuable grounding for many aspiring musicians. Angus MacKenzie – later successful as Karl Denver – was one of several singers drawing from songs of blue-collar optimism alongside material introduced by merchant seamen. The role played by these figures has been exaggerated out of proportion, the image of sailors scouring ports to bring shellac-coated manna to anticipatory hordes is largely a romantic one. When individuals returned with songs they'd heard or 78s they'd bought, these were imparted to those already interested. The seamen, many of whom enlisted as an alternative to National Service, were catalysts, not harbingers, who travelled to places where this music was more freely available.

The individual parts were set: the R&B/rock 'n' roll of Ricky Barnes and the folk/blues of Donegan's skiffle. This was compounded by newer US releases resulting in a potent stew other musicians were unable to ignore.

'I came to music through listening to guys like Gerry Mulligan,' remembers Patrick. 'I had been in the big dance bands, about fifth saxophone, but found it rather unsatisfactory. Then I heard Bill Haley's 'Two Hound Dogs Called Rhythm And Blues'. I didn't know what it meant, but I loved the sound the band was making.'

Patrick rehearsed at Bill Paterson Studios, an agency in Glasgow's Argyll Street. He knew of its reputation for offbeat characters, but was still surprised to see a group fronted by someone with long hair held in a headband.

'This was, of course, Alex Harvey, who at that time fronted a trio playing semi-wild country music. He decided they would be better with me on saxophone, but although I didn't like it at first, the more I heard what he was playing, the more I was attracted. It was Hank Williams, 'Jambalaya' and all that, but the way Alex did it was different.'

Legend has it that between leaving school and becoming a performer, Alex Harvey had more than 36 jobs. If so, some of that wanderlust was reflected in his music. He was born in Govan on 5 February 1935 and reputedly relished his first professional appearance playing trumpet at a friend's wedding. Although never its master, Alex played the instrument in a dixieland band, but left soon afterwards for a career as a singer/guitarist.

'I'd never heard a guitar played the way Alex did – he was hitting it – and he shouted more than sang. The result was very, very exciting. He tried to play in a country style while I preferred jazz, and while knocking the numbers about came up with, I suppose, Scottish rock 'n' roll.'

With Patrick now inaugurated into the line-up, the reshaped unit made its debut at the Daily Record Ballroom Championship in 1955. A part of Bill

Paterson's touring roadshow, they shared the stage with comedians and tap dancers. They were, in fact, both of the bands featured that evening. For the first set they became the Clyde Valley Jazz Band, neatly dressed in evening suits, white shirts and black bow ties.

'We sat at desks with nicely printed sheet music, which some of us couldn't read, and proceeded to play trad favourites like 'Georgia Cat Melody'. At the interval we changed into red jerseys with the legend 'rock 'n' roll' across the front and charged onstage singing 'Hound Dog' as the Kansas City Skiffle Group. The result, at first, was stunned disbelief. Then they yelled and threw things, demanded their money back and walked out in disgust.'

Antipathy towards the new beat was widespread. Dancebands resented these smaller, cheaper groups and any venue considering rock 'n' roll was fearful of the trouble it might attract. A whiff of conspiracy filled the air and many acts sought refuge away from the city centres.

'Places like Clydebank and Kirkintilloch were better,' Barnes remembers. 'In Cumnock there was a dance formation team, all kids of about 16 or 17, called the Alligators who used to follow us everywhere. They all wore black pullovers with the troupe's name on them.'

'Smaller towns and villages welcomed up-to-date music,' Patrick concurs. 'One of our first gigs out of town was in the Northern Meeting Rooms in Inverness. Within five minutes farmers in their boots were up onstage with the band, while policemen tried to throw them off.'

The dancehalls maintained their damning stranglehold as arbiters of taste, and in Edinburgh, Portobello's Inchview Ballroom splashed 'No Edwardian Dress' across advertisements. The Locarno, however, showed a measure of adventure with its Tuesday 'Jive, Be-Bop and Swing' sessions, while Edinburgh also boasted the short-lived Teenage Hall. Their counterparts in other cities would follow, but by then it was much too late as demand had pushed both performers and audience towards different venues and musical directions.

'About this time a friend of ours came back from America with a record by Syl Austin,' says Patrick. 'The first track was a thing called 'Happy Birthday' and we heard sounds we'd never heard before. Guitarists played things we thought were impossible, so did the saxophonist, and right away we knew we had to do this too.'

The Kansas City Skiffle Group thus became the Kansas City Counts, and the Clyde River Jazz Band was ceremoniously jettisoned when the group pawned the trumpet of a recalcitrant Bill Paterson. Harvey did adopt a folkier perspective with the Alex Harvey Skiffle Group, in which he was joined by younger brother Leslie, but this act was abandoned when the genre's allure faded. Meanwhile, Ricky Barnes continued to bring international pop to the traditional village hall dance, offering a set half-evergreen, half-rock 'n' roll, until enough strong rock numbers had appeared. The group were extremely loud, being one of the first to use amplification, prompting comments from a Greenock journalist that the sound resembled a jukebox. 'I told him that was my intention,' says Barnes.

The trickle of classic US singles quickly became a flood as new names – Little Richard, Carl Perkins, Jerry Lee Lewis – succeeded those of Haley and Presley. The new pop could no longer be ignored and the search began for a homegrown rock 'n' roll star. Impresario Larry Parnes took merchant seaman Tommy Hicks out of a bustling coffee bar underworld and, having renamed him Tommy Steele, recorded the ludicrous 'Rock With The Cavemen'. The song re-painted the genre by numbers, replete with the most appalling couplets – 'Stalactite, stalagmite,/Hold your baby very tight' – but Steele's later success as a Cockney Happy Harry places the blame squarely on all of the participants. However, he was British, or more precisely a Londoner, and as such attracted considerable excitement. The *Daily Record* responded in April 1957 with a competition to find 'Scotland's Tommy Steele', which the gallus Alex Harvey not only entered, but won.

'Anyone less like Tommy Steele I couldn't imagine,' said Patrick. 'Alex was a screaming blues shouter where Tommy was polite, but they were photographed shaking hands as a publicity stunt.'

The pair became firm friends over the ensuing refreshments and on hearing that Steele's former ship was berthed at Princess Docks, Alex volunteered to take the star to see his one-time crewmates. Refused admission at the gate, the pair climbed the dockyard wall, only to be apprehended by the police. 'They narrowly escaped jail,' recalls Patrick.

Rock 'n' roll had been confirmed as something more than frivolous in February 1957 when Bill Haley appeared in the UK for a tour. His arrival inspired scenes of mayhem, but rioting was assuaged by the spectacle of this paunchy performer and the now-obsolete sound of his group. Haley's departure home was unremarkable.

His visit did not extend to Scotland, but an appearance at the Glasgow Empire by Freddy Bell And The Bellboys created a telling impact. Within weeks the Ricky Barnes All Stars were using elements of the Bellboys' stage routine in their act and sporting new suits cut without lapels. By this point the line-up had changed with Joe Moretti (guitar), Bobby Taggart (piano) and Leo McGory (drums) featuring in the All-Stars, who shared the bill with the Kansas City Counts at Paisley Town Hall. Dancing was forbidden at this all-seater venue, but the thrill of rock 'n' roll proved overpowering and the struggle between the audience and management exploded in turmoil.

'The next day it was on the front page of the *Daily Record*,' recalls Barnes. 'We couldn't believe it. A riot in Scotland.'

'There had been riots in cinemas,' says Patrick. 'but this was live. The place erupted while we were on, seats were torn up, it just went mad. A police inspector demanded that everyone stopped playing. So we did, but the audience kept on rampaging. The day was saved by a young man who appeared in full highland regalia, whistling old-time Scottish songs. Within five numbers they were in the palm of his hand.' A distracted clientele was thus treated to the then-unknown Sidney Devine, who later became a popular, if somewhat derided, 'all-round' entertainer.

Despite the increased attention, there was little appreciable difference in the lives of those musicians slogging between Dornoch and Dumbarton. The All-Stars maintained their popularity, but in the absence of a record deal, were unable to break new ground. They appeared twice on television's *6.5 Special*, and later travelled south to audition for *Boy Meets Girl*. 'We didn't get it,' Barnes recalls, 'yet some of the bands that did were not nearly as well-rehearsed as us.' Crucially, a chance to appear at the London Palladium was turned down when the fee was deemed insufficient.

'It was the first time any theatre had asked a rock 'n' roll band to perform,' says George McGowan, by that point drummer in the All-Stars. 'The Palladium had to have one and this guy - John Barry - was asked to get one together. Look where he is now.'

As Tommy Steele was soon seduced into the world of pantomime, so former manager Parnes groomed a gaggle of aspirants - Marty Wilde, Dickie Pride, Billy Fury, Duffy Power - in the hope of emulating his popularity. Steele's most obvious successor was, however, Cliff Richard. His debut single, 'Move It', was certainly superb, but the singer's metamorphosis into an all-round entertainer confirms the event as a happy accident. Meanwhile, Scotland was not slow to spot the potential of matching beat with showbiz and, in 1958, Edinburgh's Jackie Dennis was launched as a kilted Elvis. The tartan ploy was an age-old prop, honed to perfection by the music hall star Harry Lauder, but in an age of gimmick it brought results and Dennis was rewarded with a Top 5 hit, 'La De Da'. A cultural stereotype had been horribly reinforced. Dennis travelled to the USA to guest on *The Perry Como Show*, a first for British rock 'n' roll, but momentum faltered with his follow-up single, an ill-advised stab at Sheb Wooley's 'Purple People Eater'. It did reach the Top 30, but the singer's fall was as spectacular as his rise. Despite his brief popularity, Jackie Dennis left little impression on the development of Scottish music.

There were other, momentary, Celtic pop stars. Henry Robinson, a former reporter at the *Elgin Courant*, was musical director of Jack Good's pivotal *Oh Boy* show and, as Harry Robinson, fronted the eccentric Lord Rockingham's Eleven. 'Hoots Mon' filtered 'A Hundred Pipers' through Johnny And The Hurricanes, but while obviously tongue-in-cheek, it nevertheless implied continued cultural reliance on shortbread and Highland Games. Karl Denver, inspired by his spell at sea, introduced a more cosmopolitan perspective at the beginning of the 60s with 'Marcheta' and 'Wimoweh', but despite his laudable ambition, the singer's vocal gymnastics quickly became parodic.

The All-Stars and Counts' English contemporaries were the groups which appeared in the late 50s and swamped England's 'transport cafe' circuit. These included Neil Christian And The Crusaders or Screaming Lord Sutch And The Savages, who barnstormed the countryside producing a frantic noise, ambushed from US singles, but splattered with an anglicised panache. Among the best was Johnny Kidd And The Pirates, whose riveting debut 'Please Don't Touch' was bettered only by 'Shakin' All Over', the consummate British, pre-beat single. Much of the latter's hookline was derived from a plucked guitar pattern and menacing solo courtesy of Joe Moretti, who had left the All-Stars for session work.

The Kansas City Counts had meanwhile tired of a name which lent itself to obscene alternatives. By 1958 they were the Alex Harvey Band; by 1961 Alex Harvey And The New Saints, both taken in deference to the frontman who had emerged as their star. However, the unit decided on yet another title under which to pursue their new direction.

'We lost all desire to be a pop band; we'd heard too many new things,' remembers Patrick. 'There was an advert for Horace Silver in *Crescendo* where they spoke about Soul Jazz. That was where we took our name from, long before Stax and Tamla came along.'

The group became known as the Alex Harvey Soul Band and, as such, defined an obsession with black urban styles that subsequently characterised Scotland's music. Material by Muddy Waters, Ray Charles and Bo Diddley became an integral part of a set honed to R&B perfection and peppered with songs that were barely known outside the States. 'We'd pick out names from American papers,' says Patrick, 'and then send away for their records.'

The highlight of the act was 'Shout', a gospel-influenced clarion-call first recorded by the Isley Brothers. Having discovered the song on a jukebox in a Wick cafe, the Soul Band decided to include it in their repertoire. 'We persuaded the owner to give us the record, which we sang on the way to the gig by way of rehearsal.' Patrick recalled. 'It made us into a heavy R&B group.'

'Shout' was always open-ended, a vehicle for improvisation or simply a means to transmit passion. It took on a different dimension in Harvey's hands. Rather than simply play favourites, his group used seemingly disparate parts to create something new and vibrant. By emphasizing personality and pursuing a specific path, they laid the foundations of a distinctive Scottish rock music.

It was at this time that George McGowan left the All-Stars for the Soul Band. 'Both worked for the same booking agent,' he recalls, 'and we'd pass each other on the road. I got to know Alex well and when his drummer left he asked me to join. His band was not as clean-cut as Ricky's; they were all readers, but it was very exciting.'

If the music was different, the cramped travelling regime was just the same. 'We were all packed in the Dormobile, the band and the equipment. You had to lie on top of the gear until it was your turn for the front seat. Then Larry, our piano player, decided to get some vibraphones. They were brand new, so he got a joiner to make him a case. It was shaped like a coffin and four of us had to lift it into the van. Old guys beside us would take their hats off.'

By the early 60s the balance between dancehalls and smaller venues was changing. Although ballrooms were still dominant, trad jazz was heard in several clubs, many of which welcomed R&B groups as fellow pioneers. These smaller venues were often open into the early hours, flourishing at the dancehalls' expense. Glasgow's groups and their prospective audience welcomed the arrival of La Cave, an all-night locale in a side lane off Jamaica Street.

'It was a low, dark place,' Patrick recalls, 'very like the old Marquee with its stage in one corner. You could eat supper or breakfast and hear good trad bands like the Steadfasts, powerful R&B from the Soul Band or modern jazz from Tubby Hayes. It was one of the first places in the city to break the stranglehold of danceband music.'

'The Soul Band played La Cave on Wednesdays, Fridays and Sundays,' states McGowan, 'and the Steadfasts had Thursdays and Saturdays. They used to show up on a Sunday and we put the two bands together. We went their way rather than they come ours, Alex could sing traditional stuff like 'Doctor Jazz', but it was absolutely amazing.'

It was at La Cave that the Soul Band made its final appearance in evening dress. Garden shears had been brought for the occasion as, one by one, the musicians symbolically cut away their suits. 'We wanted a new, definite image to match the music,' says Patrick, 'and at their peak the Soul Band was a sight to behold. We had silver lamé jackets, red shirts and trousers, white high-heeled boots and gold bow ties. It really was fantastic.'

Yet even while something strong was building, those who set the foundations were tiring of their role. 'I began to find it just a bit too provincial,' Patrick continues, 'and wanted to get south. George and I left the band and joined the Brook Brothers, who'd hit with 'Warpaint'. They were a good pop band and we toured all over Britain with them.'

McGowan and Patrick subsequently worked with a succession of visiting US acts, including the Four Seasons, Brian Hyland and Little Eva. Now based in London, the saxophonist was able to compare the music he had left behind with that on offer in that city's clubs.

'Their scene was a year or two behind and bands who became famous performing R&B were still doing pale covers of American pop. Some were catching up, Georgie Fame And The Blue Flames and Graham Bond were playing the kind of music we'd done in the Soul Band, but they were in London and so got the recognition. Bands staying in Scotland missed the bus.'

Bill Patrick's elder brother, Bobby, quickly learned that lesson and Bobby Patrick's Big Six was already a fixture on the capital's burgeoning nightclub circuit. Ricky Barnes had also opted to move south, although a group bearing his name continued for a further two years. He took whatever club work came his way, and one night was surprised to find the Big Six playing to a deserted venue.

'I recognised their bassist Archie Leggatt, who they got from me. They were doing one of my arrangements, a Louis Prima thing called 'Jump, Jive And Wail', so I opened up my saxophone case, got up on stage and joined in. When I finished Bobby called me out. They were auditioning for a German club owner. "Would you mind leaving us alone?" he said. I felt a right clown, but when I got to the bar this agent said he liked my playing and offered me a job with a band he had.'

Within hours Barnes was *en route* to Hamburg where he remained, barring short breaks, for the next 12 years. But if several musicians were abandoning Scotland, others remained, at least temporarily. The Alex Harvey Soul Band had regrouped and seemed as fresh as ever, while newer acts rose to the challenge they posed. At first there was only a handful, but the rise of Merseybeat transformed that trickle into a flood.

CHAPTER 2
BEAT CITY

Scottish music entered the 60s with a mentality still based on the previous decade. Although a mere eight ballrooms remained in Edinburgh from the 36 active before World War II, their decline was due to rival entertainments; cinema, television and bingo, rather than an upsurge of clubs. Several had been established, but if La Cave enjoyed relative longevity, many others were temporary affairs, abandoned when the profits fell or the fire department called. Nascent beat groups sprouted throughout the country, such as the Meteors, the XL5, the Bellrocks (with future Searchers' drummer, Billy Adamson) and the Cyclones, but there was little to bind them together other than restricting themselves to an anaemic Top 20.

'Even in 1962 there was nothing you could call a Scottish scene,' says George Gallagher, lead singer with the Poets. 'Ballroom dancing was still in vogue and pop bands were just an aside to the main event. When Alex Harvey left for Germany there was no group left of any real eminence.'

Tired of a sterile circuit, the Soul Band had moved to Hamburg in 1963. Ricky Barnes was, by then, an established figure there, working in the Top Ten Club as resident saxophonist and houseband leader. Another ex-patriot, Ian Hines (brother of actor Fraser), handled all the venue's bookings and, not surprisingly, several Scottish bands were presented. One such act to arrive was Bobby Patrick's Big Six, the same band Barnes had gatecrashed in London. The group even secured a recording deal, and a series of dazzling releases would appear over the ensuing two years. 'Shake It Easy Baby' and 'Monkey Time' were issued in Britain, along with the *Teenbeat: Three* EP, and together these records showed a group blending cool R&B with soul. Their final single was a sympathetic rendition of 'Comin' Home Baby', but the Big Six was the exception, rather than the rule; for most other groups recording was confined to impromptu, informal sessions.

The Top Ten Club had a studio at the rear of the building. Having finished a series of punishing sets around three o'clock in the morning, Ricky Barnes would then record for another few hours, creating singles for the in-house jukebox or commercial release. 'The Top Ten did a couple of records with Isabel Bond,' says Ricky. 'She came over with the Crescendos, but stayed behind when the group went home to Scotland. Isabel was a great singer; some nights I used to get shivers up my back, but the singles just didn't take off.'

Barnes' skills are also tucked away on numerous albums released in Germany at this time. He accompanied Tony Sheridan on the Polydor releases the singer made following his work with the Beatles, and also completed an R&B set with respected jazz musician Knut Keisavetter. Ricky's searing solos revealed a style honed to grab the attention of an audience otherwise occupied by cheap alcohol, brawling and sex. Should you pick up a copy of the *Live In Hamburg* set recorded at this time, and if it has a saxophone, it is likely to be Barnes, bolstering the raw recruits for whom Hamburg was a magnet.

'The Top Ten Club was a great place for young musicians. It made them three times, four times better than when they came in. Alex Harvey came across because there wasn't enough work for him in Scotland. He was way ahead of the competition, both as an experienced player and for his feel for the blues. None of the Liverpool groups had it – and I mean none of them – they were more like showbands. Alex built an atmosphere, it was a driving, swinging thing and you could see the excitement on the faces of the crowd.'

Early promotional poster for the Alex Harvey Soul Band

The Soul Band followed Barnes into the Top Ten studio, where they too cut several acetates of current favourites which were given a bewildering array of pseudonyms; Bruce Wellington And His Robber Band, Jimmy Doyle or Ian Other. By this point the group was exceptional, with the addition on bass of Jimmy Grimes, a long-time friend, providing Alex with a perfect foil. Early members Bobby Rankine (ballad singer), Willie White and Charlie Carsware had been replaced, and Robert Nimmo (rhythm guitar), George 'Hoagy' Carmichael (tenor saxophone) and Wally Stewart (congas) joined a prodigal George McGowan in completing a quite enthralling line-up.

Polydor agreed to sign Harvey to an 'official' contract, but although *Alex Harvey And His Soul Band* was Scotland's first rock album, there was a last peculiar twist. Harvey's backing band was not his official group, but another culled from members of Kingsize Taylor And The Dominoes, including bassist Bobby Thompson and drummer Gibson Kemp. The reason was doubtlessly contractual; these musicians were already Polydor artists, but it meant that the 'real' Soul Band was sadly never caught in full flight.

Such reservations apart, this is an authoritative album. Recorded in October 1963, Alex sings and plays with poise and confidence, the music is exciting and the set boasts several skilful arrangements. The best example, 'I Just Wanna Make Love To You', is pitched at seduction. Relaxed and mildly erotic, it is many miles from the adolescent smash and grab the Rolling Stones offered some six months later. 'Framed' is equally impressive. The familiar greeting of 'My name's Alex Harvey' sets the scene for a catalogue of set-ups and crumbling alibis as the singer wailingly protests his innocence. By coincidence, or not, the same song became the touchstone of Harvey's renaissance and final acclaim in the 70s.

Elsewhere the album glides through New Orleans jump, country blues and Chicago R&B, compressing Muddy Waters, Lonnie Johnson, Shirley And Lee and Rodgers And Hammerstein ('When I Grow Too Old To Rock') into an original, affectionate farrago. Its importance cannot be exaggerated and had the Soul Band been domiciled in London, or signed to a label with secure distribution, the commercial result in Britain might have been different. This, however, was the first in a long series of imponderables plaguing successive Scottish groups struggling through the decade. While *Rhythm And Blues From The Flamingo* by Georgie Fame was rightly lauded, Harvey's earlier, equally innovative set was all but ignored, passed over because it was authored by a group still stuck in Hamburg, a city that pop's new heroes had long since abandoned.

There was little change in fortune when the Soul Band, belatedly, began playing in London. They debuted in February 1964 at the Jazz Club at 100 Oxford Street and were later featured on the bill at (Long John) Baldry's Blues Club in a benefit for Cyril Davies' family. Davies, co-founder of the seminal

SCOTLAND'S BEAT PAPER
Lennoxbank News

BANDS — CLUBS — DISC TIME BY RAYMOND BOYD

No. 3   NOVEMBER, 1963   Sixpence

STAR OF THE MONTH

BILLY FURY

Photo by courtesy of New Record Mirror.

Band for United States

IT was announced by the Norman McFarlane Organisation, who are the sole agents for the U.S. Base at Dunoon, that the United States Navy have asked for the four top bands who entertain their men in Dunoon to be recorded.

The reason for this is that one of the major broadcasting companies in America is interested in putting on a special show using the recordings made here. It is understood that the band which creates the most interest will be flown over to the States for a week, during which they will tour, broadcast and appear on television.

The groups which have been chosen to make the recordings are **Dean Ford and the Gaylords**, **The Blue Notes**, **The Kinning Park Ramblers**, and **Steve, Cathy and the Boleros**. Recordings will be made early this month and sent over to the States.

La Cave Re-opens

AS predicted in our first issue, the La Cave, Midland Street, Glasgow, has re-opened. Now under new management the promoters hope to turn it into the equal of Liverpool's Cavern.

The policy of the Club is to present the best in Beat and Jazz bands. Bands which have so far appeared at the Club since it re-opened are the "Bathgate Crusaders," the "Steadfast Jazz Band," "Fabulous Falcons" with the McKinley Sisters, and the "Jaguars" from Cardross. The La Cave has been under the management of many promoters, let's hope that it's here to stay, so that we can spend many a happy hour at the Cave.

A Bigger and Better "Lennoxbank News"

IT'S better than ever now, thanks to your support!

All this has entailed extra costs, so the price goes up to 6d from this month's issue—

It's Great Value At That!

Lightfoot Tour

WELL-KNOWN outfit Terry Lightfoot and his Jazzmen will be doing a five-day tour of Scotland during this month. Dates arranged for Terry are at Hamilton; Whitecraigs—Giffnock; The Tech., Glasgow; Bearsden; and Dunfermline. Terry Lightfoot and his Jazzmen have toured Scotland on several occasions with great success, and no doubt the success will be repeated on this tour.

An early issue of Lennoxbank News

Blues Incorporated and a gifted harmonica player, had died of leukaemia the previous month. Harvey's appearance owed something to yet another Scots connection, as he was now represented by Glaswegian Malcolm Nixon.

'At the beginning of the 60s Malcolm took a folk show to Russia as part of a cultural exchange,' says Andy Lothian, one of Scotland's leading promoters during the 60s. 'When he came back he established an agency in London and while both Baldry and Davies were in his stable, his devotion attracted many Scottish bands.'

Nixon initially found work for Scotland's trad bands, most notably the Clyde Valley Stompers. The Soul Band joined the growing agency, but despite several appearances in London clubs and dates in Manchester, Newcastle, Glasgow and Edinburgh, they were little further forward and, as George McGowan recalls, very often hungry.

'There was a place in Soho where we went nearly every day for a college pudding and a pint of water. You ate half of it, drunk half the water, ate the other half if that was possible, and finished the water. That way you were bagged up for hours.'

A second Harvey album, *The Blues*, was recorded in Hamburg in June 1964. The sessions lasted two days, but although the driving R&B the group had pioneered was now firmly in vogue, it was virtually a solo collection and primarily acoustic. The sole support came from Leslie Harvey, who had grown from childhood aspirant to adolescent prodigy. In 1957, at the age of 11, he had formed the Kinning Park Ramblers Skiffle Group, an ambitious septet which shed its suffix and later re-emerged as a quintet. Robert (Bobby) Kerr, Thomas Graham, Donald McChristie and Pauline Boyle completed the realigned act which became a popular fixture on Glasgow's west side. Leslie subsequently led several other bands and was plucked from his school group, the Ramblers, to provide muted electric accompaniment on this particular session. The material was suitably idiosyncratic, encompassing several songs obviously drawn from Harvey's early years among the hikers. Material by Jimmie Rodgers and Woody Guthrie vied with 'The Big Rock Candy Mountain' and 'Kisses Sweeter Than Wine'. While 'Danger Zone' and 'St. James Infirmary' confirmed the blues of the album's title, the brothers also contributed two stylised originals. In itself the set is entertaining, but again an opportunity had been missed. The attendant liner notes hint at a forthcoming full Soul Band release, but by 1965 the group, tired and in debt, had been disbanded. Alex and Jimmy Grimes stayed together, vowing to explore folk-based music.

Two singles contradicted this desire. 'Ain't That Just Too Bad' caught the gusty verve of the late-period Soul Band, while 'Agent 00 Soul' was a vibrant reading of Edwin Starr's popular soul classic. Uncompromisingly uncommercial, they made little impression and a disillusioned Harvey retreated home to Glasgow.

The Scotland Alex returned to in 1966 was markedly different to the one he'd left behind three years earlier. The catalyst was, of course, the Beatles, who not only focused the ambitions of basement singers and boxroom guitarists, but threw pop at a much wider audience than that reached by rock 'n' roll.

'They saved us from obscurity,' says Pete Agnew, later bassist in Nazareth. 'We were getting Mark Wynter and stuff like that, then these guys started singing 'Please Please Me'. I thought, "Yeah, that'll do."'

In 1961 Agnew was playing in the Dunfermline-based Shadettes, who stalked the local dancehalls in Fife and Edinburgh. 'We mixed pop things with original American material. I mean we already knew 'Needles And Pins' when the Searchers brought it out because we'd heard Jackie DeShannon's version.'

In Glasgow the Poets were also forging a career, priming chart hits with their esoteric taste. 'Hume Paton and I were really into blues,' recalls George Gallagher, 'Lightnin' Hopkins, Howlin' Wolf and Sleepy John Estes. We also began writing our own material, and played it live, right from the beginning.'

Formed in 1961, the Poets survived the fallow early years to become part of the flourishing circuit which evolved in the wake of Beatlemania.

The Poets

'The Glasgow scene developed rapidly, probably overnight,' says Gallagher. 'The Sabres, the Meridians, Dean Ford And The Gaylords; all of these bands suddenly mushroomed. They must have been doing what we were trying to do, wondering where it was going, when all of a sudden...'

Most new groups took a dash of Liverpool and mixed it with pop standards. A succession of largely forgotten names, including the Phantom Five, the Chaperones, the Winklepickers, suggested the general impression that this new sound, like skiffle, would prove temporary and would be replaced by another fad within months. It was the opportunists who would benefit, as pop fever gripped a teenage generation too young to remember, or even care about, Elvis Presley's Sun releases or James Dean's death. Beat clubs sprouted everywhere, eager to snatch a piece of Mersey pie. 'Some clubs were awful,' remembers Gallagher, 'a room and kitchen knocked together. Others, such as the Gamp and the Place, were great.'

The two clubs, which faced each other in Edinburgh's Victoria Street, were central to the capital's thriving circuit. London entrepreneurs Brian and Paul Waldman had arrived in Edinburgh during the 50s and, as one-time employee Bruce Findlay remembers, were responsible for founding several crucial venues. 'The Waldmans opened Bungys, Edinburgh's first beatnik-styled club and coffee-bar, at the turn of the 60s,' he states. 'You had to look 'student-y' to get in. The Tempo Club followed, then the Gamp and Place.' The Gamp was almost home to the Athenians, the first Scottish-based beat group to record a single. Released on the Waverley label in January 1964, 'You Tell Me' had been cut to aid the students' annual charities appeal and distribution was confined to the university shop, Jeffrey's Audio House, who owned Waverley, and the Gamp itself. In truth the performance was weak, especially when compared to the group's highly positive stage show, but the self-penned song represented a start, of sorts.

The Place was, indisputably, the city's leading club. Opened in 1962 as Jazz At The Place, the venue's name mutated into the Place Jazz Club, and later, the Place. Its bohemian origins remained intact throughout its early years and whereas the Gamp was nascent Mod, its 'rival' attracted a quite different clique. 'In winter the two queues threw snowballs at each other,' recalls Findlay, reflecting a time when inter-club rivalry was confined to such simple self-expression. By 1963, however, the Place was featuring Edinburgh's early beat groups, including the Telstars, the Sapphires and the Premiers, as well as attracting the cream of Glasgow's acts, and delineation between the venues became increasingly obscured. The following year the Place was host to an ambitious blues package with Memphis Slim and Champion Jack Dupree and, when Joan Baez appeared there, the resultant concert was televised. Unlike the boxrooms generally masquerading as beat clubs, the Place was uniquely spacious, as its former DJ Linnie Patterson explained.

'The Place was on four floors. The main office was in the foyer, from where you went downstairs to two large rooms about 40 feet square, with brickwork like castle walls. One was for dancing, the other was a coffee bar. The main hall, which had a big stage, was down another set of stairs, with the discotheque below that. The atmosphere was wonderful. You'd just float about all these places through the night.'

Edinburgh's other clubs included the Kasbah in George Square, the Scene in Portobello, while Bungys itself was now established as the city's first all-nighter. Yet despite the thriving circuit, only two acts were signed from the capital by major record companies. The McKinleys were two sisters, Sheila and Jeanette, whose career began in the local Plaza and Palais ballrooms. They initially sang on a part-time basis but were encouraged by their parents, who were also musicians, to turn professional. A London-based songwriting/production team, John Carter and Ken Lewis, heard a promising demo tape and they brought the duo to EMI.

The McKinleys' debut, 'Someone Cares For Me', was issued in March 1964. The production drew on Phil Spector but, unlike most British imitations which tended to be flat, this had a marvellous vibrancy, where a cavernous arrangement gave full support to the singers' earthy voices. Their second release, 'When He Comes Along', was brash and somewhat disappointing, but its follow-up more than compensated. Spurred on by whiplash guitar lines, 'Sweet And Tender Romance' was a compulsive performance, driven at almost breakneck speed until the McKinleys' voices became lost in a whirlpool of frantic sound. 'Give Him My Love', their final single, could not be a greater contrast. The song boasts a poignancy akin to that of the Beach Boys, while its arrangement implies the uptown soul of Ben E. King. Yet despite promotional appearances on *Ready Steady Go* and *Thank Your Lucky Stars*, and photoshots bedecked in the requisite tartan, the McKinleys were unable to score that elusive hit. They later resurfaced in Hamburg, performing at a rapidly declining Star Club, but they left behind a set of accomplished British girl group-styled recordings.

It's arguable that the McKinleys' career would have happened without British Beat, that they belonged to a different ethos of well-established industry practices. The Boston Dexters, however, fought against such constraints. 'I heard Ray Charles singing 'What I Say',' their vocalist Tam White recalls, 'and that turned me on to rhythm and blues.'

White began his singing career in local cafes and clubs, before forming the Heartbeats with drummer Toto McNaughton. Although the group broke up soon afterwards, the pair were subsequently reunited in the Dean Hamilton Combo, a popular act with a considerable following. 'We played the usual pop stuff,' says White, 'but I started putting in a lot more black music.' The Combo later won a residency at the plush Kon Tiki Club. 'It was our first chance to go fully professional,' he recalls, 'but as a jumped-up Trini Lopez band.'

It was Brian Waldman who suggested creating a band, based on 30s' gangsters, called the Boston Dexters. The quartet - White, McNaughton, Johnny Turnbull (guitar) and Alan Coventry (bass) - were duly dressed in expensive, pin-striped suits, and even carried replica guns onstage. Initially unsure of this new, outrageous image, the group warmed to the scheme upon reading Damon Runyon where they discovered hoods could be crazy. 'We were even booked by Glasgow Students' Charities to rob a bank for publicity,' says White, 'but the police wouldn't let us stage it.'

Fortunately the Dexters' sound survived such tactics. Turnbull was an exceptional guitarist, McNaughton a powerful drummer, while White belonged to a line of truly soulful Scottish voices. Even at age 19 he had a husky rasp, inevitably based on his beloved Ray Charles, but with an empathy and command defeating copyist remarks. The group had much in common with the Soul Band and they picked their way through a similar repertoire; 'Night Time Is The Right Time', 'Troubles Of My Own', 'Buttered Popcorn' and 'Talkin' 'Bout You'. Few contemporaries matched their imagination, those who aspired to generally just copied it.

'We played the Place regularly throughout 1964, and Johnny Turnbull backed Champion Jack Dupree at Waldman's Blues Festival. The club was always busy when we were on, but the reaction could be strange. We played out-and-out R&B and some people thought we were being smart-arsed - "Elvis isn't good enough for them", but it was just songs we liked. In the sticks it was even worse.'

The Boston Dexters

Music in Scotland had almost turned full circle. Whereas rock 'n' roll had been accepted in rural areas, the more urban-styled R&B was not. City groups, of course, still followed the countryside circuits, but those opting for Buddy Holly or Elvis or Jerry Lee Lewis found a much warmer reception. Their counterparts increasingly looked south to London, and the first step for the Dexters was a series of demos. Six songs were completed, including 'Matchbox' and 'I've Got Troubles Of My Own', which were duly pressed on to three limited-issue singles.

'Waldman put the money up,' says White. 'He wanted to start his own company, cutting records here in Scotland to sell on to bigger labels.' The irrepressible Waverley showed a not-unnatural interest, but the group was more ambitious. Their gamble almost failed until a journalist tipped-off a friend at EMI. The Dexters were duly auditioned, and signed, in January 1965, but it was here that matters went awry.

'I remember the day we met Bill Martin and Tommy Scott,' says White. 'They were going to write us a song. They came up with 'I've Got Something To Tell You, Baby' which was nothing like the band at all. Even if it had been a hit, we wouldn't have played it.'

The release was, indeed, a blunder. The song was trite, the performance anonymous with White's voice lost in pop group harmonies. It resembled the perky Mersey bands now deemed passé and bore no relation to the real Boston Dexters. That group was thankfully captured on the flip-side. "I Believe To My Soul' was a Ray Charles' song,' says White, 'and it shows what the band were capable of. That was where we went wrong. We tried to pursue the charts and that really wasn't us. It's very difficult to combine youth and wisdom so we were maybe led astray on that one. It's like being the victims of bad taste.'

A second single followed three months later. Once again Bill Martin supplied the song, but he too seemed to have learned from the experience. 'Try Hard' was modelled on 'Go Now', a hit for the Moody Blues, and thus more in keeping with the Dexters' personal preferences. Coupled with Turnbull's ambitious 'No More Tears', the release was an artistic, if not commercial, success.

The quartet had, by this point, moved to London, hoping to pierce the circuit, supporting the Artwoods, the Cheynes, Zoot Money, and Chris Farlowe; acts playing obscure R&B, working with record deals, yet set apart from hit parade expectations.

'Waldman had opened a club in Putney called the Pontiac,' recalls White, 'and we stayed in the flat above it. The place was a hellhole, but we had some good times. We played the club at night which brought us into contact with the Animals, Long John Baldry, all the heavy rock bands of the time.'

Sadly, the break would not come. Despondent at the gulf between their live set and records, the Boston Dexters returned to Edinburgh and split in two. The Athenians, however, were still around, ever faithful to Waverley. Their second disc, 'I Got Love If You Want It', was a marked improvement on their tentative debut and the group seemed at ease with the laconic slur of Slim Harpo's original. It even came in a picture bag, although the black & white snap did little justice to those immaculate maroon velvet suits. Their surging version of 'Louie Louie' then appeared on a charities' disc, before the group closed a brief recording career with a perfunctory reading of the Shadows' 'Thinking Of Our Love'.

Changes in line-up had robbed the Athenians of their early sense of purpose, and they fell apart in 1966, surrounded by a new generation of groups led by the Images, the Hunters, the Avengers and the Hipple People. The Avengers had cut the Beatles' 'I Don't Want To Spoil The Party' on yet another students' disc, but were better known for proto-garage band material drawn from Paul Revere And The Raiders. The Hipple People had a furious sound, ideal for gutsy soul like Roy Head's 'Treat Her Right', while two photogenic lead singers inspired comparison with the Walker Brothers. The Images were billed as 'Scotland's only professional band', but this had its drawbacks, as bassist Gordon Hastie recalls. 'We must be the only group which came back from a tour in Frankfurt to play one gig at the Murrayfield Ice Rink

The Athenians' 'Thinking Of Our Love' single

10 BEAT NEWS

Musicians take note!

We are now in a position to supply all the leading makes of instruments. A few of our instruments in stock include:

CARLTON "Gaelic" — CHOICE OF CHAMPIONS

GUITARS

FENDER STRATOCASTER	£180 12 0
FENDER TELECASTER	£122 17 0
FENDER PRECISION BASS	£141 5 0
GRETSCH HOLLOW BODY	£241 10 0
BURNS TR 2	£140 14 0
BURNS DOUBLE SIX 12 STRINGS	£131 5 0
GIBSON LES PAUL JUNIOR	£ 78 15 0
GIBSON ES-335 TDC	£162 15 0
HARMONY H77	£ 99
HOFNER GALAXIE	£ 57 15 0
HOFNER BEATLE BASS	£ 57 15 0
HOFNER COLORAMA 11	£ 37 16 0
KENT GUITAR	£ 4 19 6
MADRIGIL SPANISH	£ 13 13 0

AMPLIFIERS

VOX T 60 BASS	£152
VOX AC 30 TWIN	£115 10 0
VOX AC 10	£ 47 5 0
SELMER ZODIAC TWIN	£ 94 10 0
FAL 15 WATT	£ 28 7 0
SCALA AMPS	£ 18 18 0
DOMINO AMP	£ 18 18 0
SELMER LITTLE GIANT	£ 12 12 0
BURNS STAGE ONE	£ 63
LINEAR CONCHORD	£ 16 16 0
LINEAR L 50	£ 23 2 0
TRIPLETONE	£ 15 18 9

DRUM KITS

TRIXON LUXUS OUTFIT	£176
CARLTON BIG BEAT OUTFIT	£156 7 2
CARLTON CONTINENTAL KIT	£111 9 2
JAPANESE KIT	£ 78 15 0

ECHO UNITS

WATKINS COPYCAT	£ 38 10 0
DOMINO ECHO	£ 47 5 0
SELMER ECHO	£ 37 16 0
SWISS ECHO	£ 84
DYNACHORD	£102 0 0
VOX ECHO	£ 99 15 0

CLINKSCALE BORDER BEAT SHOP

THE SQUARE · MELROSE · ROXBURGHSHIRE · SCOTLAND

Telephone : 223 - 286

The cost of musicianship as reflected in a January 1965 advertisement from *Beat News* in Edinburgh. When it was finished we got back into the van and set off for Zurich, passing through Frankfurt on the way.'

Edinburgh's third attraction, however, was the Moonrakers. They drew largely on popular material, especially by the Kinks, and their set was renowned for 'Sittin' On A Sofa' and a novelty reading of 'Alley Oop'. They were the danceband of 1966, girls even screamed at them. Their hearts were crushed, however, when bassist Derek McDonald, always the favourite, was battered senseless by a jealous gang and suffered irreparable brain damage. The group was forced to ask him to leave, having first let slip a Polydor contract in the hope that recovery was possible. The Moonies were never the same again and within months had completely disintegrated.

The Poets appeal for fan club members

CHAPTER 3
SOMETHING TO SHOUT ABOUT

By 1963 it was clear that beat was not a passing phase and record labels responded with clinical, almost carpetbagger, precision. They descended on a town, and having bought what they considered its leading talent, moved elsewhere. Liverpool, Manchester and Birmingham were each, in turn, bled dry, inspiring journalist Gordon Reed to lobby EMI on Glasgow's behalf. Two days were duly set aside at the Locarno in Sauchiehall Street which was then flooded with starry-eyed aspirants nervously eager to audition.

'EMI sent Norrie Paramour,' says William Junior Campbell, lead guitarist of Dean Ford And The Gaylords. 'He wrote the music for 'The Young Ones' and 'Summer Holiday', and had produced Cliff and the Shadows, so just to come around that revolving stage and see him sitting there, his glasses glinting in the light, frightened the life out of us.'

Although the Gaylords were barely 16, they had been together for three years, and thus bridged the chasm between danceband and beat. 'We started out in standard evening dress,' Campbell recalls, 'but when the Liverpool rage hit we threw them in a bin and reappeared looking like the Hollies. We were getting better instrumentally, but lacked a strong vocalist. One guy, Wattie Rodgers, did an incredible Elvis impersonation, but there was little future in that.'

Adverts in local papers solicited Thomas MacAlise, singer with the Monarchs, who then assumed the Dean Ford name. The new line-up - Ford, Campbell, Pat Fairley (rhythm guitar), Bill Irving (bass) and Ray Duffy (drums) - gelled into a cohesive pop band and successfully negotiated the Paramour audition. Now required to complete a demo tape, the unit submitted a song drawn from their live repertoire, a Chubby Checker tune, 'Twenty Miles'. 'EMI picked it as a single and took us to London to record it,' recalls Campbell. 'When we got in the studio our drummer, Raymond Duffy, walked over to a booth which was already set up. He came back ashen-faced and said "Jesus Christ. Look in there". We went over and there it was, the Ludwig kit with 'The Beatles' on it.'

Released in 1964, 'Twenty Miles' was promising rather than exceptional, but there was no denying the chirpy breeziness which drew favourable comparisons with Liverpudlian act the Fourmost. It stirred sufficient interest to confirm Paramour's faith, although his other Scottish proteges, the Golden Crusaders, fared less well. Formed as the Blackjacks in Bathgate, West Lothian, this showband-styled septet had been active since 1960 and stalked the Central belt offering current hits and vintage rock 'n' roll. Their debut single, 'I'm In Love With You', was heavily indebted to a now-passé Merseybeat, but it boasted a unique self-confidence and effervescent melody, while the saxophones and guitar lines had been compressed together to produce a distinctive, grumbling sound.

The song was written by Andy Doolan, a Bathgate trombonist and auxiliary Golden Crusader. He was denied another chance when the single flopped, and the group instead cut a perfunctory 'Hey Good Looking', doubtlessly drawn from their barn-dance set, which simply reinforced their anachronistic image. A third single 'I Don't Mind' was better, but by then it was much too late and the septet split up in 1965. Despite their unquestioned competence, the Golden Crusaders viewed the 'beat boom' as a culmination, rather than a new opportunity, and found themselves out of place when it gave

Lulu and The Luvvers in 1964

way to R&B. Both of Paramour's selections, for all their charm, betrayed his 'traditional pop' prejudices and unfairly suggested that Scotland was a backwater, bereft of pioneers.

Decca, EMI's great rivals, were equally zealous in their pursuit of talent. Driven on by the nightmare of having rejected the Beatles, they not only relied on the trusted method of demo discs, but sought acts though talent contests, tape-lease deals and recommendation. It was hard to ignore the publicity generated by Marie McDonald McLaughlin Lawrie, better known as Lulu. Born in November 1948 on the north side of Glasgow, she was still a pupil at Whitehill School when her photo and biography began appearing in the city's evening newspapers. Marie had sung informally with the Bellrocks, but it was with the Lindella Club houseband that she first attracted attention, having been plucked out from the audience in which she was just another dancer. 'Everybody knew I could sing,' she would later state. 'I would never shut up.'

The group, the Gleneagles, was initially self-contained, but the singer's fearsome, carefree rasp ensured she quickly became their focal point. A change was inevitable and the unit became Lulu And The Luvvers with the musicians Alec Bell and Ross Nelson (guitars), Jimmy Dewar (bass/vocals), Jimmy Smith (saxophone) and David Miller (drums) relegated to a supporting role. They were a good, but not innovatory, group. Marie's raucous intonation echoed that of Brenda Lee, rather than Motown's Gladys Horton or Martha Reeves. The Luvvers' set largely comprised established favourites, but what separated Lulu was her youth. At a time when pop was hooked on gimmicks, she was natural; a schoolkid with a fishwife's roar.

The Luvvers were later regulars at Le Phonograph, owned by Tony Gordon who had family and commercial ties in London. By February 1964 the group had secured a recording deal and almost immediately travelled to London to cut their first single. Marie had hoped for a rare Lennon/McCartney song, and returned home somewhat disconsolate when Decca insisted on 'Shout'. In Scotland the song was synonymous with Alex Harvey, and it is rumoured that Lulu was more than wary of his reaction. Her fears were assuaged watching the Beatles on *Ready Steady Go*. John Lennon proclaimed 'Shout' the pick of that week's releases.

The single was enthusiastic, not without a certain novelty appeal, and deserved its Top 10 place. However, work was in motion to prise the singer from her 'backing' musicians and television slots for Lulu alone already outnumbered those for the group as a whole. Although useful live, they were deemed superfluous in the studio where subsequent appearances were strictly limited.

Lulu's second single, 'Can't Hear You No More', was lifted note-for-note from Betty Everett's original. This was a strong, soulful performance which, although not a hit, prepared the singer for her collaborations with US producer Bert Berns. A skilled doyen in uptown soul circles, with credits on releases by the Drifters, Garnet Mimms and Solomon Burke, Berns had arrived in Britain to check on its emergent R&B scene. For Lulu he took 'There You Go', a song he'd already used with the Exciters, and having reworked the lyrics, emerged with 'Here Comes The Night'. Her slow, brooding version contained a bluesy vocal more mature than the singer had managed to date, yet the single was an ignominious flop. To add insult to injury, it was eclipsed several months later by Them, who, with Berns again at the helm, scored a Top 3 hit with the same song.

The failure was also disastrous artistically. Lulu's soulful inflection was never natural, it needed care and coaxing without which the effect was akin to blustered parody. Her debut album, *Something To Shout About*, contained interesting material, although the execution lacked imagination, with safe, rather than challenging, arrangements. It included songs popularised by the Impressions and Marvin Gaye, but the stand-out track, also available as a single, was 'Try To Understand', written by girl-group promoters Pam Sawyer and Lori Burton. Subsequent releases, including 'Leave A Little Love' and 'Call Me', showed a distinct shift towards MOR styles and a singer able to command attention yet display little empathy. Meanwhile, a depleted Luvvers (Alec Bell was the sole remaining original member) made a valiant attempt at an independent career with the exceptional 'House On The Hill', before breaking up in 1966.

If Lulu's career was guided by traditional management values, that of the Poets was markedly different. By 1964 they were a regular attraction at the Flamingo Ballroom in Glasgow's Paisley Road West and were managed by two brothers who ran a small chain of cinemas. But, as George Gallagher states, 'Nothing really happened until Oldham appeared.'

Andrew Loog Oldham was pop's *enfant terrible*. As manager of the Rolling Stones, he cultivated the band's image of revolt, manipulated parental fears and exaggerated errant behaviour. He was sharp, cool and hungry for success, both for his artists and himself.

'Oldham was heading for Gretna Green to marry a girl considered underage in England,' said Gallagher. 'He arrived at Edinburgh airport and happened to see a copy of *Beat News* with our photo on the cover. We were dressed rather flamboyantly in the Rabbie Burns style - the velvet suits, the frilled shirts - and this intrigued him.'

Oldham traced the group to their Flamingo haunt where they auditioned several original songs. 'Within a fortnight,' says Gallagher, 'we were down in London, a part of the Rolling Stones' circle, recording our first single.'

Despite the Poets' avowed influences, 'Now We're Thru' owed little to R&B. Ringing 12-string guitars and tambourines created an ethereal, Celtic

Lulu's Something To Shout About LP

drone, while Gallagher's nasal intonation showed enough impartiality to heighten a well-established sense of mystery. There had never been anything like it in pop before and for once Oldham's naive production complemented its subject. 'Andrew did very little on 'Now We're Thru' that we hadn't done before he heard it,' recalled Gallagher, 'but we were perfect for him to live out his Spector dream. Hume Paton and Tony Myles always had that echoey atmosphere in their songs. If there was any uniqueness about our sound, it was down to their way of playing guitar.'

'Now We're Thru' reached a respectable number 30, and the Poets began extensive British tours. 'We stayed at the Ayland Hotel,' says Gallagher, 'a rundown place in London. Jimmy Savile had his own suite and he helped us out a couple of times when things were tight. Them were also living there. Van Morrison and I had some sessions in the lounge, trying to out-sing and out-play Little Walter.'

The Poets' follow-up, 'That's The Way It's Got To Be', was radically different from its predecessor. 'It was our best single,' opines Gallagher. 'We used a 6-string bass and a 4-string together on the bottom line and the resultant riff was outstanding.' The introduction was, indeed, arresting, and it propelled the rest of the song at an enthralling, breakneck speed. A similar, if more

BEAT NEWS

universal dance agency

PROPRIETORS OF BEAT NEWS

present **FORTHCOMING ATTRACTIONS** in the **NEW YEAR** and **SUMMER SEASON**

RECORDING ARTISTS

COLUMBIA	DECCA	COLUMBIA
DEAN FORD and the **GAYLORDS**	**THE POETS**	**THE GOLDEN CRUSADERS**

ALSO presenting Scotland's New Top Boys—
THE SENATE
featuring SOL BYRON

ALSO from a list of 225 available Bands:—

THE APACHES with TOMMY	THE FLINTSTONES	THE M.I.5s
THE ARDENS	with PHIL	with JOHNNY LAW
THE BEATSTALKERS	THE FIREFLIES	THE MUSTANGS
BEAT UNLIMITED	THE GIANTS	THE RAIDERS
THE BERRYS	THE HAWKS	THE REIGNING MONARCHS
THE BOYFRIENDS	THE HI-FI COMBO	THE ROAD RUNNERS
THE CHEVLONS and JAY ANDERS	THE HUSTLERS	THE ROYAL CRESTS
THE CHARIOTS with MARK ANTONY	THE INTERNS	THE TRADERS with TONY
THE DROVERS	THE INVADERS	THE VAQUEROS (becoming THE LAIRDS)
THE EDINBURGH CRUSADERS	THE KIMBOS	THE VELTONES
	THE KWINTONES	THE VIKINGS

ALSO for Modern, Latin American and Old Tyme:—
THE LARRY MILLER ORCHESTRA and
THE FRANK CARDLE QUARTET
Very suitable for your Annual Ball

ALSO we welcome any enquiries for touring attractions or national artists.

HEAD OFFICE:—
John McGowan, 50 Dundrennan Road, Glasgow S2.
Tel BATtlefield 3123.

PERTH OFFICE:	FIFE OFFICE:	ABERDEEN OFFICE:
Andy Rettie, 1 Cargill Place, Perth. Tel. Perth 26358	Mrs. Mary Yardley, 239 Methil Brae, Methil, Fife. Tel. Leven 1259	Malcolm Milne, Mill of Pert, Laurence Kirk, Kincardineshire, Tel Northwaterbridge 249.

A representative selection of Scottish Beat attractions during 1965 measured, pulse later resurfaced on the Spencer Davis Group's hit 'Keep On Running', but here it simply reinforced the Poets' startling originality. Although lacking a defined melody, 'That's The Way' was adventurous and exciting, but the blanket campaign which accompanied 'Now We're Thru' was noticeably absent. 'The politics at Oldham's office probably stopped the follow-up singles being hits,' says Gallagher. 'The Stones wanted more autonomy and we were left on the sidelines.'

Yet as the Poets faltered, so Dean Ford and the Gaylords gathered momentum. Expectations on their behalf were less, and the quintet was able to develop away from the limelight. The Poets refused to compromise, but the Gaylords proved more flexible, adapting their sound without seeming opportunistic, and any misjudgements were part of a learning process.

'The follow-up to 'Twenty Miles' was 'Mr. Heartbreak's Here Instead',' recalls William Campbell, the band's lead guitarist. 'It was written by two budding Ayrshire songwriters, one of whom was Benny Gallagher. Their demo was diabolical, but we did the best we could.'

The single was disappointing, a song marred by a resigned performance and poor support from an uncaring label. 'We were allocated Studio Two from two 'til five. Finish. There was no coming back; it was in, set up, record two songs, mix and out. The producer, Bob Barrett, wasn't that particular. If we wanted to record something, fine, but it had to be done quickly. We were just another band going through their contract and there was no way we could learn the craft of recording. We weren't even allowed in the control room.'

This perfunctory approach contrasted with that of the Poets, as George Gallagher explains. 'We didn't start recording until after midnight. All the lighting was subdued, there was some booze, a couple of crates of coke - the atmosphere was very relaxed. There were no inhibitions and a lot of the songs were written, or at least finished off, in the studio.'

Such different environments helped exaggerate the disparity between both groups' finished performances. For their third single the Gaylords exhumed 'The Name Game', a Shirley Ellis song which had proved highly popular onstage during a spell at Cologne's Storeyville Club. 'That was a dreadful, dreadful record,' Campbell ruefully recounts, although this is a harsh assessment. The playing is sloppy, but it boasts an urgency missing from previous records and has all the energy of a live performance.

Although they continued to play in Glasgow whenever possible, such groups as the Gaylords, Lulu and the Poets became national acts by virtue of recording deals. However, there was no shortage of potential replacements. A second generation of groups arose, including the Chevlons, the Hustlers and the Del-Jacks. The latter featured vocalist Frankie Miller.

'I used to sing 'round the backs when I was two,' Miller recalls. 'I don't remember the songs but people used to throw me pennies and ha'pennies.

Then I heard Little Richard and he really knocked my head off. I used to try to copy him, but at first I never knew there were any words to his songs.' By this point Miller was barely in primary school, but by the age of seven he'd joined a local skiffle group. 'They were a really good band - no name - who were into rock 'n' roll and things like Lonnie Donegan.' At 11 years old Frankie was a member of the Sundowners, who played at the Territorial Army Halls in the heart of Bridgeton, and two years later, in 1963, he was fronting the Del-Jacks. 'They did a lot of rhythm and blues,' Miller explains. 'They used to play at a local club, the Manhattan, and I would go and see them. They really needed a singer and my pal told me I should get up there with them. So I did.'

The list of new groups continued to grow but the best, indisputably, was the Blues Council, formed by Bill Patrick following a spell as bandleader at Glasgow's Plaza Ballroom.

'Joe McCourtney, a local impresario, was about to open the Scene Club in West Nile Street. When I told him that jazzy R&B bands were big in London, he suggested we should get one like that together to launch the new venue.

'The group was the first of its kind in Scotland, quite different to the Soul Band; more organized, more arranged - just as wild but in a different way. There were two saxes, an electric keyboard - one of the first in Scotland - and Alex Harvey's brother, Leslie, on lead. We were cooler and more bluesy than the guitar-oriented groups, but not free blowing. It was post-Bo Diddley, much newer than what we'd been playing before.'

The Blues Council became a leading attraction in Scotland, revered by audiences and musicians alike. One of the first truly Mod bands, they even looked the part, matching sound and image in a spontaneous way. London publisher Dick James, who was quick to spot the group's potential, signed them to a production deal whereby finished masters were leased to EMI.

Their sole single, 'Baby Don't Look Down', fulfilled every promise, blending the gospel swing of Ray Charles with the hard blues of Chicago. It was rhythmic, compulsive and mature; success for the Blues Council seemed inevitable.

It came to a sudden and tragic end on 12 March 1965. The band was returning home from a gig in the early morning when their van crashed on the outskirts of Edinburgh, killing vocalist Fraser Calder and bassist James Giffen. EMI suggested pulling the single, unsure of how to react, but the parents of the dead musicians asked that it should go ahead as a mark of respect. Such a terrible accident naturally left its mark. 'I haven't played that record since the day we made it,' said Patrick. 'It's a tragic story.'

The survivors - Bill Patrick, Leslie Harvey, Larry Quinn (alto), John McGinnis (piano) and Billy Adamson (drums) - did regroup with Bill's brother Bobby, now bereft of his Big Six, and tenor saxophonist Bobby Wishart, formerly of the Soul Band. The new line-up, however, only lasted a matter of weeks before disbanding; they simply lacked the heart to carry on. Their tale sent a chill though every musician, who thought of his own crowded Dormobile and haphazard lifestyle. Many still recall it decades later, confirming the shock effect it had upon young Scotland.

The Comet

Chapter 4
'I WAS FIRED FOUR TIMES. I LEFT ON THE FIFTH OCCASION.'

The clamour for pop was not solely confined to Glasgow and Edinburgh. Other centres eagerly accepted the new music and although styles and taste in rural areas differed - bands continued to return from northern sorties bemoaning its blind affection for rock 'n' roll - Scotland's urban areas, such as Dundee and Perth, held an equally fervent allegiance to soul.

'Dundee had a lot of bands prior to the Beatles,' says drummer Donnie Coutts, 'Most of them, like Johnny Hudson And The Hi-Four or the Staccato Five, were semi-professional.' Although their repertoires were based on British chart hits, such acts generally favoured American material which proved highly popular. 'There was a big US airbase at Edsel,' says Coutts. 'All the bands liked playing there because the servicemen appreciated the music.'

Releases by the Contours, Miracles, Sam Cooke and Marvin Gaye became prized items and such material was sometimes generously passed from band to band. A sympathetic record shop could prove as vital as a local club and several groups became enthusiasts, desperately seeking pressings on Pye International, London/Atlantic or further afield.

'We used to order singles on import,' recalls Pete Agnew. 'You maybe had to wait three or four weeks, but you got it. I went from band to band on the radio listening for something I hadn't heard before.'

The Beatles were the catalyst for change, yet where their original compositions provided a new development, the fact they covered Black American pop did not, as many Scottish bands were already versed in 'Twist And Shout', 'Please Mr. Postman' and 'Money'. As Donnie Coutts notes, 'By popularising Mary Wells or whatever, they gave another dimension to what was happening anyway.'

Such factors may explain the lukewarm reaction afforded the yet-to-be-Fab Four on their first Scottish tour of 1963. Beatlemania and 'She Loves You' were still several months away when they opened at Elgin's Two Red Shoes on January 2. Hours spent in Hamburg sleazepits cut little ice at a gig in Bridge Of

Allan where, as promoter Andy Lothian recalls, 'Not many people came, but those who did fought with each other. The Beatles did not get a good reception and I collected something like 3s/10d from the stage when they came off.'

Lothian had been impressed by 'Please Please Me' which, although unissued at that point, had closed the Beatles' set. He forged a partnership with entrepreneur Albert Bonici and, having impressed manager Brian Epstein, the pair promoted every subsequent Beatles' tour of Scotland. Yet Lothian came to his trade entirely by accident. A member of the East Coast Jazz Band in the early 60s, he found that this popular act was often double-booked and began placing other bands in venues they couldn't play. His fledgling agency flourished on securing the entertainment rights for the island communities on Arran who, tired of a trad jazz diet, demanded greater variety. Having first introduced folk musicians, Lothian started to book emergent beat groups. In this way, Dundee acts began meeting with their Glasgow counterparts and discovered a common obsession with black American music, establishing a mutual understanding.

'Motown and Stax were huge here,' recalls Donnie Coutts. 'The intensity seemed peculiar to Scotland, to Dundee and Glasgow in particular , and it's seen in the to-ing and fro-ing of bands between the two. Unemployment was higher than average in both places and other areas tried to make us feel second class. The people were always proud, regardless, and maybe that's what we had in common with black Americans.'

'It's hard to get the connection between Glasgow and American black music,' adds Poets' vocalist George Gallagher. 'Maybe it's because something like Tamla came from a hard city like Detroit, it reflected something in the Glasgow character.'

Despite an occasional exception, notably the Boston Dexters, Edinburgh failed to create the same kind of obsession. It boasted its soul boys, of course, but the city's groups were largely more commercial, content to rely on favourites, rather than forge a brave new style. A popular band such as the Images did play the requisite Tamla tracks, but they favoured obvious selections. Glasgow bands were more daring and evoked a sense of anticipation where their Edinburgh counterparts opted for a well-won popularity, rather than innovation. This might explain a curious anomaly. Audiences in the Scottish capital never clapped - one song ended, the dancers turned away (or not) and the next song began. Yet the city's clubs continued to attract groups from all over Scotland.

'The Shadettes started playing in Edinburgh in 1964,' says Pete Agnew. 'That's where it was happening. We did the Place, the Gamp, the 'Nash and there were three, maybe four bands playing these places every night. You could do an early spot at one club, then get to the Top Storey, and lastly, finish off at

The Shadettes

The Place
VICTORIA STREET EDINBURGH

MONDAY 8 p.m. till 12 midnight
BEAT

TUESDAY 8 p.m. till 11.30 p.m
FOLK SINGING

FRIDAY 9 p.m. till 2 a.m.
BEAT (3 Star Bands)

SATURDAY 8 p.m. till 2 a.m.
BEAT (4 Star Bands)

SUNDAY 8 p.m. till 12 midnight
BEAT (2 star bands)

MEMBERSHIP PER ANNUM
GENT'S 5/- - - - - - LADIES' 1/-

Bungies
ALL NIGHTER

OLD FISHMARKET CLOSE
HIGH STREET, EDINBURGH.

Saturday Night is
BIG BEAT NIGHT
THREE STAR BANDS
7 p.m. till 7 a.m.

BREAKFAST
Membership 1/-

June, 1965

Two of Edinburgh's most popular music haunts

Bungys at four or five in the morning.'

'There were still places to play in Fife,' adds Dan McCafferty who became the Shadettes' vocalist on the departure of Des Haldane that year. 'There were about eight bands in Dunfermline and everyone was working.' Such acts included the Red Hawkes, the Ambassadors and the Mark Five, the last of which was party to an outrageous publicity stunt. In 1965, they set off for London, on foot, to demand a recording deal. They managed to both complete the journey and get the contract. The Mark Five produced a rousing version of the Isley Brothers 'Tango', before being dropped by their label as soon as the story ran cold.

Dundee's Poor Souls avoided such hi-jinks. They were formed in 1964 from the ashes of the Johnny Hudson Hi-Four, a pivotal act within the city's nascent musical community. Known initially as the Hi-Four, the group included Doug Martin (guitar) and John Casey (drums), but it became a stronger unit with the arrival of vocalist Johnny Moran, who took the stage name Johnny Hudson. The Hi-Four was the first group from Tayside to enjoy a spell in Germany, moving from Cologne's Storeyville Jazz Club to Hamburg's Top Ten. On their return from a later sortie abroad, the quartet joined the bill for the Beatles' show at Dundee's Caird Hall. The Poor Souls evolved when Hudson, Casey and Martin were joined by Chick Taylor, and the new combo became one of the most innovative of the era. Where the Blues Council captured jazz R&B, this expressive quartet evoked the uptown soul of the Drifters or Garnet Mimms, a cross between 'Up On The Roof' and 'Cry Baby'. In Dougie Martin the band had an intuitive songwriter, while the rest of the group were equally skilful. Their work together was touched by a radical inventiveness.

'When My Baby Cries', issued on Decca in June 1965, was not a group original, but they moulded it to sound like one. A deep ballad punctuated by piercing backing voices, its complex melody and threatening confidence proved largely uncommercial, although the single sold well around Tayside and in Glasgow. A tour of England was little help, despite a protracted spell in East Anglian US bases, and the quartet returned to a fortnightly slot at Dundee's Top Ten Club.

'The Top Ten Club grew out of the Continental Ballroom,' recalls Andy Lothian. 'Eventually the numbers grew so large that it was switched to the Palais. For the next six years, until 1969, Dundee youngsters could see most touring British and American groups.'

'It was a typical ballroom,' adds Donnie Coutts. 'A balcony at one end, the floor itself and a semi-raised stage. The public had access up both sides and round to an area at the back. It created a really exciting atmosphere as the crowd was packed in around the group.'

Local groups were often found behind a glass screen, studying the headline

The Vikings, with Alan Gorrie pictured centre

acts. They were naturally critical, applauding like-minded innovators, denigrating the merely topical, refusing to compromise their precious soul heritage. One-upmanship increased as time progressed and bands strove to find unfamiliar songs, tucked away on flip-sides or albums, which they offered exclusively on the circuit. Coutts argues that this was part of a wider evolution.

'One group I was in, the Syndicate, learned their Barrett Strong and Curtis Mayfield songs second-hand, from records by Cliff Bennett And The Rebel Rousers. This helped us look at other material by those writers. Before long we'd built our own set and although they were all covers, it was the first step towards playing original material. The discipline was the same; you had to get a song they didn't know over to the audience.'

The Syndicate were active until 1966, but lost heart when Coutts and vocalist/guitarist Mike Fraser defected to the Perth-based Vikings, 'where the material was really obscure.' The latter act was the Poor Souls' only rival, with a reputation for unearthing lost soul gems and introducing to Scotland previously unheard material by James Brown, Solomon Burke, Don Covay and Bobby Bland.

'Dougie Wightman and Roy Fleming already had a duet,' explains Vikings' bassist Alan Gorrie, 'and there was a guy in my class, Pete Hartley, who owned a drumkit. Up till then I had been flailing away at home on an acoustic guitar but I was desperate to join a band and felt I could do what they were doing. They didn't need another guitarist, so I butchered this acoustic and put four bass strings on it.' This early act, the Falcons, lasted some 18 months before Hartley's departure became the first of several changes. 'Peter decided he was going to college and we found this guy called Graham Duncan, who was like Keith Moon and Ginger Baker rolled into one. He had some good ideas - it wasn't a straight ahead thing with immaculate time - there was a lot of activity. That was the band that became the Vikings.'

'The first stuff we played was the Shadows and a bit of Elvis, but we then got a singer called Ian Jackson, a little guy with a Jackie Wilson-ish voice, a real chanter. Because this guy had a voice, we used to do things like 'My Prayer', standards updated by people like Clyde McPhatter. I started digging out other black songs and so the Vikings took on a soul music form almost right away.'

Jackson was then replaced by Johnny Taylor, aka Johnny Little, the latter name derived from his previous band, Johnny Little And The Giants. 'He was a real Sinatra-style singer,' Gorrie recalls. 'It was kind of tough because he really did want to do the standards. The ones we liked had credibility because they had been covered by soul artists. We were saying "No Jock, not the Bing Crosby version, the Sam Cooke".'

The Vikings won the '£100 Tayside Sound' contest in 1964, and cut a demo disc of 'Deep Purple' and 'At The Club'. For Gorrie, however, the pivotal change came on discovering Marvin Gaye. 'I'd heard the Stones do 'Can I Get A Witness' and saw they didn't write it. I found out who did the original, ordered it, and the day I got it played it over and over again. The sound just blew me away. It was like St. Paul on the road to Damascus - instant conversion.'

The Vikings had no peers in Perth, but Gorrie does acknowledge the influence of nearby neighbours the Poor Souls. 'That was the band we emulated,' he recalls. 'They had such a great repertoire and because Dougie and John were that bit older than us, they had a real depth. Dougie Martin was a major influence on how I sing and what I think a singer should be.' Yet the Vikings' messianic determination led to internal friction and Christmas 1965 was marked by yet another upheaval. Duncan left after a fist-fight, Fleming quit in sympathy, while new vocalist Drew Larg was poached from struggling rivals the Honours. The transformation was complete with the arrival of Donnie Coutts and Mike Fraser, and the group began the New Year in optimistic mood.

'Donnie is a walking soul encyclopedia,' Gorrie explains. 'There were several American phrases in songs that I would never quite peg so I'd blur that line. Donnie knew what the words were. He had a great Smokey-ish falsetto voice - he could do 'Tracks Of My Tears' - I sang the Stax stuff, and Drew took the Major Lance-type material. We were a complete vocal group, the first in Scotland to combine this inside an instrumental unit.'

The Vikings now comprised musicians from Perth and Dundee, two traditional rivals. Scottish music was beginning to reflect a singleness of purpose, and progress towards such unification was enhanced with the arrival of pirate radio.

Despite the all-pervasive big beat, pop on the wireless was restricted to the BBC Light Programme's *Saturday Club*, *Easy Beat* and the perennial *Pick Of The Pops*, while a commercial station, Radio Luxembourg, broadcast shows sponsored by individual record companies. The fading reception added to Luxembourg's mystique and the playlist offered a degree of adventure missing from the BBC. However, the record labels tightly controlled the acts they wished to promote on the station. Song plugger Ronan O'Rahilly, frustrated at being unable to secure a play for a single by Georgie Fame, sought an alternative outlet. Inspired by the Dutch-based Radio Veronica, he bought and refitted a Danish passenger ferry, the Frederica, which was anchored off Felixstowe. On Easter Sunday 1964, Radio Caroline began transmitting the UK's first, 24-hour, pop music station with the Beatles' 'Can't Buy Me Love'.

Within months the coastline was peppered with rival concerns, and plans for a Scottish pirate were set in motion. The principle figure was T.V. 'Tommy' Shields, who ran the TVS Publicity Company from an office in Glasgow's Renfield Street. Shields had already failed to gain an official licence to broadcast but took heart from the Caroline experience and, at a press conference on 28 September 1965, was unveiled as the managing director of City and County Commercial Radio (Scotland) Ltd. Refitting the 'Comet', an obsolete lightship, took longer than anticipated and the boat did not arrive in the Firth of Forth until 30 December. The anchor was dropped some four miles off Dunbar, and at 11.50 on Old Year's Night, Radio Scotland began transmission on 242 metres.

A head office staff drawn from Scottish Television, the *Glasgow Herald* and elsewhere assiduously sold advertising space which, when booked, required a copy writer to supply a script. 'I had to brief the one we had,' recalls DJ Tony Meehan, 'but he always came back with something terrible and eventually I wrote them myself. Once the station was on the air I began doing the voice-overs as well.'

Having proved he could broadcast, Meehan was coaxed into joining the crew, although his idyllic dream of buccaneer life was quickly shattered. 'Stuart Henry couldn't cope with the boat, he was seasick all the time, so Tommy asked me to go out in his place. The day visits had been great, there was a feeling of joviality because everyone was so happy to see a strange face, but reality was quite different. The food was poor and conditions were very basic, the work onboard wasn't even finished. There were no fires in the cabins and the only heat came from a central stove stuck in the hallway. If you wanted coal you had to go up to the bow of the ship with a bucket on a rope and climb down into the hole it was kept in. All this in a force six wind with the 'Comet' heaving up and down.'

Yet little of such hardship came over to the listener who, like the pre-DJ Meehan, imagined a life of permanent party fun, where frolics on the high seas were spliced with music and the thrill of illegality. Few guessed that the landlocked Henry taped his shows in Glasgow or that dissension was rife. The banter between Paul Young and Ugly Bob Spencer or the mayhem wrecked by Jack McLaughlin suggested an unfettered camaraderie and established an early bond between audience and station. The 242 Fan Club and related *Showbeat* monthly, with its articles and photographs of Scottish bands, added to a sense of collective purpose.

Radio Scotland, however, only had a limited amount of pop coverage. By the time its MOR, Ceilidh, Hooly, jazz and religious programmes were taken into consideration, little space was left for contemporary music. 'Choice was left to the DJ although it had to be within the guidelines of the show; pop, jazz or whatever.' says Meehan. 'You picked what you wanted out of the small library. Occasionally you were told "Don't play this", but by the time the memo arrived from head office, the thing had been played to death.'

Soul was surprisingly poorly served, but Sunday's run-down of the Stateside Top 50 suggested a hidden sense of adventure. Any Scottish group cutting a single was assured rotational airplay, but the initial impetus wasn't sustained and the saturation audience figures once claimed by the station (2,195,000) rapidly dwindled. Its programmes were increasingly aimed at older listeners.

Scotland's Sound Sensation: recorded for posterity

The company was plagued with problems. In June 1966 the ship was moved from Dunbar, through the Pentland Firth and down to Troon. But if reception in Glasgow was improved, it was now lost to Edinburgh. Boosting the signal helped a little, but the station failed to recover ground. Storms also took their toll and further panic ensued in April the following year when, after four weeks off-air, the 'Comet', now called Radio Scotland And Ireland, resumed broadcasts east of Belfast at Ballywater. Reception in Glasgow was poor.

This episode lasted a mere three weeks after which the station was closed down again. The ship began the long haul back to Scotland's east coast, where it anchored off Fife Ness. Its programmes were now extremely cosy, with pipes, tartan and country dancing the main hopes for survival. Jack McLaughlin was given the Ceilidh show, which he sent-up in merciless fashion, before being fired for irreverence. This was not an unusual occurrence, McLaughlin had already been disciplined for broadcasting thinly-veiled requests for food, and getting the sack was simply part of the job.

'I was fired four times,' says Meehan. 'I left on the fifth occasion. The van driver who collected from the boat was the ideal gauge. If he smiled, you were still hired. If he frowned, you knew he had a letter for you - "Report to Tommy Shields" or "Report to Brian Holden".'

Holden was the station's co-ordinating controller but Shields dismissed him in May 1967 following a bitter internal dispute. Four other senior staff members resigned in protest and this bloodletting marked the end of any lingering hopes that something could be salvaged from the now-doomed company. Advertising worth £15,000 had already been withdrawn and an on-air appeal for funds netted only 650 replies. Yet Radio Scotland did limp on to the end, ceasing transmission at midnight on 14 August. It was an ignominious demise caused by a misguided attempt to win legitimacy through its conservative programming policy.

Unlike Radio London, and others, Radio Scotland did not have American interests pumping money into its coffers. For better or worse it was Scottish, proudly independent, and based on a mixture of blind faith, hope and individuality. As such it was merely a diversion, recalled with affection, but never crucial. The true aficionados tuned to other stations, in particular Radio 370, where they avidly digested Mike Raven's R&B Show.

However '242' did produce two important spin-offs; the Clan Balls and the Alp record label. The Clan Balls were concerts held at various venues throughout Scotland, ranging from dancehalls, to clubs, to ice-rinks, depending on the bill. The early ventures were highly parochial and simply reflected the station's day-to-day programmes. Extensively sponsored and advertised on air, the shows were promoted by Andy Lothian.

'There was a definite split at the early Clan Balls, with no middle ground.

A small number of traditionalists came for the country dance band and they could not bear the noise of the beat groups. They eventually became rock occasions and so grew in importance.'

'Sometimes the Clan Balls were part of a national group's Scottish tour,' adds Tony Meehan. 'It was always done on a shoestring budget and we always tried to use local bands as well. They would bring their own following and you hoped a name band would do the rest.'

The meeting of groups from home and away was thus not always altruistic, but this combination was already established at the Top Ten Club. The Clan Balls created a regular, co-ordinated series of concerts and dances throughout the country which were backed by advertising on radio and in print. Groups from one Scottish city would appear at another and the shows inadvertently began the erosion of the pockets of isolationism which existed in different parts of the country. Greater contact between the musicians led to inter-city hybrids and acts were increasingly termed 'Scottish', rather than from Glasgow or Dundee.

Ironically, the Clan Balls grew in strength as Radio Scotland waned. The last official gathering was on the night of 14 August 1967, as the Marine Offences Bill, outlawing pirate radio, passed into law. Glasgow's Locarno Ballroom carried an air of gloom; the station's staff had received their final pay cheque while the crowd felt the end of an era had arrived. No-one moved in to pick up on the Clan idea and, without direction from above, the concept simply fell apart. The demise of Radio Scotland also undermined Alp Records, its last tenuous link with pop's infrastructure.

'We wanted to promote a truly Scottish label,' says Andy Lothian, 'and use the support the ship could provide. We were keen to capture the best pop and soul music in the country as well as working in traditional areas. One of our first singles was 'Radio Scotland Polka', the station's theme tune, specially written by accordionist Johnny Huband. It was played at the opening of every Clan Ball to identify the concept of Radio Scotland on land.

'We piloted Alp with the Red Hawkes' 'Friday Night'. Outside the four main cities, dancing was mainly restricted to either Friday or Saturday nightx and the song conveyed the town hall approach of the time. The Friday nights had gone shortly thereafter, and perhaps this single has more in it than we thought at the time.'

'Friday Night' was written by group member Manny Charlton, previously of the footsore Mark Five. The song had a rural dancehall feel, but this was largely due to the Red Hawkes' dated, showband sound. Purposeful, yet unexceptional, the impatience for the weekend's promise was better captured on the Easybeats' 'Friday On My Mind', co-written by Glasgow-born George Young.

Alp - Andy Lothian Productions - was not the first of Scotland's

THE COPY CATS

REPRESENTATION —
CANA VARIETY AGENCY
41–43, Albermarle Street
London W.I.
phone MAYfair 1436

— MANAGEMENT
ALBERT A. BONICI
1 North College Street
Elgin.
phone ELGIN 7058 – 7803

The Copy Cats

independent labels. It was predated by both Waverley and Norco, the latter of which was founded in Elgin by the redoubtable Albert Bonici. His major signing was Johnny And The Copycats, a quintet from Buckie, whose lone single coupled 'I Can Never See You', written by guitarist Iain Lyon, with a version of the Coasters' 'I'm A Hog For You Baby'. Released in 1964, it was a highly accomplished and professional effort but failed to make any commercial impact. They were not without northern peers, however, and contemporaries included Tommy Dene And The Tremors, of which Billy Bremner, later of Rockpile, was a member.

Other groups, frustrated at a lack of recognition, also took to cutting limited-issue singles. Linlithgow's Phil And The Flintstones belied their rather cabaret reputation with a commendable 'Love Potion No.9' while Aberdeen's Misfits cut the Beatles' 'You Won't See Me'. What separated Alp was its sense of ambition. Lothian was not content to merely service Scotland, to sell singles to fans and retire. He struck a national distribution deal with Polydor and his signings were often taken south to record. This foresight attracted the most promising of groups, including the Poor Souls, latterly dropped from Decca's roster.

'We recorded 'Love Me', one of Dougie Martin's songs, at Craighall in Edinburgh,' recalls Lothian. 'Polydor flipped for it, but although the demo had a real excitement, the final record, which we did in London, lost something of its magic.'

The demo may well be superior, but the single is sensational. Faster than the ballad style of 'When My Baby Cries', 'Love Me' soars with unparalleled confidence. The voices are superb, the harmonies incisive and the song itself moves though complex chord and tempo changes without ever losing track of its basic commerciality. Yet sales were poor, eroding confidence in both group and label. It was followed by the Hi-Fi's with 'It's Gonna Be Morning' which, although lacking the drama of the Poor Souls, was highly promising. The Wishaw group was unable to capture their soulful sound in the studio. It was left to the Vikings to try for Alp's elusive hit, with 'Bad News Feeling', a song written by US folksinger Paul Simon.

'We joined the label in 1966,' recalls Coutts, 'and were given songs to learn for a producer, a lady from Brooklyn who took her little dog everywhere. We passed the audition, but the record was a shambles. We didn't know what we wanted to do. There was a harpsichord sitting in the corner and we suddenly thought "That's a good idea." It became the dominant thing on the single. The b-side was recorded in precisely six minutes because the studio was booked for someone else. I knew it was guaranteed a play on Radio Luxembourg between 12 and 12.15 because that was the Polydor slot. I used to sit up every night and think I was a star. It actually sold about 1,200 copies.'

There never was a Simon And Garfunkel version of 'Bad News Feeling' which is not entirely surprising. It was a largely undistinguished composition, but in the prevailing folk-rock climate Polydor eagerly grabbed this hitherto hidden song in the hope it would emulate 'Sound Of Silence' or 'Homeward Bound'. The single is ordinary, rather than bad, while the fey harpsichord is unnecessary. 'What Can I Do' was superior, but in being completed so hurriedly, resembles a demo rather than a finished master.

The failure of these singles marked the end of Alp. If one had been a success, then circumstances would have been different, but even an autonomous label, supposedly able to exercise control, found the business marketplace unreceptive.

'We could not crack the bias that existed against Scottish groups and music,' says Lothian. 'Disc jockeys could not see what we saw in them.'

'It was so much effort for a Scottish band to succeed,' adds Coutts. 'Lulu had success, but she was an exception. There were much better bands who did not make the next step. The soul thing was not the same in England as it was here. It stretched for years in Glasgow and Dundee, much longer than it did down south.'

The scene in Tayside and Fife was the first of Scotland's to fade from prominence. With the Poor Souls in exile and cut to a trio, and the Vikings about to settle in London, Perth and Dundee had lost its natural leaders. Dunfermline's Shadettes had meanwhile pulled off the road to take up residencies and thus save on travel. There were, of course, many hopeful bands eager to replace them and the obsession with black music never faltered, but as 1966 unwound into 1967 the focus fell ever more on Glasgow and Edinburgh.

CHAPTER 5
THE INVISIBLE INSURRECTION

By 1966 British pop was not only a means of entertainment, it had also begun to exert a newfound independence. Having spent two months in seclusion, locked inside the studios at Abbey Road, the Beatles emerged with the triumphant and trailblazing *Revolver*. 'Although (they) have been recording for four weeks,' proclaimed a shocked *New Musical Express* midway through the sessions, 'the LP is still not complete,' a statement reflecting their hitherto unknown protraction.

Much was happening elsewhere during the Beatles' confinement. Manfred Mann singer Paul Jones had embarked on a solo career, the Yardbirds lost Paul Samwell-Smith, but gained Jimmy Page, while the Animals had split altogether, although vocalist Eric Burdon had retained the rights to the name. Some months later Stevie Winwood left the Spencer Davis Group and the police poured through the doors of Keith Richards' Redlands' cottage. Musicians were rebelling, both culturally and professionally, and of all centres outside London, Edinburgh seemed most likely to emulate such changes.

The city's reputation as a bohemian enclave was established by the Fringe, an annual adjunct to the International Arts Festival, and a conduit to performers working outside the mainstream. It was here Peter Cook, Dudley Moore, Jonathan Miller and Alan Bennett anticipated the satire boom with their revue *Beyond The Fringe*, novelist William Burroughs was part of the panel at the 1962 Writers' Conference, while folksinger Richard Farina arrived simply to busk on the streets. Yet if such figures were individuals 'in transit' , the city was also home to the Paperback Bookshop and Traverse Theatre.

An expatriate American, Jim Haynes, had opened the Paperback in 1959. The shop endeavoured to stock every softback edition in print in Britain including the notorious *Lady Chatterley's Lover*, a copy of which was purchased by a former African missionary. 'She wouldn't touch the book,' Haynes recounted in his autobiography, 'but picked it up with coal tongs and carried it out to the front. She poured some kind of liquid, probably kerosene, on top and proceeded to put a match to "this iniquitous document".' For several years the Paperback was a magnet for an unnamed alternative society, selling tickets for Fringe and University events while its walls acted as an art gallery. Haynes even staged readings and productions in the shop and a 1962 performance of Fionn MacColla's *Ane Tryall Of Heretiks* provided the impetus for a more permanent venue. It was tiring taking all the stock out, then putting it back in again the following morning.

Edinburgh did boast a small-scale theatre, the Gateway, but it was on the point of closure. Temporary sites generally housed iconoclastic thespian arts, notably during the Festival. The Cambridge Footlights of August that year was showcased in a former dosshouse and brothel, Kelly's Paradise, which was dubbed the Sphynx Club in deference to its newfound status. Sited off the High Street at 15 James Court, this tenement flat was later converted into a permanent theatre and in January 1963 the Traverse staged its first production, pairing Sartre's *Huis Clos* with Arrabal's *Orison*. During the second performance actress Colette O'Neil was accidentally stabbed, prompting columns of publicity for the fledgling concern. 'Real-Life Drama On Edinburgh Stage,' proclaimed the *Evening Dispatch*, the first of several 'front-page' stories the theatre would engender. By April Haynes had become chairman; by 1965 he was also serving as artistic director, but this joint tenure ended rancorously in June the following year, partly because of his increased commitment to events and developments in London. He took with him plans to found an alternative Edinburgh publication, *Clype*, ideas he later brought to *International Times*.

The Traverse had meanwhile strengthened its position as a haven for experimental drama. Its pop culture affiliations included the Scaffold's 1964 revue *Birds, Marriages And Deaths*, while the following year it showcased *Bubbles* with mime exponent Lindsay Kemp and future Bonzo Dog Doo-Dah Band star Vivian Stanshall. The Traverse moved to larger premises in the Grassmarket in 1969 but, as its historian Joyce McMillan states, the memory of those formative years haunts the company 'like an irritable Beat Generation ghost.'

The theatre also sponsored the 1964 Exhibition Of Contemporary Art which featured the work of, among others, Glasgow-born Mark Boyle. Another London-based exile, Boyle had been involved in a 'happening' undertaken during the previous year's Drama Conference. 'This nude crossed (the organ gallery) on a lighting trolley,' he recounted in *Days In The Life*, the reasons for which 'art school model' Anna Kesselaar explained to the *Sunday Mirror*, 'A lot of people were disappointed by the pompous tone of the conference. My friends and I thought the whole thing should be jazzed up into life.' In the midst of the resultant furore, Edinburgh Council banned an ensuing Poetry Conference and this Calvinistic attitude forced many to seek more enlightened climes.

Novelist/poet Alex Trocchi, a crucial figure in post-war literature, had long-since forsaken his native Glasgow, spending time in both Paris and New

York. An associate of Guy Debord and the fledgling Situationists, a friend and colleague of Burroughs, Ginsberg and Mailer, he returned to the UK in 1961, but although his sorties North included the 1962 Writers' Convention and a public burning of his banned *Cain's Book*, Trocchi was repulsed by Scotland's stifling parochialism. Edinburgh's *New Saltire Review* did publish his critical paper, *The Invisible Insurrection Of A Million Minds*, but this blueprint for Sigma – the author's extension of 19th century Lettrisme – was applauded in centres without the capitol and its author opted to settle in London. Trocchi, Haynes and Boyle each became crucial components of London's underground, although Boyle did return for the 1967 Festival where his lightshow illuminated 'The Lullaby For Catatonics' which featured music by Soft Machine.

Bereft of such pivotal figures, Scotland's counter-culture was, at best, fragmented and *avant garde* pretensions were confined to that frenetic three-week Festival. Music could not be divorced from this quandary and those groups wishing to progress often found themselves trapped in an artistic vacuum. Others seemed content to play a subsidiary role, and if stylistically sure within themselves, their work was rarely challenging. The conditions were ripe for the divisions between pop and progressive styles.

The Boston Dexters step out again

Groups preferring a pop appeal continued to flourish in Edinburgh. If mindless violence had halted the rise of the Moonrakers, then their eminent position was accepted by the Beachcombers, who established themselves at the Top Storey Club during 1966. The quintet's reputation was enhanced with a residency at the rival International where they unashamedly courted a partisan following. The 'Combers relied on well-known songs, but although their popularity was generally confined to within the city boundary. CBS took note of their hometown reputation, and signed them on the strength of an audition.

The Beachcombers were then taken to London, but as they lacked a substantial style, they seemed ripe for manipulation. They lost their name, becoming, instead, the Boots, and their two singles, 'The Animal In Me' and 'Keep Your Lovelight Burning', were wrapped in the full brassy sound common to several contemporary releases on the label. Interest subsequently focused on the flip of the former, 'Even The Bad Times Are Good'. Although hurriedly recorded, the song remained inescapably catchy and only corporate muddleheadedness could confine such bubblegum to b-side status. The Tremeloes obviously agreed, and their (later) version of the song soared into the singles' chart. The Boots could only wonder why the hit wasn't theirs.

The Buzz was another new act to surface in Edinburgh. Formed in 1966 from the ashes of the Boston Dexters, it featured relative newcomers Brian Henderson (bass) and Mike Travis (drums) alongside veterans Tam White and Johnny Turnbull. Within a matter of weeks, this accomplished quartet had secured a deal through producer Joe Meek.

'Meek originally wanted to sign the Dexters,' says White, 'but we went elsewhere. He gave the song he had earmarked for us, 'Please Stay', to the Cryin' Shames.'

'Please Stay' was originally cut in 1961 by the Drifters. An aching ballad, where the singer pleads with his girlfriend 'not to go, but to stay here in my arms', it was performed live by several of Scotland's earliest and most influential groups. A British cover, by Zoot Money's Big Roll Band, further enhanced its standing, while Meek's tinny remake introduced the song to yet another audience. By 1966 almost every band in Scotland played 'Please Stay' and its undying popularity with audiences and group alike ensured it remained an integral part of the musical framework.

It was thus too late for the Buzz to tackle the song. Instead they recorded 'You're Holding Me Down' which, although rather flimsy, had its faults submerged by the producer's proto-psychedelic effects. 'When we finished recording the single, Meek flooded it with echo,' White recalls. 'which took away a lot of its aggression. His b-side, 'I've Gotta Buzz', was one of the worst songs I've ever heard.'

A disenchanted Buzz broke up several months later with plans for a second release in tatters. Meanwhile, a second Boston Dexters had been formed around their original drummer, Toto McNaughton, and newcomers Robert 'Smiggy' Smith, Gus Rennie, Ally Black (ex-Athenians) and Linnie Patterson.

'I was DJ at the Place with a friend called Brian Cairns,' Patterson recalled. 'Sometimes Brian would switch the records off and I'd sing a few lines. That's how I started as a vocalist.'

Linnie was already something of a local hero. He'd once been crowned 'king of the mods' and was carried around shoulder high in a chair on the night the Gamp was closed down. As DJ his choice of material was perfect; Tamla/Motown, Stax and Sue with just a smattering of Ska, yet the crossover to that of a performer provided a challenge. Patterson was acutely nervous on his debut as group frontman. 'I had to stand with my back to the audience for the best part of the evening. I just couldn't face them.'

The reshaped Dexters remained together for nine months, but they could not survive the drummer's sense of disappointment. 'Toto was hurt when the original group broke up,' said Patterson. 'He pushed the new line-up so hard but we weren't in the same class. The musicianship was good, sometimes outstanding, but we weren't together long enough to knit. However Smiggy and I had become good friends and we moved on into Three's A Crowd right after that.'

Three's A Crowd were a supergroup long before such a term was coined, a unit drawn from the ranks of already-established musicians. Founded as a trio around Smiggy, Jimmy Bain (guitar) and Alan Pratt (drums), they were initially envisaged, in Patterson's words, as 'a Cream-type thing', but Linnie was later added to the line-up. 'We stuck it out for a while, but broke up when Jimmy took a job up north.' Bain, a revered guitarist even in these pre-virtuoso times, later resurfaced in Ritchie Blackmore's Rainbow, before forming Wild Horses with another Scot, the fiery Brian Robertson.

Unlike other contemporaries working in Edinburgh, Three's A Crowd anticipated the shift to self-expression now commonplace in London. Yet novelty was not their downfall, but rather the form it took. Esoteric soul sides punctuated well-established material - Tony Clarke's 'The Entertainer' was a firm favourite - and new acts from other cities still acquired a reputation by playing deep, faultless R&B. In Scotland the acid test remained the dancefloor, and those who failed to move the masses were quickly frowned upon.

Many aficionados gathered in Mr. Smiths, sited in Edinburgh's Lothian Road, and owned by the still-sedulous Waldmans. 'I was working in Bungys at night,' recalls Bruce Findlay, later manager of Simple Minds, 'and Brian came up with this idea to open a Chelsea Drugstore place with a boutique, a fashionable shoeshop, and international newsagent, along with a coffee-bar and record shop. I was the only one who took a stall.' It was quickly established as a Mod enclave, outside of which Vespas and Lambrettas were ranked while their owners pored over new releases. 'It was a hang-out for like-minded people,' Findlay explains, 'who were very selective about what they liked and wanted to buy.' Mr. Smiths was not in operation long and by 1966 Findlay had left the city to run a beach bar in Majorca.

Edinburgh's first truly pioneering act came from an unlikely source. Over the years several groups had laid claim to the name the Premiers, but by 1966 only one such unit remained. Its anachronistic style was rapidly falling from favour - their biographies stressed allegiance to Elvis Presley and Roy Orbison and a break between the older, more conservative members, and three newer arrivals became inevitable. Ian Ellis (bass/vocals), Billy Ritchie (organ) and Harry Hughes (drums) were determined to follow an imaginative path and broke away to form 1-2-3.

The trio made its debut, at Falkirk's La Bamba, in November 1966. Their set comprised of original songs and 'standards', but these latter pieces were studiously reshaped to become, in essence, new. It anticipated the techniques later used by America's Vanilla Fudge, but where the US group slowed their creations down for melodramatic emphasis. 1-2-3 were more concerned with swing and used the pieces as stepping stones towards self-expression, rather than a means in themselves. Yet they balanced this esoteric desire with a conspicuous focus on melody. There was nothing else remotely like it around, and an isolated 1-2-3 left for London the following February.

They secured a residency at the Marquee and were later signed to Brian Epstein's NEMS agency. The Beatles' manager was in the process of promoting a series of Sunday concerts at the Saville Theatre, many of which featured the pick of the dawning progressive era. The Jimi Hendrix Experience performed two shows on 7 May, supported by Denny Laine (with Strings Attached), Garnet Mimms and 1-2-3. It was the first of several such appearances, but Epstein's death and successor Robert Stigwood's Bee Gees concerns dashed the trio's hopes. Dropped by the agency and denied a record deal, they disappeared into a period of mediocre dates and general austerity, but a determined self-belief kept them together until the upturn arrived.

Although 1-2-3 had proved too ambitious for staid Edinburgh clubs, other new acts found success by adopting gradual changes. 'I had just left Three's A Crowd,' recalled Linnie Patterson, 'and was hanging around the Bandura, a Ukranian place where all the bands used to meet after gigs. One of them, the Jury, was looking for a frontman and asked me to join.'

Jake Scott, Jimmy Hush, Bill Scott and Willie Findlayson came from the outskirts of Edinburgh - Newtongrange, Lasswade and Penicuik - and as yet had failed to make an impact in the city. With Linnie on vocals the pieces slotted into place and by 1967 the group was established as a leading attraction. They were loud and aggressive, attacking material by Sam And Dave, the

Impressions and the irrepressible Isley Brothers (especially 'This Old Heart Of Mine'), but the quintet was also highly visual and demanding, and won almost undivided attention.

The Jury thus mirrored a new maturity evolving in British pop. The Beatles had followed *Revolver* with 'Strawberry Fields Forever', a breathtaking mesh of innovation, melancholia and studio trickery, while Ray Davies of the Kinks fused social comment and nostalgia in 'Dead End Street', 'Autumn Almanac' and 'Waterloo Sunset'. The Who bade farewell to pirate radio with *The Who Sell Out*, a montage of original material and jingles, the Yardbirds maintained a sonic attack with 'Happening Ten Years Time Ago', while the psychedelic underbelly, exposed by Pink Floyd and the UFO club, now included Family, Tomorrow and the Pretty Things.

Many of these attractions came to the new music from straight R&B. 'Where's that joint?', Mick Jagger enquired before launching into the meandering 'Sing This All Together' on *Their Satanic Majesties Request*, which confirmed their development from Chicago acolytes to narcissistic flower children. Although Scottish bands had included material by Jimmy Reed, Muddy Waters and other bluesmen in their sets, there were no crusaders for this more specialised form, no equivalent of the Cyril Davies R&B All-Stars. Scotland did not have the art-school tradition spawning such acts and thus the transition from blues-band to hallucinogenic was not, in general, an option.

There was, of course, the occasional, rudimentary lightbox. 'We mixed acetone and coloured water,' Patterson recalled, 'pressed it between two slides and projected it on to the wall.' Several foolhardy souls wore kaftans to the local miners' welfare institute, but paisley-pattern dreams were generally considered effete, and certainly alien. New acts did emerge; Chinese White, Leather Soul, and Plastic Meringue among them, but such groups were largely temporary affairs. Thus the transition to progressive styles was completed without recourse to 'Alice In Wonderland'. There would be no equivalent of Tomorrow's 'Three Jolly Little Dwarfs', but there was no Celtic 'Interstellar Overdrive' either.

White American music also began to assert itself, initially through the Byrds. The Lovin' Spoonful, the Mamas And The Papas and Jefferson Airplane followed in succession and although Scottish groups welcomed their perspectives and sounds, it would be left to another generation to fully integrate such influences. Yet it was clear, by 1968, that soul was being replaced by rock and the Jury signalled this shift of perspective by changing their name, symbolically, to the Writing On The Wall.

'Our whole music changed after we saw Family,' states Linnie Patterson, 'and we started writing our own songs. We did well in England, but at home everybody was still expecting a dance band. We lost a lot of fans until we changed their way of thinking.'

Writing On The Wall

Writing On The Wall did follow 1-2-3 to London, but only after winning the respect of their homeland. They too were managed by Brian Waldman, and their next move mirrored that of his previous protégés. 'We all got our apprenticeships,' said Patterson, 'packed our bags and headed off to London. Our base was at the Middle Earth club and for the first week we slept underneath one of its stages.'

The Waldman brothers owned this venue and, in a piece of corporate wisdom, later renamed the Place Middle Earth North. The London venue became the linchpin of the city's underground scene, showcasing bands from both Britain and the USA. Some, including Moby Grape, then found themselves in Edinburgh, playing to bemused, but grateful, west coast music aficionados. Such moments were, however, rare.

By 1969 the 'Wall had become a popular UK attraction, compounding all their musical strengths with a reputation for irreverence. This was a band which choreographed fights, during which Linnie was often ejected into the crowd. 'We smashed a bubble car onstage at the start of the Breathalyser,' he also recalled. 'I was sitting in the front seat and the rest of the band hit it with 7lb hammers. The crowd then passed it over their heads and out into the street. When the police came they thought there'd been a smash.'

The group, however, was unable to secure a deal, despite completing an exceptional demo, recorded live at the Middle Earth North. This gritty performance was the ideal introduction to the group and easily surpassed their official studio album.

'*Power Of The Picts* was produced by a guy called Dave Howison, who slept through the whole recording,' remembers Patterson. 'We were in the studio for about two weeks and nothing was working. On the last day we decided to do it all in one take, me as well. I went in and sang vocals with the rest so it was completely live. Unfortunately Howison 'came to' then, did the mix, and took all the edge off it.'

The Power Of The Picts was indeed a disappointment. The sound was flat, the group seemed lacklustre and the set failed to convey their verve and humour. Live, you laughed when Linnie yelled 'Oh God, I think I'm gonna blow my mind'; on record you blushed with embarrassment. There was only one brief spark of wit when Bill Scott introduced side 2 with some sprightly country dance band accordion. 'Bill's a fine player on the box, that was how he trained,' recalled Patterson. 'We decided to use it and then go straight to the heavy riff on 'Bogeyman'.'

The record sold well enough initially, fans were grateful to have something tangible at last, but it had no staying power and failed to attract new followers. The 'Wall were doomed to watch as groups they'd headlined over, Black Sabbath or Wishbone Ash, won superior recording deals. *Power Of The Picts* was released on Middle Earth Records, an outlet for various Waldman acts,

Tam White

including Tam White. Since leaving the Buzz he'd pursued a solo career, releasing several singles on Decca, including 'Amy', 'Dancing Out Of My Heart' and 'Girl Watcher', but these were marred by a stifling conventionalism. His Middle Earth album was a gruff, folk-nik collection, but it also failed to capture the singer's talent, especially when compared to another Ray Charles disciple, Joe Cocker. Sweet Plum, a singer reminiscent of 'Mama Cass' Elliot, Arcadium and the Wooden O completed the label's eclectic roster, but its prime acquisition was already questioning their position. They were hidebound by contracts combining recording, publishing and management.

'Chrysalis offered to buy us out,' stated Patterson, 'but Waldman wanted too much money, so they told us just to wait until our contracts with him ran out. We really shouldn't have, we should have pushed for it, because that's when the rot set in.' Denied access to recording for 18 months, the group found that, without releases, they were doomed to repeat the same gigs as before and could not make progress. They held out for the allotted period, by which time Chrysalis had grown noticeably cool and, to quote Patterson, 'Everyone had fallen out with everyone else in the band and we were all going in different directions.'

Willie Findlayson had already been replaced by Smiggy who, with Patterson, then left the group to seek a new career in California. Nonetheless, Jake Scott, Jimmy Hush and Bill Scott did continue and with Findlayson now back in the ranks, completed a final single as late as 1973. Although 'Man Of

Renown' was forgettable, 'Buffalo', its flip, was a moody, atmospheric piece and a final act of defiance. At their peak, the Writing On The Wall were truly special, but the band's calamitous progress added yet another name to a growing litany of unfulfilled potential.

The band's fate mirrored that of Edinburgh. A city which once boasted the stongest club scene was suddenly deprived of its principal venues. The Gamp and Bungys had ceased to operate, the Place/Middle Earth, although still active, lost its bearing as the Waldmans were distracted by other interests and the Top Storey was knocked down in urban re-development. The expansive McGoos featured local acts as well as visiting stars such as the Kinks and Small Faces, but it too would fold, the building left to rot, unattended. Those clubs that remained vied with static discotheques and by the end of the 60s the face of Edinburgh's pop had changed irrevocably.

One focal point for music was Bruce's Record Shop, opened in 1969 by the prodigal Bruce Findlay in partnership with his brother Brian. It specialised in 'long-hair'; progressive rock, imports and greatcoat blues; it stocked underground papers and displayed the work of local artists on its walls, rather than just plug product. Poet Alan Jackson was even invited to pen its advertorial odes. 'What is it the host of the party produces? A bottle, a joint, or something from Bruce's?' It encapsulated the era's pleasure principles and while the shop quickly lost a founding innocence, it was a welcome haven during its early months.

The new sounds, however, attracted a passive audience, who sat, listened and even applauded. Steeped in expertise, it denied the collective enjoyment held in the body talk of dancing and the exuberance of soul. In a perfect world, the two could be seen as interchangeable, alternative stimulations for the head and feet, but they increasingly sparked bitter rivalry. Progressive groups found venues less willing to accept them, which in turn enhanced the sense of outlaw chic with which its participants burnished themselves.

The few clubs remaining in Edinburgh's city centre lost members to those sprouting in the housing schemes. However, such places were not only bedevilled by residents' complaints but, more seriously, they became the focus for local chauvinism. Violence had always been present, but the growth of gang rivalry during this period was far more sinister. As territory became paramount, so demarcation lines were set. Buildings were daubed with slogans - YBT (Young Broomhouse Team) or YMD (Young Mental Drylaw) - and strangers greeted, at best, with suspicion. These neighbourhood clubs gradually dwindled in number, leaving a once-healthy scene tawdry and fragmented.

Even the one established counter-culture venue was struggling. The Combination had been founded in 1969 amid the labyrinth of passages snaking under Blair Street, just off the Royal Mile. It was the city's arts-lab - Jim Haynes was seen flaunting a Super 8 camera paid for by John Lennon - and the ambitious plans included rooms for groups to rehearse in, somewhere to drink coffee and eat, areas for painting, for plays and for films. Pennebaker's Dylan documentary, *Don't Look Back*, was an early success in an era when the film was rarely screened.

It was here that Skin played, Edinburgh's newest progressive unit, who offered complex, original material and, as a trio, were the long-haired successors to Three's A Crowd and 1-2-3. Led by Ed Jones, a local correspondent for *Melody Maker*, Skin were loud and self-assured, and secured a deal with Decca through the aegis of performer and poet Pete Brown. The label, somehow sensing lasciviousness, took exception to the unit's name, which was then changed to Human Beast. Their solitary album, *Instinct*, showed undoubted skill, but was bereft of purpose and suggested the trio was already past its best. The situation at the Combination had also declined with ego problems, 'untogetherness' and rumoured gangster involvement forcing its closure. Its demise ended the last frail hopes of keeping the capital's progressive scene alive.

INTRODUCING 1-2-3

We have made reference in previous programmes to the 1-2-3, an unique and completely individual group of musicians from Glasgow who have created an entirely new sound in "pop group" music. Musically speaking, they are exploring harmonic and rhythmic fields in much the same way as jazz musicians do, but if the "pop group" is to continue this sense of musical adventure is essential. We hope Marquee patrons will recognise the truly exciting nature of the 1-2-3 and will come and hear them this month on Friday, 12th, and Thursday, 25th. The group comprises : Harry Hughes (drums), Ian Ellis (bass) and Billy Ritchie (organ).

An item from the *Marquee Newsletter* introducing 1-2-3 to London audiences

CHAPTER 6
IT'S ALL LEADING UP TO SATURDAY NIGHT

Perhaps it was the example of Alex Harvey and the Poets, perhaps there was simply more talent, but where most of Edinburgh's beat musicians were content to follow trends, those in Glasgow preferred to set them. The city's first division contained the Gaylords, Sabres and Senate, but there were many other names struggling to gain recognition. One such act was the Arrows which included Fraser Watson.

'We were just friends from school, playing at the local youth clubs. The singer never turned up the first night, he stayed at home, shit-scared. Later on we played the Trocadero in Hamilton, doing a half-hour set between the big bands, wearing huge suits with big lapels and looking like idiots.'

The Arrows were active between 1962 and 1965, and evolved from a local attraction - 'getting the bus into town with the drumkit,' recalls Watson - into one touring throughout Scotland. The rest of the group, however, did not share Fraser's full-time ambitions and the guitarist began looking elsewhere.

In the meantime the Poets had prepared another single, 'I Am So Blue', which was issued in July 1965. A ballad, it recalled the sedate manner of 'Now We're Thru', but although lacking the latter's dazzling intensity, the song's harmonies and shifting mood confirmed the unit's peerless standing. Progress was, however, undermined by the first of several changes. Original drummer Alan Weir, upset at the use of a session musician, had already been replaced by Jim Breakey, but the departure of Tony Myles was both unexpected and unnerving. An integral part of a songwriting triumvirate with Gallagher and Paton, Myles had shaped the Poets' distinctive sound and the group, dazed by his sudden decision, opted to return to Glasgow. Their most pressing need was a replacement, and an audition was announced in all the local papers.

'I arrived at the Flamingo Ballroom at 11 o'clock on a Sunday morning,' recalls Fraser Watson. 'The manager took my name and put it at the foot of a list of about 50. The Poets were up onstage, going through a few guys, when

George Gallagher jumped down and came towards me. I'd never seen him before but he leant over and said, 'If you're any fucking good you're in.' My hair was slightly longer than anyone else's and, after a couple of numbers, that was me: a Poet.'

The group had maintained their following and their fan club continued to run four double-decker buses to out-of-town gigs. Yet they still refused to court easy popularity, preferring an original style to the all-pervasive soul. They did make forays into black music, Wilson Pickett's 'In The Midnight Hour', the Drifters' 'Feel Good All Over' or Howlin' Wolf's 'Smokestack Lightning', but the quintet's own songs were still paramount and Watson began writing within weeks of his arrival.

'I Was A fool,' ran the banner headline of a 1966 *Showbeat Monthly*. It introduced a vitriolic interview in which an embittered Alex Harvey told of fraudulent promoters, broken promises and unpaid fees. 'The scene down south needs the lid lifted off,' he added, 'to let the people see the squalid mess that's squirming underneath.' The frustrated singer was clearly disillusioned over his now faltering career and had regrouped to Kinning Park to rethink his future. Island Records did release his rough reading of 'Work Song', but Alex still harboured plans for the less formal style of 'The Blues'. These hopes went largely unrealised and instead he joined Leslie and the Patrick brothers in an all-star band at Dennistoun Palais.

The return of these exiles enhanced the whirlpool of west coast pop. Frankie Miller had quit the Del-Jacks and formed another group from the ruins of the lamented Blue Council. 'I always loved that band,' he states, 'and used to watch them at the Scene Club. They were such great musicians.' Miller took pianist John McGinnis and added ex-Luvvers' bassist Jimmy Dewar to create Sock 'Em JB, whose manifesto was quite explicit. 'We did a lot of soul stuff,' Frankie recalls, 'Otis, Sam And Dave and Wilson Pickett,' but it was a newer group, the Beatstalkers, which attracted the greatest attention. Mutual friends – Davie Lennox (vocals), Eddie Campbell (guitar), Alan Mair (bass) and Tudge Williamson (drums) – formed the latter act in 1962, but the line-up was quickly expanded to include second guitarist Ronnie Smith. The quintet then undertook a period of intense rehearsal before emerging with a weekly spot at Battlefield's Cooper Institute. 'It had two halls,' recounts Mair. The Quintones took the big one while we did our sets next door. Very few people came to see us, but it was a start.'

The Quintones were one of the city's vital feeder groups through which several accomplished musicians would pass. Singer/guitarist Alex Ligertwood left the ranks in 1964 to join the Senate, an act specifically formed to back Sol Byron. Byron, nee Billy Lochart, had been active in Glasgow's music scene for several years and, like the Poets, had been one of the attractions at the

Flamingo Ballroom. He recorded one of the city's few independent singles - an agreeable version of Marvin Gaye's 'Pride And Joy' - before jettisoning his regular group, the Impacts, in favour of this new aggregation.

Two other bands renowned for 'nursery' status were the Meridians and the Sabres. 'There were a lot of different people in the Meridians,' states Frankie Miller, who sang briefly with this Paisley-based group. 'I joined because I knew the drummer, Jeff Allen, but they seemed to change their line-up every week.' They were, under whatever guise, steeled by a messianic zeal, and a glimpse of their under-exposed potential was caught in a session for *Come Thursday*, a pop show exclusive to the Scottish Home Service which featured most of the country's leading bands as well as eager lesser lights. The Meridians offered material by Chuck Jackson ('Any Day Now'), the Righteous Brothers ('My Babe') and Mose Allison ('Seventh Son'), and by doing so not only reflected Scotland's obsession for obscure R&B, but made their instability all the more frustrating. Miller's tenure ended when he traded places with Sabres' vocalist Ian Crawford Clews. 'We exchanged,' says Frankie. 'I joined the Sabres, he joined the Meridians,' the ease of transfer suggesting that other groups were equally innovative.

The Beatstalkers also harboured pioneeing ambitions and built a following with a mixture of original songs, obscure Rolling Stones' tracks and material drawn from black America.

The Beatstalkers' 1967 single 'Silver Tree Top School For Boys'

'We wanted to do something more specialised,' recalls Mair, 'and by luck I stumbled across a shop in Battlefield - Gloria's Record Bar - which was run by a soul fanatic. I had already heard 'Gypsy Woman', but he was importing Otis Redding, the Tams, Don Covay, the list goes on and on. I just stood there - "What's this? Can I hear that?" - and he kept playing more and more. If there was one song that started the Beatstalkers' obsession it was the Impressions' 'It's Alright'. From that moment we were in the shop every week, ordering from *Billboard*.'

The Beatstalkers thus continued the established trend of scouring for songs viewed as exclusive, material no other Scottish band had discovered. They gradually built an original set, but astutely chose material which combined a furious dancebeat with strong, memorable melodies. 'Our fans were really loyal,' says Mair, 'because the set was made up of numbers you could not just go out and buy. No-one could hear those songs unless they came to see the Beatstalkers.'

The group was also highly visual, but where the Poets' continued wearing frills to maintain a sense of visual theatre, the 'Stalkers were unashamedly Mod and as such formed a tight bond with their audience. This stature was fully exposed in 1965 during an ill-starred attempt at an open-air concert in Glasgow's George Square. 'After it, rival bands said that it had been a set up,' remembers Mair, 'but you can't organize a riot.'

Their appearance was one of several lunchtime shows and the previous day the Gaylords had drawn a respectable crowd of six to seven hundred. But even as the Beatstalkers began preparing for the show, it was clear that thousands were descending on the city centre area. 'We got onstage,' said Mair, 'but every time we tried to play a number, the fans rushed forward. I think we managed three songs, but by that time the barrier that had been put up was gone and the stage was beginning to collapse.'

Mounted police scooped up the now-terrified musicians as their colleagues stopped all traffic in the streets surrounding a square which swarmed with teenagers. 'We got into the City Chambers,' adds Mair, 'which is linked to other important buildings through miles of underground passages. The police chief sent us through one which took us out in Albion Street, away from all the pandemonium. We all went back to my house, and waited. At four o'clock we were in every paper in Scotland.'

Many groups dismissed the antics of the day, but even if the group had organized something this grand, which is doubtful, they proved they were popular enough to pull it off. 'From that moment we could do no wrong,' states Mair. 'When bands came to the Barrowland, we were put on at the Dennistoun Palais to rival them.'

The Beatstalkers were now a hairbreadth from recording, without having to compromise. Word gradually filtered south telling of a Scottish Beatles, inspiring mayhem and fanaticism, and only a final nudge remained. 'Our manager's nephew was a masseur in London,' Mair recalls, 'and one of his clients was John Fenton, manager of the Moody Blues. He persuaded Fenton and producer Denny Cordell to come up and see us. They could not believe it, and the whole soul thing, the audience participation, just knocked them out.'

Within a week, the Beatstalkers had become Decca artists, but in the now obligatory fashion, it was at this point that matters went awry. 'We demo-ed two songs, the Tams' 'Hey Girl Don't Bother Me' and 'Gin House',' said Mair, 'and took them to London. Cordell said no, that they had this great composer, Tony Washington, who's written 'Everybody's Talking 'Bout My Baby'.

'We were out of our depth. We knew what we were doing in Scotland and we knew what we wanted to do in London, but we didn't have the power or know-how to stand up for our rights. 'Everybody's Talking...' was a good record, but it knocked us off course.'

Released in August 1965, it is an excellent single, set rolling by Campbell's splendid organ riff and some inspired, offbeat voices. But Cordell had decided to hedge his bets and produced a rival, paler version of the song for Roger Peacock, former vocalist with the Cheynes and later of cult group the Mark Leeman Five. Released the same day on EMI, this duplicity eroded confidence still further and, to compound the irony, within 12 months 'Gin House' was a Top 20 song in the hands of Amen Corner.

"Everybody's Talking...' sold just over 50,000 copies during its first month,' laments Mair. It should have charted, but didn't, because they were all bought in Scotland. Radio Scotland's listeners would be forgiven had they thought it was a hit as the song was featured heavily for several weeks. Other groups even played it at dances, basking in reflected glory, while the coupling 'Mr. Disappointed' was the subject of scrupulous attention, and in the process a Beatstalkers' anthem was unearthed.

---

for
the group going places
book

the beatstalkers

Contact
Manager **Joe Gaffney**
29 Wedderlea Drive
Glasgow, S.W.2
Phone SOU 0235 or MOS 8712

A typical advertisement for the Beatstalkers

'Bill Martin came into our rehearsal studio in Denmark Street,' recalls Mair.' He said "I've got this song, I wrote it specially for you" and he sings "Talk about D-I-S..." and we thought "God, this is so tasteless." However, we knocked it into shape and it became reasonable. It didn't represent the group to begin with; it wasn't 'Hey Girl' or 'Daddy Loves Baby' and all those other wonderful songs, but it became very popular because our audience could participate.'

'Mr. Disappointed' was a last-minute replacement for the original b-side, 'Never'. Although rewarded with a crowd-pleaser, the group still felt betrayed, an impression enhanced when the promise of a live album, to be recorded in Glasgow and crammed with all those 'wonderful songs', remained unfulfilled. The project was never taped, and these successive failures upset a group previously accustomed to success.

'In truth, we were struggling from that point on,' recalls Mair. 'We carried on playing to the same acclaim and were even banned from several places, but Decca didn't know what to do with us and we ended up with records which were so removed from our live set. We just couldn't get in tune with London or the London way of doing things. They, in turn, couldn't understand this Scottish group that didn't sell records in England.'

A glimpse of the true Beatstalkers was caught on record, tucked on the flip of their second single 'Left Right Left', which surfaced in 1966. 'You Better Get A Better Hold On' was written by Joe South, at that point an in-house composer for the Tams. Here his song is ripped apart by crunching, fuzz guitars, a rabid, stamping rhythm and the perky Mod arrogance usually confined to the Small Faces. This was the fury of the George Square riot and the sound responsible for such wild appreciation. Those puzzled by the tag of 'Scotland's Beatles' and those asking 'why the fuss?', could now hear the evidence, but only if they turned the record over.

Although passable, 'Left Right Left' was formula pop. Penned by the group's new producer, and fellow Glaswegian, Tommy Scott, it merely cloned the bluster of its predecessor without capturing its charm. Optimism that 'You Better...' would lead to representative top-sides proved ill-founded, even though the group's third single was pulled from the Tamla catalogue. Written by Holland/Dozier/Holland and first recorded by Martha And The Vandellas, 'A Love Like Yours' suggested success at last, but the Beatstalkers sounded curiously laboured, with sloth replacing pathos. The flip, 'Base Line', was a rousing instrumental, fun but throwaway, a piece in the process of development rather than the finished item. Composed again by Scott, it resurfaced as 'I Can Only Give You Everything' once Bill Martin had added the requisite words. The song was then passed on to Them, another of Scott's protégés, withering on Decca's indecision. It would not be importune to ask why the label, and others, were bent on placing Celtic groups with Celtic backroom staff, as if those with a similar brogue shared tastes and would automatically enjoy mutual understanding. The fact that the Beatstalkers, Them and the Boston Dexters had independent aspirations seemed somehow less relevant than their birthplace and hit singles certainly did not appear via a form of cultural zeitgeist.

The third Poet's single, 'I Am So Blue', did not restore the group's commercial fortunes and in 1966 they were removed from Decca's roster and placed instead on Immediate, Andrew Oldham's fledgling independent label. Three songs were duly noted as possible a-sides, from which 'Call Again' was chosen. Although retaining the now-accustomed sense of mystery, this particular composition lacked the arresting qualities of its predecessors and was inferior to the forthright 'Some Things I Can't Forget', issued on the flip-side. But, although Oldham had maintained his association with the group, progress was frustrated by an increasing indifference towards them.

'Everyone at Andrew's office was involved in their own arguments,' recalls Gallagher, 'and the Poets were just left to rot without any real attempt to co-ordinate recordings or any future tours. Other acts were equally hurt with his preoccupation with the Stones, we were left to the minions who just couldn't handle us.'

Five songs were readied for the Poets next a-side, four original compositions and a cover version of Marvin Gaye's 'Baby Don't You Do It', which the group often played live. Oldham was impressed with their arrangement, but was 'too committed' to produce the session and thus passed the reins to Paul Raven, then floor manager at *Ready Steady Go*, but later better known as singer Gary Glitter. 'Paul gave it the Phil Spector production,' recalls Fraser Watson, 'it was good and earthy before that, but the remix made it a bit wild and poppy.' On the final single there is considerable echo, even by Poets' standards, but this possibly helped disguise the splices required to cut down the original, lengthier take. 'Ours was far better than the one the Who did a few years later,' adds Gallagher. 'I don't think we were given credit.'

The Poets' cover version was definitive, surpassing even that of the Small Faces, wrapping its fervid plea in their distinctive 12-string drive. It captured an overpowering urgency, and a sense of total commitment, yet its commercial reward was negligible. Its failure exacerbated already simmering tensions and the group, quite simply, disintegrated.

'Hume Paton's father began to interfere,' said Gallagher. 'He was a very successful businessman in his own right but had absolutely no feel for the record industry. This rubbed badly with the London management who saw him as a total amateur. Oldham just broke all connection with us and that led to the break up.'

'George had had enough,' adds Watson. 'He didn't like the set-up with the band or management. A few politics came into it and he just got out.'

The new vocalist was Andi Mulvey, formerly of local act the Spirits. Gallagher briefly remained in the line-up alongside his replacement and a six-piece Poets toured Scotland's North Sea coast. 'George was so relaxed,' Watson recalls. 'All the tension had gone because he was getting out. The two of them were great together, just singing away.'

George Gallagher's departure was an insurmountable body blow, depriving them of a visual presence and a unique voice. Although Mulvey was a fine singer in his own right, the Poets had become a quite different prospect. Within weeks both Paton and Dawson had gone - Norrie McLean (bass) and Ian McMillan (guitar) joined in their place - as the revamped quintet, none of whom were featured in the founding line-up, toyed with dropping the Poets' name. It was, eventually, kept, but although interest in the group had not completely waned, they now had to accept a less prominent role.

Through no real fault of their own, the Poets' early rush on London had floundered. Dean Ford And The Gaylords, their erstwhile rivals, bided their time, but having replaced Bill Irving with Graham Knight, they too decided to head south. 'It was a terrible time for us initially,' recalls Junior Campbell. 'We were used to success in Scotland, but just couldn't get gigs in London because nobody knew us. We had to rely on word-of-mouth and that's eventually how we did it.'

The Poets

The group's struggle was relieved, at least partially, by their recording deal, and the previous releases had established a grounding. They had not suffered a meteoric smash and fall, thus progress was made at a more gradual pace. It may have proved frustrating, but the quintet eventually enjoyed a commercial success few contemporaries dared dream of. The first step was to drop the 'Dean Ford' and leave the name, officially, as the Gaylords. The next was to record their strongest single to date.

'We got 'He's A Good Face' through a publisher,' recalls Campbell. 'We walked into Al Gallico's and they played us this great demo which was slightly Dylan-ish, but also had Mod connotations.'

The term 'face' implied Top Mod, as in Small Faces, or the High Numbers' 'I'm The Face', but in this case it had been adopted by New York songwriting team Al Kooper and Irwin Levine, who had penned hits for Gary Lewis and Gene Pitney. Campbell's Dylan comment was pertinent as Kooper had played organ on 'Like A Rolling Stone', and such contrasting affections gave 'Good Face' its unusual drawl and vibrant hookine. This excellent single formed a bridge between the group's initially naive releases and their introspective successors.

'We were entering a new phase,' states Campbell. 'Our EMI contract was up and although they wanted to retain us, CBS were also interested. We'd also signed to the Starlite Artistes agency and now had new things to aim for.'

By this point the Gaylords' name was completely out-of-place and the quintet was subsequently dubbed the Marmalade. 'The ballgame had changed completely,' adds Campbell. 'We were working out of the Marquee and had a great student following. We weren't really underground, but we used to do all the Jazz & Blues Festivals.'

The new regime swung into blanket promotion. A publicity film was shot in which the group drove around London, jars of marmalade arrived at radio stations and a glowing testimony from Paul McCartney was avidly reproduced. The quintet set up a communal home in Archway, north London, wore paper suits or paisley-patterned trousers and generally considered anything which might attract attention. The campaign culminated in September 1966 with the release of their 'debut' single.

"It's All Leading Up To Saturday Night' was chosen by the staff at CBS,' Campbell recalls, 'while the flip-side was us trying to write something for ourselves, trying to progress. It wasn't much but at least there was the confidence to start.'

Despite Campbell's reservations, 'Saturday Night' is a wonderful period piece. A harpsichord introduction, redolent of the Yardbirds 'For Your Love', leads into the imagery found on 'Friday Night' and 'Friday On My Mind'; the restless longing for weekend freedom. 'Wait A Minute Baby' was indeed somewhat slight, but the harmonies were strong and the group's enthusiasm

REFLECTIONS OF MY LIFE

Words and Music by WILLIAM CAMPBELL and THOMAS McALEESE

WALRUS MUSIC LTD. sole selling agents KPM MUSIC, London WC2

The Marmalade

was infectious. The next release, 'Can't Stop Now' was a curious pop/soul effort, but its fussy arrangement failed to disguise a sense of anonymity. 'There Ain't No Use In Hanging On', another group original, was far superior and paved the way for the group's first self-penned a-side.

"I See The Rain' was recorded in New Bond Street,' remembers Campbell, 'and Allan McDougall, a Scottish friend of ours who worked in press, brought Graham Nash down. He liked the song and helped a bit with the production. I thought it was a great single, the atmosphere was really good. Jimi Hendrix voted it his favourite record of the year in *Melody Maker* and that was like an Oscar to us.'

It was a striking record, thanks in part to mid-60s wizardry. Skin-tight harmonies established a deceptive melody before the song sweeps into a gripping chorus. A tuned-down lead guitar line, suggestive of Duane Eddy, booms out as the group cheekily exploit the riff from 'Hey Joe', a nod to Jimi Hendrix with whom the Marmalade had shared a package tour. It captured the group at a creative peak, a factor reinforced by 'Man In A Shop', another piece cut from the self-same cloth, with its swirling tapes and wondrous harmonies. With these two singles the quintet captured the experimental aura of 1967s flower-power summer.

'Mike Smith was allegedly producing us,' recalls Campbell, 'but he'd just say "Right boys, Back at six," and leave us, which was wonderful. This was really when we learned our craft. The whole backing tape to 'Man In A Shop' was in reverse, to which we just added the voices.'

Within the space of a year the Marmalade had moved from self-consciousness to maturity, from interpreters to innovators. These records may not have been the freak-rock of a Soft Machine or Family, but they were exemplary, exploratory pop and have remained as fresh, light and inspired as they were when first recorded. In the meantime, CBS had not only added the Boots to its roster, but had also acquired the Beatstalkers, who had tired of Decca's ambivalence. However, rather than find themselves reborn, the group just exchanged one set of problems for another. Their CBS debut, 'My One Chance To Make It', was considerably low-key, lacking both flair and bite. The Beatstalkers had chosen a curious time to become suddenly self-effacing and a cluttered reading of a dancefloor favourite, 'Ain't No Sole In These Rock 'n' Roll Shoes', did little to expel doubts. Their status as a recording act still negligible, the group began strenuous efforts to establish themselves in London as a live attraction.

'If we hadn't wished to further our career, then we had everything we could possibly want in Scotland,' said Alan Mair, 'but we did want to break new ground.' A weekly residency at the Marquee Club, which spanned six months, helped bring the group a hard-core following, but the Beatstalkers were increasingly bereft of direction, a fact apparent in all subsequent releases.

They were now managed by Kenneth Pitt, whose roster also included David Bowie. 'Ken was anxious to promote his budding singer/songwriter,' added Mair, 'and as we were still puzzling over our records, he suggested we do some of David's songs.'

'David's songs' included 'Silver Tree Top School For Boys', 'Everything Is You' and 'When I'm Five', although it should be emphasized that only the first composition was actually issued as an a-side. 'The group went from one ridiculous situation into another,' opines Mair. "Silver Treetop' was not written for a soulful Scottish band and it was pitiful to watch Davie Lennox painfully rehearse the song in an English accent.'

The combination was not an artistic success. 'Everything Is You', a mock-Latin piece with echoes of the Tremeloes, was placed on the reverse of 'Rose Coloured Glasses', which itself was undistinguished. Meanwhile 'When I'm Five' typified the ingenious nonsense Bowie peddled at the time and is easily the poorest track the Beatstalkers recorded. Its coupling, 'Little Boy', was mercifully stronger, boasting proto-progressive guitar lines and, at last, a worthwhile melody. The song was written by Reg King, former singer of leading Mod group the Action, and an empathy between group and song was apparent. But the single was issued in 1969, by which time many groups were writing their own material, rather than relying on others. Time was ebbing for the Beatstalkers, and an ill-starred grab for publicity, by wearing mini-kilts, smacked of utter desperation. The end, however, was more sudden than the participants expected.

'We were about to play in Coventry,' recalls Mair, 'when Jeff Allen, who replaced Tudge, went into a post office. When he came out the van, with our guitars, amps; everything, had gone. We just didn't have the heart to continue and so that afternoon marked the end of the band.'

Despite the Beatstalkers once-fanatical standing, surprisingly few in Scotland noted their demise. They were simply one of many groups not only struggling with individual demons, but which now faced the change from pop to rock. An abiding passion for soul became suddenly irrelevant in the 1967 of a 14 Hour Technicolour Dream, yet paradoxically the Poets, once the proud vanguard of original material, became a living Tamla jukebox.

'We were doing a lot of good songs,' recalls Fraser Watson, 'a lot of gigs but it was a lean time really. We weren't a big band any more, just one of many.' Nonetheless, the group was sufficiently popular to interest Decca producer Eric Wolfson, and they arrived in London to record.

'Jim Breakey had left by that point,' Watson remembers, 'So we got in Stuart McKenzie from the Sabres. However, he disappeared with John Banks from the Merseybeats the night before recording and we never saw him for three weeks. In fact he'd bombed on pills and gone down some street smashing all the windows before getting arrested and jailed.'

The Poets completed what became their final single with the help of the Marmalade's Raymond Duffy. 'Wooden Spoon' owes much of its strength to his powerful drumming, although Watson's divebombing guitar and Mulvey's committed voice enhance its undoubted urgency. The completed master is more akin to hard-edged west coast pop/rock than soul, while 'In Your Tower' offered just a hint of psychedelia. 'It was Eric's bright idea to add the Indian flute,' admits Watson. 'We thought it sounded really horrendous, but he thought it was great and, as the producer, his view prevailed.'

The single made little change to the Poets fortunes and the inevitable changes occurred. Mulvey and McLean both left with Johnny Martin (keyboards/vocals), Hughie Nicolson (bass) and Charlie Smith (drums) joining the line-up. Within days Watson had also quit. 'I did a gig with the Pathfinders when Neil McCormack was ill,' he recalls. 'A few months later he became their manager and I was offered his job.'

The Pathfinders were, by the summer of '67, the most exciting attraction in Scotland. McCormack, another ex-member of the Quintones, had formed the group with the prodigal Clewsy, fresh from his short period in the Meridians, and the new act was quickly acclaimed for its gritty grasp of soul. Colin Hunter Morrison (guitar), Ronnie Leahy (organ) and Timi Donald (drums) completed the line-up of what became the consummate dance party, yet their vision of Tamla and Stax was couched in genuine excitement: with Clewsy the transcendent, impassioned frontman. Although their set comprised, almost exclusively, non-original material, the group brought to it a panache few rivals even dreamed of, while a distinctly heavier sound emphasised this independence. They were especially popular at the Picasso, Glasgow's latest leading club, although the competition for this accolade remained muted as the city was still unable to support a consistent club circuit. George Gallagher suggests a contributory factor.

'There was a gang problem in Glasgow at the time. It caused so much trouble in the clubs that half of them closed down.'

Glasgow's post-war housing schemes, notably Easterhouse and Drumchapel, festered with teenage discontent and Edinburgh's tearaways were tame in comparison with the fierce tribes of the west. The Tongs, Toi and Bundy guarded the shells they claimed as territory and tales of their arsenals of knives, clubs and axes proliferated freely. A religious divide encouraged tribal loyalties, but this was also the mean city of the razor kings from precious generations, a fearsome reputation which still lingered. If dancehalls had been the focus for trouble during the 'Bully Wee' 30s, then beat clubs were the target for their 60s counterparts.

'The youth clubs in the schemes could be heavy,' recalls Fraser Watson. 'There'd be one team on one side and another on the other, with fifty lassies up

The Pathfinders

front looking at you. You could feel the atmosphere building up. All of a sudden someone would cross and nut somebody and that would be it, there'd be a battle. But apart from the occasional stabbing, they all seemed to get up and walk away and by the time the police arrived they'd disappeared into the schemes, flinging bricks at buses. It was just frustration, I suppose, but if you weren't one of the team you were an outcast, so you had to get involved.'

Other regular dancers remember moments of madness when bodies suddenly scattered as fists, heads and feet flew while hot-headed tempers raged. The band played on, pretending to be oblivious, belting out a perverse soundtrack which would eventually pull the crowd back together again. The stench of violence clung to Glasgow throughout the decade, dooming the Barrowlands Ballroom, which closed in the wake of persistent fights and the reign of terror surrounding the 'Bible John' murders. A much-publicised weapons amnesty introduced an uneasy peace although the power of the gangs was more detrimentally broken when the Tongs leader was jailed for a just-for-kicks murder. 'I've done a boy in,' he reportedly bragged, having thrust a screwdriver through the heart of a total stranger.

The change came too late for many of Glasgow's venues, although those which remained often forged unlikely partnerships with local musicians. 'After the Poets I sang in a big band at the Flamingo Ballroom,' recalls George Gallagher. 'Fridays were hell because it was over-25s night and I had to sing standards, but Saturdays was rock, which was better.'

Gallagher subsequently switched to the Dennistoun Palais where he joined Alex and Leslie Harvey, Bill Patrick and Isabel Bond in a potentially enticing houseband, but one which splintered when the hall became a roller rink. 'It lasted about four months,' said Gallagher, 'after which Alex returned to London.'

The southbound Harvey was intent on exploiting a new air of experiment and in 1967 he formed the brazenly psychedelic Giant Moth. This short-lived enterprise inspired two fascinating singles which the singer completed with Jim Condron (guitar/bass). George Butler (drums) and beatnik acolyte Mox (flute). Their first release, 'The Sunday Song', had its comparatively mainstream structure peppered by finger cymbals and quasi-mystic instrumentation, while its coupling, 'Horizons', boasted offbeat rhythms, conga breaks and neo-Eastern promise. Alex then unleashed a firebrand reading of 'Maybe Someday', previously a gentle folk tune from the first album by the Incredible String Band. Subtlety was tossed aside in a delivery so maniacal that the fact the song remained recognisable was, in itself, an achievement. Backed by 'Curtains For My Baby', a bizarre re-reading of 'St. James Infirmary', the single confirmed that the performer was, yet again, out on a limb. Winter killed many empirical ventures, including Giant Moth and Alex next opted for a day job in the pit band of the London production of *Hair*.

Glasgow, meanwhile, thrilled to a new supergroup, culled from disaffected local musicians. Studio Six was studiously groomed for success and it was for this band Jim Breakey quit the Poets. Signed with Polydor at the end of 1966, the sextet did achieve popularity, although their four singles were frustratingly inconsistent. 'When I see My Baby' and 'Bless My Soul' were naggingly commercial, but while the former's chirpiness was emphasised by a dopey bassoon, the latter was hamstrung by over-ambition. Despite combining a Salvation Army Band and mock-English accents, the group failed to disguise the song's triviality. Their collective tongue-in-cheek approach was removed for 'Times Were When', but the direction this deep ballad suggested was abandoned for 'Strawberry Window', which took Studio Six into the realm of psychedelic pop. Cellos, sound effects, spoken passages and thrashing drums created an effective stew, but begged the question of authenticity. Guitarist Neil Grimshaw, the author of all his band's releases, was either a talent or pirate, but the unit's sudden demise in 1968 put paid to further speculation.

Despite the brief aside posed by Studio Six, few seriously queried the eminent position of the Pathfinders, or Jason's Flock as they briefly called themselves, before reverting to their well-established sobriquet. By 1968 several recording deals were beckoning, but the group was aware of the pitfalls entrapping many of their predecessors.

'We did some demos for Malcolm Nixon and Tommy Scott,' recalls Fraser Watson. 'They were unbelievable, trying to push us into a pop/soul thing. Ian also recorded 'Lovin' Things', the one the Marmalade had a hit with later, for CBS. The band didn't play on it, it was just him and an orchestra, but it didn't come out. Eventually we got involved with Tony Meehan.'

The former Shadows drummer was, by this point, heading a production/publishing company to which George Gallagher had submitted some new compositions. Several of his demos featured the Pathfinders in support, but it was the group, not singer, that Meehan was ultimately drawn to. He brought them to London and having financed the recordings of 'Road To Nowhere', a Carole King/Gerry Goffin song which was an integral part of the quintet's act, he took the resultant acetate to Apple.

Founded by the Beatles as a philanthropic outlet for creative ideas: be they music, film (*Magical Mystery Tour*) or a boutique, Apple became the natural focus for countless aspirants. Many were frivolous, in true 60s fashion, but the unfettered freedom the company offered was greatly welcomed. 'We were playing at the Cromwellian.' said Watson. 'When Tony burst into the dressing room and told us about Apple. He was playing it to Paul McCartney when George Harrison, who was in the next room, heard it. He came in and said "That's Great. Put it out."'

Tinkling bells had introduced Carole King's original 1966 version, but although its bitter lyric chronicled the break-up of the songwriters' marriage, she held her emotions in check. Three years later the Pathfinders unleashed the full power of their sound, leaving Clewsy almost screaming over the top, desperate to be heard above the roaring instruments and gasping volley of noise. Few records anywhere were this good, but its progress was dogged by controversy.

'The punters at Apple didn't like the Pathfinders name, so they changed it to White Trash.' explains Watson. 'The BBC objected, so all the first copies were withdrawn and repackaged with 'White' scored out.'

The group hated either name which were foisted upon them with little or no debate. The 'White' prefix was marginally contentious, coinciding as it did with Enoch Powell's 'Rivers of Blood' speech, but an attendant press release describing Glasgow as 'dirty, violent and riddled with slums', inspired self-righteous anger from rent-a-quote politicos. Their hot air cant quickly dissipated, but the squabbling undermined the band's enthusiasm. Trash then became victims of the infamous Apple blood-letting and saw their projected album shelved.

'It was good at first,' said Watson. 'We rehearsed in the studios downstairs and made a few friends, but things tightened up as time went on. We were just left sitting around after 'Road To Nowhere' bombed. No-one seemed to know what to do with us.'

With Beatles attention elsewhere, mainly their own disintegration, Apple and Trash were fast becoming moribund. Reduced to a quartet with the loss of Colin Hunter Morrison, the group was handed a lifeline by press officer Derek Taylor. 'The Beatles had just finished *Abbey Road*' recalls Watson, 'and Derek managed to do a fly one and nick one of the five acetates. He told us to go home and record it, which we did, and pick a number from it. He then wangled some studio time, sneaked us in on George Harrison's bill and somehow managed to get George Martin's original scores. That was it: 'Golden Slumbers'.'

A part of the interlocking suite which formed side 2 of *Abbey Road*. 'Golden Slumbers'/'Carry That Weight' gave Trash a melodic counterpart to the gruff drive of their debut. They made the piece their own, but Taylor's plan almost backfired when a furious McCartney demanded that the single be scrapped. John Lennon, whom the group had met during the Amsterdam bed-in, nodded his approval and declared 'It's going out.' Back in Glasgow cynics suggested that McCartney's petulance was because Trash had outplayed the Fab Four.

'Golden Slumbers' seemed a certain hit. Initial sales were encouraging and airplay was strong but EMI, who distributed Apple, chose to issue a competing version by Orange Bicycle. Although clearly inferior, this rival provided a fatal blow, and the singles cancelled one another out. Trash had tried to record without compromises: their flipsides, 'Illusions' and 'Trash Can', showed flair, but the group was now demoralised. They accepted an offer to back Marsha Hunt, an expatriate US rock/soul singer, and as such reached their biggest audience, half a million, at the 1969 Isle Of Wight Festival.

This ironic twist suggested the end of an era. With the Pathfinders reduced to supporting roles, the Beatstalkers in ruins, Alex Harvey sight-reading and the Poets playing unresponsive dives, little was left from the once-proud vanguard leading Scotland's beat challenge. 1969 had indeed been cruel, but beneath the surface was another undercurrent, slightly out of vision, building its momentum without the pressure of high expectations.

Apple recording artists' White Trash

CHAPTER 7
'. . . WEARING BLACK CHERRIES FOR RINGS. . .'

'A youth of mediocre talent. Only a completely non-critical audience, nourished on the watery pap of pop music, could have fallen for such tenth-rate drivel.' Folksinger Ewan McColl wrote this ill-tempered flagellation in the September 1965 edition of *Sing Out!* magazine. His target was Bob Dylan and such vitriol brought new meaning to the line 'Don't criticise what you don't understand.'

MacColl was born in Auchterarder, Perthshire on 15 January 1915, but grew up in Salford, Lancashire. A former dramatist, he turned to music in 1950 and not only helped found the pivotal Ballads and Blues Club, but was an integral member of the Critics Group, a workshop examining style, content and performance of the traditional song. Such orthodoxy helped inspire a mistrust of new, deviationist developments.

Hamish Henderson was another pivotal figure in the folk revival. A renowned collector, he spent much of the immediate post-war period travelling around Scotland, meeting singers, instrumentalists and raconteurs. In 1951 he joined US folklorist Alan Lomax on an extensive tour of the country and together they gathered a considerable body of songs. Lomax himself was no stranger to field trips; while assistant curator at New York's Library of Congress, he recorded both Leadbelly and Woody Guthrie and the resultant pollenisation between the US and Scotland provided source material for the campers and hikers of Balloch and Loch Lomond. Indeed Guthrie had spent some time in Glasgow during World War II when he, and fellow performer Cisco Houston, worked as merchant seamen. Other US musicians to perform in Scotland included Ralph Rizler, later of the Greenbriar Boys, and Ramblin' Jack Elliott, the latter recording a deferential reading of Will Fyffe's 'I Belong To Glasgow'.

By the early 60s a new, younger cabal of folksingers was emerging. They included Archie Fisher, Owen Hand, and Hamish Imlach; performers aware of Scotland's heritage, and voicing it in song, but who were equally conversant with American styles, as Bert Jansch recalled for *ZigZag* magazine. 'Archie Fisher used to say, "Have you heard this one?" and launch into a Reverend Gary Davis' number, which hasn't the remotest connection with the Scottish tradition.' Born in Glasgow, Jansch came to music through skiffle and Lonnie Donegan, but switched to folk on moving to Edinburgh where he discovered the Howff Club in the city's High Street. Founded as a theatre in 1961 by Jim Haynes and Roy Guest, the latter began booking folk acts when the former opted to concentrate on the Paperback and Traverse. Guests also performed, but it was the larger-than-life Imlach who left an impression on Jansch. 'He was the first real folk-singer I ever saw. I used to sit six inches away from him, watching his every move.'

The aspiring guitarist then took lessons from Len Partridge, a respected player who rarely ventured out of the Edinburgh milieu, and Jill Doyle, Davey Graham's sister. Born of Scottish/Guianan parentage, Graham was a seminal influence on British folk musicians and a pioneer of the beatnik trail around Europe, North Africa and India. His first recording, an EP for Decca entitled *Davey Graham And The Thamesiders*, appeared in 1960, a year before the artist completed his debut album, *Guitar Player*. It was, however, another EP, *3/4 A.D.*, which secured his reputation. Although buoyed by contributions from Alexis Korner, the set contains Graham's renowned 'Angi', a memorable instrumental and a piece which became an integral part of every young troubadour's repertoire.

Davey's 1964 release, *Folk, Blues And Beyond*, compiled material by Leadbelly, Big Bill Broonzy, Charles Mingus and Bob Dylan, the last-named of whom would prove inspirational to another young musician, Mike Heron. 'I had been playing in several different bands,' he explains. 'The Saracens were a kind of Hollies' imitation while the Abstracts were more Stones/R&B. There were a lot of maracas shaking there. I was also with Rock Bottom And The Deadbeats, which was very art college, and had one of the first electric banjo players.' When not involved with those acts, Mike was a member of a jazz band, which played several cafes with a repertoire based on the MJQ. It was in such haunts that he forged a solo career. 'There was a coffee bar called the Stockpot which was run on a New York basis. I played at tables and it was in the middle of all this that I discovered folk music, partly through the first Bob Dylan album.'

Heron's new interest was enhanced further on discovering a folk club founded at the Crown Bar in Lothian Street, near the capital's university. 'Archie Fisher and Jill Doyle started it on Thursday Nights,' Bert Jansch told rock historian Pete Frame, 'and Robin, Clive and I formed another one on Tuesdays.' Robin and Clive - Robin Williamson and Clive Palmer - were, by

1964, already working as an instrumental duo. Indeed the Edinburgh-born Williamson had accompanied Jansch on a first sortie to London during which the pair appeared at the feted Troubador. English banjoist Palmer joined Robin on his return and a hint of their formative years together is captured on 'Jazz Bo's Holiday', their contribution to a various artist's set *The Edinburgh Folk Festival 1965*.

By the time the album appeared the group had become a trio, as Mike Heron recounts. 'I used to go and see them at the Tuesday blues club. I was a fan, but they'd heard that I played in all these different bands and felt I'd be the ideal person to strum along with them.' The Crown had come to epitomise the feuding factions within folk. 'Archie's club became very traditionally-oriented,' Jansch explained, 'whereas ours went the other way, contemporary and more freaky.' It did, however, set a precedent for other public house venues in the city, as well as the later Triangle Club, but by that point many founding figures had moved elsewhere. The itinerant Jansch, who had followed Graham's path through Tangiers and Morocco, eventually settled in London, while Heron, Williamson and Palmer moved to Glasgow, where the latter had established a new venue. 'Clive's Incredible Folk Club was in Sauchiehall Street,' Mike recalls. 'It was one of the first all-night clubs in Glasgow, but it only lasted for about six months before the police closed it down. You had to get to it in a small lift which, apart from anything else, was lethal.'

Despite its short lifespan, the club was a magnet to Glasgow's folk subculture. Among those appearing there was Iain McGeachy, better-known as John Martyn, who had learned to play under Hamish Imlach's tutelage. 'Hamish taught me all the things I knew in C,' he told writer Andy Childs, 'and I used to go and see him all the time.' Although born in New Malden, Surrey, Martyn was raised in Glasgow as part of a musical family; his father, Russell Paterson was known as 'Scotland's Troubadour'. One of the latter's friends, Billy Synott, introduced the aspiring guitarist to Cisco Houston and Woody Guthrie, while Imlach's love of blues fostered a rootsier, Black perspective to Martyn's work, rather than the Scottish element prevalent in many contemporaries. Having played at the Glasgow Folk Centre, which had featured, among others, Alex and Leslie Harvey, Martyn gravitated to Clive's Incredible Club, before he too moved south. 'Everyone in Scotland was in awe of the London scene,' he explained in 1974, 'and that's where you went if you wanted to make it.'

Palmer, Heron and Williamson had meanwhile established a trio called, with reference to their venue, the Incredible String Band. 'Robin and Clive liked Ewan MacColl,' states Mike, 'but they also had a tremendous knowledge of early blues - Robert Johnson for example - and of jug bands. Meanwhile I brought an awareness of folk in the Dylan mould.' The combination was enticing and this fusion of disparate elements would remain characteristic of the

The Incredible String Band

group throughout its existence. The String Band also began recording, the fruits of which included a tape completed on a rudimentary console owned by Buzz guitarist Johnny Turnbull, and a fully-fledged collection undertaken in Glasgow. 'We went into this studio and put down our live repertoire,' Heron recalls. 'There was enough for an album, but I don't know what happened to it. I think the engineer was paid to forget about it.' The group was certainly being courted by several labels, including Transatlantic and Elektra. The latter's British representative, Joe Boyd, was already acquainted with Robin and Clive, having seen them perform together in Edinburgh. He felt an even greater excitement over the trio, which he signed in 1966.

The resultant *The Incredible String Band* was an enchanting compendium of the trio's contrasting muses. At times akin to a Celtic Holy Modal Rounders, at others indescribable with reference to others, the set revolutionised the notion of 'folk music', capturing its rustic traditions while imbuing the same with a wispish sense of mystery. The contrast between Heron's effervescent 'Maybe Someday' and Williamson's desolate 'October Song' is especially moving, and the pair's polar perspective was another integral part of String Band lore. Indeed Palmer is already marginalised; he only has one original song, 'Empty Pocket Blues', the traditional form of which is at odds with the rest of the album's idiosyncrasies. It was nonetheless surprising when, in the face of complimentary reviews, the String band broke up. 'Clive went to India,' Heron explains. 'He didn't want to continue, he didn't want more fame. Robin said, "I suppose that's the thing finished then. I'm off to Morocco, I might be back," and so I asked Archie Fisher to arrange a solo tour of Scotland.'

Bert Jansch had meanwhile established himself in London's burgeoning circuit. He worked out of Bunjies Coffee Bar, Les Cousins and the Scotch Hoose, where he was resident for about a year. It was, however, another exile who found commercial success. Donovan Philip Leitch was born in Glasgow in 1946, but although his family moved to Hatfield in England some ten year later, he still recalls the heritage of his early childhood. 'We'd gather together at New Year or a wedding and sing traditional Irish and Scottish songs. My father also used to recite monologues, in particular the poetry of Robert Service and it's from there I got a love of rhyme.' As a teenager Donovan became embroiled in the folk-based coterie centred on St. Albans. Mick Softley and Maddy Prior were among those playing at a public house, the Cock, while another, known as 'Dirty Hugh', taught Don the finger-picking style of the Carter Family and the flat technique of Ramblin' Jack Elliott. Alex Campbell and Derroll Adams proved influential on the young performer who was 'discovered', almost by chance, in 1964. 'The St. Albans' crowd went down to Southend to rave and sleep rough on the beach,' Don explains. 'There was a group playing there we knew called the Cops And Robbers, and their managers were there to see them.' Geoff Stephens and Peter Eden were largely conversant with the demands of Tin Pan Alley-styled pop, but the pair were attracted by the handful of songs Donovan sang during the group's intermission. They took him to London to record a series of publishers' demos which were then played to Elkan Allen, producer of the seminal *Ready Steady Go*. 'They promoted me as the new favourite of the European folk scene,' Donovan recalls, and indeed his peaked cap and denim garb contrasted the show's otherwise strictly Mod fraternity. His nimble, topical songs about, for example, that week's hit parade, made an immediate impression, and the singer's three-week residency culminated in a recording deal with Pye. The plaintive 'Catch The Wind' reached the UK Top 5 in March the following year, while further success ensued with 'Colours' and a 'protest' EP, *The Universal Soldier*.

Donovan had become a pop star, yet he was loathe to let its trappings affect him. He still played at Soho's haunts, notably Les Cousins, and for a time retained his kinship with Bert Jansch. The latter's fiery composition, 'Do You Hear Me Now', featured on *The Universal Soldier*, while the composer's version surfaced on his own album debut. Released in 1965, *Bert Jansch* confirmed the singer's premier position as both composer and musician through some startling

Donovan's 'Universal Soldier' EP

fretwork and haunting imagery. The set is renowned for 'Needle Of Death', one of the era's most chilling drugs' songs, the effect of which is heightened by Jansch's dispassionate vocal. Aficionados proclaimed the album's appearance – Jimmy Page openly acknowledges its influence on his playing – yet Bert was far from reaping the commercial rewards that Donovan enjoyed. 'That first album was sold to Transatlantic for £100,' Jansch told *ZigZag* magazine. 'I was hungry, starving and broke and that was the best deal (I) could get.'

Such penury helps explain the disdain with which some in the folk world held Donovan. He was chided for 'looking like Dylan', and mocked for embracing the pop world, yet those troubling to look beyond visual trappings found, not just a folknik, but a much deeper romanticist. If his debut album, *What's Bin Did And What's Bin Hid*, bore an affection for Woody Guthrie, the follow-up set *Fairytale* was a quite different proposition. Although recorded within months of its more derivative predecessor, this compulsive collection showed the singer shedding his Okie lilt and in its place proclaiming a more independent vision. 'To Try For The Sun' and especially 'Sunny Goodge Street', show a remarkable maturation from the Boho sage of, for example, 'Josie', and prepared the ground for the style of work to follow.

Bert Jansch also completed a second album in 1965. *It Don't Bother Me* was another strong selection, emphasising rather than denying the direction of earlier work. Jansch was part of a British folk perspective, rather than the US style eschewed by the early Donovan, and his releases were perceived within that context, rather than those of pop or rock contemporaries. Its highlights included 'My Lover' and 'Lucky Thirteen', both of which featured John Renbourn on second guitar. The pair then recorded the seminal *Bert And John* while the latter also contributed to the third Jansch album, *Jack Orion*. Ewan MacColl's 'First Time Ever I Saw Your Face' apart, this 1966 set comprised traditional material, ranging from the lengthy title song to a poignant reading of 'Nottamun Town'.

Jansch and Renbourn then founded a club of their own at the Horseshoe Pub in Tottenham Court Road. Although a haven for folk music, the venue did boast a light show, a feature reflective of the changes happening around them. Among the musicians featured at the club were Danny Thompson, Terry Cox and Jacquie McShee, each of whom joined the two guitarists in a subsequent venture, the Pentangle. This quintet became an integral part of Jansch's career, although he continued to record superior solo albums, notably *Nicola*, *Birthday Blues* and *LA Turnaround*. His influence, like that of Davey Graham, did recede, although there was no denying the craft both continued to offer.

Graham had continued to enjoy his peers' respect, but his work became marginalised. He was part of a different generation, of a beatnik culture now supplanted by the flower-child hippie. It was these naïfs who now took the trail to Kathmandu, while Donovan provided the musical version of this transformation. Having rid himself of the dying vestiges of bedenimed costume, the singer found himself embroiled in an ugly and protracted wrangle over his commercial soul. His wish to employ Mickie Most as producer resulted in an injunction, debarring Donovan from recording in Britain. The master for 'Sunshine Superman', a song already aired on television's *A Whole Scene Going*, was shelved. While other sessions were undertaken in Los Angeles, Donovan was effectively 'off the British charts' for most of 1966.

'Sunshine Superman' topped the *Billboard* Hot 100 in July that year, and a UK pressing followed in December once the legal dust had settled. This adventurous, engaging performance is one of the era's most memorable singles and was the first of many excellent recordings. 'Mellow Yellow', 'There Is A Mountain', 'Hurdy Gurdy Man' and 'Atlantis' were among the highlights in a run of stylish pop moments, while the artist's talent was extended further on a series of picturesque albums, including *Sunshine Superman* and *A Gift From A Flower To A Garden*. The latter, a double set, featured a series of acoustic performances many of which embraced Scottish themes. Songs such as 'The Isle Of Islay' or 'The Tinker And The Crab' evoked a minstrel image at which Donovan was particularly adept. While it's true his post-60s work lacked the charm of these releases, the singer continues to record material shaped by the era's idealistic dreams.

Although he'd quickly leave that impression behind, the early John Martyn offered elements apparent in the *Fairytale* Donovan. He too had become a London resident and gigs at Les Cousins presaged a spell on the Kingston Folk Barge which in turn resulted in a crucial professional contact. 'A fat man called Theo Johnson appeared,' Martyn explained to Andy Childs. 'He'd just recorded two albums of bawdy ballads for Island Records and he took me to them with a song called 'Fairy Tale Lullaby'.' The label duly signed the young performer and his debut album, *London Conversation*, followed in 1967. Given the prevailing psychedelic air which surrounded its release, the set's adherence to strict folk club formulae restricted its contemporary appeal, yet it contains several amiable tracks, including 'Rolling Home' and 'Back To Stay'. The latter's unconventional structure was indicative of Martyn's ultimate direction, although it's equally true that the follow-up set, *The Tumbler*, shared the largely traditional merits of its predecessor.

This second album was produced by Al Stewart, Glasgow-born but Bournemouth-raised, and another habitué of Soho coffee dens. Stewart had toyed with the pop world, recording an uncharacteristically whimsical single which coupled 'The Elf' to the Yardbirds-penned 'Turn To Earth'. He drew greater plaudits for producing *The Paul Simon Songbook*, recorded while the US singer was domiciled in Britain. Stewart's album debut, *Bedsitter Images*, encapsulated the melancholia of London while on his second set, *Love*

Chronicles, the singer enjoyed the dubious plaudit of being the first Briton to sing the word 'fuck'.

'I think somebody said I should have a producer, and Al probably volunteered,' Martyn explained to *ZigZag*. *The Tumbler* also featured flautist Harold McNair, who appeared on several Donovan sessions, notably 'There Is A Mountain', and the extra texture is indeed welcome. His counterpoint on the engenue 'The River' remains attractive, while 'Dusty' and 'Fly On Home' also benefit from his contributions. *The Tumbler* still bears a debt to Bert Jansch, but shows a performer beginning to assert his independence.

'I then became friendly with Jackson C. Frank,' Martyn told Andy Childs. Another ex-patriot American, Frank was feted on the London circuit and his all-to-brief sojourn left an indelible mark on his peers. 'He was an absolute fucking genius,' Bert Jansch told Pete Frame. 'A lot of the music that came out of that period was certainly due to him. He wrote one song in particular, 'Blues Run The Game', which influenced just about everyone who heard it.' Martyn joined Frank on an appearance at the Chelsea College of Art, the bill for which also included Beverley Kutner, better-known simply as Beverley. A pop-cum-folksinger, she had launched the Deram label with 'Happy New Year', before completing a gorgeous version of Donovan's 'Museum'. Another of Joe Boyd's protégés, Beverley was signed to his Witchseason publishing company, and, with this in mind, she invited John to work as back-up guitarist on several forthcoming sessions. The pairing gelled, both professionally and personally. 'It seemed obvious to go as John and Beverley Martyn,' the former explained in 1973, 'and to make an album together.' The result was the excellent *Stormbringer*, released in 1970, on which Band member Levon Helm and acclaimed bassist Harvey Brooks lent stellar support to the duo's contrasting perspectives. John's folk background brought depth to 'John The Baptist' and 'Would You Believe Me', and the same sense of continuity prevailed on the duo's next release, *The Road To Ruin*, which was otherwise marred by an uncomfortable flirtation with jazz. The notion itself was admirable, but rather than interact, the embellishments were overdubbed, robbing the set of a natural spontaneity.

The notion of experimental bravura was exemplified on Witchseason's most unconventional act, the Incredible String Band. 'Robin returned from Morocco in the middle of my solo tour,' recalls Mike Heron. 'He was revitalised and reappeared with hand drums and all these songs he'd written. We went to London with Joe Boyd and recorded those as well as my own. The results were so fresh - there's no embellishments - and Robin sings 'First Girl I Loved' with all the emotion he had when writing it.' Such material formed the basis for *5,000 Spirits Or The Layers Of The Onion*, the String Band's 1967 release. This audacious selection was rightly hailed as a triumph as Heron and Williamson grabbed whatever instrument suited the timbre of a particular song;

Typical Incredible String Band poster art

sitar, oud, gimbri or tamboura, and coloured it accordingly. While the former offered compositions indebted more to recognised structure, as evinced by the delightful 'Painting Box', the latter often allowed his imagination to rise over formal meter and the results, on 'My Name Is Death' or 'First Girl I Loved', are enthralling. The latter song, which tells of a chance meeting with a long-lost lover, manages to be moving without becoming maudlin.

Part of the String Band's attraction was this firm demarcation between the pair's songs. 'I think we wrote one together,' states Heron, 'but generally I would write a song and then take it to Robin to embellish. He was such a good multi-instrumentalist. I couldn't do so much with his unless it was a blues-y one on which I'd add harmonica. That was why I learned the sitar. It was an ideal instrument to use in that way.' The group's 1968 release, *The Hangman's Beautiful Daughter*, emphasised their differing visions while remaining firmly within what could be perceived as folk. Seven of its 10 tracks were Williamson compositions, which ranged from the fragile 'Nightfall', through the quirky 'Witches Hat' to the lightly operatic 'Minotaur's Song'. Heron's contributions included the lengthy 'A Very Cellular Song' and the ebullient 'Mercy I Cry City', the sound of which suggested it may have been a much older recording. Yet if the album suggested a honed economy, its sprawling successor, *Wee Tam And The Big Huge*, was a madcap compendium of fleeting instrumentals, lyrical musings and expansive meanderings. There's much to admire in its audacious spread, and its simpler, almost 'live', performances. Williamson offers his customary ambition, both 'Ducks On A Pond' and 'Maya' last in excess of nine minutes, but it is Heron who provides the albums' finest moments in 'You Get Brighter' and 'Cousin Caterpillar'.

'It wasn't the folk scene anymore; there were no barriers at all,' says Heron, and indeed the String Band were seen as an immutable part of the 'underground', supporting Pink Floyd at Brian Epstein's Saville and headlining at the UFO or Middle Earth, where their sense of adventure echoed that of concurrent hippie zealots. The colour photos on the double's sleeve were shot in Frank Zappa's garden while the ISB were later one of the acts featured on the bill at Woodstock. Scotland's home-based counter-culture was, at best, sparse, yet the String Band remained inseparable from the movement's international progress.

CHAPTER 8
IN THE LAND OF DREAMS

The trickle of Scottish groups leaving for London had, by the late 60s, become a haemorrhage. Yet if the Gaylords or Beatstalkers departed with little left to prove, less successful compatriots slipped away to much less fanfare, frustrated at the impasse strangling Scotland's once-proud circuit. Redevelopment, gangs and legal constraints had killed clubs in Glasgow and Edinburgh, but alternative work could be found in civic halls and corn exchanges, local venues which switched to teenage dancing whenever the weekend loomed. Yet by 1968 these outlets too were folding. 'Within two short years,' recalls Andy Lothian, 'a number of large promoters ceased operating. Border Dances, who had been running 24, sometimes 30 dances on a Friday night, disappeared. Stardust Promotions, who worked all of Central Scotland, shut down. The music scene changed completely.'

Lothian too would bow out, as did Albert Bonici, both of whom were unhappy with Beat's replacement, Progressive Rock. New entrepreneurs did appear, but they faced considerable problems, as Eddie Tobin, who helped run Music and Cabaret, one of Glasgow's leading agencies, explains. 'The type of music heard in the halls was not played on the radio. The new groups brought in guitar solos, organ solos, drum solos; they were getting louder and heavier. The numbers going to the traditional dancehalls and community centres dropped away because you couldn't dance to this music. The town councils in turn closed their doors and, as far as I'm aware, most of them never reopened'

A new generation of bands emerged - Gully Foyle, the Sleaze Band, Power Of Music - resplendent in t-shirts or rugby jerseys, a uniform showing a calculated disinterest which proudly proclaimed their mistrust of pop's demand for pretty styles. The pick of this musicianly challenge nonetheless came from those rooted in the past, but the concurrent great white blues boom, like the R&B vein which preceded it, did not inspire a serious Scottish equivalent. Edinburgh's East-West were contenders for a short while, headlining an open-air festival in Princes Street Gardens at a time when such things mattered, but many new groups preferred to build their progressive rock from the inevitable soul base. 'A lot of our early influence was black American, Tamla and Stax' recalls Alasdair 'Zal' Cleminson, who initially came to prominence as lead guitarist with the Bo Weevils. 'I was playing parts with a sound like Steve Cropper or Buddy Guy.'

Although active between 1965 and 1968, the Bo Weevils were a new, and much younger, attraction. They did not offer the burning soul of a Pathfinders, but a simpler, more upfront music where a gutsy solo was as vital as the rhythm of the song. The Weevils were punchy, loud and aggressive and held aspirations to progress. Three of the 1968 line-up - Cleminson, Dave Batchelor (keyboards), Chris Glen (bass) - resurfaced in Mustard alongside Willie Monroe (drums), ex-Beatstalker Eddie Campbell and former Poet Andi Mulvey. The last-named dropped out soon afterwards, but despite its undoubted promise, the new act proved transitional rather than an end in itself. When Campbell also left the line-up, the remaining quartet adopted a new name, Tear Gas.

'The circuit in Scotland was still pop,' recalls Cleminson, 'but when Tear Gas went on they definitely rubbed some people up the wrong way. We had a very aggressive approach which disappointed those still expecting a soul thing and that in itself gave the band a name and image.'

Drawing inspiration from Deep Purple and (later) Led Zeppelin, Tear Gas joined a growing number of aspiring Scottish acts struggling to gain a foothold in an ever-decreasing circuit, but determined to follow the progressive path. In 1970 Tony Calder, once Andrew Loog Oldham's partner at Immediate, arrived in Glasgow seeking possible signatories for a new venture, Famous Records. 'We'd got word that he was coming up,' said Cleminson, 'and a lot of bands kind of auditioned for him, playing their own material. We'd been writing a lot at that time and he obviously liked our stuff.'

Tear Gas were taken to London to record and the resultant album, *Piggy Go Getter*, was issued in November that year. Tough and raunchy, it proclaimed the group's raw sound which was built on solid riffs and a cohesive mesh of organ and guitar. Cleminson emerged as a highly skilled musician

The release of *Piggy Go Getter* coincided with the emergence of several new Glaswegian bands, including Northwind and Beggars' Opera. The latter act was the flagship of the 'rival' Inter City Entertainments agency, and as such quickly built a rabid local following. They secured a prestigious deal with Vertigo which resulted in the release of four albums. *Act One* established Opera's love of flashy instrumentation but, if undeniably adroit, the style lacked both heart and melody. It suggested a heavy-rock symphonia of which their furious reading of 'Classical Gas' was the most unfortunate recipient. *Winds Of Change* and *Pathfinder* followed in a similar manner, before the group axed much of their pretentious airs for *Get Your Dog Off Me*. By this point, the line-up had changed considerably with the revamped Opera buoyed up by the arrival of Linnie Patterson, fresh from a rejuvenating spell in California. He was an adept foil for founder member/guitarist Ricky Gardener, but the unit's early glory had long-since evaporated and they split in 1974.

Another group to unfold at this time was Power, which brought together several of Glasgow's most experienced musicians. Their singer was Maggie Bell, who began her career in the Kinning Park Ramblers, about to be swamped by Merseybeat and R&B. 'I met Alex and Leslie Harvey when I joined the Ramblers,' she recalled. 'I went up to their house in Durham Street and they were playing 'Tell The Truth' by Ray Charles with Margie Hendricks, and some great songs by Big Maybelle. Then I heard Aretha Franklin, and she changed my life around.'

The Ramblers did not survive the mid-60s upheavals, but Maggie resurfaced in the houseband at the Dennistoun Palais where she forged an impressive partnership with fellow vocalist, and ex-Rambler, Bobby Kerr. Their fiery combination was captured on two 1966 singles, '(I'm) Never Gonna Leave You' and 'Climb Every Mountain', which the duo recorded under the showbiz tag, Frankie And Johnny. Although crying out for a more subtle, rhythmic groove, the recordings showed something of the singers' spirited interplay, while 'I Wanna Make You Understand', the flip of the latter, later became a fêted item in northern soul circles. The pair broke up when Kerr began a solo career and, as her spot at Dennistoun had been taken by Isabel Bond, who had returned from Hamburg, Maggie crossed over to the Glasgow Locarno.

'Some weekends used to be pretty hairy up there,' she recalls, referring to inter-gang strife. 'You had the Fleet from Maryhill, the Tongs and the guys from the US Naval base at the Holy Loch, and tables and chairs could go flying.' Bell fronted the support band at the venue which, despite these occasional aberrations, quickly expanded its Top 20 routines to include material by the Modern Jazz Quartet. Bill and Bobby Patrick and Leslie Harvey were also in the line-up, and the alliance they forged with the singer inspired the creation of a new group.

'The four of us went to Germany,' observes Maggie. 'Bobby knew all the good American bases although we did run into a bit of trouble. They were all segregated - black servicemen on one side, white on the other, but both came on the first night to look at the band. I just opened my mouth and sang Aretha's 'Respect' and for the rest of the month we only played to black guys.'

The quartet remained in Germany for a little over a year during which time they 'ate, slept and thought music the whole time.' However, the lure of a new British scene only accessible to them on record proved too great for Bell and Harvey. 'Leslie and I had had enough,' Maggie recalls. 'We felt there was more to life than working in Germany, so we jumped into a Lufthansa jet and came home.' Now resettled in Glasgow, the pair heard about a gritty band new on the circuit, which included bassist Jimmy Dewar and organist John

McGinnis. 'We went up for a jam,' said Bell, 'and knocked each other out. Jimmy and John said that they might have a residency at a pub that was opening and would we be interested in joining them? We were, and that was Power.'

The pub in question - the Burns Howff - became a focal point in Glasgow's music scene throughout the ensuing decade. Power became established at the venue where the discipline of a prolonged stay provided time to hone a stylish cross-section of hard rock and soul. Meanwhile, Frankie Miller, former colleague of Dewar and McGinnis, had worked with his own group, Westfarm Cottage, prior to joining the Stoics. The latter quartet tempered abrasive progressive rock with interludes of quality pop, shades of which were apparent in the group's sole single. Released on RCA in 1968, 'Earth, Air, Fire And Water' was an endearing slice of commercial cosmology, but the flip, 'Search For The Sea', written by guitarist Jimmy Doris, was much stronger. Its alternating moods served to underline the songwriter's undoubted skills. The single also provided a link across the generations: 'Earth And Fire' was arranged by one-time Ricky Barnes' guitarist Joe Moretti.

Miller joined the Stoics - Doris, Jim Casey and John Wynn - after the single was issued. Although Doris was considered the principle songwriter, Miller also introduced some equally strong originals and a friction developed between them. 'Jimmy and I just weren't hitting it off,' Miller explains. 'He really wanted to do co-written songs and I felt some of them weren't good enough.' Mark London, an executive from the company managing Lulu, signed Doris to a five-year publishing deal, but Frankie was a little more reserved. 'I didn't like London. I thought he was a bit of a fly man and wouldn't sign with him.' Yet despite this disharmony the Chrysalis label was intent on wooing them. 'They took us to Germany to tour with Ten Years After,' Miller recalls, 'but in the end they offered me a publishing deal, which I took.' A split in the group was now inevitable and while Frankie laid plans for a solo career, Doris concentrated his efforts on songwriting, particularly for Lulu.

The singer's career had taken a new twist on recording 'To Sir With Love', the theme song to a film she also starred in. Although a flop in the UK, the single swept the USA, topping both the national and R&B charts and Lulumania was such that the three-year old 'Shout' was dragged back into the *Billboard* Hot 100. Such success on the black music listings was not lost on Atlantic's Jerry Wexler, who signed Lulu to his label when her contract with Mickie Most expired in 1969. Wexler, a veteran R&B producer, had already secured an artistic success with another British woman singer, Dusty Springfield, and the wedding of voice to crack soul houseband was now repeated.

Lulu cut two albums for Atlantic. *New Routes* featured the Muscle Shoals group – Roger Hawkins, David Hood, Jimmy Johnston and Barry Beckett – who had contributed to a clutch of records fervently worshipped in Scotland. Guitarist Duane Allman was also present, but the sessions were often fraught, and rumours of a tearful singer abounded as Wexler demanded a harder performance. The final work showed Lulu to be more comfortable with the pop version of soul than the real thing, and her voice invariably had all the form, but little of the substance. For the second set, *Melody Fair*, Wexler used the less imposing Dixie Flyers, but the relationship was then ended. It did provide some excellent moments, but the pick of the material came from Doris, whose deep ballad, 'Oh Me Oh My', suited Lulu perfectly. Another US smash, it was one of her most moving performances, where at last singer and material worked in harmony.

Other singers, notably Aretha Franklin, also recorded the song, but its composer would never gain the recognition his work deserved. Prone to bouts of self-doubt and depression, Doris became less and less prolific. He later died in London having been struck by a bus.

The demise of the Stoics, a group of such stirring potential, indicated yet again that talent and success were not synonymous. Something else was

The Marmalade

required, be it self-belief or even staying power, which allowed a group to survive indifference until a breakthrough appeared. For some that only came with compromise.

'The Marmalade had been offered 'Everlasting Love',' recalls Junior Campbell, 'but said no because we wanted to do our own material. Then the Love Affair took it to number 1. We'd been at CBS for two years and had four singles out to negligible return. It was, if you like, the big cop-out.' The group was told, quite bluntly, that time was running out and 'Lovin' Things', already tried, and rejected on the Pathfinders, was resurrected for one last push. 'We knew the song already,' explains Campbell, 'because Graham and I had helped out on the original session. Bill Martin recommended the song again to Mike Smith and that was it. Big hit.'

By 1968 CBS had become skilled at production-line sessions and virtually all of their UK acts, including the Love Affair, the Tremeloes, and Georgie Fame, were subjected to the sweeping, booming Keith Mansfield Orchestra. Bubblegum sweet and bouncy, 'Lovin' Things' gave the Marmalade that elusive UK hit, but at the obvious expense of their identity. The song, rather than the act, was the success, and the creativity of a 'Man In The Shop' was discarded for unabashed pop.

'It took us seven years to become an overnight success,' reflected Campbell. 'We really did work hard for it, but were a little disappointed with the way it had gone. It wasn't what we would have chosen.'

Despite this disquiet over content, the Marmalade had at last achieved a breakthrough. Although Alan Whitehead had replaced a homesick Raymond Duffy, it was essentially the same act which had moved to London and their perseverance had now proved worthwhile. 'We were the only ones prepared to turn our back on success in Scotland and really have a go where it mattered,' opines Campbell. 'We forsook money and, if you like, getting our jackets torn off in George Square. We made the grade and other bands thought that if those bastards can do it, so can we.'

Nothing was left to chance with the follow-up and the boisterous 'Wait For Me Mary-Anne' aped the formula of its predecessor. The group then closed the year with a chart-topping smash with a cover of 'Ob Li De Ob Li Da' lifted from the Beatles' *White Album*. The song was outrageously commercial, and a mock Bluebeat lilt and jokey JA vocal enhanced its infectious, good-time party atmosphere. Such consistent chart success was rare to Scottish pop and if 'Baby Make It Soon' failed to emulate the same success, at least it maintained the group's momentum. 'Butterfly', released in October 1969, was an unfortunate flop, yet it was easily their best recording since the halcyon days of 1967. The reasons for failure, however, were political rather than musical.

'The CBS contract was up for renewal,' said Campbell, 'and Decca outbid them. They also gave us free time in the studio and the first song we recorded was 'Reflections Of My Life'.' This thoughtful, self-penned ballad not only gave the Marmalade a second number 1, it also became a substantial international hit, emphasizing just how popular the group had become. 'My Little One' and 'Rainbow' followed it into the UK chart, but despite the promise offered on *Songs*, by 1971 predictability had crept into their work and one member, at least, wanted out. 'I thought the band had gone as far as it could,' Campbell recalled. 'We were good friends and had stuck together, but success seemed to change us radically and we were going in different directions. I decided to pull out and Hughie Nicholson was just the injection they needed.'

Nicholson joined from the Poets who, despite operating in a twilight zone of smart suits and Midlands' supper clubs, nonetheless retained an air of optimism. They cut demos of Hughie's excellent songs which in turn were picked up by other Scottish acts. (White) Trash had used the compulsive 'Illusions' on the flip of 'Road To Nowhere', and it was doubtlessly this songwriting talent which attracted the Marmalade. While Campbell embarked on a solo career, his replacement brought the required new perspective which, while still commercial pop, had both flair and a quirky imagination.

'Cousin Norman' and 'Back On The Road' were bright and memorable, but the best was 'Randancer', a brash piece of clubfloor chic where the male strutted peacock-like, sure of his attractive skills. The fade contained several worthwhile one-liners - 'Read your Sunday papers' referred to the groupie exposé splattered across Fleet Street tabloids which somehow decided the group was guilty of on-the-road sexual transgressions. 'Dance, dance, Ian McMillan' was a neat sideswipe at Nicholson's erstwhile partner in the Poets.

That particular group had also provided the Marmalade with its new drummer, Dougie Henderson. Charlie Smith took his place, but this realigned Poets later rejected a now-passe name, opting instead for Chapter 22. By the mid-70s the act had broken-up completely.

Ian McMillan sought new pastures by joining Cody, a Trash offshoot completed by Ian Clews, Timi Donald, Ronnie Leahy and 'newcomer' Norrie McKenzie. Recoiling from their unsettled past, the new act offered a blend of country-rock and Crosby, Stills And Nash, but only one single was ever completed, the melodious 'I Belong With You'. Their premature break-up ended the Pathfinders' legacy with Leahy moving into production and Clews leaving music to raise stud horses in Arizona.

Despite the bravura on 'Randancer', morale within the Marmalade was ebbing. Nicholson decided to leave and a stream of departures followed. Dean Ford completed a solo album before settling in the USA, and when the flurry finally died down Graham Knight was left holding the name, which he took into the dinner and dance/cabaret circuit, reliving foggy memories for ageing suburbanites.

Nicholson, McMillan and Timi Donald re-emerged together in 1973. Dubbed Blue, the trio partially fulfilled the promise of their immediate predecessors with a brand of poignant pop belying the strength of purpose within the unit. Both guitarists offered compositions which were simple yet effective, with McMillan's less introspective contributions recalling the charm of Paul McCartney's solo debut. It was, however, Nicholson's songs which made *Blue* such a compulsive release, with three in particular; 'Red Light Song', 'Sunset Regret' and 'I Wish I Could Fly', boasting the most gorgeous of tunes.

A second set, *Life In The Navy*, was recorded in San Francisco with the assistance of local resident and émigré Robert 'Smiggy' Smith. The collection lacked the sparkle of its predecessor, a fourth member had somehow upset the balance, while Hughie's songwriting had become burdened by American affectations. *Blue* was now seen as an isolated gem and the product of a burst of creativity stemming from the trio's then-newfound independence. *Life In The Navy* sounded mainstream by comparison and its creators subsequently drifted apart. While Donald became a favoured session musician, McMillan and Nicholson laid low, before resurrecting the group with two new partners in 1977, including ex-Poet Charlie Smith. Blue would score their longed-for hit with 'Gonna Capture Your Heart'. However, the undistinguished, anaemic style they now peddled bore little relation to that tenacious debut, and the band was dissolved at the end of the decade.

If determination brought success to the Marmalade, then self-confidence bore fruit for 1-2-3. They had refused to knuckle under and, by 1968, saw their perseverance rewarded when improvisation suddenly came into vogue. The Nice had become a leading act through Keith Emerson's Hammond organ indulgences, although 1-2-3 counterbalanced their extremes with meticulously crafted songs which, like those of Blue, recalled the Beatles.

The trio was playing a tiny club in south London when they were spotted by Terry Ellis. Impressed, he offered to be their manager and agent, and having renamed the group Clouds, added them to the roster of the Chrysalis company. Ellis and partner Chris Wright already represented Jethro Tull and Blodwyn Pig, and enjoyed a licensing deal with Island Records. Clouds were thus an integral part of a new and ambitious company.

Their debut album, *Scrapbook*, was issued in August 1969. The nostalgic title track was heavily orchestrated to enhance its weepy effect, but seemed the antithesis of Clouds' other, blatantly progressive, desires. Elsewhere sculpted melodies vied with an instrumental fury, but although the collection was a minor commercial success, the trio were disappointed with the outcome and returned to the studio to complete an album filled with stage favourites.

Join the crusade

GET HIGH ON THE CLOUDS

We are conducting a **crumby** promotion campaign based on the slogan 'Get High On The Clouds'.

It would be nice if we could just tell people that CLOUDS are an extraordinarily talented group playing exciting music in a totally **original** style. However, mental barriers are thrown up against anything new and uncategorised and we are forced to be **sneaky** and use an easily accepted **superhype** method of attracting attention to CLOUDS and their album 'Scrapbook'—again not what one would expect to hear, CLOUDS have successfully utilised all their talents to present a varied piece of aural **entertainment.**

Presenting something new, which you believe in, is always something of a **crusade,** although always most rewarding. So watch CLOUDS tonight, listen to their album and well . . . . JOIN THE CRUSADE.

The first album by CLOUDS released in June : 'Scrapbook'

Chrysalis production for ISLAND RECORDS

island ISLAND RECORDS LIMITED 155-157 OXFORD STREET LONDON W1 ENGLAND

Promotional material from Island Records

Released only in the USA and Canada, *Up Above Our Heads* represented Clouds' onstage repertoire, but many mourned the rejection of those wondrous strings-backed pop songs.

Clouds continued to have an impressive workload, touring with Jethro Tull and Free. They still blazed an original trail, although a second UK album, *Watercolour Days*, saw them attempt to forge a sound midway between pop and progressive, rather than explore each style individually. It was an unhappy compromise, but in truth the trio was now tiring. The set's commercial failure added to Clouds' fast-ebbing resilience, and yet another act with roots in Scotland's beat past split up.

Although dissimilar musically, both Marmalade and Clouds had displayed staying power, and helped to remove the stigma attached to tackling practices in London. NSU, a three-piece largely unknown in Scotland, somewhat impertinently played at the Albert Hall and recorded an album, *Turn On Or Turn Me Down*, for the underground label, Stable. They disappeared as perplexingly as they arrived, but their aplomb was noteworthy. The House Of Lords, which featured Alan Pratt from Three's A Crowd, travelled south to work, but the highly-promising 'In The Land Of Dreams' was, frustratingly, their only release. Glasgow's Societie had meanwhile been discovered by the Hollies' Graham Nash and Allan Clarke and the latter produced the enthralling 'Bird Has Flown'. This original song endearingly recalled the close harmonies of the quartet's mentors, but they too broke up prematurely.

Patronage also assisted Grapefruit, a new act which, although far from entirely Scottish, was led by George Alexander, a Glasgow-born guitarist, singer and songwriter. He was the elder brother of Easybeats' member George Young, but had declined the chance to accompany his family when they emigrated to Australia. Having served an apprenticeship with Tony Sheridan in Hamburg, Alexander later won a publishing deal with Apple. His early songs were superb and Grapefruit rightly garnered critical acclaim for their grasp of harmony pop. Later recordings, however, veered towards an ugly sort of funk and one by one group members defected elsewhere. Alexander joined the late-period Easybeats, but dropped out of music when Young and partner Harry Vanda took up a career in production.

Another Scottish act enjoying an Easybeats' connection was My Dear Watson, who had made the trip to London having forsaken both Buckie and their old name, Johnny And The Copycats. The Watsons completed two compulsive singles, the first of which coupled 'Elusive Face' with an exciting 'The Shame Just Drained', a Vanda/Young original. The pair also produced the group's follow-up, 'Stop! Stop! There I'll Be' and the casual listener would be forgiven for imagining it was the Easybeats themselves. However, the song was written by Watson's guitarist/vocalist John Stewart, and this bomb-bursting performance is one of pop's truly neglected classics.

My Dear Watson failed to reap due commercial reward and with Vanda and Young distracted by failures in their own career, their protégés looked to the Continent where they worked for several years. They reappeared in 1970 with a beautiful, country-influenced single, 'Have You Seen Your Saviour?', in which the energy of the group's earlier work was replaced by peace and contentment. If R&B had once been a prime influence, My Dear Watson now looked to the gentle sound of the Byrds and the Flying Burrito Brothers. Yet their new approach was tantalizingly brief, and the group became one of many Scottish bands splitting up as the decade changed. Those surviving would embrace the new opportunities with open arms.

My Dear Watson

Chapter 9
Pick Up The Pieces

Many of London's Anglo-Scots had arrived in the city from Glasgow, fleeing the dwindling Tayside circuit. 'I had to get out of Scotland,' says Alan Gorrie. 'I loved London. There was a buzz about it. After all, what should we stay for? Another week in Aberdeen? The record wasn't happening and there comes a time when you have to move. Promoter Mary Yardley - Auntie May to a lot of bands - had contacts with Peter Walsh at the Starlite Agency and so we joined their books.'

Although the Vikings were stablemates of the Marmalade, they struggled in this pop-based environment, and a final flourish as Fancy Bred failed to aid a fading career. 'Dougie liked the whimsical name - the Vikings wasn't hip in 1967 - but it was going to take more than that to fix things.' Tensions between Wightman and Larg surfaced, Coutts opted to return to Dundee, and the Vikings disbanded leaving Fraser and Gorrie to plot new ventures.

Several Scottish groups were living in a 'rock 'n' roll dosshouse' in Finsbury Park. The Senate and the Scots Of St. James were two of its occupants and both played a pivotal role in Scottish pop's development. The Senate had split from singer Sol Byron in 1966 and quickly established a reputation as the ideal band to back visiting soul singers. Their spell in support of Ben E. King reaped its reward when the latter produced the group's debut single. Both 'Can't Stop' and 'Ain't As Sweet As You' were King compositions and the combination of producer and artists inspired an authoritative performance. There were no concessions to commercial whims but the empathy and respect on display was rewarded when it become the only record by a white act to be played on *Soul Supply*, Mike Raven's Radio Luxembourg show.

Alex Ligertwood (or Alex Jackson as he briefly dubbed himself) was the group's lead vocalist and continued Scotland's soul lineage. 'Alex is the other great Scottish voice,' opines Alan Gorrie. 'He's an amazing singer but just never gets his due.' Davie Agnew (aka Mark David - vocals/guitar), Bob Mather (saxophone) and Tony Rutherford (aka Tony Mimms (trumpet) provided the nucleus for this particular Senate but it was initially bolstered by Brian Johnston of the Golden Crusaders. Ex-Viking Mike Fraser joined on his departure, while the drum spot was taken by another ex-patriot Dundonian, Robbie MacIntosh, who arrived on Donnie Coutts' recommendation.

This reshaped Senate supported Garnet Mimms on his 1967 tour and the resultant in-concert album captures both in fine form. The group's own preliminary sets were also taped and material culled from shows at the Speakeasy and Sussex University was complied to construct *The Senate Sock It To You One More Time*. It was an exciting collection of 16 unstoppable minor classics including 'You Don't Know Like I Know', 'What Is Soul?' and the inevitable 'Please Stay'. Despite moments when the unit performed rather breathlessly, it successfully captured the sweat and fluster of a mid-60s dancehall. The album was also a last testament to a golden era, begun with Alex Harvey's Soul Band. The Senate followed this with a tour of Germany, but broke up in 1968. Fraser, MacIntosh and Ligertwood resurfaced, at different times, in the Italian-based Primitives. The the latter pair joined Brian Auger, while Mike Fraser became a much-respected session musician, working with Ennio Morricone among others.

The Vikings' 'Bad News Feeling'

The Scots Of St. James also began their career in Glasgow. Originally known as the In Crowd, the group had initially included Hughie Nicholson, but he was replaced by Owen 'Onnie' McIntyre. Jimmy Oakley (vocals), Graham Maitland (guitar), Diego Danalaise (bass) and Alan Kelly (drums) completed the formative line-up, although the latter pair opted to stay in Scotland when a move to London beckoned. Norrie MacLean (ex-Poets) and Stewart Francis were already full-time members when the In Crowd took their new name in deference to the fashionable club, the Scotch Of St. James, where they were the resident band.

The quintet completed their debut single, a version of Ben E. King's 'Gypsy', prior to yet another reshuffle. 'When the Vikings broke up, I just moved into the band next door,' Alan Gorrie explains. 'I still wasn't that adventurous - it's a familiar accent - and although they weren't as good a band as the one I'd left, there was a potential.' Gorrie's predecessor, however, did not appreciate the changes. 'Norrie was a strange customer. Just after I joined the Scots my speakers were stolen. I went to the Marquee to see Norrie play with someone and there he was with my gear. I told the police, so Norrie was dragged offstage and questioned - looking daggers at me - and I was asked if I wanted to press charges. I said, "Yes, I've nothing. I'm broke. Those columns are all I have and that guy's nicked them".'

'I've heard many stories about Norrie,' Alan adds. 'He had a cynical view of life and did lots of odd and horrible things to people. He later hung himself.'

The Scots Of St. James then recorded a second single, 'Timothy', and later enjoyed a highly successful German tour, but the growing rift between the band and Oakley could not be healed. 'We went down better when Jimmy was offstage,' Gorrie recalls. 'We did a few numbers before he came on and when he did, it would sink. He didn't have the range or personality and while I wanted to get out there and be a real soul band, that didn't suit Jimmy at all.' The two sides parted company during a spell in Glasgow, but Gorrie had already eyed a potential replacement. 'Jim Drysdale, who ran the La Bamba club in Falkirk, called me up about this great band and singer. I went through and there was Hamish Stuart and it was just "Fuck me. I'd love to sing with this guy."'

At that point Hamish was leading the nascent Dream Police, but he was quickly tempted to join the Scots. 'We dropped Jimmy off for the last time,' Alan recalls, 'and went straight round the corner to pick Hamish up. It was almost as crass as that.' The group then opted to abandon their now irrelevant name and by the time vocalist Oakley had opened his solo career with 'Little Girl', his former colleagues were pursuing a new direction as Hopscotch. It proved to be another short-lived venture - the group was reduced to a quartet again when Stuart returned to Glasgow - and Gorrie readily acknowledges its misdirection. 'Hopscotch was too pop and Hamish was right. It had to be

The Scots Of St James' 1966 single 'Gypsy'

stopped.' Two singles were recorded but if 'Look At The Lights Go Up' was pleasant, but undistinguished, the follow-up, 'Long Black Veil' provided a stronger proposition. The group's reading of this traditional chestnut was inspired by that of the Band, who found inspiration blending Bo Diddley with Tamla Motown, or George Jones with Booker T. Their voices caught the poise of Bobby Bland and the surprise of the Temptations; all of which proved irresistible to Scots hearing similar influences in their own music. The dues of the Band were the dues of Hopscotch, whose version wasn't so much a carbon copy as a recognition of parallel paths.

'We were still called the Shadettes in 1968 and this was like an anchor round out necks,' recalls Pete Agnew. 'We were all in the foyer of Dunfermline's Belville Hotel and they were playing 'The Weight' by the Band, which had the line 'Just pulled into Nazareth'. We thought 'That sounds alright as a name' and stuck it on the drum.'

The Shadettes had spent the psychedelic years in residencies, unwilling to continue the grind of one-night stands. By this point, however, several members itched to get back on the road, and having jettisoned those unwilling to do so, Agnew, Dan McCafferty and Darryl Sweet were joined by former Mark Five/Red Hawkes guitarist Manny Charlton.

'Nazareth played mainly in Glasgow and the west coast to begin with,' said Agnew. 'At that time all the supposedly happening bands played at the Burns Howff and this guy Bill Fehilly came to see us there. He asked if we wanted to go full-time and make an album, so we talked about it and then said "yeah, We'll give it a go."'

While Nazareth 'gave it a go', and played with renewed purpose, Hopscotch was quietly discarded. Graham Maitland had been replaced by English guitarist Mike Travis, and the revamped unit then took a new name, Forevermore. 'Mickey took us through Robert Johnson and Leadbelly,' Alan Gorrie acknowledges, 'stuff I remembered from art college. We became a speculative folk/blues/R&B band.' Forevermore completed two albums, *Paint It Yourself* and *Words On Black Plastic* but the experience was soured by business machinations, as Gorrie relates. 'This was our introduction into making records for an American company, getting our feet wet with contracts and getting taken for suckers, big time.' Two entrepreneurs, Ray Singer and Simon Napier-Bell, had secured advances from gullible A&R boards for groups which did not, at that point, exist. Duly armed with contracts, the pair then signed musicians to complete the requisite album(s). 'I don't think we even got a session fee,' states Gorrie. 'Napier-Bell and Singer made off with all the money - $30,000 - some of which should have gone to the band.' Forevermore's music was a pot-pourri of often contrasting styles; at one point pop, at another down-home rustic and, if ultimately disappointing, the records provided valuable learning experience and helped focus Gorrie's latent ambitions. 'Forevermore was not what I was all about, it was much too light. I wanted to put horns into a real R&B band, and pull together all the elements of the Blue Workshop.'

The Blue Workshop had been set up in Perth in 1964 in conjunction with members of Dundee jazz group Free Four. 'They basically wanted to steal Perth folk club's audience and they asked me to bring the Vikings in because we were already popular. However, the jazz connection attracted people like Jim Mullen, Bobby Wishart and Andy Park and so the Workshop became a musicians' free for all. We'd have loose rehearsals on Sunday afternoon, where we'd decided who played with who, and then do our sets in the evening.' Although short-lived, the club's importance cannot be over-emphasised. It was here Gorrie first encountered Robbie McIntosh, while two musician friends from art college, Roger Ball and Malcolm 'Molly' Duncan, sat in on several occasions. Although opting to finish their studies first, the latter pair subsequently moved to London where they worked on sessions as the Dundee Horns.

By 1968 a revamped Dream Police had inherited the troubled mantle of 'Glasgow's most promising group.' Although Hamish Stuart drew his passion from soul, the group had constructed an adventurous, almost mysterious sound

Average White Band

which forged psychedelic and progressive styles in a truly exciting manner. They too found London's lure irresistible, and joined the agency representing the Marmalade, which in turn brought the two groups together. 'I recommended the Dream Police to Decca,' Junior Campbell remembers, 'and then produced 'I'll Be Home'. It had the first orchestral arrangement I'd ever done.'

Released in 1970 'I'll Be Home' could have passed for Campbell's own group and while undeniably accomplished, the single's melodrama surprised those expecting something more rumbustious. The rest of the unit's output ranged from the progressive noise of 'Living Is Easy' to the country-rock 'I've Got No Choice' which, if suggesting an act searching for direction, also showed prowess at contrasting styles. The first a-side apart, each of these songs was penned by Stuart and guitarist Joe Breen, who remained at the band's helm throughout its turbulent twists, including the loss of founding drummer - and future Blue member - Charlie Smith.

His replacement, Ted McKenna, was formerly of Bubbles, a popular group on the west coast circuit, but one losing momentum. 'We'd gone as far as we could go,' recalls McKenna. 'We were playing at St. Margaret's in Airdrie and just before we went on Hamish and Joe came in. I knew they were there to ask me to join the Dream Police.' The newcomer moved down to the Marmalade's flat in Southgate, north London, where the Dream Police also stayed, and the reshaped group attempted to relaunch its career. 'We did the Speakeasy and Blazes and recorded some stuff for Decca, although I don't know what happened to it. It was certainly never issued.' The label had clearly decided to drop its option and the Dream Police began to fragment. 'Joe Breen walked in and said that Hamish had left to form a band with Willie Monroe from Tear Gas. I immediately went and phoned Eddie Tobin, Tear Gas's manager, and said, "I hear you've lost your drummer. I'll be right up." That night we got in the Cortina estate and I was in Glasgow the next day, rehearsing with them.' Meanwhile Stuart's new venture included not only Monroe, but former Dream Police colleague Matt Irving and ex-Trash guitarist Fraser Watson.

'Matt and I had always talked about getting a band together,' the latter recalls. 'They'd be called the Berserk Crocodiles and would have Willie Monroe from Tear Gas and Hamish, as well as ourselves. Willie had come down to London at that time, and was up for it, so when the Dream Police split, the Crocodiles started to happen.'

The group shared a communal flat in Notting Hill Gate, which doubled as a rehearsal room. They would commute to Glasgow to play at the city's Electric Ballroom, then head south for subsistence, spur-of-the-moment gigs. 'We got involved with Black Sabbath's producer, Roger Bain, who did some tapes with us at Rockfield. Rolling Stones Records were interested for a while, but nothing seemed to happen.'

Concurrent with all these changes was Alan Gorrie's decision to break from Forevermore. 'It happened at a rehearsal somewhere, I couldn't keep it back. I went for a walk with Onnie during a break and told him this was my last day. It wasn't what I wanted to do. I explained about my ideas for a new group and how it involved Molly and Roger and then asked him if he would join, which he did. We went back and someone said what are we were going to do next. I said, "quit".'

Duncan and Ball had been working with innumerable singers and groups, the most notable of which was Mogul Thrash. That group's premature demise left the duo free to pursue Gorrie's venture. 'They came round to my flat in Barons Court one Saturday afternoon,' he recalls. 'I actually still have the page to my diary which says 'Average White Band formed today'.'

Robbie McIntosh, who had returned from his European sojourns, was the natural choice for drummer, while Canadian-born trumpeter, Mike Rosen, formerly of Eclection, completed the initial line-up. 'Central Sound owed me some studio time,' Gorrie explains. 'I did a lot of demo sessions there. We put down three tracks and right away we knew we'd got it. Mike Rosen had several contacts in America but although he got great reaction to the tapes, we still didn't get a deal.' Rosen left the group soon afterwards and the final piece in the jigsaw slotted into place with the arrival of Hamish Stuart. 'He was singing all the wrong stuff with the Crocodiles,' Gorrie opines.' It was doing his throat in. We rescued him and that was us on the rails.'

The sextet then undertook session work, principally for the Island label, where they became the unofficial houseband. 'Muff Winwood was toying with the idea of signing us,' Gorrie recalls, 'but his only reservation was, I quote, "It's very hard to get a hit with an instrumental band". Our manager, Robin Turner, pointed out that we had two real vocalists, but...' However, the White Band did secure a contract with MCA, who issued *Show Your Hand* in 1973. It was a quite remarkable set; here at last was a soul groove many predecessors had only aspired to, yet at the same time it was patently not a recreation of Stax and Tamla. The album's cultural reference points were Sly Stone or Bobby Womack, and an immaculate take of the Crusaders' 'Put It Where You Want It' confirmed this empathy for contemporary black R&B. *Show Your Hand* also revealed the group's remarkable vocal strengths, and 'Twilight Zone', with its contrast between Gorrie's gritty lead and Stuart's impassioned counterpoint, was an outstanding emotional achievement.

Show Your Hand was not a great commercial success in Britain and it became clear the USA would be more receptive to the group's ambitions. Alan Gorrie recalls: 'We'd done some live radio in the States, played several clubs and recorded with Bonnie Bramlett, yet still nothing was really happening for us. We knew then we'd have to spend more and more time there, sit on their doorstep, so to speak, until we got in.' Paradoxically, the break came on the day that MCA dropped the group from its roster. 'We were having a wake in a cheap Chinese restaurant. Our new manager, Bruce McKaskell, had discovered that Jerry Wexler was in town, and arranged to play him our new tape. We were all ratfaced, but went, thinking that at least we'd meet a legend. By the end of the night we had a record deal.' Wexler, the head of Atlantic Records, signed the Average White Band in 1974, reinforcing Tayside dreams of the previous decade.

The group was teamed with veteran producer Arif Mardin who brought a commercial edge to their sound. 'Personally, the kind of music I love has the same sound as *Show Your Hand* states Gorrie, 'but you could never have got to US radio with it in the way Arif did with the White album.' *AWB*, aka the White Album, continued the group's intuitive and rhythmic understanding of black music, but infused with a greater sense of discipline. 'That was something Arif taught us,' Alan continues. 'Rather than cut up tape to tighten the songs, we shortened the arrangements.'

The White Album was a marked progression from *Show Your Hand*. A succession of superb originals, 'Pick Up The Pieces', 'You Got It' and 'Person To Person', plus a sublime cover of the Isley Brothers' 'Work To Do', signalled that the empathy the group felt with urban black music could be translated into a sound held in common, rather than one in which the former drew from the latter. All the years of hope were caught on this single, exciting collection; only a tragedy could cut them down.

On 23 September 1974, the Average Whites completed a week's work at the Los Angeles Troubador by attending a party thrown at the home of millionaire Kenneth Moss. Several guests, including McIntosh, were given what they assumed was cocaine, but which turned out to be heroin. They were all violently ill but, with care, the majority recovered, pacing the rooms to avoid becoming comatose. The drummer, however, was unable to vomit and retained the poison in his system. Physically wrecked from the punishing residency, he slipped into unconsciousness and died in the early hours of the morning.

The rest of the band were shattered, but having toyed with dissolving, stayed together 'for Robbie's sake'. 'What a great legacy to leave behind,' says Gorrie, referring to *AWB*, and it's no doubt that much of its fire comes from McIntosh, whose syncopation gave the set its unerring, unflinching backbone. 'Robbie's drumming was his whole personae. He was a huge person to have around and be around. If I was the organizer, he was the heart and soul of the whole thing and when that's plucked out.'

'To this day I still catch myself thinking what would Robbie do here. He encompassed everything - the Al Jackson sound, the (Pretty) Purdie stuff, Clyde Stubblefield - all rolled into one.'

Despite its international success, the White Album was not an immediate best-seller. 'The first single, 'Nothing You Can Do', didn't really happen. It wasn't until November 1974 that word was filtering through that 'Pick Up The Pieces' was getting played in discos.' Atlantic duly issued the track as a single and, within weeks, both it and the album were topping their requisite charts. The success of 'Pick Up The Pieces' which, bar its titular chant was an instrumental, gave Gorrie a riposte for Muff Winwood. 'I had to put it to him. "Muff, it's very hard to get a hit with an instrumental band." The whole irony of it was something else.' By this point the group was heard on every ghetto radio station, but although Steve Ferrone, a black session drummer, had been added to the group, the first signs of a professional coldness had set in. It would be convenient to pinpoint Robbie's death as the source of this decline, but the White Album was such a perfect statement, any subsequent work would have struggled match it. 'It never quite got as good again,' states Gorrie. 'There are moments on *Show Your Hand* and *AWB* that I'd quite frankly stack up against anyone. But rather than put out another track as a single, Atlantic pushed us into the studio to cut a new album.'

Cut The Cake, was dedicated to a dear lost friend, but although the title track crackled with a hard funk redolent of the Brothers Johnson, the set in general showed an understandable lassitude. Nonetheless, it was another best-seller and the White Band became an immutable part of 70s soul. 'Because we liked Black music, it was very easy for us to accept the fact that black people wanted to buy our records or come and see us play. It was the biggest, and most flattering, accolade we could get.'

The group's in-concert fire, captured on *Person To Person*, helped counteract the disappointment each new studio set engendered. Yet a spark was, on occasions. kindled, particular during a joint project with Ben E. King; *Benny And Us*. 'We were having a hard time making *Warmer Communications*,' Gorrie recalls. 'We were halfway through and it was bogged down in the mud. Benny was brought down to do a single with us, 'Star In The Ghetto', and it was so much fun we thought "Let's do an album", anything rather than go on our own record. It was a weight lifted off us and, since we were already working with Benny, it was a chance to bring in other people.' Guests included Luthor Vandross and ex-Senate singer Alex Ligertwood, by this point a member of Santana. 'It was very creative,' adds Alan; 'Everyone's ideas were tried and we went back to our own album with a bit more steam.' Yet despite the temporary relief it brought, *Benny And Us* could not repair the cracks opening in the line-up. '*Warmer Communications* was the first signs of us straining,' says Gorrie, 'and from then it seemed like we needed outside influences to keep ourselves from squabbling. The common influences that united us at the beginning were all starting to fray.'

Average White Band

Feel No Fret, released in 1979, nonetheless suggested that matters could be saved. It was easily the group's strongest set since *AWB* and where 'Atlantic Avenue' suggested the style of Earth, Wind and Fire, a sumptuous rendition of Dionne Warwick's 'Walk On By' showed their interpretative powers to be intact. 'We had a great time making that album,' confirms Gorrie. 'We all got away to the Bahamas and decided we needed to do it without Arif, which he took very graciously. I had to 'phone and ask him if he'd mind if we produced ourselves - but could we take Gene Paul, his engineer? The ultimate in impudence.'

Feel No Fret marked the end of the group's association with Atlantic, from where they switched to Arista for *Shine*. 'Clive Davis wanted to sign us, but he successfully managed to emasculate the band by putting us with David Foster. I had a great time writing with David, but his production, in retrospect, leaves me cold.' 'Let's Go Round Again', a gorgeous invocation of the classic 'Philly' era, nonetheless gave the group a surprise hit single. It was, however, their creative swan song, as the following album was little short of disastrous.

"Cupid's In Fashion' was the band tearing itself apart, you can hear it. There's almost nothing there except the sound of breaking glass. I can't listen to it; it's too painful. Hamish and I started fighting in the studio, I was driving home at four in the morning, drunk. You had to get drunk to stand the album - it's something you would just want to forget.'

The Average White Band split up soon after that album's release in 1981. Hamish Stuart resurfaced in the Paul McCartney Band, paradoxically singing John Lennon's lines when Beatles' songs come up. In the Dream Police he had taken Macca's role. Alan Gorrie completed a solo album before reforming AWB with McIntyre and Ball in 1989. 'I like to be in a group of people, a machine that's working. Where can you play if you don't have your own band? We do little tours, basically for fun, and let some people hear funk for the first time.' The messianic element, prevalent in Gorrie's previous work, remains a contributory factor. 'You don't go to your grave with your money. You go with the music you've made.'

CHAPTER 10
PLEASE SING A SONG FOR US

Although many admired the eccentricity inherent in the Incredible String Band, few embroiled in Scottish folk would follow their path. Edinburgh trio Bread, Love And Dreams did cut three 'flower-power and trinkets' albums, but these fey selections are period-piece curios rather than something with vision. Fife singer Rab Noakes made his debut on Decca with *Do You See The Lights Go Out*, but his perception of folk was merged with a love of a pop and rock tradition. He loved Dylan, Leadbelly and Woody Guthrie and was greatly impressed by Bert Jansch. The Everly Brothers, however, were another influence, and Noakes would also follow the exploits of home-based beat groups the Beatstalkers, Pathfinders and Poets. He attracted attention within folk circles when three of his songs, including 'Somebody Counts On Me' and 'Together Forever', surfaced on *Thro' The Recent Years*, a 1969 collaboration between Archie Fisher and Barbara Dickson. *Do You See The Lights Go Out* grew out of this interest, but it also anticipated Noakes' subsequent drift towards a style loosely defined as 'singer/songwriter'.

Indeed several Scottish acts came to folk music from mid-60s combos, opting for a genre which continued a song-based tradition rather than the multi-media blitz of progressive psychedelia. Benny Gallagher and Graham Lyle had been members of a Salcoats-based act the Tulsans which, in time-honoured tradition, spent the early 60s playing Tamla and black American pop. The group auditioned for Decca alongside Lulu And The Luvvers, and the label issued two Gallagher/Lyle compositions as a-sides, 'Comes The Night' and 'With My Baby'. Another of Lyle's early efforts, 'Mr Heartbreak's Here Instead', would of course become that controversial second single for Dean Ford And The Gaylords. By 1966 the pair had moved down to London where they hoped to pursue careers as contract songwriters.

Within 18 months they had secured a deal with Apple Publishing. A weekly stipend allowed the duo to hone their skills, and one of the resultant songs, 'Sparrow', was recorded by Paul McCartney protégé Mary Hopkin. In 1970 Gallagher was invited to join McGuinness Flint, a new act formed around

Tom McGuinness from Manfred Mann and ex-John Mayall drummer Hughie Flint. Benny insisted that Lyle be added to the line-up and the pair wrote many of the group's best-known releases, including the chart-topper 'When I'm Dead And Gone'. They quit the group in 1971 and, barring a brief spell in Ronnie Lane's Slim Chance, spent the rest of the decade recording in a folksy, harmony style, evocative of the Everly Brothers but fused with the pastoral ease of the Band. Acoustic guitars, accordions and mandolins provided the perfect bedding for Gallagher and Lyle's homespun compositions, the most successful of which were 'I Wanna Stay With You' and 'Heart On My Sleeve', both of which reached the UK Top 10 in 1976. An attendant album, *Breakaway*, also provided successful and although the title track was a minor chart entry in its own right, a version by Art Garfunkel was a major US hit.

Gallagher and Lyle sundered their partnership at the end of the decade, having discovered they could no longer write songs together. The latter has since maintained his career as a songsmith; in 1984 he co-wrote Tina Turner's 'comeback' smash, 'What's Love Got To Do With It'.

Paisley-born singer/composer Gerry Rafferty initially followed a similar path to that of Lyle. 'The first thing I remember hearing that struck me was 'Rock Island Line' by Lonnie Donegan,' he told journalist Jerry Gilbert. By the early 60s Rafferty was playing guitar in local bands and through this rudimentary circuit came into contact with Joe Egan. 'He was singing in a band called the Censors,' he continued, 'who only played at weekends. They needed a rhythm guitarist and vocalist so I filled that space. Something sparked off between Joe and myself because we'd both been keen on the Everly Brothers, and we could sing quite well together.' The pair subsequently switched to another Paisley band, the Mavericks, which in turn evolved into the Fifth Column. This last-named act signed to EMI in 1966 and their sole single, 'Benjamin Day', was part-written by Rafferty and Egan. Although largely undistinguished, the song's blend of harmony and acoustic guitars anticipated the direction its co-composers would later follow.

Whereas Egan took up a day-job on the Fifth Column's demise, Rafferty maintained a full-time commitment to music. A friend and folksinger, Danny Kyle, introduced him to the Humblebums, a duo renowned for its humorous songs. Their first album, *A Collection Of Merrie Melodies*, had proved popular on the folk circuit where, as Gerry recounted, 'People actually sit down and listen.' The 'Bums initially comprised Billy Connolly and Tam Harvey but, in 1969, Rafferty was asked to join them. 'We worked as a threesome for about six or seven months,' he explained, 'then things came to a head.' Harvey was axed; Connolly and Rafferty kept the group's name, and together completed two excellent albums, *The New Humblebums* and *Open Up The Door*.

Both sets contrasted Billy's throwaway jibes with his partner's gift for McCartney-esque pop. 'Billy never took (his songs) that seriously,' Rafferty recounted for *ZigZag* in 1975. 'In a sense he could never show his true mettle on record in the same way I could never show mine on stage.' The first album is a gem, with 'Please Sing A Song For Us' and the wry 'Her Father Didn't Like Me Anyway' among its strongest cuts. Its success, however, brought problems. 'At that point we were still playing folk clubs as a duo,' Gerry continued, 'but two or three of the songs called for more than just Billy and I so when we attempted to do them onstage it was impossible.' *Open Up The Door*, which featured the poignant 'Shoeshine Boy', was a more pop-conscious collection, its content fleshed out by several session musicians. The 'Bums label, Transatlantic, suggested they form a backing group but this in turn altered the balance between the two main protegenors. 'The thing that existed between Billy and me, which was very, very fragile, had been destroyed. He didn't feel equipped, musically, to cope with the thing and it was after that we decided to go our own separate ways. It was a mutual decision.'

Connolly returned to the Scottish folk scene where a between-songs patter became the act itself and led to his highly successful career as a raconteur nonpareil. Rafferty meanwhile, teamed with Rab Noakes in an embryonic version of Stealer's Wheel. 'We did gigs just as a duo to earn some money,' Gerry recounted in *ZigZag*, 'and then I met up with Joe Egan again. I'd been out of contact with him all the time I'd been working on the folk scene, but he was doing gigs at weekends on the Mecca circuit, singing in front of big bands.' Egan needed little persuasion to join the new group, which was expanded to a 4-piece with the arrival of Roger Brown, when it decamped to Tunbridge Wells. 'We rehearsed for about two or three months (but) Rab decided that he didn't quite fit into the thing and wanted to work on his own.' Brown too left the line-up which was eventually completed by Paul Pilnick, Tony Williams and Rod Coombes. In the meantime Rafferty completed his contractual obligations to Transatlantic with *Can I Have My Money Back*, before taking his new act to A&M. They completed an eponymous album under the aegis of famed R&B producers Leiber And Stoller, but the marriage was not without its problems and the experience drained the group's founder who quit and returned to Scotland.

Two singles, 'You Put Something Better Inside Me' and 'Late Again', were released to scant attention, but a third 45, 'Stuck In The Middle With You', reached the UK and US Top 10 in 1973. 'That gave me a lift,' Gerry confided to Jerry Gilbert, 'and I (re)joined the band because it looked as if the whole thing was going to be good. But it was the same old shit.' Guitarist Luthor Grosvenor had 'replaced' Rafferty in the interim, and he remained a member on the latter's return, despite the imbalance this created. Egan, who had been required to become an unwilling frontman, was now prepared to quit, at which point Rafferty snapped. 'Stealers Wheel was always myself and Joe,' he continued, 'and since we were sick of the whole fucking muddle we decided to

Gerry Rafferty

do it on our own.'

The pair completed the second Stealer's Wheel album in 1974. Dubbed *Ferguslie Park* after Paisley's notorious housing scheme, the set's melodious charms did not disguise the irony of its lyrical content, something particularly apparent in the bittersweet 'Star'. Although Jerry Leiber was no longer involved, Mike Stoller still handled production chores and thus age-old problems resurfaced. 'It was songwriters versus songwriters. They'd been immensely successful and weren't going to take notice of Egan and Rafferty, who had proved nothing so far.' Mentor Williams produced the duo's third album, *Right Or Wrong*, but the collapse of Stealer's Wheel's management company brought the group to a close. Both musicians then embarked on solo careers - Benny Gallagher and Graham Lyle assisted on Egan's 1979 release *Out Of Nowhere* - but it was Rafferty who enjoyed commercial plaudits with 'Baker Street' and his *City To City* and *Night Owl* albums.

Rafferty and Egan made cameo appearances on three solo albums by former colleague Rab Noakes; *Rab Noakes*, *Red Pump Special* and *Never Too Late*. Despite the passive, personal element pervading his work, Noakes was an outspoken, sometimes difficult character. Commercial success eluded these early 70s releases, and a potentially regenerating deal with Ringo Records coincided with punk, when the singer's craft was deemed out of favour. He nonetheless continued to record and play live, before securing the post of executive producer at BBC Scotland.

Stealer's Wheel

Released in 1969, Fairport Convention's *Liege And Leif* changed the notion of folk music by electrifying traditional material. Many new groups, including Steeleye Span, Fotheringay and Lindisfarne - who recorded two Rab Noakes' songs - blurred further an increasingly hazy dividing line. In Scotland Five Hand Reel brought a rock-based perspective to 'A Man's A Man For All That', 'Aye Fond Kiss' and 'The Bonnie Earl O' Moray', while lead singer Dick Gaughan continued their ambitious sweep on a solo career which happily wedded Joe South's 'Games People Play', the lilting 'Flowers O' The Forest' and the Socialist clarion-call 'Handful Of Earth'. The dilemma between acoustic and electric styles was one faced by all folk-based acts, including the Incredible String Band.

The group's 1969 album, *Changing Horses*, showed a quartet on its front sleeve; Christina 'Liquorice' McKechnie and Rose Simpson had seemingly joined the accustomed Williamson/Heron duo. The latter argues this was not a preconceived plan. 'I don't think that marks a point when they were fully involved. I associate them with 'Painting Box' and things like that.' Indeed, both made contributions to the duo's subsequent three albums and Mike feels that Liquorice was always an integral part of their thinking. 'Licky was definitely in the group. She was with Robin in the early days and began to be more involved in his songs. I introduced Rose on a different level.' Although the contrast between Mike and Robin's songs remained. there was now a more collective aspect to the group, and what became its extended 'family'. 'I had a little house near Broxburn,' Heron recounts, 'but Robin and the rest tried to do this communal living thing in Wales. Rose and I went down but didn't stay. From that the idea came that perhaps we could have separate houses but next to each other; close but not sharing kitchens. So we all moved to Glenrow - and 'String Band Street'.' The commune, sited in the Borders near Peebles, was a natural magnet for other musicians, including the Irish group Dr. Strangely Strange, who shared the String Band's mystic muse.

Its two lengthy pieces aside, *Changing Horses* also included the emotional 'This Moment' and the tongue-in-cheek 'Big Ted', but the set lacked the group's erstwhile obscure solicitudes. *I Looked Up* featured a rousing version of 'Black Jack Davy', while Heron's 'The Letter' confirmed the band's slippage into rock; Rose's bass work was supported by Fairports' drummer Dave Mattacks' distinctive precision. The group's experimental face was captured on *Be Glad (For The Song Has No Ending)*, the soundtrack to a film melange of concert material, interviews and fantasy, and *U*, a surreal pantomime which the ISB took on tour with dance troupe Stone Monkey. '*U* never really excited me,' Heron recalls, 'but I liked to see Robin do that stuff. I didn't contribute much but rather picked ideas to write about. I stood back a bit, rather than be fully involved.' The extravagant album nonetheless contained worthwhile moments, including Robin's 'Queen Of Love', while Rose took lead vocals on

Mike's 'Walking Along With You'. It would be one of her last contributions to the group; in 1971 she was officially replaced by Malcolm LeMaistre, who had already contributed to *U*.

Heron's solo album, *Smiling Men With Bad Reputations*, also appeared that year. 'I had all these rock-sounding songs,' he explains, suggesting they did not fit String Band thinking, 'and Joe Boyd called up these different musicians to play on them.' John Cale, the Who (bar Roger Daltrey), Richard Thompson and Dr. Strangely Strange are among the cast of thousands featured on what was a highly-liberating set. Heron had lived in Williamson's shadow, 'Smiling Men' provided a self-confident statement.

Two successive String Band albums, *Liquid Acrobat As Regards The Air* and *Earthspan*, followed in 1971 and 1972. Their release was punctuated by Robin's solo debut, *Myrrh*, which recalled the transcendental nature of the 60s period. The next ISB release, *No Ruinous Feud* marked the official arrival of newcomer Gerald Dott. 'Gerald came in when Licky left,' remembers Heron. 'We never replaced like with like. I'd known him from an Edinburgh skiffle group which also featured Mike Travis. Robin had also played with them, but at a different time from me.' Stan Lee (bass) and Jack Ingram (drums) were then promoted from the road crew to the group, while ex-Powerhouse guitarist Graham Forbes replaced Dodd for *Hand Rope And Silken Twine*, the String Band's final album. The decision to split was announced in Autumn 1974. 'We'd become a rock band,' Mike explains. 'Everyone in the group had to be written for and a lot of Robin's stuff just didn't work that way. We were under pressure to tour the rock circuit and he was gradually pushed out. He did some electric fiddle tunes and a couple of token songs but he was out on the edge, on his own. We did start another String Band album before Robin left, but when he did we decided to carry on. That then became *Mike Heron's Reputation*.'

Williamson and Heron have since remained active. The latter completed *Diamond Of Dreams* (1977) and *Mike Heron* (1980) while his songs have been recorded by such disparate acts as Manfred Mann's Earthband and Bonnie Tyler. Robin initially moved to California where he formed his Merry Band, the traditional aspect of which set the tone for subsequent work. The group was disbanded at the end of the 70s and, having returned to the UK, Williamson has since recorded Celtic Harp music, spoken word cassettes, incidental soundtracks and original material. His catalogue is as challenging as always and maintains the eclectic vision marking the String Band at its finest.

Chapter 11
Keep On Dancing

The AWB provided the final link in a soul music chain forged by Alex Harvey, the Boston Dexters, Poor Souls and Blues Council. But if they represented purity, an antithesis was found in the Bay City Rollers, who stripped pop to its bare essentials and aimed it squarely at female adolescents.

Formed in Edinburgh as the Saxons during the mid-60s, they initially scuffled around the city's lesser venues. Where others were demanding, the group - Nobby Clark (vocals), Neil Portoeus (guitar), Dave Pettigrew (organ), Alan Longmuir (bass) and brother Derek (drums) - offered simple hits of the day, intercut with well-worn favourites discarded by others as distinctly out-of-fashion. They were safe, but a pretty-boy image assured them of a following, and the group began looking for a suitable manager.

'I wanted to be in a rock 'n' roll band after seeing Ricky Barnes and Alex Harvey,' recalls Tam Paton. 'I formed my own, the Crusaders, but later found out that they only kept me around because I got them work. I was a terrible, terrible musician, but could really sell an act.'

Paton subsequently became bandleader at the Palais de Danse in Fountainbridge. He cut the resident group down to a manageable number and developed a showband routine revolving around that particular week's chart. 'We copied every record, number 30 right down to number 1,' he recalls, 'but we didn't go down well on teenage nights and that's when I started bringing in groups.' One such act was the Saxons, although the impression they initially left was decidedly mixed. 'What I heard was ghastly, but they obviously had something because the audience was screaming and shouting.'

Paton had, on one occasion, met Brian Epstein, who pressed upon him a byword: image. Despite all technical improprieties, the Saxons possessed a raw appeal and thus their request for assistance was granted. The group's manager immediately discarded their old name, conjuring Bay City Rollers in an effort to suggest something American, and later abandoned interest in the Jury and Hipple People in order to concentrate fully on his new protégés.

New members were brought in. Greg Ellison replaced Porteous, a second organist, Keith Norman, was added, while Mike Ellison shared vocals with Clark. This line-up also proved temporary and both Ellison and Pettigrew were later axed to incorporate ex-Beachcomber Davie Paton and relative newcomer Billy Lyall.

The Rollers also held a Sunday night residency at Edinburgh's Top Storey, which they latterly transformed into a stomping ground. There was no denying their popularity, but even during this embryonic stage the group lacked credibility and were roundly denigrated by rival musicians and older audiences. Undaunted, the Rollers welcomed their teenage following, and while largely avoiding the west coast circuit, blanketed its more malleable eastern counterpart.

'I realised we couldn't keep playing in Scotland,' recalls Paton, 'and so tried hard to get a deal in London. I spent 14 days going round the companies, coming back to a van each night which I slept in, wrapped up in newspapers. I had no tapes, just photographs, and was trying to sell the group on that.'

It was 1971 before the Rollers secured a recording contract, by which time Paton and Lyall had been replaced by Archie Marr. The deal was won by luck when Dick Leahy, MD at Bell Records, was fogbound at Glasgow airport. He drove to Edinburgh in the hope of a connection but flights from there had also been suspended, and a now-stranded mogul enquired if any groups were playing in the city. 'Ronnie Simpson, the agent, suggested that if he wanted a laugh, he should see the Bay City Rollers,' Paton recalled. 'The club was packed, there were queues outside and the band was going down a storm. Dick Leahy pulled me to the side and we did a deal.'

The group was then introduced to Jonathan King, who disinterred 'Keep On Dancing', a 60s' hit for the Gentrys, on their behalf. His limp production emphasised an atmosphere of temporary, pliable pop, while the perky performance, if eager, sounded amateurish. Nevertheless, the single was a major hit, reaching number 9, but this considerable coup was undone when successive follow-ups failed to sell.

"Keep On Dancing' kept us going for the next few years,' said Paton. 'We brought out lots of other records that flopped miserably and I was beginning to think we were one-hit wonders. But I wouldn't give up on them; I had slogged for the Rollers to the point I almost thought I was a member.'

Paton's confusion was understandable. His charges changed line-up with frightening regularity and if the alterations left the rhythm section and vocal spot intact, some 27 different members had passed through the ranks. 'Only two were ever actually sacked,' Paton added. 'The rest left to get engaged, married or whatever.'

'Whatever' would include remuneration - or lack of it - a gripe of many departing dissidents, as well as choice of material. Nobby Clarke was particularly frustrated over the Rollers' direction, and balked at recording

'Remember', a Bill Martin/Phil Coulter song. He walked out of the group and it was his replacement, Les McKeown, who took lead vocal on the finished take. Eric Faulkner, Stuart 'Woody' Wood and the ever-faithful Longmuir brothers completed a line-up literally on its final chance.

'Bell were seriously thinking of wiping us off,' said Paton. 'I knew something had to be done. At that time there were magazines like *Pop Shots* where fans could write in for stuff on the Osmonds, David Cassady or whoever. They printed the names and addresses of all these teenage girls so we got lots of copies together, had photos of the Rollers made up into postcards and sent them out. We wrote on them "Hi there. We're The Bay City Rollers. Our new record, 'Remember' is out on Bell..." and the response we got was incredible.'

Within days their single had out-sold its first pressing. A second mailout encouraged fans to order copies as a stopgap, and the ambitious ruse was rewarded when 'Remember' reached number 6 in February 1974. There would be no faltering this time around and over the next two years the quintet racked up eight more Top 10 hits, including 'Shang A Lang', 'Bye Bye Baby' and 'Give A Little Love', the last two of which were chart-toppers. Rollermania had been introduced, a whirlwind teenybop phenomenon which

The Bay City Rollers

would envelop Britain's first post-Beatles generation. Tartan-trimmed, short-fitting bell-bottoms blossomed while plaid scarves were tied to wrists to echo current football fashion. It was another version of the Jackie Dennis trick, yet the clan-like image bonded an audience and group maligned by supposedly wiser council. Derision was nothing new, Alan Longmuir had faced it since the days of the Saxons, but contemporary attitudes were particularly harsh, with several showing distinctly racial overtones. Paton's mother hen stories of milk before bed were certainly unhelpful, yet the Rollers were simply a part of pop's continuing traditions, no more gauche than Mud, the Sweet or Hello, and certainly less pretentious. Of course, when combined with the noxious Middle Of The Road, Scots purveyors of 'Chirpy Chirpy Cheep Cheep', the charge of Celtic trash was made much harder to refute.

The squeaky-clean image on which the Rollers perched could not be held down forever and the years of rabid popularity were interspersed with controversy. McKeown ran down and killed an elderly pedestrian and the volatile singer was also charged with firing an airgun at a persistent admirer. Alan Longmuir and Eric Faulkner allegedly attempted suicide and despite Paton's strenuous efforts, tales of dope and madness began to filter out. In between all this came success few could match. 'Saturday Night', a song culled from the 'flop' era, became a monster US hit and the Rollers duly appeared on prestigious shows, at first by satellite, and later live. They were signed by the eminent ICM Agency and played a series of US State Fairs. If the group's appeal was waning at home, the rest of the world awakened. An audience of 125,000 saw them perform at Toronto's North Phillips Square and the Rollers chalked up further success in Australia, New Zealand, Japan and Europe. The pressure, however, proved too great and Alan Longmuir quit in 1976, too old at 25, he opined, to be a pop idol. (He'd return some two years later). Ian Mitchell, then Pat McGlynn, would replace him, but the rot merely continued. The group's first single of 1977 was the adventurous 'It's A Game', a song written by former folkie busker Chris Adams and originally recorded by his prog-rock band String Driven Thing. This unconventional choice suggested that Eric Faulker's demand for 'heavier' material was, in part, answered. However, the record stalled at number 16 and became the Rollers' last Top 20 hit in Britain.

While their manager struggled with a mental breakdown, his charges became ungovernable. Les McKeown was ousted in 1978 - the rest of the band simply hated him - Faulkner fought a weight problem, Mitchell indulged in frottage with passing room service and suddenly it all seemed tawdry. Paton was sacked, McKeown returned and left, while the Longmuirs desperately tried to keep something together, even if it played to a diminishing audience. As an influence the Rollers were negligible, yet their persistence and commercial success deserve recognition.

Scottish 70s pop was not solely confined to their efforts, although those of Pilot were inextricably linked. The group was formed in 1973 by two ex-Rollers, Davie Paton and Billy Lyall, although it also included session guitarist Ian Bairnson. Two Top 10 singles, 'Magic' and 'January', established their crafted, witty style, but rather than build on this promise, the unit simply repeated the formula. Their albums were more imaginative, but when the hits dried up, so too did Pilot's enthusiasm. While drummer Stuart Tosh, once of the late-period Athenians, joined 10cc, his former colleagues became respected session musicians. Paton, in particular, enjoyed a high profile for work with Alan Parsons and Pete Bardens, and joined Bairnson on (William) Lyall's 1976 album, *Solo Casting*.

The Glasgow hard-rock circuit, once avoided by the Rollers, was largely dead by the early 70s. A working knowledge of current hits was essential for survival and reputations were forged according to the group's development within such restrictions. 'We decided to create an act that would be popular at the Electric Garden,' recalled agent Eddie Tobin, 'and that was Salvation. They were a pop group, but an aggressive one and they became immensely popular

Pilot

in Glasgow. However, they'd been made to perform rather than record.'

Salvation - Kevin McGinley (vocal), Jim McGinley (bass), James 'Midge' Ure (guitar) and Kenny Hyslop (drums) - formed in 1972, but the line-up was later expanded to include Billy McIsaac (keyboards). Frontman Kevin left for a solo career two years later and with Midge now leading them, the reshaped quartet took the name Slik. They remained favourites locally, but now wished to progress beyond the hits, although a series of demo tapes made little impression. 'The only deal we could get was through Bill Martin,' Ure recalls, 'who saw us playing in a Glasgow club.' Slik's debut single, 'The Boogiest Band In Town', was a commercial flop, and thus little was left to chance over a follow-up. The backing track was completed before the quartet stepped into the studio and, although the baseball shirts and caps had been their own idea, an air of compromise saddled the proceedings. 'It was the best we could get at the time,' Ure later admitted, although the group was initially grateful for the chart-topping place their second release, 'Forever And Ever', gained. The song was riddled with clichés, but if Slik hoped that success would grant them artistic leverage, then such thoughts were dashed with the grandiloquent 'Requiem'. A moderate seller, it was followed by two flops and by 1977 the group was deemed passe, discredited by the cheap pop tactics obscuring their genuine abilities. They were dumped, half-forgotten, beside a string of other pretenders - Bilbo Baggins or Rosetta Stone - many of which were groomed by Paton in a vain attempt to clone his best-known charges. The Rollers were unique, and having developed out of Edinburgh's less-purist attitudes represented the exaggerated apogee of the Moonrakers and Beachcombers, just as the sound of Dundee and Glasgow soul culminated in the Average White Band.

Slik

Chapter 12
Tomorrow Belongs To Me

As the club and village hall environment dissipated, so groups of an underground hue looked to universities as possible outlets for their music. The Students' Union took the place of many tired and trusted promoters, but the fact that the general public was generally barred from such gigs led to another artificial schism in an already fractured circuit. 'College bands' became a popular euphemism for those working outside the hit parade and survival for an ambitious act, such as Power, was made less difficult.

'Power had been together for about a year,' recalls Maggie Bell, 'when Leslie was called away to tour America with Cartoone. He'd known the guys for years, they all grew up together, but they'd never played live before and their guitarist, Mike, didn't want to go.'

Glasgow's Cartoone - Mike Allison, Mo Trowers, Derek Creigon and Chic Coffils - signed a contract with Atlantic on the same day as Led Zeppelin. Despite a previous incarnation as the Chevlons, they were a largely unknown quantity until a tape of their original songs had reached Mark London who in turn brought them to the label through his connections with Lulu. Released in 1969, *Cartoone* showed promise, but despite considerable help from guitarist Jimmy Page, the set lacked a sense of identity which, when wedded to the quartet's anonymity, meant that sales were far from encouraging. This was not, in itself, uncommon during the progressive era and many UK acts sought to salvage moribund careers at home by touring North America.

'Leslie came back with two new Gibson Les Pauls, a suntan, and peace and love,' recalls Bell. 'He introduced us to the music he'd been listening to out there and Power began to play in a more American style. Mark London wanted him to stay with Cartoone, but Leslie said no, that he had a girl-friend and a good band back in Scotland.' An intrigued London thus arrived in Glasgow accompanied by Led Zeppelin manager, Peter Grant. 'They sat in the Burns Howff,' Bell adds, 'their big limousine parked at the back door, ready to make a quick exit for the airport.'

Within weeks Power had secured a recording and management deal, although their somewhat lacklustre name was changed to Stone The Crows. The core quartet - Bell, Harvey, Dewar and McGinnis - was augmented by Colin Allen, one-time drummer with John Mayall. The revitalised unit began work on their debut album. *Stone The Crows*, released in 1970, confirmed the musical and personal bond between the singer and guitarist, with Maggie's rough, raspy voice cushioned by Leslie's textured, economic style. He was a superb player, but the role of Jimmy Dewar should not be under-estimated, as his husky delivery was crucial to the group's overall approach. 'He's one of the finest singers I've ever heard,' Maggie later opined and when the pair traded lines, Stone The Crows roared with an unshakeable confidence.

The set has much to commend it, from the searing, tense version of the Beatles' 'Fool On The Hill' to the ambitious, sprawling 'I Saw America'. Here Leslie's impressions of that first, whistle-stop tour formed fleeting images which were, in turn, tied to deeper, more lasting emotions. The track required its expansive length, 18 minutes, to capture the vastness of its theme, and the instrumental interplay invoked the same spirit of adventure.

The same line-up completed *Ode To John Law*, but although the songs are enjoyable in isolation, it is less satisfying as a set and lacked that initial, exciting reciprocity. There were, nonetheless, several telling moments and, taken together, these two records display blues/rock at its finest, whether in the swaying, fervent call of 'Gospel Zone' or the emotional depth of 'Blind Man'. 'That was always a favourite of mine', said Maggie. 'I saw Alex (Harvey) doing it in La Cave. We thought we could sit down and write something as good, but nothing came up to match it.'

Ode To John Law marked the end of the original group. Frustration had crept into the ranks, and Dewar doubtlessly felt diminished in what was, at best, a supporting role. He was offered a place in Jude, a new group formed by guitarist Robin Trower, formerly of Procol Harum, and Frankie Miller. 'I had to go with Jude to get Jimmy Dewar in the band', the latter recalls. He was doing nothing in London, and I really wanted to try that two-vocal thing, but the vehicle wasn't right. We must have been together for 10 months but the co-written stuff was a bit contrived and I was getting on better with my own. The best thing to do was for Jimmy to sing with Robin in a 3-piece, Hendrix-type thing and for me to go on my own.' Dewar duly remained with Trower until 1980, taking their power-trio format to the US astrodome circuit while remaining largely unrecognised, and unheralded, in Britain. He is another great lost Scottish voice.

Frankie Miller meanwhile took full advantage of London's flourishing pub rock circuit, which welcomed a back-to-basics traditionalism as a foil to the pyrotechnics of progressive rock. It was during this period that the singer came into contact with genre doyens Eggs Over Easy and Brinsley Schwarz. 'I met the Brinsleys at the Tally Ho in Kentish Town,' he recalls. 'One night they were at Eggs Over Easy's house, playing this country-rock stuff, and I was singing with them. Then they asked me if I'd do an album with them down at Rockfield.'

The resultant *Once In A Blue Moon* was a wonderfully informal set, capturing pub-rock's natural, good-time feel perfectly. Miller's original songs were highly effective - indeed his talent for composition is often overlooked in the rush to praise his voice - yet the highlight was 'After All (I Live My Life For You)', a plaintive ballad co-written with Jimmy Doris during the Stoics' era. Lulu had already tackled the song, but the unfussy arrangement and restrained support herein gave full rein to Miller's emotional delivery.

The easy, understated sound characteristic of his debut set, contrasted the style unveiled on Miller's second album, *High Life*. 'Chrysalis wanted me to get a good producer, and Alan Toussaint was the only one I could think of. I never wondered who produced Ray Charles or Little Richard, but I always knew who'd done Lee Dorsey's records. I didn't think he'd agree because he'd never worked with a white singer, but he came back and said yes.' The combination was an artistic success; the singer was completely at ease with the demands of the Crescent City style and drew fresh inspiration from its loping rhythms. 'Toussaint asked me what I wanted to which I said "as rough as we can get". When we finished it was really punchy but then Chrysalis went away and remixed the tapes at Philadelphia because the Philly sound was in. I always hated that stuff. I didn't want anything to do with them and I really didn't want to have anything to do with the album either. I still have the real mixes.' Despite Miller's reservations, *High Life* remains a triumph, with the pulsating 'Brickyard Blues' one of the singer's finest performances.

The Rock marked the debut of the Frankie Miller Band, which included two ex-members of Irish band Eire Apparent, Henry McCulloch and Chrissie Stewart. 'A Fool In Love' deftly fused the group's ambitions with gripping R&B and was underscored by nagging, pumping horns. This taught approach was also heard on *Full House* which blended Miller originals with choice interpretations. John Lennon's 'Jealous Guy' - 'I always thought he could have been angrier' - allowed Frankie to work with established material, while Andy Fraser's 'Be Good To Yourself' was perfect for his gritty intonation.

Two songs were resurrected from the singer's immediate past. 'The Stoics did some demos for Chris Thomas,' Miller explains. 'He always liked 'Take Good Care Of Yourself' and wanted me to do it on the album.' Frankie's own affection for this Jimmy Doris composition is equally clear, but it is 'This Love Of Mine', written during the Jude era, which best exemplifies the artist's skills. Beautifully understated, this impassioned performance invokes the Otis Redding of 'I've Got Dreams To Remember', wherein the aching lyric is offset by muted, yet sympathetic, support. 'I had Otis in mind when I was writing the song,' Miller confirms. 'It was a thing I dedicated to him internally, but never said too much about it.'

From there Frankie has maintained his blues/rock style, irrespective of transitory fashion. His voice was always splendid, even on the maudlin 'Darlin', which gave him a Top 10 hit in 1978. 'That song lost me a lot of following,' maintains Miller. 'We were doing well anyway but suddenly grannies and kids were coming to our concerts and they drove away the hard-core fans.' Yet although Miller did not maintain this overt commercial success, he continued to write and record. *Dancing In The Rain* from 1986 contained several compositions co-penned with Brill Building veteran Jeff Barry, whom Frankie met when a plan to re-record the Crystals' 'Da Doo Ron Ron' was mooted. 'Barry always wanted to do the song slowly,' Miller recalls, 'but when the record didn't happen we began writing together and had a great time. He doesn't like working at a piano, but would just sit down, sing a melody, then ask what guitar part would I put to it.' Frankie also enjoyed a minor UK hit with 'Caledonia', a hymnal folk-song brought to prominence by a television advert. This emotive paean unsurprisingly topped the Scottish chart in 1992, since when the singer has enjoyed success collaborating with country star Clint Black. 'I met him in Nashville,' Miller recounts. 'We had a good time - he knows how to have fun - and we cut 'Burn One Down', an old thing I'd had for ages.' The song was later lifted as a single and Black's popularity in the USA has ensured substantial sales there.

While Miller's career continues unabated, so contemporaries Nazareth also became a truly international act. They too survived initial disappointments, as Dan McCafferty explains.

'*Nazareth* and *Exercises* were recorded in London, but we were never happy with those records and decided to do the third one at home. We'd been using an ex-government storeroom for rehearsals - we called it the Gang Hut - and brought in a mobile.' Deep Purple bassist, Roger Glover, instilled a tighter, more purposeful sound and the resultant album, *Razamanaz*, was a commercial success. Nazareth then enjoyed a string of international hits as successive releases, *Loud 'n' Proud*, *Rampant* and *Hair Of The Dog*, became international best-sellers through a judicious cross-section of hard-rock and commerciality. They had survived the demands of scout-hall beat, and years of struggle had fostered a sense of togetherness. Nazareth found an early groove and stuck with it, but having secured UK Top 10 placings with the self-penned 'Broke Down Angel' and 'Bad Bad Boy', by 1973 they were displaying equal skill at re-interpreting material drawn from contrasting sources; be they psychedelia or singer songwriter. 'Joni Mitchell's 'This Flight Tonight' was always a band favourite,' explains McCafferty, 'so we just decided to cover it instead of doing another 'Bad Bad Boy'.'

Whereas the original was a sweet homage to a wistful memory, Nazareth transformed 'This Flight Tonight' into a celebration of stolen love. They would

Nazareth: Sheet music for Broken Down Angel

subsequently punctuate original material - 'Shanghai'd In Shanghai' or 'Holly Roller' - with other interpretations, including Randy Newman's 'Gone Dead Train', Tomorrow's 'My White Bicycle' or the Everly Brothers' 'Love Hurts', the single which broke the group in the USA. They clearly relished the artistic freedom such choices offered, but the band were never merely opportunist, grabbing at some well-established song to secure an easy hit. 'You don't just cover a song,' Pete Agnew declared. 'I don't know how many times we tried Roy Wood's 'Wild Tiger Woman', but it still sounded like the Move with a different singer. 'Love Hurts' and 'This Flight Tonight' are so removed from the original versions, if anyone cares to listen, that we felt we'd done something to make them our own. We stayed interested and that's what kept the band going for so long.' Given that the Shadettes were formed in 1960, Nazareth's longevity - McCafferty, Agnew and Daryll Sweet are still featured in the line-up - is indeed remarkable.

John McGinnis departed from Stone The Crows at the same time as Jimmy Dewar. The remaining trio regrouped around organist Ronnie Leahy, fresh from the defunct Cody, and bassist Steve Thompson, Colin Allen's former colleague with John Mayall. *Teenage Licks* showed a further change in style, tough but less bluesy, as the quintet pressed towards a more mainstream direction. Lulu - as 'Wee Marie' - joined the Dundee Horns in fleshing out a sound which still exuded confidence. *Teenage Licks* was the band's best-selling set to date - they even appeared on *Top Of The Pops* plugging the abrasive 'Big Jim Salter' - but they were still unable to translate their undoubted popularity into real commercial success. 'We worked hard, seven nights a week if we wanted it,' recalls Bell, 'but we were a people's band and could not conform to being goody-goody hitmakers.'

A live album, the perennial salvation for gigging bands, was one likely option for a group revered on the student circuit. On 3 May 1972 they were onstage at Swansea's Top Rank Ballroom, switched there from the local university to accommodate demand. Leslie was preparing to begin the set, fingering his guitar, tuning up in readiness, when he touched a live mike and was electrocuted.

Maggie Bell was grief-stricken, whereas Scotland had lost an innovator, her loss was more personal. Stone The Crows did work for another year with child prodigy Jimmy McCulloch from Thunderclap Newman joining for *'Ontinuous Performance*. The set was technically proficient but cold, and Leslie had, unsurprisingly, proved irreplaceable. With her group now fractured, Maggie Bell looked to a solo career and became yet another Scottish act signed to Atlantic.

'Jerry Wexler produced 'Queen Of The Night',' she recalled. 'We spent five days listening to song after song - we must have heard 300 - before choosing the final tracks. He has such a good ear for music and the album worked out well.' The material was indeed excellent, while support for the singer's fervent delivery was provided by the cream of New York's session musicians; Richard Tee, Steve Gadd and Cornell Dupree. Bell simply sounded natural and, inspired by an understanding of black music, revealed herself to be a gifted, interpretative stylist. This was particularly apparent on 'A Woman Left Lonely', a song irrevocably linked with Janis Joplin, a singer with whom Bell was often compared. Conscious of this, Maggie chose a more reflective style which displayed a vulnerability not often apparent in her work. Material by John Prine, J.J. Cale and former cohort Ronnie Leahy, who supplied the title track, was equally powerful. Yet somehow the album's undoubted promise was allowed to slip away. Gaps were left between releases and it was 1975 before the disappointing *Suicide Sal* appeared. Later releases lacked focus, and Bell's pre-eminent position was briefly taken up by Maggie Reilly, vocalist with Cado Belle, whose soft-funk withered on their record label's bankruptcy. Reilly later surfaced as part of Mike Oldfield's coterie, and although Bell latterly enjoyed a hit, partnering B.A. Robertson on a tongue-in-cheek 'Hold Me', it was scant reward for her stirring, individual voice.

Leslie Harvey's premature death galvanised his elder brother, who returned from London determined to reclaim a career becalmed by the artist's refusal to follow a cognisant path. Alex had remained with the cast of *Hair* for several months and even completed an album of songs from the show, before recording *The Joker Is Wild*, an idiosyncratic pop set only issued in Germany. He then joined a new-wave jazz collective, Rock Workshop, members of which appeared on Harvey's 1969 release, *Roman Wall Blues*. It was a curious hybrid, in which songs from Delaney And Bonnie, the Rolling Stones and *Hair* were pitted against the singer's more intuitive originals. Where it worked, on tracks like 'Hammer Song', the sense of experimentation was genuinely exciting. Elsewhere the combination seemed uncomfortable.

Alex then guested on the first Rock Workshop album, before fronting a trio completed by Ian Ellis from Clouds and ex-Fire drummer Dave Dufont. He was still determined to breach the musical barriers, and although some describe the band as 'universally unpopular', others recall them as excellent. Whatever, it was a distinctly uncommercial prospect, and as Harvey's interests drifted towards a tougher, dramatic sound, his manager, Bill Fehilly, began to search for a complementary backing band.

Tear Gas had been disappointed with the reaction afforded *Piggy Go Getter*, but the arrival of Ted McKenna rekindled hope. They nonetheless retained a sense of mischief - offstage and on. 'We were a really loud band,' he recalls. 'In fact we used to open with Jethro Tull's 'Love Story' which started very softly and the crowd would drift towards the front. Then we'd turn the volume up and blow everyone out of the hall.'

A second album, *Tear Gas*, issued in 1971, showed a group approaching music with renewed vigour. 'I was really into Jeff Beck,' explains Zal Cleminson, 'especially the early songs he did with Rod Stewart. So we did the arrangement of 'Jailhouse Rock' they'd done on *Beck Ola*. I think the album worked well. It had a real excitement.'

Commercially, *Tear Gas* was not a success and the group still found itself in penury. 'We stayed six to a room in Shepherd's Bush,' McKenna recalls, 'and now and again Tony Calder would give us a tenner for food. We'd eat either at the hot dog stand or O'Hara's Cafe on Goldhawk Road, then put on our best gear and pose about at the Cafe Des Artistes.' More importantly, Dave Batchelor was proving incompatible and the itinerant Ronnie Leahy played keyboards on that second set. 'Dave wasn't as strong a singer as the rest of the band were with their particular roles,' states McKenna. 'My cousin Hugh, who had been working with Hughie Nicholson from the Poets, joined Tear Gas to extend the harmonic ability of the band. We became a 4-piece with Hugh singing lead.' Nonetheless, the group's workload had shrunk to almost imperceptible levels and what little money they did earn was spent paying off equipment costs. They limped back to Glasgow in 1972, and once more a potentially excellent career seemed doomed to flounder prematurely

'That's when we got the call from Eddie Tobin,' Cleminson recalled, 'telling us that Alex needed a band. We met in the Burns Howff - he walked in with his guitar slung over his shoulder - and then wandered off into a rehearsal studio nearby. Alex started to play the riff for 'Midnight Moses' and said "Can you play this?" Of course everybody just leapt in and started hammering the shit out of it and he thought "Yeah."'

'We didn't know if it would work,' adds McKenna. 'Tear Gas had supported Alex at the Marquee when he had that trio and so we didn't know if we could play the kind of songs he wanted us to. When we heard 'Midnight Moses' we said "We can play THAT" and then we knew we could believe in this guy.' The partnership was forged that night, although as Tear Gas were already committed to several live dates in Arran and the Isle Of Man, plans were put into place to make initial gigs joint affairs where both acts completed individual sets before combining to close the show. All that now remained was a name.

'Alex was always influenced by people like Gorgeous George,' said Cleminson, 'who talk themselves into a situation where people can't deny they're brilliant. You'd see posters with 'The Incredible Fantastic Temptations' or 'The Fabulous Four Tops', and so Alex said that we should call ourselves 'Sensational' and make that part of our name.'

Those first forays were far from perfect. 'The audience hated Alex,' McKenna recalls. 'It was, "Who's this guy coming on with Tear Gas?" They booed and shouted; he shouted back and swore – I thought it was the end of the world.' However, it quickly became clear that the garrulous Harvey thrived on such adversity, viewing it as something to overcome. 'Alex was abrasive, he intended to challenge people,' states McKenna, 'but he was determined they were not going to forget him. Then, because Mountain management had opened doors with Nazareth, we simply played and played, and in that way developed a grass-roots following.'

The Sensational Alex Harvey Band began recording almost immediately. The resultant album, *Framed*, was completed within three days, reflecting something of the urgency felt by both parties. It was a controversial record – 'A lot of people said it was dreadful,' Zal remembers – and many, recalling Alex as the great innovator, refused to look behind the gut-wrenching stomp Tear Gas brought to his music. It was their loss. *Framed* may have been basic, but it was also exciting, fuelled by a wild thrill and undeniable arrogance. It is certainly hard rock, but unlike much of that style's proponents, the album had a surrealist touch, a facet more freely explored on later releases.

The title track joined 'I Just Wanna Make Love To You' in alluding to Harvey's past. Both had been staples of the Soul Band set and their inclusion herein reinforced the concept of artistic rebirth. Tear Gas, of course, ripped them apart, but saved their most savage assault for 'Midnight Moses', which was initially cut on *Roman Wall Blues*. That first version now sounded positively polite as the band exaggerated its seminal riff to the point where its introduction simply teemed with anticipation. '*Framed* got us off the ground,' declared Cleminson, 'but *Next*, for me, had the best combination of songs.'

Issued in 1973, this second album was a triumph, and included many surprises, not the least of which was a frantic version of 'Giddy Up A Ding Dong'. The song, of course, is irrevocably linked with Freddie Bell And The Bell Boys. However, this was not just a tribute to the group which excited the Glasgow audience all those years ago, but a celebration of the event itself. Alex then placed this homage beside 'Next', Jacques Brel's tortuous vision of mobile army brothels, and a song perfect for Harvey malevolent leer. The atmosphere of unease was reinforced by a perverse string quartet, as if the injection of this touch of class could divert its essential sordidness.

The other highlight was 'Faith Healer', a piece also hinged to an irresistible opening. 'Hugh and Alex went off to a flat for a while and wrote several songs,' recalls Cleminson. 'They brought 'Faith Healer' to us as a demo, just piano and voice. When we got to the studio Alex had this machine, a Heath Robinson device, which basically made a pulse. It pumped away in a weird time signature and we just added this big guitar figure.'

'Faith Healer' is a track of manic proportions as Harvey implores, then demands, to place his hands upon the recipient, the menace in his voice leaving their willingness open to question. Such powerful inclusions established, *Next* as the Harvey Band's most popular release and the set formed the backbone of their constant, heavy touring schedule. 'Alex had learned a lot from his time in *Hair*,' McKenna explains. 'He'd found out how a director brought a performance on to the stage, how to focus the band and how to show the audience where to look. He'd come on in a dressing gown and glasses, his hair slicked back, picking petals off a rose. When there's not a lot happening you have to make it happen and he knew how to put a whole room under his spell.' Lighting, posture and dramatic effect were thus married to Harvey's gifts as a showman and the urgent, enveloping sound of his group. The Sensational Alex Harvey Band live was thus a radical blend of noise and theatrical effects.

'I used to pull faces to mimic the stupid expressions guitar players did at the time when they were bending notes,' Zal recalls. 'Our manager Bill Fehilly suggested I should do something so that my face could be seen at the back of the hall. I went to see several mime acts, including Marcel Marceau, until I got round to the white face, but as soon as I did it gave me a definite role within the band.' Cleminson's clown-like make-up, with its double-edged aura of sadness and joy, was the perfect foil to Harvey's several stage personae and added an element of mystery to the group.

SAHB's third album, *The Impossible Dream*, was another demanding set, and if 'Anthem' brought to mind Scottish patriotism, Alex balanced this with 'Sgt. Fury', a vaudevillian homage to a comic book hero. Elsewhere, the combination of 'The Tomahawk Kid', 'Vambo' and a hard-rocking take of 'Money Honey' not only suggested the unit's eclectic ambitions, but confirmed their ability to fulfil them. It was thus no real surprise to hear them tackle 'Delilah'. 'Alex thought, "Tom Jones? Yeah, why not?"' recalls Cleminson. 'There were no rules about the band and what we should be playing.'

'We could play anything if we took it seriously enough,' adds McKenna. 'Every day was an escapade and many gave us ideas for songs. Some didn't come across on record, pieces with sections and different tempos, but we could be whatever band Alex wanted. Yet he was conscious of the ridiculousness of his role as 'rock singer', and we got a hit with a joke. It was as much to do with us in the broad sense, but if we tried to make pop records we couldn't do it.'

SAHB's 'Delilah' was hilarious. They took the pompous original and exaggerated every nuance, singing the chorus like rabblehouse drunks, celebrating this squalid crime of passion, while Harvey's mock-seriousness merely heightened the effect. A Top 10 hit in 1975, it became the first of their chart singles, but the band was unable to sustain success as a recording act.

'Alex did three days at the Apollo that Christmas,' said Eddie Tobin, 'which sold out instantly. They were, in retrospect, the highlight of his career. SAHB could ask for, and get, thousands a night, but not sell anything like that in albums because they were writing for the stage. Instead of writing for a record and performing it live, they did it the other way round which didn't come across well.'

The Sensational Alex Harvey Band

This dichotomy was apparent in *Tomorrow Belongs To Me*, wherein 'Stoneater' brought Harvey's comic fantasies to a crazed conclusion, and 'Action Strasse' or 'Compliments To The Chef' indicated a music growing ever more complex. The title track, meanwhile, was a Nazi anthem and, while suggesting a touch of perversion, its inclusion fitted a set which caught the band at its most teasing and ambitious. Nevertheless, the album left little space for cohesive musical development, and suggested that SAHB had reached a creative impasse. 'Alex's reaction was "We've done all that,"' McKenna explains. 'The fact you could do it didn't matter. He wanted something else and we were flying around in different directions. Alex wanted to invite the audience to a rehearsal or play a grate or rake and/or play without cymbals or even a kit. He was touching all these extremes and we couldn't keep up with him. I was still coming to grips with a kit and he was telling me to throw it away.'

Live was an obvious ploy given the band's unquestioned in-concert appeal. It captured the atmosphere of a gig, and showcased several songs in quite radical settings. The highlights included a burning 'Faith Healer', a cheeky 'Delilah' and an expansive 'Framed', which had grown from the protestations of an unfortunate spiv to those of a greater magnitude. In Germany. Alex appeared onstage as a gaffer-taped, gagged Hitler, taking a proclamation of innocence to more questionable extremes, but such a dramatic effect served only to confirm how important the group's visual impact had become. No studio album could hope to capture the appeal of a painted guitarist and commanding singer who ruled his audience as if they were part of some extended family. Similarly, the reciprocal warmth and respect could not possibly be caught on record; in short, SAHB were fighting a losing game.

The group continued to mark time with *The Penthouse Tapes*, their first release of 1976 and a sideswipe at the trend of vapid stars to fashion albums culled from favourite songs. SAHB, of course, were suitably irreverent, and combined Irving Berlin's 'Cheek To Cheek' with the recurrent 'Love Story', while throwing in 'School's Out' (Alice Cooper), 'Runaway' (Del Shannon) and 'Goodnight Irene' (Leadbelly). Commercial suicide perhaps, it was nonetheless great fun and the group's reading of the Osmonds' 'Crazy Horses' remains one of rock's truly epic moments.

SAHB Stories, the legitimate follow-up to *The Impossible Dream*, represented something of a compromise. Simpler than its predecessor, it showed a group showing signs of fatigue and although 'Dance To Your Daddy' and 'Boston Tea Party' were undoubtedly worthwhile, much of the set lacked their erstwhile fire. 'Live work was taking its toll,' McKenna remembers. 'Alex was in his 40s, but lived like the rest of us, who were 15 years younger. The pace was hectic and the morale of the band fluctuated up and down.' In the autumn of 1976, Harvey entered hospital. He had injured his back during a live performance, but a recurrent liver complaint was also becoming a problem. The rest of the band worked on in his absence, performing as SAHB (without Alex) and releasing a 'solo' album in 1977. It is worth finding for the sleeve alone, which shows a gagged Harvey tied and bound, crouched behind an amplifier. Sales were, however, slim, and Alex felt the pressure to return.

'He came back out of hospital too early,' Chris Glen stated later, and it's undeniable that Harvey simply tried to do too much. SAHB undertook the singer's first live appearances in a year and a new album, *Rock Drill*, was also completed. A bleak and half-forgotten work, it featured Tommy Eyre in place of Hugh McKenna who, so often, had been the musical pivot for Harvey's ideas. His departure was a crucial loss, adding yet another strain upon an increasingly tense group. 'Hugh and Alex were totally different, they had a love/hate relationship. One day Hugh was late for a rehearsal, but when Alex picked him up on this, Hugh turned round and said "How would you know? You never wear a watch," which was true. Alex put his hand above the table - that day he did. Hugh just put on his jacket and left.'

McKenna also recounts the trauma surrounding the sessions for *Rock Drill*. 'Alex wanted me to lift all preconceptions, and turn everything on its head. He was reciting a poem with ferocious lyrics and I was trying to play, trying to make sense and Alex was wanting it not to make sense, and eventually I cracked. I picked up the kit and threw parts of it around the room and Alex went "That's it! That's it!"' The SAHB Band then began a European tour, midway through which Harvey perceptibly began to tire. 'Chris Glen came up to me and said Alex won't go on,' recalls McKenna. 'I went backstage, did an Alex on Alex - he was a great bandleader and motivator - but we eventually had to pull gigs and cancel the tour.' The group did complete two festivals, at Bilston and Reading, where the *Framed* personae now became Christ. Between those dates Harvey acknowledged the emergent punk rock with a performance at London's Vortex, where he sang a Scottish traditional song 'The Galloway Hills', accompanied by two pipers. 'Alex wanted us to play places like the Vortex when punk was taking off,' Zal Cleminson recalls. 'He knew he'd been a part of what was starting, where you just got up and did what you wanted to. That's what Alex was saying all along.'

In October 1977, during a rehearsal for 'Sight And Sound', Alex finally snapped and, unable to face the up-coming schedule, walked out of the group and refused to return. 'This time I was late,' says Ted McKenna. 'Alex tore a strip off me then turned round and said "That's it. I'm finished." I left my riser and sat down beside him. We'd both lost belief in the situation and when I mentioned the cab that brought me there was still around he went out and got into it. I shook his hand and said "It's been fucking great Alex" and he left.

'I went back inside and told them Alex was away home. I can't remember

ALEX HARVEY

polydor

Alex Harvey as a young man

exactly what happened and what was said, but I didn't care anymore, I knew I had to get out as well.'

In retrospect Ted McKenna pinpoints the death of manager Bill Fehilly, who was killed in an air crash in 1976, as another factor in the group's eventual demise. 'I've thought a lot about why it was doomed to go wrong. Bill was a warm-hearted, charismatic guy and was the only person who could handle Alex. You felt confident when he was around. When he died it was like the sun going down, it was a big blow to Alex, but that's when we realised that the management didn't really know what it was doing; at our expense. We lost a lot of money playing in America, no-one was taking care of business.'

SAHB did remain together awhile under a new name, Zal, but they crumbled after a mere five months. The guitarist then joined Nazareth, while McKenna and Glen were later reunited in the Michael Shenker Group. Meanwhile Harvey, although still not fully restored to health, entered 1978 fired by a newfound desire to build a library of social history. The first in his series of ambitious recordings was based on the Loch Ness Monster.

'This posse went up to Invermorrison,' recalls Eddie Tobin, 'and interviewed everyone who had either seen the monster, or would take a drink for saying so. K-Tel, of all people, felt that an album of this would sell on a world-wide basis.' Unfortunately, a new managing director was appointed just before the album was shipped, and it was dropped from the company's schedules. Harvey's management were left holding 10,000 copies, which were then pressed into every conceivable outlet - from village shop to monastery - in an effort to sell them to tourists.

The album is, of course, a curiosity, but it holds an uncanny fascination as Alex links the low-fi interviews with narration and whimsical songs. On a more conventional tack, he also formed the new Alex Harvey Band, and commenced recording and gigging. The pace was now less frantic and it was 1979 before an album, *The Mafia Stole My Guitar*, was issued. The set itself was generally low-key, although the title-track, which recounted a real-life incident on tour in the USA, was worthwhile. Alex then began to tour more extensively and it was at the end of a four-week spell in Belgium, on 4 February 1982, that he suffered a massive heart attack. Although rushed to a Zeebrugge hospital, Alex Harvey died soon after arrival, a day short of his 47th birthday.

'We all went back to Alan Mair's house after the funeral,' recalls McKenna. 'The guys from Glasgow who were ages with Alex - Ian Campbell, Grimes, Bill Patrick - were all in one room. Everyone was drunk and singing and I went in and asked them to do 'The Galloway Hills' for Alex. I'd no idea how the original went and they played it as a traditional song, the way he would have heard it sat by a campfire up the Trossachs.'

The death of Alex Harvey closed two decades of pop in Scotland. It had moved from the corn exchange into amphitheatres, taking with it its audience and a love for US R&B. But the music and performance was now distant; passion had been supplanted by safety. There were few surprises and even less venom. Punk would blast this all aside, its local heroes in temporary venues playing live and raw to a handful of fans.

PART TWO
New Thing In Cartons

CHAPTER 13
DERANGED, DEMENTED AND FREE

In common with Merseybeat, folk-rock or New Thing jazz, punk contained many internal contrasts and the phrase reflects a prevailing mood rather than binding manifesto. Thus, if the Sex Pistols offered anarchic mayhem, then the Damned simply strove to party, and while the Clash embodied political chic, the Slits proclaimed sexual liberation.

It's now difficult to appreciate the dullness of the immediate pre-punk era, wherein the once-bright hopes of a generation became immersed in stultifying complacency. The cultural schism between pop and rock proved detrimental to both forms and while one became increasingly trivial, the other was riddled with the spurious notion of high art. Neither satisfied the underclass which burst out, with such cathartic effect, on the release of 'Anarchy In The UK', and during the ensuing cultural melee. Yet for all the proselytising of the new, and indeed a great deal of token revisionism, Punk - the movement - was indebted to the fag-end of 60s idealism with its rhetoric inspired by Situationist literature and its fashions shaped by the disenchanted flotsam of King's Road chic. 'Never trust a hippie,' declared Malcolm McLaren, but the Pistols' svengali did so from experience, rather than ignorance. He assiduously wrecked havoc on pop's Establishment with a manifesto inspired by the antics of starmaker Larry Parnes, and came to his new protégés following a spell guiding the New York Dolls.

Darlings of their city's Mercer Arts Centre, the New York Dolls embodied the trash aesthetic, combining the panache of the Rolling Stones and the streetlore of the Shangri-Las with a smattering of concurrent glam-rock. Poutingly decadent, they derided many contemporaries, espousing a classic bygone era and in turn becoming mentors to newer acts, including Patti Smith and Television. The latter group featured Richard Hell, whose spiked hair and ripped shirt, tacked together by safety pins, was seized upon by McLaren as a statement, not of poverty, but nihilism. This was the image he brought to the

Pistols, and in particular Johnny Rotten, but if this visual impact was daring, the group's music was initially less assertive, relying heavily on 60s teen-angst chestnuts by the Who ('Substitute') and Monkees ('I'm Not Your Stepping Stone'). This musical blueprint was quickly discarded, but the idea of forging a new direction by invoking the style of the previous decade already echoed throughout the UK. This wasn't the pub-rock entertainment of England's Home Counties, but a desire to return to a point in time where the group decided matters had gone astray. From there they could follow a truer path than that which history decreed.

'If you looked at the music that was going around when we formed, there was nothing very inspiring,' recalls Sheilagh Hynde, better known as Fay Fife, singer in the Rezillos. 'We looked back at a time we thought had a lot of fun in it, when people went to a place to dance and enjoy themselves.'

Although officially founded in March 1976, the Rezillos evolved out of the Knutsford Dominators, an eccentric party band formed the previous year at Edinburgh College of Art. 'We only did about 7 gigs,' recalled lead guitarist Jo Callis, 'but our reputation sank rather than grew.' Renowned for expansive guest lists and a set only intermittently competent, the Dominators fell apart when half its number opted for academia, leaving Callis and vocalist/drummer Alan Forbes to follow alternative ambitions under the respective sobriquets Luke Warm and Eugene Reynolds. They pieced together a new act, based on their erstwhile group's aspirations, but one with considerably more panache. 'It was our idea of the ultimate rock 'n' roll group,' explains Reynolds. 'When we were at art college we made up these posters with 'Beware, the Rezillos are Coming', even before it existed. We got members by going up to people and saying "You look like a candidate for the Rezillos." They would either look at us sideways or say, "Yeah. I know what you mean."' Hynde joined the pair as Candy Floss, before opting for her Fay Fife stage name, while former Knutsford roadie Mark 'HiFi' Harris joined on second guitar, a position ensured by his vast collection of blues and 60s ephemera. D.K. Smythe and 'Angel' Patterson took over on bass and drums respectively, but although Gayle Warning augmented the early line-up as a second woman singer, Eugene later opined that 'It looked like the male with two female backing vocalists which I don't think we were pleased with. We didn't want to put across that subservient image.' Gayle's amicable departure ended that particular dilemma, and the group was ultimately completed by itinerant saxophonist William Mysterious, whose cameos were so frequent that he became a permanent member. This informality was indicative of the group's initial attitude. 'We stepped into the thing with naiveté,' recalls Reynolds. 'We wanted to play something revved-up, and in a sense that idea pre-dated punk, but we weren't writing original material.'

The Rezillos took a jaded Edinburgh by storm. They came across like the

The Rezillos

mutant bastard offspring of the original Roxy Music and a greasy Dr. Feelgood, an early 60s cornucopia of motor bikes, wrap-around shades and winklepicker shoes. They worshipped Joe Meek, Merseybeat and vintage rock 'n' roll - their set was a cocktail of the Dave Clark Five, the Piltdown Men and Fay's beloved girl groups - but the unit was never reverential, opting instead to exaggerate nuances of both the song and performers. 'We were a hybrid of what we saw as 60s pop,' Eugene recalls, 'but it was our creation. We were colourful, almost science-fiction, and by not copying the latest fad invented a new-wave attitude to music.' 'It was our idea of what the 60s were like,' Fay opined in an earlier interview, 'which is not necessarily what is was like at the time.'

Within months the group had accumulated several stylish original songs, the majority of which were penned by Callis. The most immediate was 'I Can't Stand My Baby', which combined wonderfully throw-away, depreciative lines with a rapier-speed tempo de riguer for the demands of punk. Issued in the summer of 1977 on the local Sensible label, owned by the band's then-manager, Lenny Love, the single was a dramatic success. Yet if this was due, in part, to a new-wave audience, the performance bore no debt to the calculated ire of a Rotten or Strummer. Rezillos' music was rooted in a specific capsule, within which lay its unique appeal.

Although easily the best of Scotland's early independent recordings, 'I Can't Stand My Baby' was not the first such release of its era. The Drive and Exile completed early home-made singles, but their tepid music reflected pub-rock groundings rather than the determination of some brave new experience. The same was largely true of the Jolt - Robert Collins (vocals/guitar), Jim Doak (bass) and Iain Sheddon (drums) - who rose from relative obscurity upon supporting the Jam on the Glasgow leg of their UK tour. ''70s group have not been a musical influence, so much,' opined Sheddon when quizzed about his group's penchant for such pre-year zero material as 'Route 66', 'Whatcha Gonna Do 'Bout It' and 'Somebody Help Me'. Their own material reflected this interest, irrespective of the speed they played them. Having survived the rigours of a lacklustre debut ('You're Cold'), the Jolt shook off their dalliance with punk, donned matching suits and in 1978 completed an album indebted to Mod affectations which, if not original, was more convincing.

By comparison, those Scottish groups donning the Sex Pistols' mantle were younger and more disaffected. Heritage for them was the aforementioned Roxy Music, but unlike the Rezillos, who shared the former act's pop iconolatry, the punk sub-culture focused on their overall élan, drawing succour from its seemingly haphazard visual image. This facet was, of course, mutated beyond an initial, plastic glam-rock pose, but with it the concept of anti-rock had been established; a means of expression beyond a rapidly decaying art form. Xeroxed fanzines proliferated, the best of which was Tony D's *Ripped & Torn*. *Hanging Around*, *Kingdom Come* and *Jungleland* were among those arriving in its wake, but Lindsay Hutton's *Next Big Thing* would be the genre's sole survivor from this early outburst, a voice for rock 'n' roll malcontents from several different eras.

Once again Glasgow produced the emphatic musical talent, including the Back Stabbers - Rev Volting (vocals), Jimmy Loser (guitar), Colin Alkars (bass) and Far 2 Young (drums) - and Johnny And The Self Abusers, a pivotal aggregation which evolved in suitably unconventional manner. 'We used to go to a pub called the Doune Castle.' recalls vocalist Jim Kerr. 'Another group of people sat in the opposite corner with plastic raincoats and Dave Vanian hairstyles and they looked pretty exciting. One of them came over one night, pretty drunk, and asked us if we'd ever heard of Johnny And The Self Abusers. Charlie and I said no, and he told us it was this imaginary band that they were going to make real.'

'Charlie' was Charlie Burchill, a friend of Kerr's from school who was already developing talents as a guitarist. The pair's formative influences were early 70s eccentrics, Eno, Bowie, Alice Cooper - 'People that looked like they came from Mars,' as Kerr remembers. 'Then someone would tell us about the real thing, the Velvet Underground or the New York Dolls, and music just took over. If I saw a show that impressed me, I wouldn't be able to think about anything else for a month.' Unwilling to succumb to a nine-to-five regime, Kerr and Burchill left for a hitch-hiking tour of Europe. 'It was our emancipation, our version of Kerouac I suppose, but by the time we came back there was this feeling in the air.'

The duo accepted an invitation to join the embryonic combo. 'We rolled Charlie's amp about half a mile to John Milarky's house,' Jim recalls. 'He'd no microphone stands, they were taped to the ceiling, hanging down, and these amazing characters seemed like a law unto themselves. The manager at the Doune Castle had agreed to give a concert for Johnny And The Self Abusers. All Milarky had to do was form the band.'

Despite a sense of anticipation, any direction the nascent culture offered was strangled by bureaucracy as the city fathers, in their role of licensees, made life uncomfortable for pubs willing to promote punk rock in the face of tabloid fury. The assault was not the result of the expletives unleashed by the Sex Pistols on *Today*; the show was not transmitted in Scotland, but the glue-sniffing craze suddenly endemic among teenage malcontents in crumbling housing schemes. Cretin-rockers the Ramones, elder statesmen of the new noise, celebrated the practise in several songs and correct political noises were required in rebuff from the governing Labour administration. Most Glasgow nightclubs would thus opt for disco while the Bungalow Bar in neighbouring Paisley became a favoured punk haunt almost by default. The repression merely served to intensify the sense of the outsider, but local groups and venues did occasionally evade the prohibitive net, particularly during the movement's early days.

'We turned up to play our debut gig,' states Kerr, 'and there was a queue about a quarter of a mile down the street. No one had played a note and yet you couldn't get in.' Once onstage the Abusers answered expectations with girl dancers and a frantic pulsebeat; style over content perhaps, but carried off with considerable panache. 'We thought we were the city's first punk band,' Kerr relates, 'then we heard about the Jolt. But as they were from Wishaw we felt they weren't, technically, Glaswegian.'

'You'd meet Rev Volting or Jimmy Loser in the record shops,' he adds. 'They'd be talking about forming a band and buying 'Metallic K.O.'. We'd never travelled out of our part of the city but when you went to the shop, and then to the pub, there'd be people from Townhead or wherever, and it was like a big party. For a year we had a taste of what the 60s must have been like.'

The hubbub beginning to surface from Scotland eventually attracted wider attention. In a decision curiously echoing the major labels of the previous decade, two London-based independents, Stiff and Chiswick, launched a co-operative 'challenge', wherein acts auditioned in rotation at various centres throughout the UK. As Glasgow was a largely no-go area, Edinburgh's Clouds hosted the procession of Scottish hopefuls from which the Abusers and the Subhumans (later the Subs) emerged as front-runners.

The Abusers signed with Chiswick, but the fragile truce which existed between the band's different factions ruptured. Schoolfriends Tony Donald (bass) and Brian McGee (drums) sided with Kerr and Burchill, leaving Milarky and Alan McNeil to argue a quite different corner. A split was inevitable, and in a gesture of almost theatrical proportions, the sextet was disbanded the day its sole single was issued in October 1977. Both 'Saints And Sinners' and its coupling 'Dead Vandals' suffer from the contrasting desires of the participants, although the collision adds a frisson to what are largely undistinguished songs.

The Subs meanwhile surfaced on Stiff's One-Off subsidiary, a clear signal their's was not a long-term project. 'Gimmie Gimmie Your Heart' was a good song, but as more than one wag remarked, 'It's their only fucking song,' and the quartet also broke up in April 1978. Indeed drummer Ali MacKenzie quit before their final gig, for which Brian McGee was temporarily drafted.

Homebased companies were thus left to document the fledgling scene, but although Sensible had established itself with the Rezillos, owner Lenny Love was unable to balance success with other, personal commitments. Procrastination cost him the Cramps, whose singer Lux Interior handed the masters for 'Domino' and 'Human Fly' to Eugene Reynolds. 'Lux wanted them on Sensible,' he recalls, 'and to have followed us with something like that would have been perfect. However, Lenny just didn't see it.' The adventurism of the label's only other release, Neon's 'Bottles', was not matched by sales and Love was quickly eclipsed by Bruce Findlay, who's Zoom label enjoyed immediate success with the Valves 'For Adolph's Only'. An accelerated R&B act, this Edinburgh group defied punk logic, with its long-haired drummer, Gordon Dair, and ageing part-time poet/singer, Dee Robot. They were undoubtedly popular, but their style confirmed a nagging suspicion that many new-wave devotees preferred a souped-up reading of traditional pop, rather than something demonstrably more challenging. The Valves second offering combined the punning 'Tarzan Of The King's Road' with a Jan And Dean pastiche, 'Ain't No Surf In Portobello', but both sides were marred by a lifeless production and the single was a commercial flop. The quartet's brief ascendancy faltered when a piece in *Sounds* emphasised Dee's bellicose imbibing and a showcase gig ended in fiasco. The Valves did enjoy another release, 'It Don't Mean Nothing At All', but folded soon after its release.

Zoom's second signing was PVC2, a thinly-veiled pseudonym for the ailing Slik. Bereft of any credibility in the wake of their dalliance with Martin/Coulter bubblegum, the group had lost founder member Jim McGinlay, although newcomer Russell Webb had joined by the time the quartet repaired to a deserted Glasgow hall where they cut 'Put You In The Picture'. Frustration spilled out of this venomous performance which suggested the aggression they had brought to cover versions in their previous Salvation incarnation. The single was an artistic triumph, but it marked the end of Midge Ure's tenure in the band as he prepared to join the London-based Rich Kids. Willie Gardener - a cousin of Alex Harvey - was brought in to a revamped act which threw away both its former appellations, and re-emerged as the Zones with 'Stuck On You'.

'I saw the immediate punk explosion falter,' recalled Bruce Findlay, 'and I knew Zoom had to get financial support to survive.' Independent outlets rightly became more discerning and having delivered the Zones to Arista in 1978, Findlay then secured a marketing deal with the same company. The singles which followed were largely undistinguished and included early power-pop releases by the Questions, later adopted by the Jam's Paul Weller, and Nightshift. The crucial exception, however, was Simple Minds.

The fall-out from the Abusers' split resulted in two, contrasting acts. John Milarky led the first to surface and, by dubbing them the Cuban Heels, duly revealed a penchant for 60s revivalism. The quartet's debut, 'Downtown'/'Smok Walk', invoked the sound of greasy Merseybeat and showed yet another Scottish group retreating from new possibilities. Milarky's former colleagues were much more guarded, and when launched as Simple Minds in December 1977, indicated they would be the more adventurous. Their influences were now firmly pre-year zero - what journalist and early mentor Ian Cranna described as the 'Twinight academy of Bowie, Harley and Verlaine.' The Doctors Of Madness, Van Der Graaff Generator and Roxy Music should be added to this list, but each guru was fashioned in an obtuse manner suggesting empathy rather than theft. A painfully thin Kerr, framed in ill-fitting Oxfam suits, bowl-cut hairdo and mascara-ed eyes, fronted a group jockeying for position as two guitarists, Burchill and newcomer Duncan Barnwell, goaded one another, struggling to gain supremacy over the keyboards of recent conscript Mick McNeil. Former Subs' bassist Derek Forbes, who had replaced Donald, and drummer McGee, completed this adventurous line-up which, when combined with a rudimentary light show, suggested a theatre of the macabre. There was nothing remotely like it in Scotland and, as a gap between the Minds and other compatriots became quickly apparent, so Zoom began courting their affections.

The furore of punk was ebbing by 1978. Few maintained the previous year's shock tactics - where now Bread Poltice And The Running Sores? - and a disenfranchised audience of bondage pants and mohican haircuts later courted Oi, the same bastard offspring of spit-and-throttle that heavy metal was to blues. The Exploited, led by former soldier Wattie Buchan and fuelled by gargantuan guitarist Big John Duncan, fulfilled a demand, but their style, unveiled in 1981 on *Punk's Not Dead*, was as much an anachronistic curio as loon pants and space-hoppers. The quartet paradoxically clung to a sound they had not helped forge while those who did moved elsewhere. Yet where Simple Minds progressed at a determined, albeit measured pace, the Rezillos found their sudden acclaim more difficult to sustain.

The success of 'I Can't Stand My Baby' was not confined to Scotland and within months of its release the group had signed with Sire, home of the Ramones. A second single, '(My Baby Does) Good Sculptures', re-emphasised their quirkiness without extending their appeal, although a rigorous fortnight in London's pub/club circuit - the Roxy, the Vortex and the Nashville - was well-received. The quintet was then flown to New York where they completed *Can't Stand The Rezillos*. 'We did most of that album at night during cheap recording time,' Eugene recalls. 'We'd hang around CBGBs and Max's, waiting for a telephone call, then rush over to the studio, sometimes only for four hours. Most of it was done in one take.' Despite this haphazard approach, the set captured many of their best-loved songs, including 'No', 'Cold Wars' and 'Top Of The Pops'. The latter became a Top 20 single and its sense of irony was heightened when performed on the eponymous television show. However any enthusiasm was undermined when Sire, caught in the throes of a distribution battle, delayed the album's release, cancelling a promotional tour in the process. This simply exacerbated problems within the line-up and while William Mysterious succumbed to a 'flying saucer attack', a schism between Callis, who wished to pursue a heavier direction, and Reynolds and Fife, who favoured a visual, more irreverent approach, grew more marked. 'All groups have factions,' Eugene declared, 'and, as Fay was my girlfriend, we were on one side while the others formed their own unit. We found it difficult to communicate at that time. Fay and I didn't want it to slip into 'just another group', but lacked the experience to articulate how we should do it. It just ended up as friction and little splits became great gashes.' A sudden high-profile also brought problems to a group formed in such an unconventional, informal manner. 'The Rezillos did not begin with a serious intention. We didn't give a shit about chart success, but now there were pressures to keep the ball rolling. Joe felt constrained by the style of 'Can't Stand My Baby' and didn't want to write to order. He felt that the formula was tired and wanted to go in a direction which Fay and I didn't necessarily want to follow.' Such problems were masked when the set was belatedly issued and those outside the immediate unit were unaware of the simmering tension. Indeed the quintet maintained an outer confidence, one often perceived as arrogance, and the two singers were not especially popular with other Scottish acts. 'What will you call your debut album,' a writer once asked Valves' bassist Pada Scott. "Can't Stand The Rezillos Either," was his immediate retort.

'We were difficult to deal with,' Reynolds admits, 'her more so than me because she became Fay Fife. We did what we spoke about and a lot of people couldn't take it. We were direct, hot-tempered, with a somewhat abusive stance, but it was also very punk.'

Sadly, the band's internal conflict became insurmountable and an appearance at the Glasgow Apollo on 23 December 1978 - documented on a posthumous, disappointing live set - also marked the end of the Rezillos. 'It was a fantastic concert,' recalls Eugene, 'but the record didn't show it off to best advantage. Here you had a group, split in two, but with one faction mixing it with Fay and I brought in, just for a day, and in no position other than to say "We hate it."'

regular music present	regular music present for THE EDINBURGH ROCK FESTIVAL 1978
the Rezillos + support	***the Rezillos* + support**
Clouds,	Clouds,
West Tollcross	West Tollcross
Friday 25th August	Friday 25th August
Tickets: £1.50	*Tickets: £1.50*

Ticket for the Rezillos as part of the 1978 Edinburgh Rock Festival

'It meant that Joe and I, who were the best of friends, ended up hating each other for a couple of years afterwards. We became competitors and only spoke to each other through lawyers' letters.' The tension was exacerbated by the fact that the pair still shared a flat. 'That appealed to my bizarre sense of humour.'

If the Rezillos' career had run aground, that of the Skids was unfolding. Formed in March 1977, they evolved when two members of Tattoo, Stuart Adamson (guitar) and Bill Simpson (bass), were joined by extrovert vocalist Ricky Jobson and aspiring drummer Tom Bomb (née Tom Kellichan). At 16 the singer was one of Fife's few punks, and a collective working class background ensured that the movement's socio-political element was just as prevalent as its adrenaline rush. 'Stuart had already been working with other groups,' Jobson recalls, 'but he asked me to audition with these other guys. Word quickly got around that we'd formed the first punk band in Fife and a guy called Pano, a Hell's Angel, came along and looked after us. He found us a rehearsal hall in Dunfermline and got us some concerts. Our debut was at the Bellvue, where I stood with my lyrics in my hand in front of 300 people. It was quite mad really.' Adamson's firm R&B roots gave the Skids an early muscle, but Jobson's hewn features and aggressive rasp enhanced a sense of muscular urgency. 'I'd dyed my hair black and white and wasn't afraid to do anything,' Ricky later confided, but his naive panache gave the group much of its early image. 'The most important concert we went to see was the Damned at Clouds in Edinburgh. That changed everything for us. It was chaotic, wild and angry - everything we were and we found ourselves.'

The Skids first drew attention outside Fife at the 'Stiffwick' challenge. 'It was a complete nightmare,' Jobson opines. 'It was so aggressive. Luckily we had a following through from Dunfermline and while they went berserk, we insulted some of the journalists and harangued Stiff's Dave Robinson.' However, rather than go with Chiswick, who showed interest, the quartet sided with local retailer Sandy Muir. 'He was the one who stocked indie singles,' Jobson explains, 'and he took an interest in us because we were regular buyers.' The group had already amassed a sets' worth of original songs - 'We never did any covers, it was always our own material' - and Muir offered to finance their debut EP, 'Charles'/'Reasons'/'Test Tube Babies'. Although the collection paid lip service to punk, the opening song also revealed a grasp of tough, but pliable, melody. "Charles' came out classier than the others,' Jobson confirms. 'It marked the start of the Stuart Adamson guitar sound.'

By this point the Skids were a popular attraction throughout Scotland, in part through a series of support slots, notably with the Jam and Rezillos. 'A local promoter, George Duffin, had sent us to a barn dance in Perth,' Ricky recounts, '...and to make up he gave us these really crucial gigs.' They then headed for London and having set up a squat in West Hampstead, ploughed a furrow through the city's punk and pub minefield. 'At the end of the trip we returned to play at the Red Cow,' recalls Jobson. 'The place was packed solid, word had got round, and there were lots of record companies there.' Virgin signed the group in 1978, after which they completed two releases; *Sweet Suburbia*, a homage to the Fife newtown of Glenrothes, and a second EP, *The Saints Are Coming*. However Jobson remains adamant that matters were already awry, even at this early stage. 'We should have stopped making records, or at least should never have signed to a major label. We had a ridiculous contract - eight albums cross-collaterised with a publishing deal and a £5,000 advance.

'Things started to go ominously wrong. *Sweet Suburbia* came out in the ugliest sleeve I've seen in my life, while *The Saints Are Coming*, which had another terrible cover, included throwaway songs. 'Wide Open' shouldn't have been on it.' It did, however, feature 'Off One Skin', one of the singer's first compositions. 'Stuart wrote all of *Sweet Suburbia*,' Jobson recalls, 'while I wrote lyrics which were more obscure, more insular, quite different to Stuart's social topics.'

The Skids nonetheless increased their following and having become a popular act both in Scotland and in London, embarked on a tour of UK clubs and colleges. Work on a debut album commenced, but progress faltered when an unhappy Adamson suddenly quit the band during the sessions. 'Stuart and I

The Skids' second album; *Days In Europa*

were always very close,' explains Jobson, 'but one morning I woke up and he'd vanished back to Scotland. That was the first sign of tension between us and his sudden disappearances haunted the Skids to the end.' Friends and associates persuaded him to return and the finished piece, *Scared To Dance*, not only survived the traumas, but somehow drew strength from them and it remains one of Scotland's most compelling punk collections. 'Initially Virgin put us in the studio with Mike Howlett,' states Jobson, 'which was an absolute nightmare. Dave Batchelor, who used to be in Tear Gas, was much better and at last we'd found someone we could work with.'

Two Top 10 singles, 'Into The Valley' and 'Masquerade', followed in 1979, both of which were marked by ringing guitars, propulsive rhythms and Ricky's dramatic vocal. Yet the same stirring combination quickly became mannered and the Skids second album, *Days In Europa*, added little to what the group had already achieved. Producer Bill Nelson (ex-Be Bop Deluxe), did bring polish to a sound altered by the loss of drummer Tom Kellichan. 'Tom was the kindest, most human element of the Skids,' Jobson acknowledges. 'You could talk to him about life in general without an integral plot going on.' Ex-Rich Kid Rusty Egan took his place, but the internal wrangles continued. 'I had moved to London,' Ricky explains, 'but on the few occasions I came back to Dunfermline I fought with the bassist. We had a big argument on the set of a TV show and he left.' The departures of these founder members brought the group to a crossroads. New musicians introduced a different perspective to what had become an immutable niche but, as the singer confirms, 'At that point it wasn't a band anymore.'

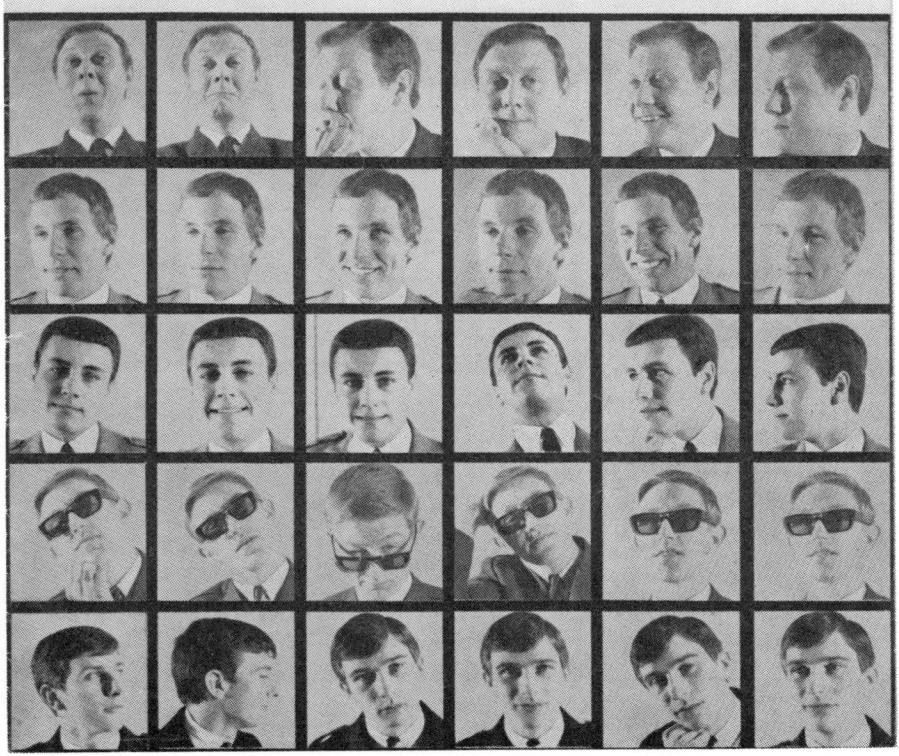

Cover of beat News, June 1965

HISTORY OF THE COPYCATS

The Copy Cats were formed in December, 1962, and first played as a fill-in group during dance intervals. They made such a big impression during this period that with the financial assistance of the local branch of the Round Table they turned semi-professional soon after Christmas of that year. At this time, two of the group were still at school. In the Spring of 1963 they achieved national publicity by being the left out group in the abortive Scottish Finals of the National Beat Championships at Hamilton. They however went on to win the re-run Finals in Perth and a month later they ended up second in the National Finals in London.

The Copy Cats celebrated their first anniversary this year by turning full-professional. Since then, they have appeared in most of the main cities and towns in Scotland and the North of England, and on Pop Shows with the 'Ronettes' and the 'Hollies'. They have also had several appearances on Television and cut their first disc 'I can never see you' c/w 'I'm a hog for you baby'.

To those of you who are interested, you'd maybe like to know that to enable them to keep their many engagements, the Copy Cats have a specially constructed van containing:—
* reclining seats for sleeping, and fitted wardrobes.
* radio, portable tape recorder, and record player.

They also have a collective headache from listening to the radio, record player and tape recorder all playing together.

The people behind the Copy Cats:
Musical Direction: Alex. Sutherland.
Road Manager: Ken Smith.
Personal Manager: Alex. Stuart.
Personal representation, publicity and management:
ALBERT A BONICI
1 North College Street, Elgin.
Telephones Elgin 7058 and 7803.
ALL ENQUIRIES TO THIS ADDRESS

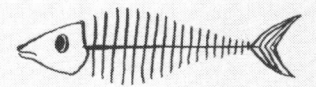

Just Released!
by NORCO RECORDS Ltd.
ELGIN

JOHNNY and the COPYCATS
I CAN NEVER SEE YOU c/w
I'M a HOG FOR YOU BABY
ON SALE NOW!

Johnny And The Copycats, an early press release

Johnny And The Copycats

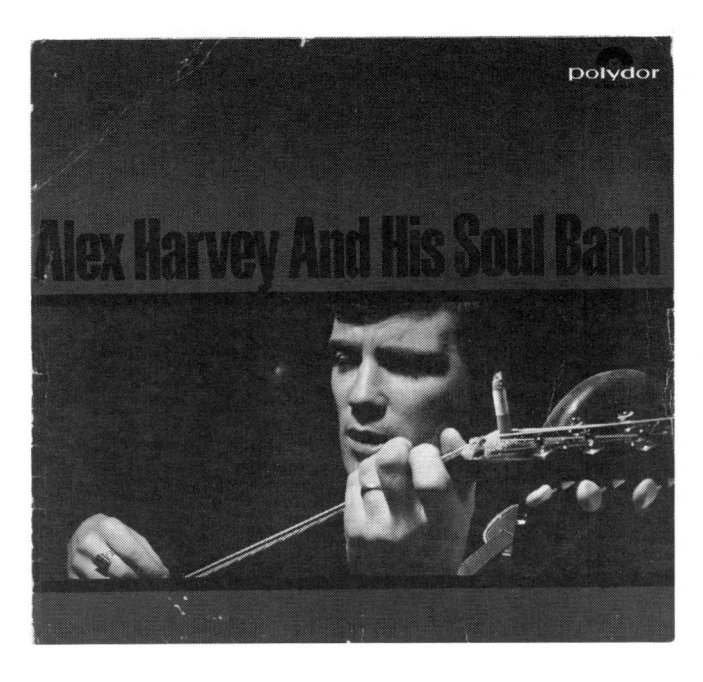

The highly collectable Alex Harvey debut album, 1964

SHOWBEAT, SEPTEMBER, 1967 — Page 15

LULU'S BACK IN TOWN

Alex for the Dream Police

ALEX SCOTT has taken over the management of the Dream Police and The Gladiators. He has high hopes for both groups.

With his experience of Jason's Flock behind him, he should have little trouble boosting them to the top.

The Dream Police are rehearsing three nights a week just now, before just taking on too many dates.

And The Gladiators are hard at work writing their own songs. They insist on original material for their stage act.

But the ever-energetic Alex is not happy yet. He is considering taking on a third outfit. But he's not revealing which one.

Rumour has it that The Gladiators may have their name changed. As the boys are all just over 5-feet tall, if the name change comes off, it could be an interesting one.

Cartoon are no joke

"THE CARTOON" formerly known as The Chevlons have always been reckoned to be one of the best groups in Scotland.

Now that they have changed their name, and policy, added a lead singer and got themselves a new bassist they are even more worthy of this recognition.

The group now do four and five-part harmonies when playing in a mixed-age group. Numbers include Rag Doll and Silence is Golden as well as the usual 'rave' material.

They are doing well at their residency in the Olympia Ballroom, East Kilbride and the crowds are increasing all the time.

THE cartoon

Management
G. ALLISON
22 Garbisdale Street
Glasgow N.

'Phone day and night
(041) SPR 7857

LULU'S back in town —with a bang. She has a great show for the Piccadilly Club in Glasgow at the beginning of September.

The girl from Glasgow is back in her home town after capturing the hearts and imagination of America.

The top men in America saw her and took to her immediately.

What with criss-crossing the Atlantic, and British TV appearances, Lulu has discovered that success brings hard work as well as rewards. After her appearance on the Monkees show in London, Lulu found that her already great British following had expanded to cover the world.

And the world wants Lulu.

In fact, it looks as if it will be a long time before she returns to Scotland for a show.

This bouncing vivacious girl will not forget her fans up here. Her top fan is her mother, who stays in the city.

So playing in Glasgow is more than just another job. It is more of a homecoming.

So, welcome home. For a little while at least.

The Oracle

Congratulations . . . . . to Ringo Starr on his part in producing a son. Jason . . . to Doug Carmichael on his engagement . . . to Mr. and Mrs. Adam Faith but black marks for allowing photographers into their bedroom the morning after the wedding. What are they trying to prove?

Come back **Bob Shaw**, all is forgiven. P.S. Bring the telephone with you . . . **Rolling Stones** new record "We Love You" dedicated to the Butler's Association, **Lord Parker** and **London Airport Taxi Drivers** . . . **Mick Jagger's** chicken pox prevented a visit to the 21st EIF.

Searchers don't like having their photographs taken . . . **Juryman** took a nosedive off stage at a recent barbeque. All part of the act? . . . **Showbeat Editor** looked thirsty at "dry" Sunset Clan Ball . . . **Hoagy Carmichael** is the greatest. Pirate radio back with a **Yak and a Mouse** . . .

Lost — **Bob Spencer**. Will finder return to Showbeat Monthly . . . Monkee's film for Edinburgh? If you like Bill Haley, you'll love the Dollyrocker Band . . . The Poets' loss is the pie-making industry's gain . . . Has **Ernie Collinson** been Slade? **George Harrison** went to San Francisco 'out of curiosity'. Is there nothing he would like to see in Glasgow . . . Radio Scotland DJ **Richard Park** offered a job with Grampian TV . . . **Gene Pitney** thinking of making his permanent home in Britain.

Studio Six moved to London on August 31 . . . **Sandie Shaw** doing well, but whatever happened to **Chris Andrews**? . . . **Tam Paton**, bare - foot - driver. Does that mean he **Hippies** when he walks. If anyone would tell me what happens in the North of Scotland, I'd insult groups there, too . . . A clog and tulip holiday for **Jason's Flock** . . . with rumours that **Sammy Juste** and **Mickey Deluxe** are married, are Top of the Pops looking for a new disc girl?

'bye now,

A page from Showbeat, September 1967

Lulu

Donovan

IDIOTS ARE FREELANCE

OVER SIXTY DELICATE, WITTY AND MOODY SHORT POEMS BY THAT MASTER OF THE MODERN EPIGRAM, EDINBURGH'S OWN

Alan Jackson

40p FROM THE SHOPS OR FROM THE POET HIMSELF.

BY POST FROM: RAINBOW BOOKS, BOGENJOSS HOUSE, DYCE, ABERDEEN.

ARENA

* DENIM BAGS from £4.25
* DENIM JEANS from £4.95
* EMBROIDERED DENIM SHIRTS £6.50
* CHEESECLOTH SHIRTS from £3.50
* CHEESECLOTH TOPS from £2.25

11 East Fountainbridge
30 South Clerk St.

Amidst all the cultural Maya find the

Spiritual Exhibition

10:30 am - 10:30 pm
Depicting Man's search for enlightenment
pure foods served during day
8.0 pm films, dance, music, food for the soul
25th August - 1st September
ZETLAND HALL
11 Pilrig St. off Leith Walk.

Alice
FOR CORD AND CHEESECLOTH

Alice
FOR FADED DEMINS

Alice
FOR LOONS IN 30 SHADES

Alice
FOR FALMERS

Alice
FOR SOUTH-SEA BUBBLE

Alice
For More Than Ever

GREYFRIARS MARKET, 14, FORREST RD.
MONDAY-SATURDAY   10-6 pm.

Display ads of the times, from fanzine Cracker, 1973

THE HISTORY OF SCOTTISH ROCK AND POP 175

Back cover of fanzine Pastelism, from the late 80s

Ex Incredible String Band member Robin Williamson

Top, Alex Harvey And The Big Soul Band, early 60s and the Bay City Rollers early 70s

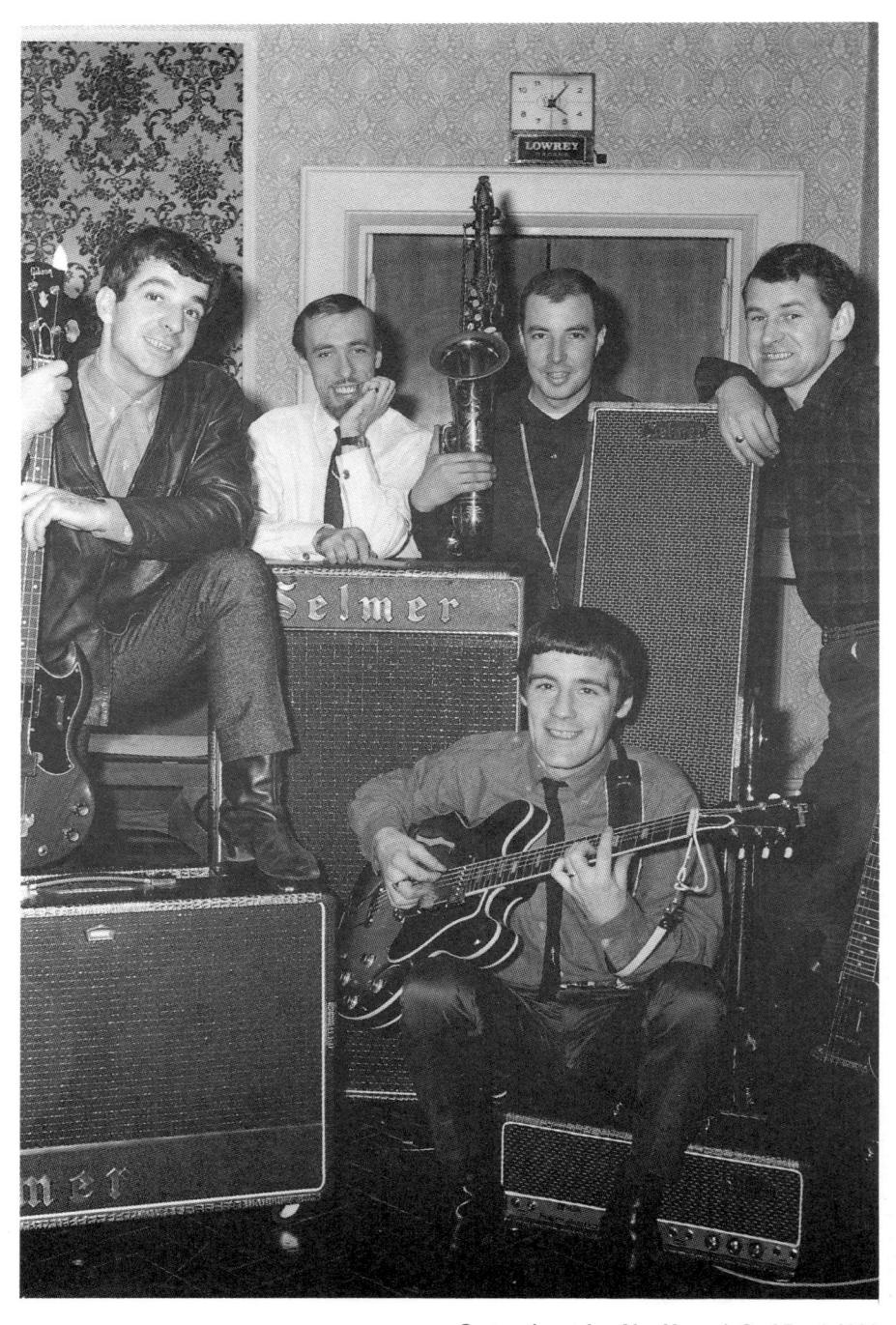

Contrasting styles: Alex Harvey's Soul Band, 1964

Wet Wet Wet, 1989

top: The Skids, bottom: Big Country

top: Jesus And Mary Chain, bottom: Hipsway

top: Josef K, bottom: the Rezillos

The Big Dish

top: Deacon Blue, bottom Altered Images

Clare Grogan of Altered Images

hoochie coochie

SUN 9 — del Amitri — **June**

SUN 16 ON 2 FLOORS LIVE FUNK FILMS & the Proclaimers

marc riley with the creepers

FUNK a
FRI certain
21 ratio

SUN 23 ALONE AGAIN OR & Tomato

Hoochie Coochie club poster

top: Del Amitri, bottom: Mike Heron's Incredible Acoustic Band

Roddy Frame of Aztec Camera

Jim Kerr of Simple Minds

top: Orange Juice, bottom: the Pastels

Fish

left and right: the Proclaimers

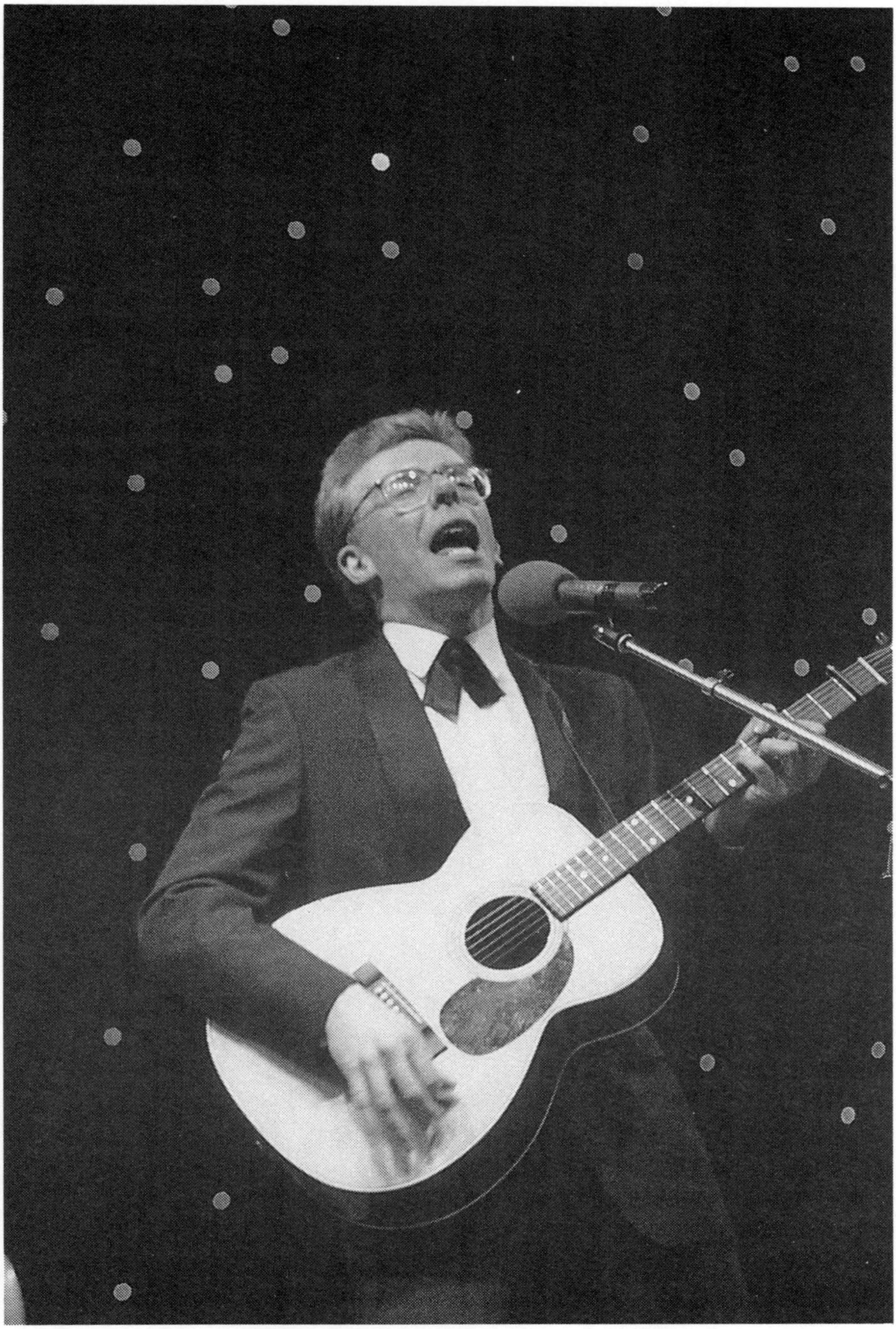

the Primitives, 1969

Bobby King of the Scars

Texas

Teenage Fanclub

Lloyd Cole

Chapter 14
Goodbye 1970s

Simple Minds spent 1978 reaping effusive praise. Local fanzines, generally, fell under their sway, while correspondents in the music press announced the arrival of a major talent. The group meanwhile refused to bow to pressure and appear on London's regular club circuit, preferring the larger stage of Scotland's colleges and universities where their grandeur could be more easily showcased. The group's ambition was clearly apparent, even when dole cheques had to be pooled to keep a crumbling van on the road or maintain a Heath Robinson light show.

Zoom's interest buoyed confidence at a time when major record companies had surprisingly rejected a series of early demos. Findlay's label appeared to offer the intimacy of an independent but, through its deal with Arista, promised international exposure, and an agreement was eventually reached. Extra funds in order to secure the band were made available, although a separate contract was required, one which would have unfortunate repercussions on the minor party.

Simple Minds were signed to Zoom in December and within a month were recording their first album. *Life In A Day* entered the UK chart in March 1979, prior to the group's London debut, and an air of suspicion not only greeted that long-delayed appearance, but also the collection itself. Despite a lengthy, laudatory review in *New Musical Express*, most critics rounded on its lifeless, sterile sound, and the group also voiced disappointment with the final result.

The title track apart, *Life In A Day* was comprised of old songs, written with two guitarists in mind, but recorded following an amicable split with Duncan Barnwell. It is thus possible to argue that the set was recorded too early, before the realigned group had found focus, or too late, by which time the material had grown stale. Jim Kerr offers a different perspective. 'I'd say it was recorded wrong. People would not do it now - you take a band from Toryglen and you put them in Abbey Road. We did want to be taken out of our environment, but we had a shoplifter mentality; we didn't know when all this was going to go away. So we bought the big PA, we put our name on the flightcases. It was something we had to do but I don't think it did the music any favours.

'We were bored with the songs. We'd written new ones and although I think people do make the glorious debut album, they are usually spontaneous. We went from punk to pro with nothing in between.'

The overwrought synthesiser swathing these recordings emphasised just how jaded the band had become, and the lynch-pin selections, 'Pleasantly Disturbed' and 'Murder Story', suddenly lost focus. 'Chelsea Girl' was meanwhile re-arranged, as if to inject a new determination, but by dropping down on the chorus, rather than rising, the band undermined the song's natural development.

Life In A Day exposed the influences Simple Minds brought to their music, but failed to expand upon them. The ensuing criticism of a group accustomed to accolade caused undue frustration, much of it aimed at Arista, who had marketed the quintet in stereotyped fashion, rather than explore the avenues of mystery they preferred to follow. Denied the critical allure of a Joy Division, Simple Minds began the long courtship of populist acclaim through a punishing touring schedule, determined to prove the validity of their own, unyielding, self-confidence.

Simple Minds in their days with Zoom

A second set, *Real To Real Cacophony*, was completed and released by the end of the year. 'We went to Rockfield for that album,' Kerr relates, 'and all we had to work on was sounds and atmosphere.' The quintet deliberately kept work-in-progress secret, denying access to almost everyone and steadfastly refusing to furnish demos, arguing that the release of sketchbook material had helped prejudice attitudes towards *Life In A Day*. 'It's there and you never capture it again,' declares Kerr. 'Too many people had heard early versions of the material on our first album, and it was too easy to say it wasn't as good.' Few were thus prepared for the shock the dense *Real To Real Cacophony* produced, nor the contrasting atmospheres it offered. No longer a malleable template, Simple Minds had become less penetrable, with only three tracks, 'Changeling', 'Premonition' and 'Calling Your Name', continuing the thread of previous work. 'Cacophony', 'Veldt' and 'Film Theme' toyed with ambient soundscapes as the quintet explored new directions by confronting their preconceptions about music. This more daring approach brought plaudits, but negligible sales, straining an already fragile relationship with Arista. 'They couldn't believe what they got,' Jim explains. 'There was no 'Chelsea Girls' as such, but it was a record which not only got good reviews, but was accepted on a more specialised level.'

By 1980 it was clear the parent company regretted its deal with Zoom and decreed that they, not Findlay, would decide its future releases. Taking the impudent bait, Bruce demanded a release from his contract, which was duly given, but as Simple Minds had been acquired on a separate deal, they remained an Arista signing despite the label's horror over the album. Decisive pressure was now necessary, their A&R department - one completely different from that which signed the group - made several fatal overtures, the most farcical being a thinly-veiled implication that the Minds look to the success of Mod/Ska signings Secret Affair and the Beat. The resultant rebuttal doomed all hope of reconciliation, but not before the group completed *Empires And Dance*.

This third selection was inspired by the quintet's forays into Europe and echoed the repetitive, pseudo-disco approach of German groups Kraftwerk and DAF. 'The months leading up to *Empires And Dance* were the first time we'd got to travel as a band,' states Kerr. 'The songs were a travelogue - in soundscapes and lyrically - postcards from wherever we'd been.' Their newfound dance-oriented sound was especially effective on 'I Travel', where a sound-system punch was under-pinned with newsreel paranoia, and the more personal 'Thirty Frames A Second'. However, it was the measured 'Today I Died Again' and 'This Fear Of Gods' - on which Derek Forbes' bubbling bass was particularly effective - which pointed at future developments.

Empires And Dance confirmed Simple Minds' rebirth following their disastrous debut, yet now they were criticised for forsaking a form of Scottish stereotype. But by adopting funk patterns, the group was simply finding a similar empathy in black styles to that discovered by a previous generation of Scots' musicians. 'Richard Jobson suggested that we were betraying our heritage' said Kerr at the time, but Simple Minds had always stressed an abhorrence of petty nationalism.

Jobson's remark seemed somewhat inopportune, particularly in the light of the Skids' second album, *Days In Europa*, and such tracks as 'The Olympian' and 'Dulce Et Decorum Est'. They reflected his growing confusion between retaining his roots and progressing, a dilemma assuaged in the wake of hit singles, notably the gregarious 'Working For The Yankee Dollar'. This could not, however, disguise the fraught relationship developing between singer and guitarist. 'I was more forthcoming than the others and the press started coming to me,' states Jobson. 'I'm sure that hurt Stuart. He was the nucleus of the Skids and is a brilliant person when he wants to be, but when his interest drifted it was a major problem. By this point we were a million miles apart.'

Rusty Egan's stop-gap inclusion ended when *Days In Europa* was completed and the quartet's third album, *The Absolute Game*, featured Russell Webb (bass - late of the Zones) and ex-Insect Bite Mike Bailie (drums) alongside the quarrelling founder members. 'That album contained accessible, commercial songs but they lacked passion,' says Jobson. 'There are elements which are fine; 'Circus Games' and 'Hurry On Boys' have threads, but the rest are just a mesh of ideas and nothing more.' Jobson grew increasingly hostile to the role he was required to take and sought solace in the literature of Jean Paul Sartre and Jean Cocteau. By doing so he further alienated his prospective audience, much of which hankered for the easy foolishness of 'TV Stars', later dubbed 'Albert Tatlock', an early favourite in which Ricky recited the names of characters from television's durable soap, *Coronation Street*. 'I had found a new niche,' Jobson explains, 'but it was so far removed from what the Skids were doing.'

Simple Minds followed the Skids to Virgin in 1981. Freed from Arista's mismanagement, the quintet entered the new decade infused with creativity. *Sons And Fascination/Sister Feelings Call* showed them ingenious with the twin-demands of chart-oriented pop ('Love Song') and cerebral challenge ('Themes For Great Cities'). 'There was an abundance of ideas on those records,' Jim Kerr confirms. 'Looking back we might have been better honing it down, but there were so many things we wanted to try.' 'We grew up at that point,' adds Charlie Burchill. 'For the first time we realised we were capable of making music which could reach a bigger audience.' Part of this newfound confidence came from a brief working relationship the group fused with Steve Hillage, a former member of hippie acolytes Gong. Hillage had become one of Virgin's favoured producers and it is fair to comment that the combination of Euro-futurists and pot-head pixie raised several eyebrows. The producer understood the mechanics combining the mental and physical, and both sides shared affection for German bands Can, Neu! and La Dusseldorf. This empathy generated a mutual understanding and common direction. 'The first time we met Hillage he was playing a Michael Rother album,' Kerr recalls. 'We connected right away.' The double set allowed Simple Minds scope to experiment, although the wide palate later grew increasingly focused.

The prosperity the quintet now enjoyed contrasted the Skids' sharp commercial decline. Kenny Hyslop, a second refugee from the now-defunct Zones, had replaced Mike Baillie in April 1981, prompting Jobson's sanguine remark that the group was now 'like a close family'. Yet within four months of this proud boast, the unit suffered the crucial loss of Stuart Adamson. 'Our potential was of phenomenal quality, but we couldn't find that blend. During rehearsals for our next tour Stuart said he never wanted to work with me again and kind of sacked me. I felt OK, sensing that now I could get on with another life, but I then got a call to come back to Scotland.' Over the ensuing few days Jobson was dismissed, and re-instated, on two further occasions while Hyslop was also asked to leave. 'Things were terribly wrong,' Jobson recalls, 'before Stuart finally walked out saying he hated me and couldn't work with me anymore. That was it.'

Russell Webb remained with Jobson in the final Skids' incarnation which was completed by flautist Paul Wishart alongside sundry friends and colleagues. The dour *Joy* was their final album, but while openly proclaiming a vaunted Celtic heritage, the set lacked the ringing sparkle Adamson brought to such patriotic material. Morose rather than uplifting, this mis-titled collection simply confirmed that the Skids had lost a once-impassioned direction and their demise was officially confirmed in January 1982. '*Joy* sold 3,000 copies, then Virgin withdrew it,' states Jobson, but despite this somewhat discouraging end, the Skids remain an integral part in the development of Scottish pop.

Another Pretty Face were the third Scottish act signed by Virgin during this transitional era. The core figure of this Edinburgh-based act was singer/guitarist Mike Scott, former editor of *Jungleland*. Although born in the capital, Scott established his first groups in Ayr, to where his family had moved when he was aged 12. Formed in 1975, Karma were, by its founder's own admission 'a living room band'. Fellow guitarist John Caldwell then formed the momentary Aaargh, whereas Scott's next venture, the Bootlegs, have since acquired a somewhat mythical status. However, as Mike relates, they were also a somewhat temporary abstraction. 'The Bootlegs were a one-off band. We played two gigs and did one recording session.' Guitarist Alan McConnel and bassist Wart Clog completed the line-up immortalised on a retrospective single released in 1979. Puckishly credited to DNV, 'Mafia' and 'Death In Venice' were culled from a marathon 21-song spell undertaken on 4 September the previous year at a small Ayr studio. Recorded live, the coupling offered a fragile intensity and while the flip showed Mike's blossoming songwriting talent, the topside was a Tapper Zukie song learned from a Patti Smith bootleg.

'I came back to Edinburgh with John Caldwell with the intention of forming a band,' states Scott although he also enrolled at the city's university, studying English Literature and Philosophy. He later dropped out, commenting he was 'more interested in what Joe Strummer was saying than William Shakespeare.' Although undoubtedly attracted by the fury of UK punk, Scott's inspiration was also derived from Bruce Springsteen and the aforementioned Patti Smith, whose reappraisals of rock's mythology were often echoed in his own work. 'I admired those acts in 78/79 when I was starting Another Pretty Face', he now concurs, 'but they haven't really lasted. I still like those I liked beforehand - the Beatles, Bob Dylan - they have always been my favourites.' Nonetheless, his assertive review of a Smith live concert, published in *Kingdom Come*, contained a quite telling assertion. 'Commercialism is the killer of art and mediocrity the lowest common denominator of mass acceptance.'

The original APF line-up - Scott, John Caldwell, Jim Geddes (bass) and 'Crigg' (Ian Walter Greig - drums) - surfaced at the end of 1978. They enjoyed critical acclaim the following year when their debut release, 'All The Boys Love Carrie', was declared 'single of the week' in *New Musical Express*. Recorded with William Mysterious as producer and saxophonist, both sides acknowledged Scott's musical mentors, but the passion he brought to his art was already well-established.

'Carrie' was issued on New Pleasures, a label run by Edward Bell, the group's first manager and a friend of Scott's from university. Bell also released the DNV single, but both sides then severed their relationship, precluding further archive material, and other companies quickly offered deals. Zoom financed a set of demos, but Virgin duly won the battle, although their victory was anything but sweet. 'Virgin had a particular idea for us as a popular-type band,' Scott recalls, 'but we had it in our heads to be harder and more angry.' One single was issued, wherein 'Whatever Happened To The West' was coupled to a new rendition of the Bootlegs' 'Goodbye 1970s'. The latter was a particularly powerful piece, with Scott dismissing the comfort of nostalgia and urging those who heard him to avoid its temptations.

AFP then completed an eleven track album, with Only Ones bassist - and former Beatstalker - Alan Mair as producer. 'Virgin didn't like the final results,' Scott explains. 'They refused to release it and we felt they should, although having listened to it in retrospect, they might have been right.' At the time, however, relations between company and artist became notoriously fraught and in a fit of exasperation, the label not only dropped the group, but allowed them to take away the master of that projected album.

Scott aside, John Caldwell was APF's longest-serving member, and the pair began looking for other ways of releasing the album. A liaison with Rough

Another Pretty Face

Trade was briefly mooted, but in the end they formed an independent outlet, Chicken Jazz, and began releasing singles culled from the aborted set. The first combined 'Heaven Gets Closer Every Day', arguably his finest, most poignant song from this period, with 'Only Heroes Live Forever'. The second featured 'Soul To Soul', a title dropped from the proposed album when it proved too awkward to mix. The song itself evolved from the DNV version of 'Mafia', while two newly recorded compositions, 'A Woman's Place' and 'God On The Screen', completed the coupling.

These releases were punctuated by an 8-track cassette, *I'm Sorry I Beat You, I'm Sorry That I Screamed...But For A Moment There I Really Lost Control*, which compiled several of the remaining Virgin titles, some live material, and a handful of studio songs. When combined with that final 45, it effectively closed this mercurial group's career.

Scott's next creation, Funhouse, surfaced in 1982. 'It was really the same band as APF,' states Scott. 'We had signed a deal with Ensign, but found there was another band called 'Another Pretty Face'. After much deliberation (including a spell as The Noise! The Jazz!) we settled on Funhouse.' By this point the pair had quit Edinburgh's penury and were living in London. The deal with Ensign was struck following APF's John Peel session which featured a version of the apocalyptic 'Out Of Control'. The song, which also appeared on 'I'm Sorry I Beat You...', impressed the label's MD Nigel Grainge and a new version was cut for the sole Funhouse single. 'This Could Be Hell', another composition from that cassette, was re-recorded for its flip-side, despite a lyric inspired by the Virgin debacle. It was, however, quickly clear that Scott viewed this venture as a temporary stepping stone, and later in 1982 he recorded a series of demos on his own. The results were artistically liberating - indeed 'December', 'Gala' and 'The Three Day Man' would eventually be released - and having parted company with Caldwell, who returned to Edinburgh to form the Collector, Mike dissolved Funhouse altogether.

His new act was initially dubbed the Red And The Black, but this was changed to the Waterboys after a handful of live appearances. Scott's first recruit was saxophonist Anthony Thistlethwaite. 'I heard him on a record by Nikki Sudden from the Swell Maps,' Mike recalls. 'He played this fabulous solo on it and I decided I had to find this guy' The first release by the new group was 'A Boy Called Johnny', a wonderfully crafted song which paid tribute to Scott's early mentor, Patti Smith. It seemed an appropriate manner with which to introduce a new era.

Another group tenuously linked with Zoom was the Associates, although this only lasted the time it took to pass on the tape they approached them with, a warped version of David Bowie's 'Boys Keep Swinging'. Formed in Dundee around a nucleus of Billy MacKenzie (vocals), Alan Rankine (keyboards),

Michael Dempsey (bass) and John Murphy (drums), the quartet had eked a living in the city's nightclubs, playing contemporary hits for ageing patrons before deciding on a more constructive direction. 'Dundee was evil,' winces MacKenzie. 'You could have been in the Jurassic age. There were no decent gigs and rather than help the younger set, older musicians laughed and made them feel like outcasts.'

Undeterred by rejection – and the fact that Bowie's original was barely off the chart – the Associates issued their demo privately and those troubling to listen beyond the material itself heard an undeniable self-confidence. Many did, however, query the choice itself. 'We were getting nowhere fast,' McKenzie explains, 'and we knew that to bring that out in such a pathetic form, three weeks after the original, would cause uproar.' Although not a conspicuous commercial success, the single resulted in a tour support slot with the Cure, which in turn inspired a recording deal with the latter act's outlet, Fiction.

'The Affectionate Punch' captured an Associates determinedly forging an individual style. David Bowie remained a crucial influence, particularly the austere *Station To Station*, but any lingering sense of plagiarism was swept aside by MacKenzie's remarkable voice. The singer's sense of drama was exceptional and his multi-octave range, akin to that of Tim Buckley, allowed him to swoop or soar dependent on mood or instinct. Yet this progress was suddenly undermined by the losses of Murphy and Dempsey, the latter of whom had opted for the Cure.

Now reduced to a pairing of MacKenzie and Rankine, the Associates cut their ties with Fiction and opted for Situation 2, an independent noted for its adventurous catalogue. The duo then completed a set of five singles, later complied on *Fourth Drawer Down*, which gave full rein to their sense of innovation and challenge. These songs were, however, recorded in scurrilous fashion as MacKenzie and Rankine would score studio time from major labels having suggested they were keen to sign to them. 'We'd do (a master) in one night,' Billy explained to *Cut*, 'and then hawk it around other companies.' Indeed other projects were undertaken concurrently, including a version of Simon Dupree's hippie hit, 'Kites', which was backed by an early blueprint for the Associates' 'A Girl Named Property'. This particular single was released under the guise 39 Lyon Street, while 'Nocturnal Operations', MacKenzie's single with singer Christine Beverage, was credited to Orbidoig.

The Associates, nonetheless, remained the core act and the most memorable of their angular performances – 'Tell Me Easter's On Friday', 'Kitchen Person' and 'White Car In Germany' – were quite startling, offering a sense of drama only marginally undermined by obtuse, dense melodies. Freed from the constrains of convention, MacKenzie glided around each composition in almost operatic fashion, while Rankine provided empathic support. Although not a conspicuous commercial success, these releases engendered considerable interest in the group, which was then signed to Warner Brothers.

The Associates' 1983 set, *Sulk*, was buoyed by an attendant hit single, the effervescent 'Party Fears Two'. It was, however, an unorthodox performance, with a hookline derived from a repeated keyboard passage, rather than its verse or chorus. It suggested that MacKenzie's generous intonation was, artistically, more satisfying on less formal songs. When confronted with material closer to the mainstream, his style veered towards self-parody. There is no denying his exceptional gifts, MacKenzie remains one of Scotland's finest-ever singers, but his work has been bedevilled by inappropriate material, mercurial temperament and record company politics.

The first major schism in the Associates' career was the departure of Alan Rankine, who would forge an idiosyncratic solo career. MacKenzie retained the rights to the group's name, which next surfaced in 1985 with *Perhaps*. This disappointing set was partially drawn from an earlier album WEA had rejected, and although fellow Dundonian, Steven Reid, collaborator from 39 Lyon Street, joined for several tracks, the overall effect lacks the pairing's earlier sense of purpose.

MacKenzie's career was unhinged further when Warners refused to release a 1988 album, *The Glamour Chase*. A high-NRG take of Blondie's 'Heart Of Glass' did appear as a single, but it was 1990 before another set, *Wild And Lovely*, was issued. The voice still startled, the material did not, leaving the artist marooned in a commercial wasteland. In 1992 he abandoned the Associates' name, and began a 'solo' career with *Overground*.

Scotland's post-punk indie-to-mainstream acts thus found different degrees of success. 'Struggle' and 'compromise' were increasingly heard in interviews and, with this in mind, many others turned towards autarkic directions.

CHAPTER 15
'GET ON WITH YOUR LIFE OR YOU'LL END UP LIKE MEAULINES'

Punk's abrasive simplicity and clockwork vitriol justified the disturbance it caused. If complacency was ruffled, so much the better, but those pioneering one-chord wonders not only fuelled a legion of malcontents, parroting boredom, they also inspired individuals already working at the cutting edge, who used the new uncertainly, to push at different barriers and challenge alternative expectations.

It was a time of cross-pollination in the arts. Don Letts and Amos Poe produced cinema-verity shorts of their respective London and New York subcultures, while a gum-chewing bard, John Cooper Clark, fused the metres of rhyme and rock in a manner unknown since the days of the Scaffold and Liverpool Scene. In Scotland Alan Jackson completed his privately-printed *Book Of Punk Poetry*, and in doing so bridged a gap between ideals and nihilism. Only the 60s Diaspora could fully understand the sense of frustration voiced by the new generation.

Musicians struggling outside rock's mainstream welcomed the freedom and Glasgow's eccentric Chou Pahrot released several records bearing little relation to anything around them. Some portions resembled the obverse of Captain Beefheart's Magic Band, others the 'Oor Wullie' comic strip, but their sense of adventure and fun was completely enthralling.

Chou Pahrot's playfulness with awkward tempos and time-signatures mirrored those of the Bristol-based Pop Group. The latter lacked their comrades' self-deprecating humour, but compensated with a sound of frightening intensity. Dubmaster/producer Dennis Bovell intensified the resonant bass-lines in order to create an anchor for the group's soaring aspirations. Their album, *Y*, was often wilfully obscure, but a rampaging single, 'She Is Beyond Good And Evil', captured their ambition and challenge. This sense of experimentation was also heard in the Subway Sect and Slits, two acts featured on the barnstorming 'White Riot' package of 1977. Headliners the

Orange Juice

Clash were punk's social conscience, co-hosts the Buzzcocks its populists, yet their foot- of-the-bill companions portrayed a greater diversity and sense of danger. The tour opened at the Edinburgh Playhouse, a date also marking the performing debut of Slits' guitarist Viv Albertine, although her aggressive amateurism was indecipherable from that of her colleagues, themselves musical novices. Their ensuing anarchic thrash celebrated a liberation from cultural and sexual stereotypes, while the less-flexible, yet still thrilling sound of the Subway Sect showed an imaginative use of punk devices while remaining apart from its clichés. Such performances galvanised young Scotland.

'Both groups really appealed to me,' recalled Edwyn Collins, at that point a member of Glasgow's Nu-Sonics. 'It seemed that now anything was possible.' Collins' own group was already part of the firmament, taking its name from the model of Burns guitar he had found second-hand. Schoolfriends Steven Daly and James Kirk - formerly of the Machetes - joined original bassist Alan Duncan to complete an act which emerged from relative obscurity supporting Steel Pulse and Johnny And The Self Abusers at Satellite City, a small venue located above the renowned Apollo. Conventionally far from competent, the Nu-Sonics were nonetheless fired by the same sense of purpose espoused by the Slits and Subway Sect, and looked to local contemporaries to be equally principled. 'We expected commitment from performers,' Collins declared, 'and were angered when such beliefs were undermined.' These views were easily misinterpreted as arrogance, a perception which increased when the Nu-Sonics took a new name in an effort to distance themselves from music's slide into either complacency or Oi. 'Calling ourselves Orange Juice was part of the sense of mischief which, in essence, describes our career,' Collins explained. 'It sounded absurd in the context of punk.'

Collins, Daly, Kirk and new bassist Dave McClymont emerged as Orange Juice in 1979. By this point they had befriended Alan Horne, botany student and former publisher of local fanzine, *Swankers*. 'Stephen organised a coach to go through to Edinburgh for the 'White Riot' tour,' Alan recalls. 'He couldn't sell 20 tickets - that's how much interest there was in punk in Glasgow - and I knew Edwyn as part of this gang of familiar faces.' Horne's dogmatism echoed that of Collins, but he also possessed a clutch of essential archive records, including the Byrds, Love and Velvet Underground, as well as classic 60s soul. Alan's box, as Edwyn later termed it, became a valuable education as Orange Juice wedded their scratchy technique to the joy of west coast melody and the rhythmic discipline of southern soul. 'This trunk had original singles on Elektra, Stax and Atlantic,' Collins recalls. 'We loved the sound of those records and had long debates whether or not we should record in mono, because we wondered if stereo made the sound less dynamic.' 'Things had changed dramatically from the Nu-Sonics' Horne adds. 'Orange Juice were prepared to look back into the past.' 'We were probably reacting against the macho image punk had degenerated into,' continues Collins. 'The original ethos had been debased.'

The revived group made its first official live appearance in 1979, partnering Edinburgh's TV Art, whose guitarist Malcolm Ross had met Stephen Daly at a concert. 'They got talking to each other,' relates Paul Haig, vocalist/guitarist with TV Art, 'and Stephen mentioned he had a group called Orange Juice. We arranged to play together in Edinburgh and Glasgow.' Besides Haig and Ross, TV Art comprised of Gary McCormack (bass) and Ron Torrance (drums), but the former, who switched to the Exploited, was replaced by former roadie Davie Weddell. 'We taught him how to play bass,' Paul adds,' and at that point we changed our name to Josef K.'

The two groups duly took the headlining role at reciprocal gigs in their respective hometowns, although Orange Juice were much less visible during the ensuing months. This was partially explained by internal strife as Daly, in particular, voiced frustration at what he looked upon as a lack of formal progress. The drummer subsequently left to join the Fun Four, which featured former Backstabbers' guitarist Jimmy Loser, now known as James King. Stephen Daly had also become a committed supporter of Josef K, and agreed to help finance their debut single. 'We had this one song, 'Chance Meeting', that Stephen really liked,' Haig recalls. 'He borrowed money to put it out as a limited pressing single.' Released on the Absolute label in 1979, 'Chance Meeting'/'Romance' revealed spiky, post-punk ambitions, buoyed considerably by guitarist Malcolm Ross's atonal interjections. It was a highly promising beginning.

Orange Juice, meanwhile, recorded several demos but, as Horne recalls, their development was clearly more erratic. 'They were on the verge of breaking up and we wanted something to stand as a permanent memento.' The first idea was a new fanzine, dubbed *Strawberry Switchblade* from an OJ song. 'Each issue would be different,' said Horne. 'We had plans to include anarchy posters, an article on sex change, material by Bruce Smith of the Pop Group and Viv Albertine, but the first was to feature an Orange Juice flexidisc.' It was here the idea for Postcard Records evolved. 'The label was based along the lines of Stax and Motown,' Collins recalls. 'Alan saw himself as a cross between Berry Gordy and Andy Warhol. We were a bunch of eccentrics - there was no business acumen there - but that didn't matter.'

Although generally perceived as Horne's creation, the label was initially a co-operative. Collins and McClymont provided half of its capital, some £500 in total, as the OJs installed themselves in John McLarty's tiny Paisley studio, sited below his clothing business, to record 'Falling And Laughing'. The session, which was co-produced by Malcolm Ross, marked the return of Stephen Daly. 'We'd driven down to London together to distribute the Fun Four single,' explains Horne, 'and on the way back I asked him if he would drum for us.' The result was an intriguing, fascinating release which defied all preconceptions of what constituted Scottish pop. The influence of 'Alan's box' was heard in passing, in particular the abrasive jingle-jangle and mock syncopated soul drumming, but the group's passionate commitment to their art made such references superfluous. What mattered was the quartet's vision, enhanced and made more endearing by their fragile musical ability. 'We didn't learn our chops in Hamburg,' said Collins, apologising for this rare lapse into 'rockspeak'. 'Our formative years are there for all to hear.' 'We made a record that we thought was fantastic,' added Horne, 'flawed, but breaking new ground musically.' 'Falling And Laughing' was indeed an artistic triumph and the acclaim it garnered in the national music press, particularly from Paul Morley, enforced its sense of occasion.

As the Fun Four single, 'Singing In The Showers', had made no commercial impression, Steven Daly opted to rejoin Orange Juice. The tension, however, did not disappear. 'We were always squabbling,' Edwyn freely admits, although at this point anger seemed to enhance the frisson which marked the group's overall sound. Their second single, 'Blue Boy', developed the precocious spirit of its predecessor, yet its feverish energy was not the result of coincidence. 'With 'Blue Boy' we took a more considered approach,'

Josef K

Collins recalls. 'We wanted the excitement of a 50s/60s recording.' 'There was a great deal of pre-production in that single,' Horne confirms. 'Everything was planned and discussed beforehand, even the notes for the solo.' The finished piece nonetheless sounded fresh, blending hooklines with boundless raw enthusiasm, a sparkling combination enhanced by its sympathetic, yet unobtrusive, production. 'We weren't Luddites,' Horne explains. 'We were striving for perfection and used Castle Sound studio because, when asking around, we were told it was the best.'

Josef K made its recording debut as a Postcard act on the same day. 'Radio Drill Time' toyed with the cold modernism of Cabaret Voltaire as Malcolm Ross's accustomed metallic jangle fought for space with some distinctly impulsive synthesiser. Haig's metronomic delivery added to its atmosphere of alienation, but in truth the awkward juxtaposition failed to ignite. Its flip-side, the ravaged 'Crazy To Exist', was far superior.

Released in 1980, 'Blue Boy' proved that 'Falling And Laughing' was not simply a gifted, but transient, moment. It remains a pivotal release, a breath of fresh air, the cipher lifting the burden of a conventional soul/rock heritage which, however admirable, stifled any means of alternative self-expression. While historians rightfully cite the liberating influence of 'Anarchy In The UK', it was 'Blue Boy' which emancipated Scotland's pop, providing undreamed of directions and hope to new, aspiring musicians. After it nothing could be the same again, yet its release was almost cancelled.

'Geoff Travis at Rough Trade loved 'Falling And Laughing',' recalled Horne, 'and offered us a marketing and distribution deal if the next Postcard singles were 'as good'. We brought him 'Blue Boy', the Go Between's 'I Need Two Heads' and Josef K's 'Radio Drill Time' and he went 'Oh I don't know...I don't like Josef K, 'Blue Boy's not as strong as 'Falling And Laughing'...' and Edwyn and I stormed out.' The rebuttal was a devastating shock and the frustration was heightened by Collins' suggestion that they approach major companies with the singles, an anathema to the obdurate Horne. 'I felt I was being betrayed,' he later reflected.

Although Horne's parents stepped in to finance the releases, economies were still required and a reversible sleeve was printed up, applicable to Orange Juice or Josef K dependent on the fold. 'We coloured all of them by hand with fluorescent pens,' says Horne, 'we couldn't afford it any other way.' 'The cartoon of a wooing couple leant itself to that in-house, idiosyncratic style,' adds Collins, and finished copies were then mailed to selected journalists. The ensuing effusive praise resulted in Travis' sudden volte-face. 'He changed his mind,' said Horne, not without irony. 'He loved the singles after all and as a result gave Postcard a favourable deal.'

In fairness, Alan's commitment to Josef K was also questionable and the group was only signed thanks to Steven Daly's persistence. 'The whole thing

WHY DON'T YOU NITE CLUB IN APRIL

upstairs at the playhouse ~ fri., sat., sun.

THE NITECLUB

9 till late ~ the live disco ~ late bar

FRI 4 ANOTHER PRETTY FACE
PLUS TV 21

SAT 5 EVEREST AND The Delmonts
THE HARD WAY

FRI 11 JOSEPH K
AND Orange Juice & THE gobetweens

SAT 12 SKANITE
WITH TWO OF SCOTLAND'S BEST
THE RUDE BOYS + ALL THE RAGE

at last, the sound of
HEAVY METAL! THURSDAYS FROM APRIL 3RD

The sounds of young Scotland

was geared to get Orange Juice noticed,' Horne admits, 'That was my only concern, my sole reason d'être. Josef K were pawns, there to make the label seem more solid and bring Orange Juice more attention. I felt I could build excitement by creating this package around them.

'It was an incredibly exclusive scene and we spat on anyone who came near us. Postcard didn't glorify Glasgow as the centre of anything, it glorified ourselves and we were very conscious of that.' Collins, however, offers a more conciliatory perspective. 'People wanted to put us down as elitist, but we were quite introverted really and that was often misinterpreted as brattishness.'

The label's third signing, the Go-Betweens, were Australian. 'I noticed their first single, 'Lee Remick', on the Rough Trade wall,' said Horne. 'Edwyn told me he'd heard it, and that it was good.' The pair duly left a note, explaining about the label, inviting the group to come and record when they returned to the UK. The offer was duly accepted and the Go-Betweens - Grant McLennan and Robert Foster - completed their sole release on Postcard with the help of the assiduous Steven Daly, before pursing their mercurial career elsewhere.

The third Orange Juice single, 'Simply Thrilled Honey', emphasised the group's quite staggering maturation, and once again superlatives, quite rightly, heralded its release. Precocious he may well have been, but Edwyn Collins displayed an endearingly off-kilter vision of pop, and his ability to bring seemingly incongruous progressions back into a hookline was abundantly clear. Horne, of course, was ecstatic, but his promotional line that 'the group feel they are the reincarnation of '69 Velvet Underground' is tempered by the fact that all contemporaneous Postcard bands were given this tag, albeit with a modified year. This was not, however, the only time Horne invoked the ghost of that fabled New York group. 'Rough Trade wanted photographs of Orange Juice,' he explains, 'and of course I didn't have any. So I cut out pictures of the Velvet Underground from Nigel Trevana's book and sent these down instead.'

Josef K, meanwhile, discarded the bleak landscapes of 'Radio Drill Time' and completed 'It's Kinda Funny', itself ironic and melancholic, but which fused its endearing melody to some perfectly understated instrumentation. Paul Haig harbours reservations - 'We weren't pleased with it at the time, the pressing was really dull,' - but the song nonetheless retains its fragile charm. Together these new Postcards maintained the label's exceptional quality, and confirmed its proud boast to be 'the Sound Of Young Scotland'. Yet it was equally true that the effusive praise heaped upon such releases came from south of the border. 'Postcard wasn't heralded in Glasgow,' Horne declares. 'Nobody would give Orange Juice a gig. We tried the Third Eye Centre, brickwall; we tried to get a support with Pere Ubu, that was cancelled. It was obvious we had to get out, go to London and bring the press up to us. The 'Sound Of Young Scotland' was something to hang those articles on.'

Orange Juice thus followed a by-now well trodden path to Paisley's Bungalow Bar for their occasional concerts. 'People were quite bemused by their first sight of Orange Juice live,' Collins states. 'They imagined that we'd contrived this charming, amateurish approach, but it wasn't affected at all. My brain was quite scrambled; we'd always be late so we didn't have time to soundcheck. When we played at the Bungalow Bar just after 'Blue Boy' was issued, I had ask the audience if anyone had a plectrum before starting our rip-roaring show.

'If there was a passage James thought too difficult to play, he'd turn his volume control down and mime the riff while pointing furiously at the monitors as if it was the sound technician's fault.'

A handful of singles and hubristic manifesto combined to give Postcard its vital image. Orange Juice and Horne riled as many as they enthralled but their unequivocal stance did much to assert a Scottish independence.

CHAPTER 16
'THE COMMODITY ITSELF MADE THE LAWS.'

Alan Horne's bravura was certainly admirable, but his was not the only Scottish label to enthral. Fast Product, launched in Edinburgh in 1978, pre-dated Postcard, and whereas the latter evoked a quixotic, yet affectionate aura, its predecessor was much more detached. 'I started Fast Product with no real idea of what I wanted to do with it,' recalls founder Bob Last. 'I didn't even know if it would be music, or something else, I just had it as a corporate identity.' The previous year, Last had been working at the Traverse Theatre, taking time out from an architectural course. It was here he first came in to contact with the Rezillos. 'I met Jo Callis when he was doing some part-time work there, he recalls, 'and I got involved in building their dalek.' Last was employed as stage manager for the venue's travelling productions, but both he and colleague Tim Pearce quit to become the Rezillos' road crew. 'By the end of the tour, somehow or other, I was managing them.'

Despite this new responsibility, Last was still intent on founding his own company, although its function was now being determined by concurrent circumstances. 'I began to make contacts as we toured further south,' he explains. 'It was still a relatively small scene and connections were made relatively easily.' Fast Product thus became a record label, and its first signing, the Mekons, was introduced to Last through his involvement with the Rezillos.

'Never Been In A Riot' was recorded on a 2-track in a cottage in the Borders,' Last recalls, which may in part explain its pugnacious, raucous howl. Few singles from this or any other era sound so raw and primitive, yet it invoked the passion punk had initially implied and which, by 1978, was hurriedly evaporating. 'I still like the record,' says Last, 'but we did meet resistance. Geoff Travis says he absolutely cannot remember this but when my partner, Hillary Morrison, took a suitcase full to Rough Trade, he said 'These people can't play. I'm not going to stock this, it's terrible.' That was a shock because we thought that if you had some kind of attitude and wanted to

Roddy Frame of Aztec Camera

communicate it, that was it. You could get the musical element together later. However, in some ways it helped us focus what we did because we now knew we couldn't rely on these people down there.'

The Mekons hailed from Leeds, and other English signings, the Human League and Gang Of Four, followed. This was, of course, an intriguing development - a Scottish-based label signing acts from south of the border - but Fast's importance was not due to this geographical twist, but arose from the adventurism of its acclaimed releases and in the way each was packaged. Where Postcard boasted an intangible notion of a collective sound or attitude, 'We're the only punk rock label - we're not new wave' - Horne declared in an opening salvo, then Fast offered a highly-visual image which clearly defined an attitude permeating each release. Last juxtaposed material and slogans like an intriguing cross between Kim Fowley and Marshall McLuhan. 'The image pre-existed the music, in a sense, because I already had the logo and name, and knew it would involve into some form of communication,' he explains. 'I had several ideas of how it should be approached, some of which were specifically visual. The important one was the actual marketing of any artefact because this was conventionally seen as something negative, something against the artist and out of their control. I thought this was wrong.

'Half the pleasure of a record was buying the marketing; the package,' Last continues, 'but because entrepreneurs looked upon this as a necessary evil, all areas of the media were becoming bland. I saw no reason to do that. It was a part of the product, therefore we would get as excited and as interested in the presentation and make sure that the whole thing relates and makes sense.'

The term 'Product' was thus not simply a suffix of convenience. It expanded on the consumerist themes established by Linder (Linda Mulvey) and Malcolm Garrett for the Buzzcocks, particularly the former's striking use of collage and juxtaposition. "Spiral Scratch' was a role model,' Last confirms, referring to the above group's debut release, 'but there is another consistent thread, the Situationists, who we'd all read.' Indeed Fast not only reflected the intellectual process behind punk, but exploited it with considerable panache. 'There were people who took the packaging thing seriously,' Last opines, 'and enjoyed it, but we played with it more openly.' Of course, in purely vulgar terms, the notion of corporate identity encouraged fans to buy every release, complete the set so to speak, irrespective of artist or, more perversely, merit. 'That became a major point within the record business,' states Last. 'Stiff were thinking in the same way but from a different ideological basis and perspective.'

However, it was equally true that Fast, having established an undoubted oeuvre, then sought to diminish it. This was especially apparent on the *Earcom* series, three various artists' sets which included material drawn from a variety of sources. 'We were seen as a new wave in pop,' Last declares, 'but the term 'new wave' had become an excuse for all sorts of tosh, so we weren't quite certain what to do. We didn't want to cling to our artists and indeed we encouraged all of them to go if they could get bigger resources. It was time to refresh ourselves and stop being precious about a label everyone was already starting to mythologize.

'It was also a response to the fact that, by that time, we were getting deluged with tapes from all over the world, which was interesting but, in some ways, depressing. The best tended to be the most quirky.' Those featured on the *Earcom* sets included Joy Division and DAF, as well as Scottish acts the Flowers and the Prats. The former showed potential, but had yet to emerge from a crippling debt to Siouxsie And The Banshees, while the latter was an Inverness quartet barely into puberty, who included a young Adamski. The Prats' amateurism was certainly refreshing, but their ramshackle incompetence quickly lost its appeal, unable to rise above mere novelty. 'Some of it is difficult to listen to now,' Last admits, 'but we deliberately wanted to make them disposable. It was intended to be like a magazine and the idea was that you got it, listened to it a couple of times, then got the next 'issue'.'

The Scars were another young group signed to Fast. They had been active in Edinburgh since 1977, but learning their art in public had brought an unfair share of derision. Many were thus taken aback at the commitment shown on the quartet's debut single, particularly 'Adult/ery', wherein the fumbling once apparent during live performances was replaced with a vibrant, self-assured sound. 'We never consciously went out for Scottish material,' Last explains, 'and the Scars simply evolved out of the scene. They were kids who hung around at our flat during the early days and signing them seemed the logical thing to do.' Bobby King (vocals), Paul Research (guitar), John Mackie (bass) and Steve McLaughlin (drums) - who replaced Calumn Mackay - later surfaced with an album, *Author! Author!*, but it lacked the sense of jagged inspiration of their debut. 'I think they became scared of their glam roots,' Last suggests, 'which was a mistake.'

The Dead Kennedy's 'California Uber Alles' became Fast's next single, and this US-licensing deal confirmed how the label had proved that something based in Scotland could function internationally. It was also its final release. 'I knew there would be no more Fast Product singles after that,' Last explains. 'I didn't see anyone coming that was right for us and I didn't want to sign just for the sake of it.' Its roster had moved to major labels as Last was now managing the Human League, the natural move was to forge a new outlet. 'Pop Aural was already lurking there with a slightly different attitude,' he explains. 'It was principally intended as a response to the fact that what we'd been stirring up at Fast Product had filtered into the mainstream. We needed to get ourselves on the radio.'

The new venture lacked the visual identity of its predecessor, and despite moments of undoubted excellence - 'They all had their moments,' - Last has reservations on its overall merit. 'We never got the right focus, which was as much our fault as the artists. We couldn't bring the magic to it to pull it off. We also began developing more Scottish acts which, in retrospect, was a bad move.' Fast protégés the Flowers, with Hillary Morrison on vocals, was the only act to feature on both labels, and the compulsive 'Life After Dark' showed a marked maturity from previous, derivative releases. Pop Aural will, however, be recalled for the furiously inventive Fire Engines.

'Punk made so many things possible,' recalls the group's guitarist and singer Davey Henderson, who concurs with Alan Horne and Edwyn Collins with regard to the role of White Riot tour. 'The Slits were so alien,' he recalls, 'and the Subway Sect were one of the scariest things I'd seen, like a bizarre Twilight Zone. Then I knew I could be in a group and do exactly what I wanted.' An excited Henderson began making contact with those similarly beguiled, including Bobby King from the Scars. 'I met him at a Buzzcocks' gig, and it was Rab who introduced me to Bob Last and Hillary Morrison.' Henderson became a habitué of Cockburn Street's 'punk pub', the Wig and Pen, which was the scene of his performing debut with the Talkovers. 'We did this song called 'Harmony Hairspray Psst Psst',' relates Henderson. 'Rab drummed like Palmolive, while we jammed on top.' Another ad hoc clutch of dissidents was subsequently gathered for an infamously brusque performance supporting the Rezillos. 'Our set lasted barely a minute,' remembers Henderson. 'We performed '98-99-100', then left, but the audience was so excited we went back onstage and repeated it.'

The Fire Engines supporting the Delmontes

Another group, the Dirty Reds, quickly followed. The original line-up had included Hillary Morrison, who also worked with Henderson in another act, the Warm Jets. She and sundry Reds later split to form the Flowers, while drummer Russell Burn retained the former name and forged, what Davey terms, 'the real Dirty Reds.' This pivotal act - Burn, Henderson, Graham Mair and Russell's brother, Tam - was dissolved in 1979, but they remain an integral part of the abiding mythology. 'We had a bad reputation around Edinburgh,' admits Henderson. 'They thought we were beat-up fucks or something, but we were just going through our Burroughs, experimental phase - we'd read 'Junky' - and would stay up all night talking like we imagined Neal and Jack did.' Although the Dirty Reds did not record, Alan Horne did approach them with a view to cutting 'Dine In My Mind'. The idea was dropped upon the group's collapse.

With Tam Burn opting to pursue acting ambitions, the remaining three musicians added guitarist Murray Slade from Station Six to form Fire Engines. 'His brief was quite straightforward,' recalls Henderson. 'You're not allowed to play chords. I was very Richard Nixon about it.' The group's name was derived from a song by the 13th Floor Elevators, and the noises prevalent on the original recording - siren-like wails, frantic voice, thundering rhythm and amplified jug - were similar to the spiky intensity the new group offered. Undeterred by their rudimentary skills, Fire Engines created a spontaneous frenzy which drew inspiration from Richard Hell's Void Oids and New York's No Wave movement. 'We wanted to be like James White; super-sparse,' Davey recounts. 'We played to our strengths, which were minimal, but as a band it somehow merged.' The resultant thrill was exhilarating. Guitars crashed and collided at random, Henderson shrieked with similar abandon and together the group created a sound both expressive and exciting. 'It was violence without people getting blooded,' adds Henderson. 'pure aggression, attitude and hate. Russell used to start the songs and the strength of his adrenaline rush dictated the speed that everyone else played at. Because we were hyped up as well, the energy was unbelievable.'

'Get Up And Use Me', issued in 1980 on Codex Communications, captured their furious assault. Recorded in a cottage in Fife with producer Wilf Smarties - who extols them to 'just keep going' after the opening fumble - the single was another essential part of Scotland's diverse, but evolving, musical milieu. Paul Morley, again, provided ecstatic reviews, while Alan Horne pleaded with the group to join Postcard. 'I desperately wanted them on the label,' he recalls, 'but they'd already agreed to go with Bob Last. I even put them on with Orange Juice and Josef K hoping that people would think they were a Postcard band.'

'Alan has never been able to accept the fact that the Fire Engines were on our label,' adds Last. 'What he failed to take account of was that although they had a lot of the same reference points as Postcard, they had been hanging around with us and our groups for several years beforehand. Davey Henderson's take on visuals, word play and packaging was very much in line with our own ideas.'

Last signed Fire Engines in 1980, following their appearance in a theatre production of 'Why Does The Pope Not Come To Glasgow?', and they immediately began work on an 8-track mini-album. Released on Pop Aural's Accessory Series, *Lubricate Your Living Room* offered the same impulsive creativity of that stirring debut, although by re-recording 'Get Up And Use Me', the group revealed how much tighter their sound had become over the ensuing months. The angular twists were still evident, but critical acclaim had robbed the quartet of innocence. 'Suddenly we had to think ahead,' Murray Slade later remarked, and the devilment marking early work was replaced by a more cognitive approach.

The unit's next single, 'Candy Skin', was noticeably different, with Henderson taking the melody in orthodox fashion, rather than use his vocals as an adjunct to the overall noise. It was not, however, a conventional song - the group retained the right to experiment - but Simon Best's string arrangement did much to sweeten its choppy framework. Fire Engine's drift towards the prosaic was confirmed with 'Big Gold Dream', their most commercial offering to date. The resultant compromise between avarice and aspiration was enjoyable, if flawed, and its irony was captured on the self-depreciating front cover which showed the group draped in raw meat, redolent of the Beatles' infamous 'Butcher's' sleeve. 'We had never seen the original,' Davey claims, 'but the following week Simon produced a copy of it.' Indeed the Fire Engines intentions were mischievous rather than idolatry, as Henderson recounts. 'We were all in Bob's Saab with Hillary in her role as official photographer. Both had just become mega-vegetarians and, while discussing where to do our next shot, we all spontaneously demanded it should be in the slaughterhouse in Fountainbridge. 'Get the details, get vats of blood and we'll do it with our tops off; we'll do it naked'.' This plan did not come to fruition and a local Safeways was used instead.

In retrospect the Fire Engines' unselfconscious brio would inevitably be short-lived, and they split up in 1981. 'Bob told us he wasn't going to release any more Fire Engines records,' recounts Henderson, a fact Last happily endorses. 'I felt that they couldn't go on repeating the formula; in retrospect it would seem less magical. The gesture had, in fact, been done.' Henderson then joined Hillary Morrison and pianist James Locke in a new project, Heartbeat, but this short-lived act proved unsatisfying. 'I hated it,' he admits. 'I wasn't the prime mover and it wasn't the place to be.'

Pop Aural also issued material by Shake, one of two splinter groups formed in the wake of the Rezillos' implosion. Jo Callis, Simon Templar and Angel

Patterson were herein joined by guitarist Troy Tate, and having fulfilled contractual obligations to Sire with an EP and single, the quartet issued 'Woah Yeah!' as Jo Bopnik in 1981. By this point, however, the group had lost initiative. 'We never found our feet in terms of direction, music and image,' Callis later related. 'Basically, we just wanted to play, and didn't do a lot of that.' Meanwhile, interest had temporarily switched to another act, Boots For Dancing. Formed in 1979, this post-punk funk act was led by vocalist Dave Carson, whose affection for 70s black music; James Brown, Sly Stone and Funkadelic, was clearly evident in two early singles, 'Boots For Dancing' and 'Rain Song'. The group's unholy allegiance to radical dance anticipated the style's revival some years later, but commercial progress was hindered by an intemperate personnel. 'They were totally self-destructive,' Last remembers. 'Their playing was quite limited, but there were some games going on, and they were also disrespectful to that Scottish soul tradition.' Paterson and Callis were both members for brief periods - the latter also served as manager - but by 1982 Carson had been joined by a third ex-Shake acolyte, Simon Templar - who'd also served time in the Flowers.

The Scars

While Callis found fame as a member of the Human League, Angel Paterson began a new career with TV 21, an Edinburgh power-pop act completed by Norman Rodgers, Ally Palmer, Neil Baldwin and Dave Hampton. Two singles, 'Playing With Fire' and 'Ambition', appeared on the quintet's Powbeat label, before a one-off tenure at Demon spawned 'On The Run'. In 1981 they were signed by Deram, but although this ill-fated liaison produced a worthy album, *A Thin Red Line*, the group and company were constantly at loggerheads. In 1983 TV 21 supported the Rolling Stones for three Scottish dates, but they broke up, demoralised, at the gulf which lay between them.

The remaining offshoot from the Rezillos' demise featured vocalists Reynolds and Fife. 'I had to learn how to play guitar and Fay started playing keyboards,' explains the former. 'and we carried the flag for what the initial concept of what the Rezillos was.' There was, however, a problem over a name now owned by Sire. 'They let us out of our contracts after nearly a year, but only on the expressed understanding that we did not perform as the Rezillos. We agreed, and the day we got out of the contract I went to Virgin and said, 'OK. We're now the Revillos.'

The 'new' group also featured HiFi Harris as well as Reynolds' brother, who assumed the drum stool as Rocky Rhythm. Backing singers Jane White, Jane Brown and Tricia Bryce augmented the unit as the Revettes. They were, inevitably, unbending, and Eugene immediately attacked pop's preconceptions by declaring an intention to gig solely at weekends. 'The concept was as important as the music,' he explained, ideas were given full rein upon securing a recording deal. 'We played 'Where's The Boy For Me' and 'Motorbike Beat' to Din Disc (a Virgin subsidiary) and they went crazy.' The ensuing deal allowed the septet its own label, Snatzo, and the former song became the Revillos debut single in September 1979.

The group maintained the trash aesthetics of its predecessor on a series of dazzling singles, including 'Motorbike Beat', 'Scuba Scuba' and 'Hungry For Love'. They even returned to Barclay Towers, Tony Pilley's tiny studio sited in his top-floor tenement flat, where the Rezillos had first recorded. A maniacal album, *Rev-Up*, was issued in 1980 and this entertaining pastiche confirmed the promise of the previous act's debut. Yet its strongest cuts, 'On The Beach', 'Bobby Come Back To Me', work best in isolation. 'When you're on spikes, trying to push yourself in different directions, there are bound to be successes and failures,' states Reynolds. 'It's not an easy album to listen to, it's a snapshot of our first year, a creative portfolio with some brilliant ideas and some crap.'

Din Disc dropped the group later in the year, but they quickly secured alternative finance. 'Superville was a mixture between a company called Super Music and the Revillos. It was run by people we very quickly didn't get on with.' Nonetheless, several more stellar releases appeared, including 'She's

Fallen In Love With The Monster Man', 'Bongo Brain' and a second album, *Attack*. But if the group's recording progress seemed obscure, their differing line-ups were perplexing. Reynolds, Fife and Rhythm were the only constant members and while sundry Revettes came and left with regularity, guitarists Kid Krupa and Max Atom and bassists Felix and William Mysterious also passed through the ranks. 'Those changes didn't matter,' Eugene asserts, 'and it was usually bass players anyway. They'd come and say "I've got some really bad news for you. I'm leaving," and we'd say "Good. Fuck off." One bassist left 10 minutes before a gig but we went onstage anyway. It sounded good, just like the Cramps.

'After William left I realised any setback was a creative opportunity to improve or vary what you were doing. It was always something to celebrate. If they had to leave it meant they weren't good enough to be in it.'

The Revillos demanded commitment, both from its members and audience. They financed several tours of North America, traversing the continent in a group van, before their sci-fi preferences attracted EMI, who came into the frame when a genre movie was mooted. The group's releases included 'Bitten By A Love Bug', but the film and impetus subsequently faltered. Eugene Reynolds: 'Without creative impetus you have no momentum; without momentum you stagnate. We were sitting in a tour van, arguing, and we decided then that was the end. Part of what we did required an audience to feed off and that side of things was no longer there. Just to preach to the converted seemed irrelevant.'

The Revillos' demise was all but unreported and while Fay briefly resurfaced in the feminist-inspired Destroy All Men, Eugene forged two successive projects, Rockatomic and Planet Pop. He also rekindled a partnership with Jo Callis, but his interest in music vies with another passion; vintage motorbikes. A return to performing is not, however, improbable.

'We'll split up after our debut album' was a common quote bandied about in contemporary Josef K articles, and when they did the remark took on an almost mythical significance. 'Yes, but we didn't actually say that,' Paul Haig explains. 'We said that we thought that all the best groups break up after two albums and somehow this was inverted into us splitting up after one. We'd no intention of doing that - we didn't want it to go too far - but perhaps it was fate. Certainly things weren't fun anymore.'

Part of the problem lay in the group's icy relationship with Alan Horne, who made little effort to disguise an ambivalence towards them. Tension was doubtlessly enhanced upon hearing the master tape to their debut album. 'It was bland, smooth...' Horne argues, '...awful,' yet Josef K were equally appalled with the final outcome. 'Everything we did in Castle Sound sounded great when we were in there,' Haig relates, 'but afterwards it seemed really dull. The bass and drums seemed to take over and when the album was finished we all hated it. We decided to shelve it and make a rock one.'

In the meantime Josef K had made contact with a Belgian label, Les Disques De Crepescule. 'Michel Duval at Crepescule invited us over to Brussels,' Haig explains. 'so Josef K and Orange Juice played at the Plan-K centre on New Year's Eve 1980. It was seen as some kind of punk event and Orange Juice, who were sweet and jangly, were hated and had things thrown at them. We went on and started a riot.' Two days later the headliners entered the Huit Pistes studio to record a new version of 'Sorry For Laughing', the title track to the abandoned LP. Although this ambiguously packaged single bore few references to it, Postcard assumed responsibility for its UK distribution. 'They only had it in this country,' Haig explains. 'Elsewhere it was on Crepescule.'

The fourth Josef K single was a new version of 'Chance Meeting', which featured Malcolm's brother, Alasdair, on trumpet, and in April 1981 the group returned to Belgium to reattempt a debut album. *The Only Fun In Town* was certainly more animated than its predecessor, and each selection was fired by an amphetamine-like rush. Several tracks, notably 'Fun 'n' Frenzy' and 'Forever Drone', benefited from its resultant, trebly sound, although several commentators felt it failed to catch the Josef K oeuvre. 'We wanted to sound livelier,' explains Haig, 'and for some reason mixed the vocals down. A lot of people who had been behind the band, Paul Morley for example, didn't like the album and felt it was somehow trashy.' By August that year the quartet had split up, despite completing an acclaimed promotional tour. Weddell and Torrance formed Happy Family - a venture abandoned when the latter joined Boots For Dancing - while Haig embarked on a solo career.

'Postcard Records are about to release singles we are genuinely happy with,' declared a 1981 press handout. 'We have now been going a year in which we released six scrappy, half-baked singles which got too much press attention for their own good.' The polemic was typical Horne; always unafraid to cross the line between self-depreciation and hauteur, but there can be no denying the excitement which surrounded the release of the fourth Orange Juice single. 'Poor Old Soul' was simply breathtaking; a metronomic beat kept discipline while guitars and voices cascaded around a song which spilled over with enthusiasm and possibilities. There was so much happening the group cut two quite different versions, the second of which boasted the threat of 'no more rock 'n' roll for you'. It closes with found-sound screams, as if inverting the Byrds' equally ironic single, 'So You Wanna Be A Rock 'n' Roll Star'.

'Poor Old Soul' was released in conjunction with 'Just Like Gold', the first offering by new signing Aztec Camera. 'We were supporting the Rezillos at Paisley's Bungalow Bar,' recalled guitarist/vocalist Roddy Frame, 'and Alan,

THEATRE P.K.F.
+ Fire Engines

WHY DOES THE POPE NOT COME TO GLASGOW?

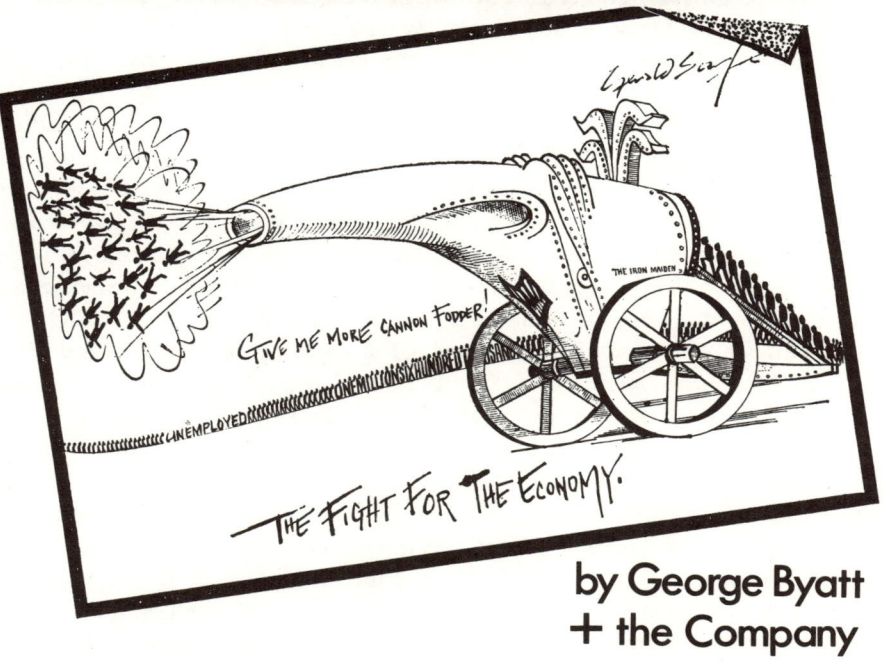

by George Byatt
+ the Company

EDINBURGH FESTIVAL FRINGE 1980 Aug 18th to Sept 6th at NAPIER COLLEGE, Colinton Rd. enter by Mardale Cresc. 7pm Guest spots.   7.30pm Main show.   9pm Discussion. TICKETS £1 only.   Concessions .. children, OAPs, claimants.

The Fire Engines appearing with Theatre P.K.F.

Edwyn and Malcolm Ross were in the audience.' Frame, plus Alan Welsh (bass) and Dave Mulholland (drums) - offered a fragile, lyrical style, suggestive of the innocence of Californian sunshine pop, and it was already clear that Roddy possessed a precious talent.

'Before Aztec Camera, I was in an East Kilbride band called Neutral Blue,' he explains. 'We used to play half of our own songs and half Clash cover versions. I suppose we were kind of Bowie/Joy Division influenced, but I was also beginning to listen to psychedelia - Chocolate Watchband, 13th Floor Elevators - the more adventurous the name the better.' From there Frame and Neutral Blue drummer Mulholland formed Aztec Camera whose early demos surfaced on a cassette-only release, *Urban Development*, prior to their association with Postcard. 'The first demos we made still sounded like Joy Division to me,' states Frame. 'On the second we were forging our own sound a bit more, they were more guitar-oriented. The songs included 'Green Jacket Grey', 'Remember The Dock' and, I think, 'We Could Send Letters'. They were recorded at Sirroco in Kilmarnock and we had to walk home from there. It was quite romantic really.'

Urban Development also featured Edwyn Collins' bedroom demo of 'Blue Boy', recorded in 1978, but included without permission. Thinly disguised as 'No-one's Listening' by the Unknowns, its appearance on the tape brought the two bands closer and was perhaps the reason for the Postcard posse's appearance at the Bungalow Bar. 'There were some DJs in the audience who said we were the worst group they'd ever seen,' Frame remembers. Alan said "If they don't like you, you must be good," and he signed us to the label.'

Aztec Camera's willowy debut was followed by the equally haunting 'Matress Of Wire', but if Frame shared Collins' 60s reference points, he was already pursuing a more introverted path. Unbeknown to its participants, the single's release in September 1981 brought Postcard to a close. Other projects had been mooted; an album by Aztec Camera (*Green Jacket Gray*), an album and single by Orange Juice (*Onwards And Upwards* and 'Wan Light'), while Horne had also hoped to issue Laurie Anderson's 'Oh Superman', a plan scotched by Warner's late decision to release it themselves.

'Orange Juice was the only group I ever cared about,' admitted Horne, and thus overtures by major outlets signalled the demise of their former label. 'We were already in the midst of recording the first Orange Juice album,' Collins explains, 'which was going to be on Postcard, but we were persuaded by the producer, Adam Kidron, to tout it about for a major deal. I think Stephen Daly also had a lot to do with that - I had my reservations at the time - but Polydor pretended to offer us complete control and so it was an offer we couldn't refuse. We thought we could be as self-indulgent as ever, plus have some money.' Horne admits there was friction, between himself and Daly. 'Stephen was always pushing to sign groups he thought would be successful,' and while the Bluebells and Altered Images were among those declined, neither act fulfilled the ethos Postcard avowedly espoused.

A revamped Orange Juice - Collins, McClymont, Daly, Kirk plus Malcolm Ross from Josef K - duly signed to Polydor in 1982, armed with a pre-recorded album, *You Can't Hide Your Love Forever*. The set was a disappointment, with the abrasive ambition of previous releases obscured by overdubs and an aura of compromise. 'We shook hands with the beast,' stated Collins, and the resultant tension broke the band in two. Daly and Kirk left, while Zeke Manyika joined as drummer.

Postcard itself ended when Aztec Camera switched to Rough Trade. 'I got bored,' Horne admits. 'I'm sure Roddy to this day thinks I neglected them. He went off because I went on tour with Orange Juice rather than Aztec Camera. I think his band was good, but it wasn't that exciting. I was bored with myself and my life at that time and they were just part of it.' Alan had lost interest in a creation which, bereft of its reason for existing, no longer served a purpose. 'We were very young,' he recalls as a way of summing up this inspirational label. 'When you're that age the only thing that's important for you is to be hip. And we had that in buckets.'

CHAPTER 17
ELECTRIC HEAT

Postcard's sudden disappearance left a vacuum in Scottish pop, one exacerbated by Pop Aural's exit in the light of Bob Last's managerial ties. Several individuals tried to fill the gap and having recorded a second Cuban Heels' single ('Little Girl'), John Milarky established a new label, Cuba Libre, with new drummer and ex-Sub Ali MacKenzie. The pair secured a marketing deal with Virgin for their venture, which not only released their own group's *Work Our Way To Heaven*, but also *Skin 'Em Up* and *Celts And Cobras*, two albums by rockabilly trio the Shakin' Pyramids.

Given the 60s' predilection apparent in the Heels, this combination of acts left Cuba Libre with more than a whiff of revivalism and it was thus the antithesis of its predecessors' brave new world. Their most virulent signing was James King. 'He was there at the beginning of punk,' McKenzie declared in a BBC interview. 'He was a character and a great songwriter.' A 'solo' single, 'Back From The Dead', was completed with the aid of Heels' guitarist Laurie Cuff, bassist Nick Clark and the ever-helpful Stephen Daly, before the singer forged a full-time unit, the Lone Wolves, with James Mason, Colin Neil and Fraser Scott. This new act also drew from rock's traditional pantheon, but in truly delinquent style, and their greaser image, captured on 'I Tried', mirrored life, not art. 'The guitarist's in jail' was the caustic reply to one writer inquiring why the Wolves had not been appearing live, and the group's ritualised trashing of hotel rooms and offices was an important factor in the cooling of Virgin's affair with Cuba Libre.

Several other pretenders briefly emerged, including Statik, home of Positive Noise, and Tony Pilley's Barclay Towers, which issued two singles by Metropak, 'You're A Rebel' and 'Here's Looking At You'. Postcard's chief aspirant, however, was Edinburgh's Rational, founded by Allan Campbell, ex-manager of Josef K and former contributor to *City Lynx*, a worthy but flawed attempt at a northern-styled *Time Out*. 'In common with all Left-bias magazines,' he recalls, '*City Lynx* was short of money and I got involved in organising benefit concerts for them. The first included the Dirty Dossers, with the then up-and-coming Simple Minds in support, while the second featured the Only Ones.' The ad hoc Dossers comprised of sundry Valves, Eddi Reader, later of Fairground Attraction, and were 'led', euphemistically speaking, by Stuart Nisbet, subsequently guitarist with the Proclaimers. However, although such charitable events failed to save the publication, they kindled Campbell's interest in promotion and he opened the Aquarius Club in Grindlay Street. 'It ran for 10 weeks,' he recalls, 'and featured two or three acts a night including the Scars and Metropak.' This ever-closer association with Edinburgh acts led to the founding of Rational Records, whose first signing, the Delmontes, Campbell also managed. Their two endearing singles, 'Tous Les Soirs' and 'Don't Cry No Tears', were well received, although many recognised a second-hand riff from the Elevator's 'You're Gonna Miss Me' on the former. 'Almost everyone pointed out that it was not dissimilar,' Allan remembers, 'but we still got good press.' The Delmontes later enjoyed a tour slot with The Teardrop Explodes, but their Alan Rankine-produced album, *Thursday*, was canned when a projected deal with WEA fell through. The group split up soon afterwards although drummer Bernice later resurfaced in the Pastels.

Rational also released two singles by the Visitors, a powerful, uncompromising group which had already issued the Fall-influenced *Electric Heat* EP. 'John Peel was very supportive over the Visitors,' says Campbell 'and their second set was licensed from a BBC session. However, like many groups, they carried inbuilt seeds of self-destruction.' It was Allan's friendship with Josef K's singer/guitarist Paul Haig which provided the label's most lasting releases in the shape of Rhythm Of Life. 'It was a working title for different projects,' Haig explains, 'a group, a record label and productions. I really didn't want to be in the forefront.' James Locke and Steven Haines (ex-Metropak) were the singer's co-conspirators in this project and two 1981 singles under its banner, 'Soon' and 'Uncle Sam', duly ensued. The second featured a local artist, Sebastian Horsley, as vocalist, but this temporary frontman then opted to pursue his skills as a sculptor. Horsley later became a close associate of Jimmy Boyle at the latter's Gateway Exchange which, for a brief time, helped salve the artistic and political aspirations of a capital city in the throes of social despair. Rehearsals, practices and exhibitions were held amid advice and counselling services in a manner curiously similar to the failed Combination arts lab. The Gateway too would ultimately close, yet the focus it provided was welcomed by those it assisted.

Despite its undoubted promise, Rational failed to secure a safe financial footing. 'The label didn't make money,' states Campbell, 'and to make matters worse it was based in Gutter Music, a shop run by the actor Andre Thornton-Grimes. He owed Rough Trade, who distributed my records, for stock, and they cross-collaterised Rational funds.' There was, however, a final grand gesture in the shape of a boxed-set which in essence captures this particular era.

The Delmontes

'We had, for some reason, remixed the second Delmontes single, of which there were several left. We packaged them with a typed note from Mark E. Smith, some used tickets from Josef K and Fire Engines' gigs, an unissued demo version of the Associates 'Dogs In The Wild', and a couple of made-up bands.'

The dissolving of Postcard, the abandonment of Fast/Pop Aural and the collapse of Rational suggested yet another shift in the presentation of Scottish pop. Yet while its struggling underclass was effectively fragmented, attention became focused on established acts and those struggling to make the transformation from indie stars to mainstream players.

Simple Minds lost founding drummer Brian McGee following *Sons And Fascination/Sister Feelings Call*. He subsequently surfaced in Endgames, whose nominal link to Samuel Beckett failed to disguise a trilling new romanticism. Former Zones/Skids drummer Kenny Hyslop took his place for the triumphal 'Promised You A Miracle', which evolved from informal riffs and improvisations to become the Mind's best-selling single to date. Its success confirmed the realigned quintet as a truly international attraction. 'Playing live is great encouragement,' Kerr confides, 'but you also have to prove yourself, the audience has to be fought and won. That year (1981/2) we just played non-stop and we could feel ourselves getting across.' The singer pinpoints an Australian tour as a key part of this development. 'Echo And The Bunnymen arrived at the same time and one of the newspapers wrote that it was a toss-up between us and them which was the more obscure.' Within five weeks the group had become a major attraction. 'We arrived to that scrap of paper, and left with a gold disc. That gave us encouragement and focus for the next stage.'

The uplifting bravado of 'Promised You A Miracle' was continued on the attendant album, *New Gold Dream*, which took the elements regarded as a 'Simple Minds' sound' and accentuated them, concentrating on McNeil's dextrous keyboard fills, Forbes' pulsating bass and a lush, extravagant production. There were moments of passivity, notably 'King Is White And In The Crown', and others of immodest bravura, but the group had not only caught their sense of ambition, but did so with warm, almost seductive, music. 'The songs were less quirky,' Charlie Burchill confirms, 'and the whole sound was more cohesive. It was a phase when we weren't sacred of beautiful melodies.' 'We still had our influences,' adds Kerr, 'but something new, something 'us', was growing through them. *New Gold Dream* was where we came into our own.' 'Someone Somewhere (In Summertime)' best exemplifies a sound which, although immutably derived from those first recordings, provides a different emotional effect. Gone was the early years' austere, sometimes discordant tension, and in its place was textured, mellifluent rock.

By the time *New Gold Dream* was completed the group had not only lost Hyslop, but also his replacement, Mike Ogletree, and it was funk pragmatist Mel Gaynor who eventually secured the drum position. The next Simple

Minds album, *Sparkle In The Rain* (1984), was produced by Steve Lillywhite, who introduced a dynamic, often contrasting perspective, quite unlike the panoramic standpoint of its predecessor. This division undermined a previous subtlety - some critics dubbed the 'new' sound superficial - and it is true that while undeniably crafted, the passion exposed on some of the tracks was compromised by a desire to simply project, rather than enchant or mystify. Where it worked, however, the album demanded attention and there is no denying the opulent power of 'Waterfront'.

Obstensively a eulogy to Glasgow, this powerful song celebrated much wider aspirations. 'You always see your home-town differently when you come back,' states Kerr, as he relates how the lyric evolved during a walk amid the ruins of the Clyde's once-thriving shipbuilding industry. 'That era is defined as the city's halcyon days, but as great as they undoubtedly were, a lot of stuff for war was built on the Clyde; everything is relative. There just seemed to be a calm and quiet that night and walking around the broken buildings it was easy to believe it was the end of something. But the river was still flowing, there was a fantastic sunset, and I just became aware of a grander scheme of things.'

Sparkle In The Rain also included a rare cover version. Lou Reed's 'Street Hassle' was an established band favourite, yet they chose to discard two of the song's three sections - the first, in which the protagonist's meet, and the third, in which the girl succumbs to a drugs' overdose - while retaining the section in which the couple make love. Where Reed's orgasmic vision is born of convenience, a last hurrah before death, Simple Minds' focus on the song's moment of optimism, a recurrent motif throughout their canon.

This seventh album topped the UK chart, and now few could possibly deny Simple Minds' popularity. In 1985 they enjoyed a US number 1 with 'Don't You (Forget About Me)', a seemingly inconsequential piece written with the group in mind. They spent several months avoiding it - 'We just couldn't see the connection with us at all' (Burchill) - but pressure was applied to accede, particularly as the song was to be included on the soundtrack to the film *The Breakfast Club*. 'It wasn't going to be the lead track at the time,' states Kerr. 'We thought we'd be tucked away where no-one could see us, but at the same time our label would think we were playing the game. We were just looking for a fair crack with our next record.' Nevertheless, something seemed to transpire when the group came to demo the song. 'At that point it gained a different shape,' states Burchill, but despite inventing a new start and adding the 'La La' refrain, a collective ambivalence remained. 'I guess we were guilty of being a little precious,' Jim admits, 'and really, if there was any problem, it was because they were not the words I would have written.'

The song's US success was duly repeated elsewhere in the world, and Simple Minds gradually became aware of its significance as the means by which a much wider audience discovered them. 'I know the pleasure it has given

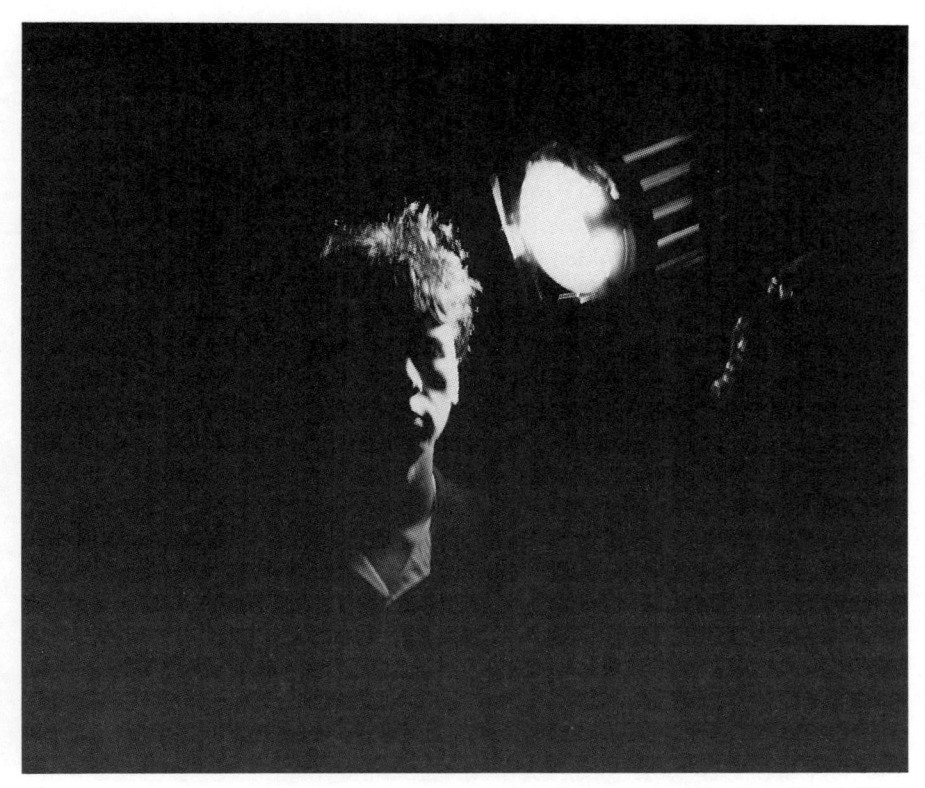

A moody shot of Jim Kerr, Simple Minds

people,' says Kerr, 'and played live it takes on a different dimension.' It became the lynch-pin of their performance at that year's *Live Aid* and remained an integral part of the group's set long after other hits had been dropped.

Once Upon A Time, recorded in the USA with producers Jimmy Iovine and Bob Clearmountain, inferred that the group had openly invested in America's rock marketplace. The combination's unambiguous recording techniques certainly brought a transatlantic burr to the Simple Minds' sound, although the set's brash power perplexed those recalling a group prepared to take on edgy experimentalism. Nonetheless, 'Ghostdancing' created an admirable racket made all the more significant when the proceeds from its sales were donated to Amnesty International, whose humanitarian cause the group openly espoused. Elsewhere the anthemic 'Alive & Kicking' contrasted the melodic twists of 'All The Things She Says', yet the persistent feeling remained that the group was refining its strengths, rather than challenging them.

Despite their international status, Simple Minds still maintained links with Glasgow. They re-opened the historic Barrowlands Ballroom with three sell-out concerts and in 1986 controversially headlined at Rangers' Ibrox Stadium.

As avowed fans of city rivals Celtic, the group ensured their allegiance was made evident. 'I wish someone like Alan Bleasdale could have captured some of these moments,' states Kerr. 'For a start we took the visitors' dressing room, even though the other one was twice the size and laid out with all the grapes and statues. They were all going "Oh no. You can't," but we said, "No no. We change where Celtic change."' Rumours of more scurrilous activity abounded - none of which involved the group directly - but tales still circulate of Holy Water being sprinkled in the goalmouth, and crucifixes buried in the turf. 'It became mythical,' Jim concedes.

The enmity between these teams draws from a religious and cultural divide. At that point Rangers had yet to sign a Catholic player, while Celtic's attendant symbolism, notably the tricolour, is linked to the Republic of Ireland. 'At that time the flags of all the countries we'd played in flew above the stage,' explains Kerr. 'The one for Amnesty International, white with a dove on it, was in the centre. Of course we'd been to Ireland, so very naturally the tricolour was there, only as we got to Ibrox, it seemed to get into the middle a wee bit - as a wind-up initially. That caused a problem and we were told that we couldn't put it up. We said, "Why not?" but they wouldn't say, "You know why not." So we asked them to write the reason down, on headed notepaper.

'The tricolour went up first,' he continues, 'and I think it went up at the Govan end. We were merciless. I don't know if this is true, but I heard the dressing room keys were returned in a keyring of the Pope.' Yet Kerr also reflects on the unifying nature of the Ibrox date. 'Usually one end is singing one song while the other sings another. That night they all sang the same song.'

Further changes ensued and the departure of Derek Forbes robbed the group of a distinctive anchor. Session bassist John Gilbin took his place, but while latterly tempted elsewhere, the newcomer introduced Kerr to the melody forming the core of 'Belfast Child'. 'He was at a piano,' the singer recalls, 'picking out this bewitching melody. When he finished I asked him when he wrote it and he said "About 150 years ago."' The piece in question was an Irish folk song, 'She Moved Through The Fair', popularised during the late 60s by Fairport Convention. Its poignancy was self-evident to Kerr who put new words to it based on his reactions to the continued strife in Northern Ireland and, in particular, the Inneskillen bombing. 'Rather than documenting it,' he explains, 'I was thinking about the future of Belfast, and what was in store for the kids born that night.'

'Belfast Child' became the core song of the *Ballad Of The Streets* EP, which rose to the top of the UK charts in 1989. It captured a period when Simple Minds' sentiments, although previously voiced, now became unequivocal. 'The issues were loud and clear,' states Kerr. 'I felt like most people with an eye on the world around them. We didn't want these feelings to pass us by.' The group had already expressed their allegiances by participating in the previous year's Mandela Day concert and the 'title' song, written for and previewed, at the event, was also a part of that political set. As lyricist, however, Kerr avoided pinning the song to temporal events and instead opted to proclaim a growing awareness of Mandela's ideas. 'Instead of singing about him being in jail, I wanted to sing about freedom. You can lock up the man, but you can't imprison his legend, his myth and his values.'

The attendant album, *Street Fighting Years*, also reflected this period's turmoil. 'Every song seemed to be about conflict,' Kerr stated to writer Alfred Bos, 'and the set described this age of chaos, the battle to try and remain intact with all this hurricane around us.' Yet the set's reflective restiveness was also explained by the lengthy sabbatical the group had taken prior to recording. 'We knew there was something wrong,' Kerr recounts. 'We were getting all the symbols of success but couldn't feel it; it was like going through water without touching it. We were absolutely knackered - physically and artistically - and it was time to stop. In doing so we essentially shut the door on ourselves in the States. They were ready for a new record, but we said 'No, we're not doing it. See ya.'''

The album's content, in particular the title track and 'This Land Is Your Land', shows little sign of compromise, and having rediscovered a focus, Simple Minds created their most cohesive set since *New Gold Dream*. Yet the personal and professional turmoil did not abate. Kerr's marriage to singer Chrissie Hynde collapsed, the group's relationship with manager Bruce Findlay was sundered and Mick McNeil, an integral part of the Simple Minds oeuvre, walked out. 'Mick had made his discontent with everything, the lifestyle, the music, us, very clear,' explains Kerr, 'but we still felt he'd go home, get fed up and a month later would be back. Then two amazing things happened. Firstly, Mick wasn't back, and secondly, Charlie had written a lot of stuff and was playing keyboards.' Sessions thus began on *Real Life*, a tentative set, understandably so given the circumstances. 'We didn't even know if we had a band,' says Jim, 'but when we played the new songs to people close to us no-one said "This doesn't sound like you."'

'*Real Life* was made very fast,' he continues, 'and it may suffer in places because of that, but although we didn't have Mick's banks of keyboards to seduce us, we knew we could go on.' 'For me it was the most enjoyable album to record,' adds Burchill. 'It was like being back at the beginning when we wrote our first album, but with much more experience. We still didn't know where we were heading, but it put a seal on the 80s mythology, clearing the way for something else.'

Simple Minds' ascendancy from parochial act to institution was followed by other acts, who now realised it was perfectly possible, not only to live in Scotland, but to be managed from there too. Stuart Adamson's departure from the Skids was inspired, in part, by his desire to remain based in Dunfermline, although the most pressing reason was that clichéd hyperbole, 'musical differences'. He then rekindled an acquaintance with guitarist Bruce Watson and, having bought a drum machine, the pair began taping new, rudimentary compositions. Some weeks later they emerged fronting an all-Scottish quintet, but when consensus declared the rhythm section inappropriate, this early incarnation folded. Undeterred, the two friends entered a studio using session hands Tony Butler (bass) and Mark Brzezicki (drums) who, as members of On The Air, had supported the Skids on a national tour. The classic Big Country line-up was thus in place.

'Harvest Home' was an inauspicious debut, but the quartet scored national success with 'Fields Of Fire'. This single, and a corresponding album, *The Crossing*, relied on the same urgent style of the Skids, while embellishing this basic pattern with ringing, 'bagpipe' guitar lines and piquant images of Scottish patriotism. 'In A Big Country' typified this rousing approach, but despite a genuinely affectionate popularity, the group quickly found themselves restrained in a self-parodic straight-jacket.

There were moments of surprise, including a live rendition of the Miracles 'Tracks Of My Tears', one of Adamson's favourite songs, but his adopted style obscured a genuine desire to address social issues, evinced in the title of a second album, *Steeltown* and an earlier flip-side, 'Belief In The Small Man'. The former topped the UK album chart in 1984 and in doing so represented a commercial peak, coinciding with international tours and a saltire-decked Hogmanay concert at the Edinburgh Playhouse. A third set, *The Seer*, included a cameo by Kate Bush as the titular prophet, while Communards' drummer June Miles-Kingston supplied backing vocals on other selections. However, in merely tinkering with the formula, Big Country only undermined their strengths.

A two-year break ensued, before the group was relaunched with 'King Of Emotion' and the attendant *Peace In Our Time*. Both reinforced the impassioned nature of early releases, suggesting that Adamson had failed to solve the problem of balancing progress with expectation. An ambitious concert, staged from within the USSR embassy in London and broadcast live on Radio 1, was followed by five dates at Moscow's Palace Of Sports. But these well-intentioned events could not obscure the withering of Big Country's commercial appeal. Adamson then faced controversy in Scotland on endorsing Tennant's brewery's decision to sponsor competitions for novice acts. Viewing music as an escape from possibly drudgery - group co-founder Watson had previously scrubbed out nuclear submarines - the guitarist saw nothing amiss in corporate sponsorship if it aided young ambition. Yet many other figures, including Jim Kerr, were loathed to equate rock with alcohol in such a formal manner and Adamson was more often required to defend his position, as opposed to proclaiming potential merits.

The guitarist's ex-foil, Richard Jobson, had meanwhile resumed recording. Since the demise of the Skids he had undertaken different projects, most of which furthered his aesthetic aspirations, including plays, poetry and monologues. 'The experience was rewarding,' Jobson explains, 'but you're on your own in the dressing room.' His solo debut, *The Ballad Of Etiquette*, featured recitations underscored by some delightful music by Virginia Astley and John McGeogh. The Belgian label, Crepescule, then followed this with four, sometimes guileless, sometimes pretentious sets, the most notable of which was the autobiographical *16 Years Of Alcohol*.

Fired by Adamson's success, Jobson formed the Armoury Show with McGeogh, John Doyle and longtime friend Russell Webb. 'Stuart had piled through by this time,' the singer states, 'and the competitive element in me wanted to work in a group again.' *Waiting For The Floods* offered a passion noticeably absent from *Joy*, but the overall impression was that of response, rather than purpose. The unit was nonetheless active for three years, splitting up in 1988, and the following year the singer unleashed his first solo 'rock' album, *Badman*. It was not an outstanding selection and Jobson then opted to pursue a career as television pundit, hosting magazine programmes and, more improbably, *Men Talk*.

A more conspicuous rival to Big Country's implicitly Celtic perspective was provided by the Silencers. Its guiding force, Jimme O'Neil, had enjoyed a brief solo career as the punningly titled 'Jimmy Shelter', before forging a lengthier vocation as a songwriter and leader of post-punk act Fingerprintz. The group's three albums took peculiar routes, but their course through fractured pop, dub and funk was marked by his oblique, sometimes perverse, perspectives and a grasp of chilling melody. O'Neil subsequently co-wrote and produced *Sob Stories* for singer Jacquie Brookes, before forging the Silencers with Fingerprintz guitarist Cha Burnz in 1986. Joe Donnelly (bass) and Martin Hanlon (drums) completed the founding line-up, which secured a management deal with Schoolhouse, at that point home to Simple Minds.

'We decided we wanted to write only about serious subjects,' O'Neil reportedly declared, and *A Letter From St. Paul* fulfils that ambition. More guitar-based than the singer's previous work, the album conveys personal demons without seeming phobic and its expansive tone, although redolent of U2, was somehow less contrived. The Irish group was one of many the Silencers supported, but this high-profile did not result in commercial acclaim. Their second set, *A Blues For Buddah*, made no difference to this trend, and if commentators praised the unit's sparkling sound, they felt unnerved by O'Neil's sometimes ominous intonation.

A different, but expanded line-up, still based around O'Neil and Burnz, produced *Dance To The Holy Man*, where a concern with simplicity reversed a previous trend towards blind anthems. The album was launched in Paris at the Locomotive Club, and indeed the fervent popularity the group enjoys in France has been crucial to its survival. They, like Big Country, have been plagued by an 'unfashionable' tag, yet this may in time produce greater longevity.

CHAPTER 18
'ONE DAY I'M LISTENING TO WES MONTGOMERY, THE NEXT IT'S JOHNNY THUNDERS.'

If Simple Minds and Big Country forged grandiose visions, those seeking expositors of a simpler Scottish pop sought solace in Altered Images and the Bluebells, the same two acts rebuffed by Alan Horne. His apprehension is not unfathomable, and if both acts took fragments of the Orange Juice jigsaw - the former their naiveté, the latter a knowledge of 60s ephemera - neither boasted its crusading zeal.

'We were all at school together,' recalls Altered Images' bassist Johnny McElhone, discussing the formative trio providing the crux of the group's initial line-up. Tony McDade (guitar) and Michael Anderson (drums) plus McElhone were together some six months before being joined by two girl singers. 'They were both really shy,' Johnny relates, but the admirable assumption that any perturbation would thus be halved did not transpire. Within weeks Claire Grogan, the sister of McElhone's elder brother's girl-friend, was the quartet's sole lead vocalist.

Altered Images - a name derived from Malcolm Garrett's design company - made their live debut at Glasgow's Mars Bar in August 1979. 'The first night was great,' McElhone attests, 'but the second was a disaster. We knew how to tune our instruments individually, but we didn't know they had to be in tune together.' This innocence is quite understandable, given both the group's juvenility and the residue of punk's 'do it' ethos. They duly followed the west's dwindling circuit, and became a quintet with the addition of a second guitarist, 'Caesar'. By contrast Claire was concurrently filming her role of Susan in *Gregory's Girl*, having been spotted serving meals at the Spaghetti Factory by acclaimed director Bill Forsyth.

A demo tape, produced by former Simple Minds' sound engineer David Henderson, found its way to Siouxsie And The Banshees via their fan club.

Altered Images

Altered Images were duly invited to guest on the latter's upcoming date at Glasgow's Tiffanys where the juxtaposition of nascence and gothic doom proved highly popular. The arrangement was maintained on a low-key British tour - the Banshees masqueraded under the pseudonym Janet And The Icebergs - but the Images' crucial early appearance was at the first Futurama festival in Leeds. 'John Peel was there,' explains McElhone, 'but he missed our performance. However, everyone was coming up to him to say how good we were and he booked us for a radio session.' The experience highlighted just how young the group members were. 'My brother Gerry drove us down to the recording,' recalls Johnny. 'We did it, got back into the van, and drove back home to be at school the next day.'

The quintet then recorded a demo for Polydor, who turned them down, although the understandable disappointment was quickly dispelled. They secured a support slot on a New Year bill at London's Moonlight Club and although there to check another act, CBS A&R scout Simon Hicks found Altered Images irresistible. 'Of course,' McElhone recounts, 'once one label wants you, everybody does, but we stayed with CBS because they were the first to show interest.' Banshees' guitarist Steve Severin was invited to produce the group's early singles and thus 'Dead Pop Stars' and 'A Day's Wait' revealed an obvious debt to their mentors. This was particularly true of the former song, on which Grogan's jerky intonation mirrored that of Siouxsie Sioux. Meanwhile its release, so close to John Lennon's shooting, raised a few querulous eyebrows.

Jim McKinven, formerly of synthesised pop attraction the Berlin Blondes, replaced Caesar prior to the Images' debut album, which paired the group with producer Martin Rushent. His commercial instincts transformed the group's sound and career, notably through the insouciant 'Happy Birthday'. 'That was the perfect song for him,' McElhone opines and the resultant Top 3 place in 1981 confirmed the promise of their collaboration. The single had merits in isolation, but successive follow-ups, including 'I Could Be Happy' and 'See Those Eyes' accentuated Grogan's little-girl voice at the expense of a more collective approach, and her skittish, Barbie-doll image obscured the group's genuine grasp of bubblegum pop. A cover of Neil Diamond's 'Song Sung Blue', a thin joke taken to abstraction, suggested a loss of confidence and McKinven and Anderson left the line-up in the wake of the disastrous *Pinky Blue*. The remaining trio added Stephen Lironi for a third set, *Bite*, as Altered Images set about dismantling their early personae. 'Don't Talk To Me About Love' did reach the UK Top 10 in 1983 as the group offered a less contrived sound, but it proved a hopeless task. The continued promotion of Clare Grogan, albeit as Audrey Hepburn rather than Lolita, trivialised the notion of a band and accentuated the idea of packaged product. 'The first two years were fabulous,' states McElhone, 'but it was too much too soon. We were inexperienced – we were so young our dads had to sign the deal – and suddenly it stopped being spontaneous. We had to live up to things and the overkill was too much.

'We were offered a US tour,' he adds, 'and this brought us to a crossroads. We had a meeting at Claire's house and agreed to break up that morning.'.

The Bluebells revolved around Robert Hodgens – better known as Bobby Bluebell – whose involvement in music began on founding a fanzine, *Ten Commandments*. The name was derived from a Prince Buster song, while the notion was inspired by John Dingwall's bedroom publication, *Stand & Deliver*. An unabashed Hodgens looked up its address. 'I chapped on his door,' he recalls, 'and said, "Excuse me. Do you do a fanzine? I want to do one too. Can you help me?"'

'I wrote the first one more or less on my own,' he recalls, 'but then I met this couple, Robert Sharp and Kirsty MacNeil, who worked for the *New Musical Express*. They helped with the next issue, but as we were doing it we seemed to run out of good Glasgow bands to write about. So we started making some up.' The prank seemed to backfire when Hodgens' effusive prose intrigued another pamphleteer, John Gilhooley, who wanted one of these acts, 007, for a compilation tape. 'Rather than admit what we'd done,' Bobby continues, 'I recorded a song at home with a drum machine and gave him that.'

Hodgens was already friendly with Alan Horne and Gerry McElhone, both of whom encouraged him to take his music further. 'Gerry took me in his car to this church hall,' he recounts. 'There were a couple of guys playing guitars, drums and bass, with this girl, Alicia, a friend of Clare Grogan's, singing. He said "Right. This is going to be your band," and then drove away and left us to rehearse.' Dubbed by McElhone the Oxfam Warriors, the group supported Altered Images at the Bungalow Bar. 'We were really terrible. The girl was too shy to sing and so after our second concert I started doing the vocals.' This arcane situation could not be sustained, a fact made plain to Hodgens at a lunchtime appearance at Glasgow Art School. 'Edwyn Collins, Alan Horne and Robert Sharp were in the audience with hit and miss cards like *Juke Box Jury*. All the songs were voted a miss.

'They all told me the band was shit, that I should chuck them all. So I did, and then formed the Bluebells with these other guys I'd met at an Altered Images concert.'

Brothers Ken and David McCluskey, previously of punk band Raw Deal, joined Lawrence Donegan (bass) and Russell Irvine (guitar) in the new group's original line-up, while Hodgens began penning a string of melodic songs. 'We played with Orange Juice and Aztec Camera,' he remembers, 'and because of this Postcard connection we were in *Sounds* straight away. There was even a picture of us in *New Musical Express* after our second concert. Nick Heyward

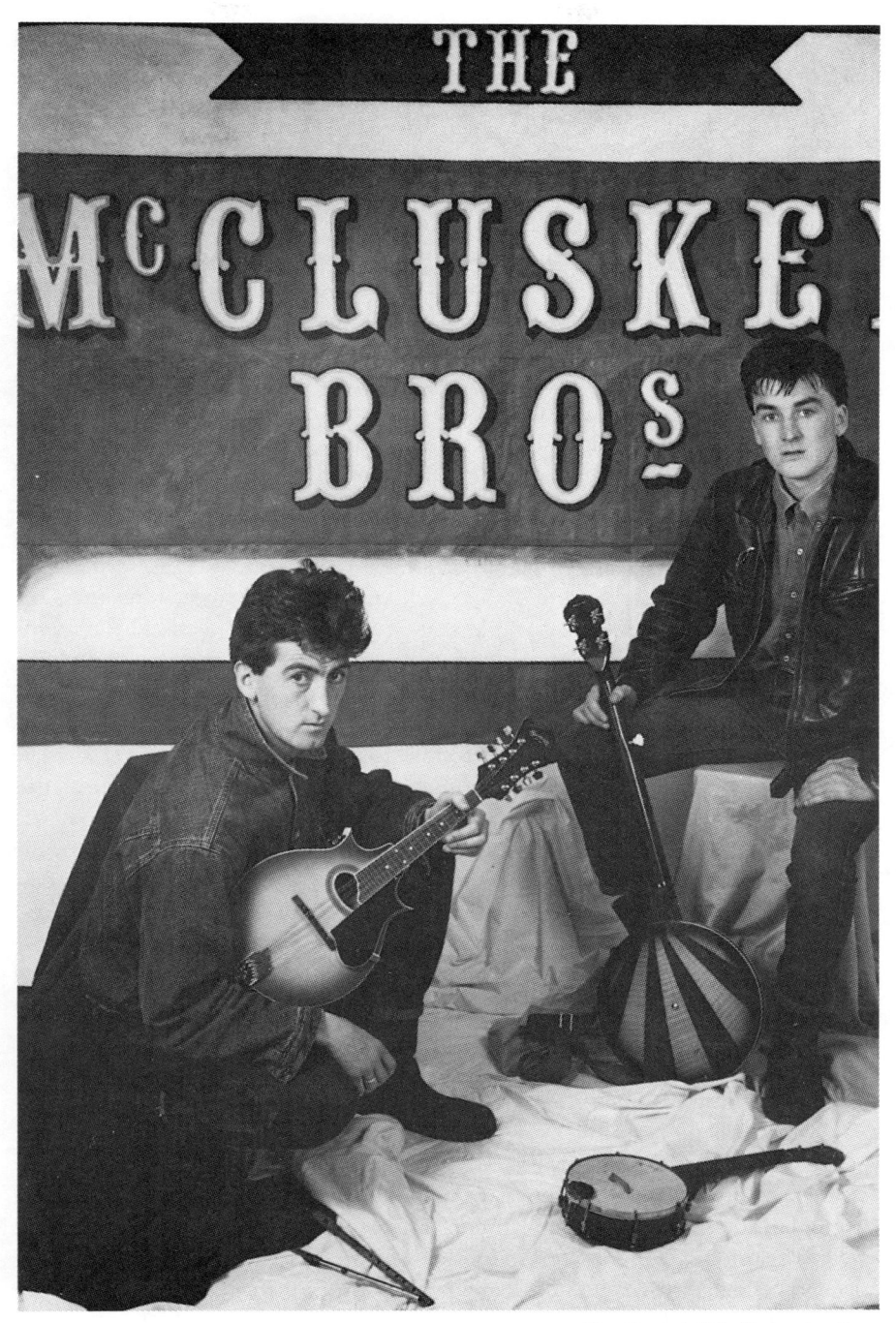

The Bluebells' McCluskey brothers

saw it and because he liked my guitar, he phoned up and gave us a support slot with Haircut 100.'

That particular tour was the first in a series of fortuitous events which took the Bluebells from provincial obscurity to hit band status. 'Everything we did at the time was blessed', Bobby concurs. 'Elvis Costello came to see us at London's ICA. We were rotten that night, but he still wanted to produce us. He said we were just like the Byrds because we dressed the same and had 12-strings. I think he wanted to patronise us because we were basically incompetent. He thought of us as quite cute.' Such attention led to friction with one-time friends. 'The more successful we got the more Alan Horne resented it; and Edwyn too to some extent, because they were obviously good and yet we were getting all the breaks they should have been getting. So there was a parting of the ways and we signed with London Records.'

With hindsight Hodgens now admits that it was here the group's luck began to change. The release of their debut single, 'Forevermore', was delayed when Mme. Bluebelle of the Parisienne Bluebelle Girls took out an injunction. 'The charge was that our appearance and general demeanour reflected badly on the name,' Bobby explains. 'I had to stay outside the court because our lawyer said I prejudiced the case. I actually was scruffy and unkempt. However, the judge dismissed her action by saying that at least we wore clothes.' The same single's progress was further hampered by another legal quandary revolving around the picture sleeve, which showed a still from the Ken Loach film, *Kes*. The original photographer objected, and subsequent pressings featured the Bluebells' roadie, Paddy, mimicking the famed v-sign.

Elvis Costello produced the single's coupling, 'Aim In Life', and this relationship was maintained on a projected follow-up. 'Some Sweet Day' was selected as the likely a-side, although that intention was undermined when the group's mentor took ill. 'We decided to do this jokey song I'd written as the b-side ourselves,' Hodgens recounts. 'It was a riposte to Rod Stewart's 'Maggie May' called 'Cathie Kay' - with mandolin parts and everything - which we then shortened to 'Cath'. We finished it in three hours.' Work on 'Some Sweet Day' resumed on Costello's return and the resultant finished master was presented to an enthusiastic A&R department. 'They asked us if we had a b-side and so we played them 'Cath'. They loved it and immediately wanted to put that out instead. Elvis was far from chuffed.'

'Cath' was not the hit everyone anticipated and the Bluebells were then paired with Cliff Richard producer Alan Tarney for 'Sugar Bridge'. 'That was the start of the rot,' Bobby opines. 'He didn't want the band on it at all. He just wanted Ken singing it and me there. There was a personality clash straight away.' The glossy results were indicative of Tarney's work with A-Ha, rather than the Bluebells own desires. Paradoxically, the fact that success had still not transpired allowed the group some freedom. 'We went up to Inverness to record,' Hodgens recalls, 'and this time we did everything ourselves. 'I'm Falling' and 'Young At Heart' were done up there, as well as most of the album.'

The Bluebell's perseverance reaped reward when 'I'm Falling' reached number 11 in March 1984. It was succeeded by the nonchalant 'Young At Heart' - replete with scraping fiddle and breezy harmonies - which deftly captured a summer's fairground innocence. A Top 10 hit, its carefree qualities stemmed, in part, from Hodgens' initial view of his composition. 'I'd actually written it for Bananarama who did it on their first album as a northern soul thing. For some reason I wasn't credited on it, so we recorded it, again as a b-side, so I could reclaim my song.'

A revived 'Cath' became the Bluebells' third significant chart entry and, imbued with their new status, the group then toured the US and Europe. Their album, *Sisters*, maintained the folk stylings of recent releases, and included a version of Dominic Behan's acerbic Republican anthem, *The Patriot Game*. The Irish writer and raconteur was a family friend of the McCluskey brothers, which in part explains its inclusion, although the melody became an immutable part of 60s folklore when it was appropriated by Bob Dylan for 'With God On Our Side'. That particular period was an integral influence on Hodgens' musical perceptions, and he still equates the Bluebells' legacy in terms of one of the period's icons. 'For six months we were the Lovin' Spoonful. It wasn't a plan on our part, but rather our nature. It was the sound of the songs and the way we looked.'

The group's brief tenure ended in 1985 following the release of 'All I Am (Is Loving You)'. A fracas with London ensued over the promotional video in which Ken McCluskey posed as a stripping priest. Relationships were further soured when the label paired the group with Wombles' producer Mike Batt. 'That was a disaster,' Hodgens declares. 'Then we did some work with Andy Paley, who was a lovely guy, but by this time Ken and David were into their own kind of music and I was losing interest so we split up.' Indeed the McCluskeys had begun an independent career during the units' final months. *Aware Of All* further explored the siblings' folk persuasions, and included Hamish Henderson's 'John MacLean's March' and Woody Guthrie's 'Union Burial Ground' alongside several songs co-written with Dominic Behan. Late-period Bluebells Craig Gannon and Neil Baldwin (ex-TV 21) moved elsewhere; the former, who'd left Aztec Camera, later surfaced in the Smiths. London meanwhile clung to Hodgens for another, unproductive, year, but freed him when vocalist Holly Johnson extracted himself from a punitive contract and set legal precedence in the process. Bobby returned to Glasgow and having withdrawn from music for several years, formed a new group, Up. The project did not last and Hodgens has since pursued a career as a dance DJ. He operates under the title 'Bob's Full House'.

Between acts such as the Bluebells and Altered Images were those scattered in the wake of Fast and Postcard. Orange Juice survived the trauma of major label accommodation and emerged from the disappointment of *You Can't Hide Your Love Forever* with the tighter, more open *Rip It Up*. The title song gave the group a bona-fide hit in 1983, to which Edwyn reacted in suitably ironic manner. 'We weren't surprised,' he confesses. 'It was the first time we'd made a video, it was the first time we'd had a properly organised campaign. There were give-away cassettes with early Orange Juice material and all the other commercial jiggery-pokery they had in those days.' 'Rip It Up' became the group's sole Top 10 single, but they were required to write an apologetic epistle to 'Top Of The Pops' producer Michael Hurll when McClymott - 'our cheeky bass-player,' to quote Edwyn - headbutted Jim Foetus, who was playing saxophone on the session. There was no denying the songs undoubted charm, yet follow-up releases, 'Flesh Of My Flesh' and 'Bridge', were equally persuasive. The fact they failed commercially was seen as Polydor intransigence, rather than dubious quality. It in turn intensified an already smouldering hostility.

Orange Juice in 1980

'There were times when I was deliberately perverse,' Collins subsequently admitted, citing the second major upheaval within the OJ ranks. The departures of Ross and McClymont seemed, on the surface, fatal, yet in truth Edwyn was liberated, freed to pursue a less-compromised path. 'It was really a different band,' he adds. 'There was a different ethos behind that line-up.' *Texas Fever* was completed with the aid of Manyika and dubmaster Dennis Bovell, the architect of those mesmerising Pop Group recordings. Its expansive sound was continued on *The Orange Juice* (1984), arguably Collins' most cohesive work to that point, which included the enthralling 'What Presence?' and an obliquely autobiographical gem, 'The Artisans'. 'All the rest are just also-rans, compared to the fabulous Artisans,' Edwyn intones in what became a swan-song. Polydor showed little patience with this undoubted artistry, and in a final perverse act, held Manyika to his contract while agreeing to let Edwyn go. 'We felt we'd done a little cracker, but they thought us a spent force and said so in as many words. We were disappointed the album didn't get the push we thought it deserved.' Orange Juice remained active until January 1985 when Collins announced the end of his creation at a benefit for striking miners. 'We were the first post-punk group to have a monopoly of roots music,' he declared when asked to précis their appeal, 'things like *Blonde On Blonde*-period Dylan and Buffalo Springfield.'

These elements were also apparent in Aztec Camera, although the line-up recording the group's debut album, *High Land, Hard Rain*, was markedly different from that of the Postcard era. Bernie Clarke (keyboards), Campbell Owens (bass) and Dave Ruffy (drums) joined Roddy Frame for a set which retained the melodic charm of 'Just Like Gold', but in forging a warmer sound, lost the edge of its less-polished predecessors. This contrast is clearly heard on 'We Could Send Letters', which Frame recut for the album, and although the new version has merits, in becoming 'more professional', the singer sacrifices part of its poignancy.

Released in 1983, *High Land, Hard Rain* announced the arrival of a crafted songsmith, and although cynics unfairly dubbed it 'new-wave Bread', the album's honeyed tones were deceptive. Where 'Oblivious' and 'Pillar To Post' were buoyantly memorable, 'Walk Out To Winter' and 'The Bugle Sounds Again' revealed an aching vulnerability. 'About half of that album was written while still living in Scotland,' Roddy explains. 'It was recorded in Eastbourne, at International Christians Communication Studio. While we were there, all these choirs were bussed in and out. We used to have conversations about Jesus with the people there; it was quite weird, but there's a spiritual feel about some of the songs, especially 'Back On Board'.' Frame's instinctive ability to construct and arrange a song brought plaudits from several quarters, including Elvis Costello and Mark Knopfler, the latter of whom produced the group's second set, *Knife*. Aztec Camera was thus welcomed into mainstream rock.

Although the new album was issued on Warner Brothers, the artistry apparent on *High Land, Hard Rain* was equally prevalent here. However, the singers' intimate appeal was gradually lessening as a wider audience beckoned, a process culminating when the mellifluous 'Somewhere In My Heart', reached the UK Top 3 in 1988. 'Funnily, that track almost didn't make it on to the *Love* album,' Frame admits. 'I didn't know if it was good enough.' However a cover version of Van Halen's 'Jump' showed that Roddy was not prepared to bow to expectations, as he recounted to *TLN*. 'I was becoming angry at being seen as the sensitive young man with the fringed jacket.' Yet despite a succession of rich accolades and plaudits throughout the 80s, Frame's disparate references remained largely those which he brought to Postcard, albeit in a more conventional manner. 'I've got pretty eclectic taste. One day I'm listening to Wes Montgomery, the next it's Johnny Thunders. The thing that does run through my music and what dictates the style is the guitar, because that's the instrument I can express myself on.'

Despite the injection of different members, including Malcolm Ross, Frame and Aztec Camera are indivisible. Though the use of a collective name implies a certain externalisation, releases reflect the attitude of its guiding light, as evinced by a 1990 single, 'The Crying Scene'. 'That is one of the most cynical songs I've ever written,' Frame related at the time. 'I used to pontificate a lot, I used to read Jean-Paul Sartre where now I read Warhol's *From A to B and Back Again*. He said that one of the most useful things he ever learned to say was "So what?" I kinda live by that - don't think about it, do it.' Frame's collaborations with ex-Clash guitarist Mick Jones, or Japanese ambient practitioner Ryuichi Sakamoto are further proof of this pursuit. Yet if the original Aztec Camera was less challenging, musically, than compatriots Orange Juice or Josef K, its subsequent incarnation enjoyed greater commercial success.

Edwyn Collins' solo career has meanwhile reflected the maturation of a wayward, but gifted, talent. He made his solo debut in 1987 with 'Don't Shilly Shally', the first of two low-key singles, before the Cologne-based White House studios invited the singer to record there. The resultant set, *Hope And Despair*, showed his skill undiminished, a facet enhanced by its mercurial successor, *Hellbent On Compromise*. 'Two maverick figures came out of the 80s; Edwyn Collins and Morrissey' Alan Horne recounted for BBC radio. 'Neither have had their day - it's yet to come - and I have this vision of them at the graveside of the pathetic music business, sniggering to themselves.'

Postcard's savant enacted Frame and Collins by leaving Glasgow in the early 80s. 'London Records offered me an office and a budget,' he explains when asked about Swamplands, a flawed but under-rated venture set up under this aegis in 1985. In truth he resurrected some of Postcard's capriciousness, albeit on a bigger budget, a combination he hoped would bring commercial success. There was thus a place for James King And The Lone Wolves, who emerged from the Cuba Libre debacle with the 5-track *Texas Lullaby*, issued on a self-financed outlet. The group's sole single for Swamplands, 'The Angels Say', strained jangly pop through a rockabilly rattle, but King was characteristically blunt about the record. 'I hated it,' he related in a 1987 interview, while being similarly scathing about the era. 'I don't know why (London) signed the Lone Wolves, because they couldn't stand us, personally or musically.' 'The whole thing was a complete nightmare,' Horne stated as a rejoinder, but he retains respect for King's pivotal role in the evolution of Glasgow's punk underclass. A Lone Wolves' album, produced by John Cale, was completed but not released and the disillusioned group then disbanded. James subsequently surfaced with Fun Patrol, whose 'The Right To Be Wrong' somehow encapsulated his unyielding intransigence.

Swamplands' strongest moments came from acts already linked to Horne's mythos. Memphis comprised of Orange Juice refugees James Kirk and Stephen Daly and their lone single, 'You Supply The Rose', captured the postulant charm of their erstwhile group. They were, however, a temporary aberration and the label found a greater consistency with Win, a new act formed by ex-Fire Engines' stalwarts Davey Henderson and Russell Burn. Although Henderson had quit the Heartbeats, he retained his songwriting partnership with Hillary Morrison and indeed one such composition, 'Love Bomb', became the first single for the Bob Last-managed Claire Grogan. Performing, however, remained of paramount importance.

'We called ourselves Win, which was the worst name ever,' he recounts, 'but we thought that people would be attracted magnetically to this beautiful thing we hoped to create.' The new act was completed by Ian Stoddart and, conscious of Paul Morley's love of their previous incarnation, Win initially completed a 4-track demo for ZTT, for which the writer acted as P.R. The cassette later surfaced at London Records, where Horne discovered it quite by accident. 'Alan was walking down the corridor when he heard our tape coming from another office,' Henderson explains. 'He recognised my voice, 'phoned Russell and signed us up to Swamplands.'

Win remained a curious hybrid throughout its career. Superficially similar to the quicksilver pop of Heaven 17 or ABC (two acts, coincidentally, also part of Bob Last's coterie), the group attempted to accommodate ideologies within a more accessible framework. Henderson remains quite clear about their motives, yet is sceptical over the final outcome. 'We created a vibey, Neanderthal, post-punk funk, but for some reason we also wanted to be pop stars. Yet we didn't go all the way and wanted to intellectualise too much over the forms of the songs and their reasons for existing. There were lyrical references to people we loved through art, but were like dilettantes, and rather than being subversive, we subverted ourselves.' Nonetheless, the audacity of 'Super Popoid Groove' - 'chewing gum for the ears' as it proclaims itself - joins the enveloping riff of

'Un-American Broadcasting' in displaying the craft of this capricious group. Both tracks were issued as singles, the latter with a peel-off American flag, 'just like the Velvet's *Banana* album' to the artistic delight of both group and label.

The ensuing album, *Uh! Tears Baby (A Trash Icon)*, worked within the same stylistic parameters. This 1987 release is now chiefly recalled for 'You've Got The Power', a pulsating dance track appropriated by McEwan's Lager as part of their televised sortie on a youth market. Their stylish advertisements required a soundtrack but, forbidden to use established acts in such a sensitive arena, the company instead approached emergent talent, yoking together a sometimes controversial relationship between the brewing industry and rock music.

Win featured in what was known as the 'Esher' promotion, and the McLuhan-esque communion of their talent and commercial communication fulfilled imagery cultivated by Fire Engines. However, if McEwans enjoyed its titular celebration, they failed to spot its lyrical conclusions - 'To Generate Fear' and 'To Censor What's Real'. 'That was important for us,' Henderson agrees, while remaining disappointed with the final collection. 'It was unrepresentative of what we really were,' he opines, yet there's little doubt that Win's debut was at least partially successful. Its seditious qualities are discussed as openly and as often as its endearing twists between Marc Bolan and Prince.

Swamplands was meanwhile caught in internal politics as London queried rising costs and lacklustre sales in 1986. Horne declared his intention to shoot a movie, *The Beat Hotel*, and issued a single ostensibly drawn from its soundtrack. Paul Quinn, ex-vocalist with the Jazzateers and Bourgie Bourgie, joined Edwyn Collins for a reading of the Velvet's 'Pale Blue Eyes', but this was perceived as a foppish whim by a frustrated parent label. The commercial impasse surrounding Win brought matters to a head.

Promotional sticker for Win's 'Un-American Broadcasting' single

London closed Swamplands down, leaving Horne with years of litigation ahead of him in order to gain a just settlement. Its roster was meanwhile scattered to the winds. 'We gave them an OK Corral,' recalls Henderson. 'London had to commit themselves by six o'clock on Friday. In fact, they hadn't actually signed us, we were a Swamplands act, and as the label didn't exist any more, we were free to go anyway.'

Win switched to Virgin where they recorded *Trigger Finger*, a release for which Henderson has much more affection. 'There was an element about the people involved in that album that I really love,' he states, although the guitarist still harbours some regrets. '*Trigger Finger* was a reaction to the previous release so we never put on vinyl what we really meant, and never realised our true ambitions.' While containing the uncompromising 'What's Love If You Can Kill For Chocolate', this second set is generally less burdened by manifesto, and thus avoids its predecessor's claustrophobia. However, it is equally true to state that Win could not rid itself of the Fire Engines' legacy, and all their releases were perceived as reflections of that past, rather than new developments. They split up in 1989, although Russell Burn, who retreated to Barcelona, re-emerged as Piefinger three years later with the diffuse *Dali Surprise*, on which Henderson appears. The sad demise of Win brought Edinburgh's immediate post-punk hopes to an end, in the way the collapse of Orange Juice had closed the Postcard dream.

CHAPTER 19
WISHING I WAS LUCKY

It would be a mistake to assume that Scotland's pop, imbued with the ragged edge of a Fire Engines or Orange Juice, immediately dismantled its pre-punk heritage. Although Oily Records provided a natural home to north-sound new-wave acts the Tools, Squibs and President's Men, the Aberdeen-based label also introduced APB, whose indebtedness to Black America was apparent on early, albeit minimalist, recordings. Their debut single, 'Shoot You Down' (1981), fused a punchy riff to de rigeur octave bass-lines, to provide a rhythmic bedrock for its extended, scratchy guitar break. Recognition was initially confined to Britain's indie ghetto, but a copy somehow found its way to an FM radio station in Philadelphia, from where it was picked up by New York clubs. A cult following ensued - APB even supported James Brown - reaffirming a musical link established by the Average White Band.

While early APB releases were recorded at Tony Pilley's Barclay Towers, the bulk of the group's work was completed with Wilf Smarties. Having flirted with Gang Of Four-styled agit-funk, the founding trio - Iain Slater (bass/vocals), Glenn Roberts (guitar) and George Cheyne (drums) - was eventually augmented by pianist Neil Innes and percussionist Mike Craighead in a less ambiguous unit determined to create a solid dance groove. Their unpretentious style was captured to varying degrees on *Cure For The Blues*, yet APB failed to secure a major deal suited to the music they purveyed. By the 90s they had jettisoned a somewhat lacklustre name, but rebirth as the Loveless has not resulted in commercial approbation.

Punk may have caused a temporary limbo, but rock and soul continued to offer havens for those to whom the rattle of guitars or self-immolation proved alien. If the newfound freedom new-wave pioneers engendered was generally welcome, many found its overall trappings unacceptable. The importance of a cultural movement is equally gauged by those who rally against it, as well as individuals embracing its possibilities. The upsurge of soul in Glasgow during the 80s was clearly due to the former, as James Grant, leader of Love and

Money suggests. 'There was a reaction to the Postcard and post-Postcard 'jingle-jangle'. We thought, "Let's turn it around and do something upfront and proud."' Grant's comments, however, are not borne of malice, and instead acknowledge how the era helped shape his musical path. In the late 70s he was playing guitar in bands popular at the Doune Castle or Dial Inn. 'We were called Stage initially, and then we went through another phase as Kashmir. We used to do some of our own stuff, as well as 'Hey Joe', 'All Along The Watchtower' or 'The Wind Cries Mary'. It sounds good in retrospect, but because this was during punk, I suppose we thought we were going against the grain.'

Grant subsequently joined a theatre company at Glasgow Art Centre as part of a YOP scheme. 'Their ad said 'Young people wanted to play guitar and act.' I thought "Fuck the acting part. Wouldn't it be amazing to get a job playing guitar?"' James duly wrote music for two plays - and secured his equity card - while the artistic environment also left an indelible impression. 'It was a very good year,' Grant explains, 'I was encouraged to be ambitious and creative, and it was here I met Harry Travers, who became a strong influence. He played me Orange Juice and Echo And The Bunnymen, before that I was a 17-year-old Led Zeppelin fan, and he knew the people from Friends Again.'

Friends Again - Chris Thompson (vocals/guitar), Paul McGeehan (keyboards), Neil Cunningham (bass) and Stuart Kerr (drums) - was an aspiring Glasgow act which revolved around the first named's insular compositions. They required a lead guitarist, a position which appealed to Grant who had already seen the group live. 'I arrived at the audition and Chris and Paul were playing something like 'Sweet Jane'. I joined in for a while, then they turned to me and said, "That's fine. Do you want to go to the shop?" I suppose that was me in the band. They never actually said anything but then, they were never good at expressing themselves in a normal, colloquial way.'

'Chris was truly inspirational,' James continues. 'He is the closest thing to an enigma I've come across. He thinks and acts differently from other people, but not in a pretentious, calculated way.'

The quartet hung around the periphery of the Postcard milieu, but were never adjudged to be part of it. 'It was a bitchy time,' the guitarist recounts. 'It was great fun but nobody had a good word to say about anyone else. Pub bands were looked upon as the darts' players of rock.' Grant's new group did appear live more frequently than their more feted counterparts, and such sorties helped finance the demo which brought the group a publishing deal. 'We recorded two songs, 'Sunkissed' and 'Honey At The Core',' he explains, 'which Dave Scott, the ENTS convenor at Strathclyde University, took to CBS.' Their recording debut followed soon afterwards, but the release of *Trapped And Unwrapped* failed to mark the divisions already appearing within the ranks. Bob Sargent's bouffant production gave the songs an airy, almost winsome, sound which undermined Thompson and Grant's often brittle perspectives. 'I was writing more and more,' explains Grant, 'and it seemed unfair to use Friends Again as the platform for this. I was edging into the limelight - it sounds so obnoxious and loathsome - and Chris and I weren't getting along terribly well at the time. As the rest of the band and I socialised as well, he was increasingly left as the outsider.' Grant left Friends Again in 1984, after which the group suddenly imploded. Thompson subsequently formed the Bathers which, like Roddy Frame's Aztec Camera, is a group in name only and serves as an outlet for the founder's vision. *Unusual Places To Die* (1987), which features support from Grant, best captures Thompson's unique brand of existentialist introspection.

Rather than concentrate on his own new project, Grant was initially involved in helping shape Hipsway, which evolved from the fallout of Altered Images. 'On the same morning that we split up,' Johnny McElhone recalls, 'the White Savages did the same.' The latter act, which had supported the Images on tour, included Grant's early mentor Harry Travers and vocalist Graham 'Skin' Skinner, another refugee from the original Jazzateers. 'By the afternoon,' McElhone continues, 'We'd formed Hipsway.' Guitarist Tony McDaid completed the founding line-up, but when he opted to drop out, Grant stepped in to assist. 'James played guitar in the band's early stages,' says McElhone, 'and might even have joined had he not had his own songs, and his own idea of what he wanted to do.' Eventually Pim Jones completed Hipsway's line-up, and having found stability, the group began forging a soul-based style. 'Skin liked dance music,' McElhone explains, 'and we were influenced by the different things we were listening to, such as the Gap Band or Sly And The Family Stone.'

Hipsway's eponymous debut album appeared in 1986, some 18 months after the group was formed. Although promising more than was actually delivered, the set displayed a brash self-confidence, particularly on 'The Honeythief', its much-reprised single, and 'Tinder', an imaginatively arranged composition marked by ringing guitar and an edgy brass section. The track was another purloined on behalf of the McEwans company but, as with Win, the advertising campaign did not produce a hit. Nonetheless, Hipsway did enjoy considerable concurrent coverage and were one of the support acts on Simple Minds' Ibrox bill. 'We changed in the boot room,' McElhone wryly recalls but the bassist retains fond memories of that particular day and the tour they undertook with the Eurythmics. 'That was one of the highlights,' he states. 'The Eurythmics were really good to us.' However, rumour of internal problems began to leak from the Hipsway camp and contemporary reports suggest that factionalising was rife, with McElhone and brother Gerry, their manager, on one side and the remaining trio on the other. A split was denied, then confirmed, yet McElhone feels the parting was not as rancorous as press articles had implied. 'We had different ideas on which way the second album should go,' he explains, 'and all we were doing was cancelling each other out. I decided to leave rather than continue to fight - I didn't want us not to be friends - and once that decision was made the atmosphere was much better.' McElhone's departure was followed by that of Travers, although the latter was the subject of laudatory praise on the second Hipsway album, *Scratch The Surface*. In the interim the group had scored belated transatlantic success when 'The Honeythief' was a US hit, but the reshaped line-up - Skinner, Jones and newcomer Steven Ferrera - failed to match the potential of its predecessor, and the group subsequently disbanded. Its vocalist and guitarist remained together as Skin and Pim, while Jason Roberston (ex-Win) completed the line-up of an act which struggled to retain a settled name. Having dubbed themselves Burn This, they were required to change it again to avoid an airplay embargo during the Gulf War. *House Called Love* appeared under the sobriquet Witness, in 1991.

Friends Again

Hipsway's brief ascendancy coincided with a period wherein several Glasgow groups assiduously courted the city's soul traditions, albeit with original material. Freed from the sense of compromise which had bedevilled Friends Again, James Grant forged Love And Money with McGeehan, Kerr and Cunningham from the former act, although the last-named was later replaced by Bobby Paterson.

This new group was also unashamedly brash. 'We shared an attitude with Hipsway,' James explains. 'Both groups had this upfront, dance groove. We were part of a new generation with a strong image and strong sound.' The quintet was signed to Phonogram within weeks of its inaugural demos, although sadly the label proved more tardy in finding a suitable producer. A frustrated Grant sought to fill the gap with a one-off single. 'I wrote 'Candybar Express' in the back of a van halfway through a Friends Again tour. To me it was just a joke – I actually thought it would be a good thing for Wham! to do – but when Graham Wilson from the Sub Club offered to let us put something out on his label, we recorded it ourselves.' The plan to issue the song under a pseudonym was thwarted when Phonogram heard the finished tape. 'It had turned out well,' Grant concedes, 'considering how effortless it was. The record company loved it, but it was a year and a half from the time we first recorded the song before Phonogram released it. That defeated the purpose, and the joke backfired.' Grant's reservations concerning this fervid composition stem from its inception as a rebuttal to the pensive Friends Again. Like Hipsway's 'The Honeythief', its brazen sexual acclamation was couched in metaphor, yet the exuberant performance left little to question. It was not, however, a commercial success, thanks in part to Phonogram's dithering, and a similar problem bedevilled *All You Need Is Love And Money*. By the time the album was completed, its creator had outgrown its content. 'I can't listen to our first record,' Grant states quite unequivocally. 'I just don't think its very good.' Certainly several of the songs mine Candybar's ebullient noise, with rampant horns and stinging guitar, and the pervasive image of Americana, heard in 'Cheeseburger' and 'Love And Money', now seems artificial. 'I had a knack of convincing people I had this political scheme, an anti-American propaganda, that I did nothing to dissuade. In reality it was just complete chancerism.' Nonetheless, there was much to admire on the record, in particular 'Pain Is A Gun'. Despite its awkward analogy – and Grant's own misgivings – it showed its creator shedding his group's inceptive trappings and developing a more individual approach.

Released in 1986, *All You Need Is Love And Money* featured two contrasting producers. Duran Duran guitarist Andy Taylor worked on three tracks, including 'Candybar', for which he had great affection. 'He was the ideal person to produce that song,' Grant opines. 'He was an exponent of the corruption I was singing about.' Tom Dowd, a legend through his years with the Atlantic label, completed the remainder and if the use of the former was purely expedient, the latter suggested a made-in-heaven combination. Grant, however, feels it was ultimately disappointing. 'Tom Dowd was so arithmetical...it was a big deal if you played through a song three seconds faster than you had the day before. Yet at the same time we were more critical of our music than he was.' The accumulated travails affecting the launch of Love And Money were far from unique, as evinced by trials of contemporaries Wet Wet Wet.

Bassist Graeme Clark was the motivator who, in 1982, began piecing this particular group together. Schoolfriends Tom Cunningham (drums) and Neil Mitchell (keyboards) were quickly absorbed into the fledgling unit, but a fourth member proved more difficult to find. 'Several people floated in and out,' recalls Cunningham, 'and we had umpteen guitarists. There were times when Neil tried to sing before Marti became a solid member of the band.' Marti Pellow, née Mark McLoughlin, another alumnae of Clydebank High, duly completed the line-up, although he admits that performing wasn't itself an ambition. 'I was never into being in a band at all, but I loved to sing and wasn't afraid to.' The quartet showed remarkably diverse musical interests - Clark loved the Ramones, while Mitchell reportedly favoured Frank Sinatra - and early rehearsals must have presented a somewhat awkward confluence. 'I hadn't the money to buy my own records,' states Pellow, 'and all I listened to was my parents' collection. I heard Bacharach And David and Patsy Cline and that's where I got my love for arrangements and melody.' When Pellow did begin to buy singles he opted for Earth, Wind and Fire, Chic and Al Green, and this affection for soul became one of several unifying forces.

The group, temporarily dubbed Vortex Motion, played its debut gig at a local community centre, offering a set drawn from records by Magazine, Squeeze and the Clash. Pop was thus another pivotal influence, as Cunningham recounts. 'I remember growing up in the late 70s/early 80s and being told "It's rubbish now." Looking back, bands like Squeeze, Madness, Blondie and the Beat were wonderful. They might not be the most credible things now, but I think it was a very fruitful time.'

These two elements - the aspiration of 70s soul and the sensibilities of 80s pop - became the key elements in the quartet's development. Eschewing any further live appearances, they opted for studious rehearsals and spent much of 1983-84 composing and honing original songs. An assault on London was then undertaken but although largely unsuccessful, encouragement from Rough Trade's Geoff Travis helped bolster self-confidence. By the time of their second live date, at the Wednesday Club at Night Moves in Sauchiehall Street, Vortex Motion had become Wet Wet Wet, acknowledging the repetitive line in Scritti Politti's 'Getting, Having And Holding'.

'They were abysmal,' promoter Elliot Davis later declared in Q magazine, recalling the rudimentary demo tape through which he first heard the group. Something, however, must have proved attractive as he subsequently booked them for a support slot. 'Elliot was managing Sunset Gun,' Pellow explains, 'but when he put us on he realised we were better. We'd been working on our songs for two years before we did that gig. We didn't want to go out and play covers, we wanted people to like our own material.' Now converted to this new act, the budding entrepreneur not only folded his club, but also became the Wets' manager. Davis was already blooded in the music business - his clients had included the Wake and aforementioned Sunset Gun - but his new protégés inspired a more concerted effort. A label-cum-management company, the Precious Organisation, was inaugurated, bringing a sense of cohesion to their collective ambitions. Three groups, Wet Wet Wet, Moroccan Cocao and the Floor became its founding roster. 'Elliot's initial idea was management constancy,' states Cunningham, 'but over the next three months he pulled all three bands' instruments together and set up rehearsals in his bedsit. It became obvious it was a unit within itself and achieving something. We decided that whoever got the deal first would somehow help the other bands and finance things like offices.'

Showcase gigs stirred interest in Wet Wet Wet and the group undertook a series of demos at Wilf's Planet, the Edinburgh-based studio hand-built by the ubiquitous - and some say eccentric - Mr. Smarties. The results captured the quartet's strengths, in particular Pellow's already distinctive phrasing, and a sometimes scurrilous bidding war broke out between several major labels once the resultant tape began to circulate.

Wet Wet Wet joined Phonogram in 1985, but despite diligent pre-planning, encountered the problems they had hoped to avoid when the subject of a producer was mooted. The band foresaw no difficulty, naively proclaiming names culled from their favourite albums - Thom Bell or Goffin/King - but these were rejected as passe with respect to contemporary pop. The quartet were instead saddled with John Ryan, 'hot' on the strength of a hit with Animation, but the results were little short of disastrous. A liaison with Pet Shop Boys' svengali Stephen Hague was equally moribund while an increasingly fraught A&R director drove an irrevocable wedge between himself and Precious by throwing a second Smarties demo back at the band. Salvation arrived, albeit after a year, when Wets' publisher, Jill Steen, approached Willie Mitchell.

At almost 60 years of age, Mitchell can rightfully be described as a veteran. Based for most of his career in Memphis, Tennessee, he led numerous versions of a tough, rhythmic dance band during the 50s and 60s, before becoming vice-president and house producer for the Hi label. Al Green, Ann Peebles, Syl Johnson and O.V. Wright were among the peerless vocalists he worked with, and it was this impressive pedigree which attracted Wet Wet Wet. The results continued the musical affection engendered by Frankie Miller's collaboration with Allen Toussaint, or when the Average White Band signed with Atlantic. The Glasgow quartet acknowledge the value of their Memphis experience. 'We found ourselves working with legends,' states Cunningham. 'The studio was still run in the way it had been in the 60s - get the feeling, get the vibe - rather than constantly watch the clock. It was imperfect compared to today's standards, but it has a warmth and emotion that makes it timeless.'

Despite the group's ardour, Phonogram rejected the final tapes. They sensed the producer's mistrust of modern technology, but where the portions featuring synthesisers sound compromised, those retaining the whiff of classic southern soul are engaging. Rumours of a 'too black' epithet abounded, and group and label were again pitched into negotiations. Once more Davis argued in favour of the Smarties' demos and a beleaguered A&R staff eventually consented. New parts were overdubbed on 'Wishing I Was Lucky', which in turn rose to the number 6 spot in 1987, some two years after its initial recording.

The single's success helped deflect the scepticism surrounding Wet Wet Wet. The protracted wrangles enhanced the feeling of hype felt in rival Scottish quarters, and a situation which otherwise might have provoked solidarity was more often treated with scorn. Much of this was due to their manager's abrasive manner. Yet his group had not only survived, but prospered, and the uncompromising Precious Organization had reaped commercial rewards.

'Sweet Little Mystery', completed with new producer Michael Baker, became the quartet's second single. A Top 5 hit, it was the subject of further controversy when Van Morrison detected two lines obviously drawn from his own song, 'A Sense Of Wonder'. 'We did it to pay homage,' Pellow declared to Q, but their mentor was unmoved, and a settlement was reached only in the wake of table-top skirmishes. Sensing a minor scandal, some critics accentuated the whiff of plagiarism by pointing out that 'Sweet Little Mystery' was itself the title of a John Martyn song, or that the parenthesis-bound qualification of 'I Don't Believe', 'Sonny's Lettah', came from Linton Kwesi Johnson. When another Wets' original, 'Angel Eyes', contained a couplet taken from 'Heartbreaking World' by Squeeze, the words 'thieves' and 'magpies' were suddenly everywhere. The fact that the latter act had sanctioned the compliment cut little ice.

The transformation of 'Angel Eyes', from ill-focused canter to tender ballad, signalled a newfound maturity. Another Top 5 hit, it consolidated the success of the Wets' debut album, *Popped In Souled Out*, which did little to deflect detractors, yet delighted legions of newfound aficionados. A chart-topping smash, it wiped clear the debt accrued during the fraught two-year hiatus and helped lessen the pain of its ensuing traumas.

'With A Little Help From My Friends', recorded on behalf of the

Childline charity, was the group's final affirmation. Initially one of several contrasting acts featured on a reworking of the Beatles' *Sgt. Pepper* album, 'Sgt. Pepper Knew My Father', the Wets' contribution was later lifted as a single. 'Childline was in financial trouble,' Tom Cunningham explains. 'The album sales weren't going to be enough. Billy Bragg and ourselves thought about putting our tracks on a b-side to make money for it in a hidden sort of way, but then we thought why not do a double 'A', and that way reach the indie market with Billy and at the same time get over to the TV appeal we were having at the time.' When the group's emollient interpretation became a number 1 single, Phonogram duly exhumed the Mitchell recordings - now dubbed *The Memphis Demos* - which were issued in their own right in 1988. Undoubtedly meritorious, the set nonetheless reveals a quite different perspective to the group which achieved success. It is not a matter of better or worse, merely that of contrasting approaches.

Where the Wets had embraced the Radio 1 factor, and were perceived as chirpily 'playing the game', Love And Money steered a more awkward course between art and commerce. 'The whole reason behind Love And Money was contradiction,' James Grant explains. 'Contradiction between good and bad, between upfront noise and heart-rending ballads, between corporate image and me.' A second album, *Strange Kind Of Love*, issued in 1988, showed the maturation of a remarkable talent. Produced by former Steely Dan catalyst Gary Katz, the set revealed Grant's skills as a composer and lyricist as well as his hitherto well-masked vulnerability. The title song alone enthrals; Grant's delicately sonorous voice flows across its intricate arrangement, and the same qualities appear on two other key inclusions, 'Shape Of Things To Come' and 'Inflammable'. The group had not shed its affection for dance-based material, as evinced on 'Hallelujah Man', 'Razorsedge' and 'Up Escalator', although these were less convincing, as Grant concurs. 'It's a good set of songs but we didn't go the whole way. It still clung on to a rock/funk sort of thing.' James is also critical of some of Katz' procedures. 'He made me feel I couldn't sing. Some of the tracks we did 30 times and at the end of the day we were dropping in on syllables. Parts of it were really enjoyable - he was a really lovely guy - but in retrospect I've had this paranoia about my voice ever since.

'The sessions dragged on and on,' he continues. 'It was the record that was never finished. The songs were already a year and a half to two years old by the time we got to work with Katz, so again the new stuff I was writing was moving in a slightly different direction.'

It was during a UK tour in support of the album that Grant confronted this particular dilemma. 'I was very depressed,' he admits, 'and was ready to give up. We were doing a couple of nights at the Glasgow School of Art and I sat everybody down and told them I wasn't happy and that things would have to change.' Love And Money's answer was an acoustic set which was slotted in midway through the programme. This simple solution galvanised Grant and restored his enthusiasm. 'I was getting something out of it again,' he states. 'It was more honest, more me.' The group toured for eight months out of the ensuing twelve and then repaired to Glasgow to recuperate and plan a third collection.

Wet Wet Wet had meanwhile completed a second album, *Holding Back The River*. Although armed with the commercial success of its predecessor, the group wished to redress a commonly-held perception that their glossy style lacked conviction and thus the concept of an adult premise flourished. 'We are first and foremost a soul band...in attitude and direction,' they had lustily proclaimed on that debut album, but their ambition now was loftier. Yet however calculated, the gamble failed because *Holding Back The River* not only sold less than *Popped In*, but was largely mauled by critics. The group's US outlet, MCA, did not even bother to release it. 'We should never had produced that album ourselves,' Neil Clarke opined in *Vox*, 'but you live by your failures as much as your success.' 'We wanted to get a bit of credibility,' added Pellow. 'We wanted to grow our hair and be a bit less manufactured, but Phonogram were saying we would alienate our early fans. Maybe they were right.'

Holding Back The River lacked focus, but where the version of Rod Stewart's 'Maggie Mae' was woefully misguided, the title track offered potential. 'We were in a Glasgow pub called the Saracens' Head,' Tom Cunningham explains, 'and we got talking to this elderly guy who'd suffered from severe alcoholism. He'd lost his family and his friends and was like a down-and-out. He was drinking this drink you get in there called a White Tornado and having told us this story, he lifted up the glass and said "There's no holding back this river."' While obviously sympathetic, the Wets' couplets reveal how much they still had to learn in the art of honing incisive lyrics. The song suffers from ill-focused ambiguity, a charge which could be equally levelled at the album itself.

Subsequent backroom intrigues were largely, by their nature, held in-camera, but rumours of a serious rift between Precious and Phonogram abounded. These became more intense when a brace of singles, issued as tasters for the forthcoming third album, failed to hit commercial paydirt. These flops, which included 'Make It Tonight', a song sculpted around *Popped In* trademarks, intensified the friction and the release of *High On The Happy Side* was postponed while the group rushed into Glasgow's Ca Va studio to complete an accompanying 'give-away' set of cover versions. Historians took note that one such inclusion was initially cut by the Average White Band.

The trauma ended with 'Goodnight Girl'. The Wets' promotional appearance on *The Des O'Connor Show* is largely credited with launching this chart-topping single, but its crafted simplicity is surely a more relevant key to its subsequent success. The simple arrangement allowed Pellow's voice to soar and fall unfettered, while the strings combined with the group's finely-wrought harmonies to create the perfect counterpoint. Where the Wets might have previously over-elaborated, here they allowed the melody to flow in a way which captured all their strengths. Not for the first time, the group had teetered on the brink, only to turn and prove their critics wrong.

Wet Wet Wet remain an undoubted paradox. Despite the increasingly mature slant prevalent on *High On The Happy Side* (1992), they have yet to secure the adult approbation they assiduously court and the success of 'Goodnight Girl' rekindled the spectre of more temporary, teenage-based, trappings. Yet their dogged perseverance deserves respect and the image of four schoolfriends, still together making music, is alluringly romantic. Elliot Davis proudly stresses their commitment to Scotland; the group live in Glasgow, Precious is still based there, and the complex boasts a recording studio as well as several new, as yet unproven, signings; Boom, Walk Don't Run and Worldwide. Wet Wet Wet may never solve their artistic conundrum, but less than 12 months on from their 'last chance' single, they appeared live to a reverential audience on Edinburgh Castle's esplanade.

The dilemmas facing Love And Money during 1990 proved even more acute. Personal relationships had been torn apart in the wake of the previous year's touring circus. Grant's emotive musical reaction, chronicled on *The Mother's Boy*, caused corporate apoplexy. 'I wanted to change the way the band was perceived,' he admitted to *Vox*, 'but I really went overboard. It was nervous breakdown material, I was really getting into a misanthropic swing, and was like (a combination of) Bukowski, Celine and Rimbaud.' The resultant tapes were shelved, but having expunged those particular demons, Grant commenced work on what became *Dogs In The Traffic*. 'This time I knew what I was doing,' he states. 'No dance or funk tracks, we had arguments about that, but I said it was time to make that break.

'The record was personal,' he continues, 'but the cathartic element wasn't as strong as I would have liked it to be. During the time it was, but the record company were so desirous of a single that they kept putting us in again and again.' The concord between group and outlet collapsed to such an extent that the former's wages were stopped to force Grant into the studio - the resultant vitriol spread into the press - but James, in retrospect, is now more sanguine. 'We were having a bad relationship but we're not an easy band to A&R. If you're going to be signed to a major record company, you have to take what's going with the territory.'

Dogs In The Traffic was issued in 1991 to universal acclaim. Where *Strange Kind Of Love* was sleek, this is edgy, intense and troubled. Grant's pungent lyrics and meticulous melodies wove an intricate, introspective path, but the final impression, of scarred betrayal, was genuinely moving. 'Much of the record is like an open wound,' he explains. 'People have said it's grim and depressing and I take that as a compliment. I'm glad that's come across. It's the first record I've made that I felt truly represented me and the way I feel. If people want to know who I am they'll find out a lot more from *Dogs In The Traffic* than they will from the previous albums.'

An exhausted Grant refused to tour to promote the album's release, a situation which again caused strife with Phonogram. The gulf appeared irreconcilable yet, to the amazement of several parties, the label picked up its option for a fourth album. A trimmed-down line-up - Grant, Paul McGeehan, Douglas McIntyre and Gordon Wilson - duly began work in the singer's home-based studio, the results of which should confirm James Grant's position of one of rock's most beguiling talents. 'Our records are all so different,' he states, 'and to me that's the most natural thing to do. An album is like a painting - it's complete, it's done, don't paint it again.'

CHAPTER 20
TRUCKLOAD OF TROUBLE

'I think, when you're taking about anything from the 60s that's common to us, I would say something like the Rolling Stones...'Satisfaction'.' - Jim Reid, Jesus And Mary Chain, *Cut*, 1987.

It's difficult to remember those same Dartford renegades as pop's enfants terribles, or the fear and loathing their image and music so often inspired. Age begets respectability, and like the Chuck Berry riffs which provided its inspiration, the classic Rolling Stones' catalogue now flirts with the veneer of cliché. Yet 'Satisfaction' was once dangerous, and by blurring cultural and sexual frustrations, including an allusion to menstruation, declared war on a succession of taboos. Some 16 years later the Jesus And Mary Chain proved equally subversive.

'We tried all over Glasgow for a gig,' Jim Reid stated in 1987, when recalling the group's early months. 'We were asking all these shitty groups, "Can we support you?", and they just laughed.' Derided by a circuit relieved of zealots in the absence of Postcard or Fast, the Mary Chain, as residents of East Kilbride, were doubly hampered through being outsiders. The group's core, brothers Jim and William Reid, thus spent the formative early 80s preparing home-made demos, sacrificing formal progression for the greater goal of self-expression. 'We were hungry for new music,' Jim explains, 'and the lack of a record to buy was as much our motivation as anything else.' 'Our father was made redundant,' adds William, 'and we bought a porta-studio. That was when we realised we could do it.' Demos, some reportedly under the name the Poppy Seeds, brought no response, even from Postcard, but an ensuing sense of frustration enhanced the pair's already defined determination. They were also not alone and, while fragmented and largely unaware of each other's aspirations, a new generation of groups emerged, kicking against what they saw as stifling complacency. Among these was the Pastels, led by Stephen McRobbie, better known as Stephen Pastel.

A fan of melodic pop - the Ramones, the Buzzcocks and the Modern

The Pastels

Lovers - Stephen formed the Pastels with Brian Taylor, aka Brian Superstar (guitar) and Chris Gordon (drums), 'who had played in Orange Juice before Stephen Daly'. Gordon left the line-up soon afterwards and although several bassists also proved equally temporary, McRobbie was determined to record as soon as was feasible. 'We felt that by the early 80s the rules were changing back,' he explains, 'and that was why we wanted to issue things. We knew we'd get laughed at because of our musical ability, but we didn't care. We wanted to stand up and represent something quite different.' The Pastels intention to learn in public began in October 1982 with 'Heavens Above!'/'Tea Time Tales', which was released under the title *Songs For Children* by the London-based independent Whaam!. The fascinating outlet was founded by Dan Treacy and Edward Ball of the Television Personalities, and the importance to young Scotland of this latter act cannot be overstated. Their quirky pop melodies and ingrained irony inspired several willing disciples. If early singles, including 'Part-Time Punks' and 'Where's Bill Grundy Now', acknowledged late 70s tribulations, they did so with a sound for which 'amateurish' was barely applicable. The songs themselves, however, were distinctly memorable, invoking the ghosts of other-era classics, and the TVP's were equally quick at addressing 60s icons. 'I Know Where Syd Barrett Lives' and 'David Hockney's Diary' are two more memorable titles in what evolved into an enthralling catalogue, but the strongest is arguably 'Someone To Share My Life With', a fragile refrain beloved by those later dubbed, somewhat derisively, 'anorak' bands. The implicit symbolism - floppy fringes, trainspotting pop and winsome immaturity - was an unfortunate generalisation. It offered a disservice to the aspirations of another disenfranchised generation, one preferring simple observations and self-disparagement to cultivated angst. 'Hearing our early stuff,' Stephen Pastel later observed, 'reminds me of what an effete 20-year-old I was, but I'm quite proud of what we were, or what we perceived ourselves to be.'

The Pastels' association with Whaam! began in the most straightforward manner. 'I noticed Dan was putting out records by more and more groups,' Stephen explained, 'and I sent him a tape of *Songs For Children*. He wrote back straight away to say he'd like to put it out.' The label faltered when Treacy succumbed to a nervous breakdown, and the Pastels' second single, the bubbling 'I Wonder Why', appeared on Rough Trade in April 1983. Its release, however, caused several problems. 'We didn't particularly like that song, nor the way it was recorded,' Stephen admits. 'Rough Trade were trying to throw off their amateur tag and somehow thought they could make the Pastels glossier and get them into this Paul Morley 80s pop boom. We never cared for that.' Despite these reservations, the Pastels were clearly becoming more confident, and while still coming to grips with technique, showed an undoubted desire to create something within their own framework. The

Alan McGee and the Laughing Apple EP

quartet was obviously more than a whim, and as such became one of the first to sign with Creation, another London-based label, though run by expatriot Scot, Alan McGee. 'Alan was a fan of the Television Personalities,' Stephen recalls, 'and was very enthusiastic about what he saw as a whole movement of bands that were rudimentary, but tried to be melodic within their means. There was some bad feeling over our second single - Geoff Travis had wanted us for blanco y negro, but it appeared on Rough Trade because they had accumulated the bill - and so Alan said "record for me." We made 'Something's Going On', which is the first of our records that I really liked.'

Although best-known for his activity-in-exile, McGee's musical taste was well-defined before leaving Glasgow. Punk inevitably provided the impetus, but this particular obsession was tinged by a hint of regret. 'It was great to be destructive about things,' he recalls, 'but I also loved the Lynyrd Skynyrd concerts, and punk sadly killed a lot of people's imagination.' By 1978, Alan's sole desire was to join a band, an ambition realised, by chance, on tuning to Radio Clyde. 'Brian Ford ran an advertisement for a group called the Drains,' he recalls. 'I telephoned the number and Andrew Innes answered.' Guitarist Innes had attended the same school as McGee and, unbeknown to either, shared a similar taste in music, although third member Pete Buchannan proved less compatible. 'We did two rehearsals then kicked him out,' states McGee, 'and then brought Bobby in.'

'Bobby' is Bobby Gillespie, another school friend, although he now argues his role within this group was largely decorative. 'It was really Andrew's band. They had guitars and could play punk rock songs and I'd roll about the floor, screaming.' Innes and McGee later abandoned the group's unimaginative sobriquet and became instead Captain Scarlet And The Mysterons. An offer from another quarter brought this equally short-lived liaison to an end. 'Ian Donaldson from Screw asked me to be bass player in H2O,' recalls McGee. 'He said it would be like the New York Dolls so I got Andrew Innes to join. After four gigs it was obvious it was more like Kajagoogoo.' Donaldson's desires eventually found commercial succour with the anodyne 'Dream To Sleep', while his prodigal ex-partners formed NuSpeak with Neil Clark. 'We played in Glasgow for about a year,' adds McGee. 'It was great fun for a while - we were like a fourth division XTC - but by 1980 the city was being suffocated. The Cuban Heels were a tip for the top and that was really depressing. We thought "Fuck it, let's go to London."'

By this point McGee and Innes had formed the Laughing Apple, a trio which completed three 7-inch releases. *The Ha Ha Hee Hee* EP was recorded in 1980 at Kilmarnock's Sirocco studio, 'with thanks to Govan CND', while 'Participate' followed some months later. Both were issued by McGee on Autonomy, which he established on moving south, and the tracks reveal an undoubted confidence, albeit one bereft of common purpose. The final release, 'Precious Feeling', appeared on Essential Records, but his relocation to London had altered McGee's priorities. 'I'd lost interest in being in a band, and my musical taste had changed. I was massively into the Byrds and Syd Barrett and loved the TVPs and all these English pop-art bands.' Alan then established the Communication Club, and attendant fanzine *Communication Blur,* but these early ventures proved both premature and uncommercial. 'I was working for British Rail,' he recalls, 'earning £70 a week, which I'd lose promoting the Go-Betweens. I did, however, learn a lot.' Having abandoned these projects, McGee founded the Living Room at the Adams Arms in Tottenham Court Road. As he freely attests, this particular venue would change his life. 'We called it the Living Room because it was so small - the place held about 150 people - and we opened just when something in music changed. It was full when the TVPs played whereas a year before only 20 would have come. There hadn't been an indie club in London before and now here was this little, exclusive mad place right in the city centre.'

Within six months the Living Room was running at a profit and in 1983 McGee founded a label to showcase groups he liked. Reverentially named after the 60s mod-pop act, Creation drew its inspiration from two seminal sources. 'The close-knit thing was definitely Postcard,' McGee recalls, 'whereas the artwork was Dan Treacy.' Creation's first releases were, like those of its mentors, highly striking. Their wrap-around jackets were visually distinctive, although once again a lack of funds determined the style. 'Those first releases were 7-inch only because we couldn't afford anything else. Bobby knew a printer in Scotland who supplied the paper cheaply and we stayed up for nights folding the sleeves. It was a boutique label - the club supplemented any losses - and the early singles were just records, rather than careers.' Having launched the label with rock scribe the Legend's '73 in 83', McGee then unleashed 'Flowers In The Sky', the sole, yet haunting, effort by Revolving Paint Dream, a group centred on Andrew Innes. The fourth release was 'Fifty Years Of Fun', the debut by Alan's own concoction, Biff Bang Pow!, which by 1991 had completed a myriad of singles and six often transfixing albums. Despite this prolific output, McGee maintains the group was always just a hobby. 'However we did do a couple of German tours and pulled in 4-500 people a night. It got a bit frightening and I began to get delusions that maybe I was Bob Dylan and not Andrew Loog Oldham.'

Creation's first longer-term project was the Jasmine Minks, a group from Aberdeen later bolstered by ex-TVP Dave Musker. Their first single, 'Think', was followed in December 1983 by the Pastels' 'Something Going On', which was, without question, the group's strongest recording to date. Faintly west coast guitars buoyed a purposeful solo, and if the skills remained rudimentary, Stephen's sense of ambition was clearly revealed as boundless. Indeed the subsequent release, 'Million Tears'/'Baby Honey', gave a lie to the 'anorak' cliché, contrasting its effortless topside with a riff-laden flip quite unlike anything the Pastels had previously attempted. The result is quite magnificent and the latter remains a lynch-pin in the Pastels catalogue, in part through several subsequent revivals. 'It's just a riff we like playing a lot,' Stephen explains, 'and I never felt we'd done it justice on record.'

Creation's burgeoning reputation did not go unnoticed in Scotland, particularly among those close to McGee. Having played bass briefly in the Wake, whose Joy Division inflections found reward in a deal with Factory, Bobby Gillespie had resumed his role as vocalist in Primal Scream, a group he instigated with guitarist Jim Beattie. Their name was a phrase Bobby had picked up - 'It sounded kinda mythical, like a weird gang,' he later recounted - although the mystique remained when they discovered its source was a form of exorcist psychotherapy, the techniques of which inspired the *Plastic Ono Band* sets by John Lennon and Yoko Ono.

'The first-ever Primal Scream gig was at the Bungalow Bar in Paisley,' recalls Beattie. 'We supported the Laughing Apple. Only one song in the set was ours, and I remember it as just total noise.' Gillespie does concur with that last statement, but takes issue over its relevance. 'That wasn't a real gig,' he states. 'It was a joke. There wasn't any shape to it at all' Yet from this rudimentary start the founder members looked for other musicians to complete a line-up normally bolstered by whoever was around.

'We wanted to make a real jump,' states Gillespie, 'and do 12-string Byrds-type things and play structured pop songs with real melodies.' To this end he and Beattie turned up at the Candy Club, run at Lorne Hotel by Nick Low and Stephen Pastel. 'Nick Low was a friend of Andrew Innes,' Bobby recounts, 'and we told him we were trying to form a band.' Not unnaturally Low was in receipt of many aspirants' cassettes, and he duly passed on a tape he'd recently received from what he assumed was another duo, the Jesus And Mary Chain. 'We'd sent this guy our demo,' recalls Jim Reid. 'which we taped on the other side of a Syd Barrett compilation. We thought we'd get a gig out of it, but he wasn't interested in having us so he gave the cassette to Bobby.' 'I only got it because he thought I might like the Syd Barrett stuff,' adds Gillespie, 'but I was blown away by the other side. I played it to Jim and he felt the same way.' For a moment it seemed that Primal Scream had found ideal new recruits, but on calling the contact number on the box, they spoke to the third Mary Chain member, bassist Douglas Hart. 'In fact all they needed was a drummer,' Bobby recalls, 'but we spoke for two hours about all the things we were into; music, films and stuff like that.' Yet if discovery of mutual musical interests inspired both parties, it proved more crucial to the Mary Chain. 'We're lazy people,'

The back cover of the Jesus & Mary Chain's 'Upside Down'

admits William Reid, 'and I don't know how long we'd have sat on our arses.' 'Talking to Bobby was so important,' adds Jim, 'We didn't know anyone who was into garage and psychedelia and here we'd discovered somebody else had the same taste.'

The Mary Chain were suddenly in demand. Not only had a Glasgow gig materialised from a quite independent source, but Gillespie had persuaded McGee to put them on at the Living Room. It gave the Reids yet another impetus. 'We didn't actually have a band,' explains William, 'and we'd only written four songs. Now we had to rehearse and write more material.' 'We were up on the stage,' adds Jim, 'doing this supposed soundcheck. We'd been getting on each other's nerves all day and just stood there making a racket screaming at each other. We thought we'd blown it and were ready to go home but McGee said it was brilliant.' 'After one song I knew they were genius,' Alan confirms, and the group was immediately offered a recording deal. In retrospect the brothers disagree on the merits of their subsequent performance, with William declaring it 'Fucking deep with noise...we were flying,' in a later interview. 'Shite' was Jim's memory, but despite this apparent inconsistency, McGee not only signed the group to Creation, he also became their manager.

The Jesus And Mary Chain made its recording debut in 1984 with the carthitic 'Upside Down', a cavernous slab of barely-controlled noise, with screaming feedback, basic bass and drums, and eerie, disengaged vocals. 'It wasn't a plan,' explained Jim. 'It wasn't "let's turn the feedback up". This was just the natural way for us to make music. There was no discussion about it, that was the way it sounded from the first rehearsal.

'We recorded that single in some grotty London studio in the middle of the night when it was cheaper,' he adds. 'We did three songs; 'In A Hole' turned out crap, but 'Upside Down' was exactly the way we wanted to be. We slipped out at six in the morning with a classic rock 'n' roll track.' If the instrumentation invoked the Stooges or Velvet Underground, the harmonies were Californian surf, and indeed the melody, like those of fellow sonic terrorists Hüsker Dü, was instantly memorable. 'We loved noise,' added William, 'but we also love good songs. The contrast never really occurred to us. A lot was instinct, stumbling about towards the next recording. We're too self absorbed to by analytical.' Meanwhile the flip, which was produced by (Slaughter) Joe Foster, another TVP refugee and now working in-house at Creation, paid homage to a mutual talisman through a suitably anarchic rendition of Syd Barrett's 'Vegetable Man'.

'Upside Down' was rightly hailed as essential, confering adulation on both label and performers. The Mary Chain were suddenly feted and Glasgow venues from which they'd once been barred now clamoured to offer headline slots. There was, however, a more pressing problem as drummer Murray

Dalglish had been axed immediately the single was completed. Several vital live appearances loomed, and the Reids invited Bobby Gillespie to step in, unconcerned by the fact he couldn't play. 'Neither could Murray,' they grimly attest. On 11 October 1984, at Glasgow's Venue, Primal Scream completed its set as support - one which Bobby feels marks the group's official debut - whereupon he took up a standing position for the Mary Chain's set. Gillespie remained in the line-up over the next 15 months.

The group then switched outlets to WEA via its blanco y negro offshoot. A series of stellar singles ensued - 'Never Understand', 'You Trip Me Up' and 'Just Like Honey' - while the Mary Chain and controversy seemed inseparable. The most glaring example occurred in March 1985 at North London Polytechnic, when a riot broke out in the wake of a customary short, intensive, set. Bobby had kicked open the doors to allow entry to frustrated ticket-holders, but his gesture merely exacerbated tension. Billed as Art As Terrorism, the event degenerated quickly, ending when the audience symbolically trashed the group's equipment. Further conflict followed two months later when a planned flip-side, 'Jesus Suck', was abandoned in the face of recalcitrant pressing plants.

Such recurrent problems did not deflect the Mary Chain vision. Released in November 1985, *Psychocandy* was a quite startling collection, combining aural assault with moments of genuine vulnerability. Nowhere was the contrast more marked than between the delicate 'Cut Dead' and piercing 'In A Hole', re-recorded to the group's satisfaction. Yet despite a perceived nihilism, it was clear the Jesus And Mary Chain were passionate adherents of true pop culture. In the same way as Orange Juice had offered a warped interpretation of Love and the Byrds, so the Reids suggested a darker, more desolate Beach Boys. Or, in the case of 'Sowing Seeds', something akin to the girl-group genre of the Chiffons or Crystals. 'Anger was a big reaction to the music scene at that time,' Jim explains. 'It was the end of *New Musical Express*' cocktail thing with Kid Creole And The Coconuts. That repulsed us. We didn't consciously think of it in that way, but it was us doing the opposite of all that shit.' *Psychocandy* encapsulated attitude and sound, and having embraced William's machine-gun technique, the listener is left to bask in what are exceptional tunes.

Creation continued to evolve with passion, despite the defection of the Mary Chain, and the Pastels maintained their inexorable rise with 'I'm Alright With You'. Better still were its couplings, 'Couldn't Care Less' and 'What's It Worth', the latter of which revealed an enchanting melancholia. Yet, as Stephen Pastel recalls, the group's progress was highly informal. 'We were rarely in the same location at the same time. Martin Hayward and Bernice Swanson were at St. Andrews University, I was at Strathclyde and Brian was working. It was quite haphazard.' The single marked the end of the Pastels' spell with Creation whose next crucial acquisition was Primal Scream, still fronted by Bobby Gillespie despite his commitment to the Reid brothers. He and Beattie had been joined by bassist Robert Young, while Tom McGurk was one of several impermanent drummers. 'Robert had been in a band called Black Tuesday,' Beattie relates. 'We got him for a gig at the Glasgow School of Art. He was only in for one song, but after four he left them and joined us.'

The early Primal Scream was clearly balanced between Gillespie and Jim Beattie. These co-founders determined the group's direction wherein Beattie's affection for Byrds-like chimes supported Bobby's engagingly languid intonation. 'I didn't know I was going to be the singer', he relates, and indeed an early session featured a quite different vocalist. 'We did a song called 'The Orchard',' recalls Beattie. 'Judith (Boyle) was playing violin with us and as Bobby had a cold we got her to sing. This meant a girl was singing a lyric about a girl...we burnt the master tape.' Gillespie argues it was just another demo - 'not important' - whereas Jim states it was a possible single. But Primal Scream's debut release, 'All Fall Down', was much more orthodox. and, although primitive, offered an enthralling atmosphere. Beattie, however, has some reservations. 'It wasn't the classic it should have been, but we just didn't

Primal Scream's debut release; 'All Fall Down'

have the necessary experience. I borrowed this 12-string Rickenbacker copy which had an original neck that was once owned by Jim McGuinn, and when the engineer asked what kind of sound I wanted I said "Imperial, majestic". He really didn't have a clue.' The flip-side, 'It Happens', was just as strong although Gillespie feels it failed to come near their aspirations. 'We wanted it to sound like Love's 'She Comes In Colours', and when you know that you know why it didn't work.'

Despite its intrinsic merit, 'All Fall Down' did not boast a sense of occasion and was seen simply as another strong Creation single in line with releases by the Loft, Slaughter Joe and Meat Whiplash. The last-named, like the Mary Chain, were from East Kilbride. Having taken their name from the Fire Engines and a cue from 'Upside Down', Paul McDermott (vocals), Stephen McLean (guitar), Eddie Connelly (bass) and Michael Kerr (drums) completed a noise-infested offering, in which 'Don't Slip Up' and 'Here It Comes' recalled the brattish power of their mentors. 'The Mary Chain gave them a gig at North London Polytechnic,' recalls McGee, 'and during the set Jim Reid's cousin threw a bottle into the audience. A guy got up onstage and all the band ran off leaving Eddie on his own. At that point I offered them a deal. They were a truly terrible band,' he adds, 'which is why the Mary Chain play on the single, but 'Don't Slip Up' is a classic song.'

Bobby Gillespie remained in the Mary Chain until February 1986. He completed tours of the Continent and USA, but when Jim and William Reid demanded a full-time commitment, the singer opted for his own group. 'I really had to think about it,' he now recalls. 'I never really enjoyed being in Primal Scream at the time and it was a hard decision. But the Mary Chain is Jim and William's band and I knew I could express myself better in Primal Scream.' 'The situation couldn't have gone much further,' adds William Reid. 'Primal Scream were pretty frustrated because he was pissing around the world with us. It was also at a time when we wanted to change; use a drum machine or do something different.' Indeed, the immediate post-*Psychocandy* period was one of turmoil in which the Reids not only parted company with bassist Douglas Hart, but also Alan McGee. 'Douglas was a friend,' states Jim. 'He was into the same music and had the same sense of humour, but he was never a studio bass player. We had to show him what we wanted and then he'd play a terrible version of it.' Despite the composite credit, Hart was only present on half the Mary Chain's debut, notably those already honed live. Meanwhile, the group's break with their manager, although rancorous at the time, is now seen more dispassionately. 'Alan had just set up Elevation,' states Jim, referring to a new label undertaken with WEA. 'It seemed he was getting busier with that and maybe neglecting us.' 'It was inexperience on my part,' confirms McGee. 'There's no room for anything else when you're involved with the Mary Chain,' but adds 'Creation would not be the success it is without them.'

Bobby's loyalties now unambiguous, Primal Scream was further enhanced by the addition of John Martin, aka Martin St. John (tambourine). 'He brought an attitude to the group,' states Gillespie. 'We'd be working out the arrangement to a song and he'd sit there with his tambourine encouraging us, helping get a vibe going. He was into the Cramps and because Alex Chilton produced them he found the third Big Star album which was a big influence on the band.' The revitalised quintet celebrated its founding with a single, 'Crystal Crescent' which, although of interest, failed to fulfil its undoubted potential. 'Velocity Girl' however, was a quite different proposition, and its combination of ringing 12-string and propulsive rhythm was later taken, wholesale, by a piratical Stone Roses for their inferior 'Made Of Stone'. The final inclusion, 'Spirea X', proved somewhat prophetic.

In September Bobby was one of a group of people responsible for founding Splash One, an alternative venue much welcomed in Glasgow's otherwise torpid pub circuit. 'It wasn't just me,' he stresses, 'there were five other people involved in it,' and Karen Parker, Derek Louden and Grant McDougal were also part of the committee responsible for this pivotal nightclub. The Mary Chain, the Pastels and Sonic Youth were among the showcased acts, while an extended licence allowed Gillespie scope to air his extensive, and eclectic, record collection. 'There was nowhere in Glasgow to see those bands or hear that kind of music. I didn't like all the groups we put on, but if you talk to people they'll tell you the place was a focus.'

Primal Scream had meanwhile welcomed, and lost, new guitarist Paul Harte - another Splash One inaugurator - while his replacement, Stuart May, later made way for Andrew Innes, whose arrival tilted the delicate balance of a group struggling to realise its artistic ambitions. McGurk was then replaced by Gavin Skinner, St. John dropped out altogether and thus, by 1987, Primal Scream was a markedly different act to that featured on 'Crystal Crescent'.

The realigned group then completed two singles for Elevation. 'Gentle Tuesday' was a gorgeous slice of folk-rock whimsy, while 'Imperial' offered a quite sumptuous melody line and almost aching tenderness. However, the relationship between group and the label's parent company, WEA, was not particularly happy. But, as Alan McGee suggests, it was a valuable learning process. 'It was good for Primal Scream to be on a major because they realised they could never fit.' The quartet then repaired to Rockfield to begin work on an album but sessions there were little short of disastrous. 'Residential life did not suit us,' claims Beattie, 'and it got really bizarre. We started saying things like 'That cymbal hit's not right' and began changing clothes for every solo. In fact I threatened the producer, Stephen Street, that I would play guitar in the nude, just to see how far we could take him.' Primal Scream abandoned this first effort and instead opted to begin again with exiled Texan Mayo Thompson, one-time member of the dissonant Red Crayola and Pere Ubu.

'We loved the racket on 'Hurricane Fighter Plane',' declared Beattie, admiring one of the former act's releases, while the American had already produced work by the Raincoats and Cabaret Voltaire. *Sonic Flower Groove* was, however, a little austere with Thompson's mathematical inclinations inhibiting the group's natural flair. 'Mayo's a great guy,' states Bobby, 'but although he's not really a producer, he did give us some encouragement.' 'It was too mechanical,' opines Beattie, but there are, nonetheless, several excellent inclusions, notably the chimerical 'Love You' and buoyant 'Treasure Trip'. However, once again potential had been undermined by an almost ill-focused blend of reverence and impetuosity. The sense of disappointment weakened an already fracturing line-up. 'We still didn't know what we were doing,' argues Gillespie. 'We tried to arrange the songs ourselves and I don't think we were very good at it. The group was too uptight. It needed to break up and find another thing.'

'We supported New Order at Wembley Arena which was fabulous,' recalls Beattie, 'but I then wanted to rest and write new songs. However, McGee had arranged another tour, which I started, but one night I left - it was just mental.' While acknowledging he still is not sure why Beattie quit, Gillespie offers another explanation. 'I felt what we were doing was too limiting and wanted to extend the group. I think Jim had a problem with that, and a problem with the other guys. It was never said outright, but in weird coded ways. It certainly didn't have anything to do with touring.' Whatever the reasons, the guitarist returned to Glasgow, exhausted, while Gillespie decided to settle in Brighton. Control of the group Beattie had co-founded was now out of his hands, and the subsequent development of both individuals show how estranged the one-time friends had become. 'Jim was a great folk-rock guitarist,' opined the singer, 'but Robert, who'd switched from bass, had a more bluesy and funky approach. We'd become a rock 'n' roll band.'

With Skinner also in absentia, Bobby introduced two new recruits, Henry Olsen (bass) and Philip Tomanov (drums), and began forging a style redolent of Detroit brats the Stooges and MC5. This aggressive sound was launched with 'Ivy Ivy Ivy', released on Creation in 1989 following the collapse of Elevation. Despite Gillespie's brave contemporary assertion 'Fuck you if you don't like it,', Primal Scream had merely adopted a new set of clichés and, however honestly they were portrayed, such trappings proved as restrictive as those they'd sought to abandon. The attendant album, *Primal Scream*, contained several similarly abrasive songs but suffered from a lack of conviction. While acknowledging its faults, Gillespie nonetheless welcomed the opportunities it offered. 'Primal Scream really only started with that album. We had to find new people for bass and drums and didn't get concerts until the record was out. We'd write songs then record them, and I think most of it suffers because of that. If we'd done it at the end of 1989, rather than the start, it would have been much better because we'd have played it live.' The ballads - 'You're Just

Dead Skin To Me', 'You're Just Too Dark To Care' and 'Kill The King' - were much stronger, oozing a fragile malevolence quite at odds with their brash counterparts. 'On acoustic guitar those songs sounded really nice,' says Bobby, 'like the Shirelles or something like that.'

'There's a certain art to writing rock 'n' roll songs,' he continues, 'and we were learning it on that album. There are certain melodies that don't go with Johnny Thunders' guitar and we had to make sacrifices. A lot of the songs were too pretty for their own good.' The gulf between frisson and melancholia resulted in a curiously schizophrenic set which bemused as many as it enthralled and suggested the group was unsure of a coherent direction. The solution lay in adopting quite different parameters.

Cut loose from the drummer, bassist and manager they were accustomed to, the Reids entered uncharted territory. For 18 months they handled their own affairs until, as William remarked, 'It was better to have someone else argue over promotional posters than have to do it yourself.' Replacement musicians were also sought and in one memorably mischievous appeal, the brothers demanded that the ideal drummer was required to know, by heart, Ginger Baker's solo from 'Toad' on Cream's *Wheels Of Fire*. 'We got some who did,' Jim ruefully recalls.

Successful applicants remained members on a purely temporary basis as the group embarked on a new direction. Their gradual retreat from white noise, apparent on successive singles, suggested a desire to avoid cliché. 'April Skies' released during its titular month in 1987, relied heavily on an enchanting refrain as the Mary Chain embraced a cleaner, less abrasive sound. This was not so apparent on its coupling, 'Kill Surf City', which offered quite overpowering distortion and the resultant contrast showed how defined the new métier had become. Many voiced disappointment when *Darklands*, a surprisingly skeletal set, appeared five months later, but the duo remain largely unrepentant. 'Looking back, my only regret is that we more or less decided that it was to be nothing like *Psychocandy*,' Jim declares. 'Everyone was raving about the first album, telling us to split up because it was perfect, and to try and make another record surrounded by that is next to impossible. Records should be made without expectations and it's a shame we weren't as uninhibited as we could have been.' '*Darklands* shouldn't have been a surprise,' William adds. 'We'd been telling people we were influenced by Burt Bacharach and Lee Hazelwood.'

Although more sombre than its predecessor, *Darklands* maintained the direction suggested on 'April Skies'. References to the Beach Boys still abound - 'Cherry Came Too' borrows illiberally from 'Surfin' Safari' - and the group's habit of writing on acoustic guitars made more sense in this less clamorous environment. This in turn suggested other styles to follow. 'We had the songs,'

Jim remembers, 'but then we'd listen to Suicide and think "why not make it an electronic album?" In some ways I wish we had because our version of it would have been nothing like a synthesizer record.' Now divorced from all the contemporary consternation, *Darklands* can be seen for its own merits and, in 'On The Wall', the set contains one of the group's most bewitching recordings. The last analysis, however, remains with Jim. 'I love *'Darklands'*. To be honest I prefer it to *Psychocandy*.'

The title track and 'Happy When It Rains' were subsequently culled as singles, and hidden on variants of the former's flip-side were 'Surfin' USA' and 'Here It Comes Again'. The first of these wedded samples of a fundamentalist preacher to Brian Wilson's celebratory ode, while the latter track toyed with dance rhythms. By 1988 Jim was openly voicing an interest in hip-hop and thus the joyful explosion unveiled on 'Sidewalking' was not completely surprising. 'It was a conscious attempt to modernise,' explains William, 'without degenerating into a Faces rip-off. Too many people love rock 'n' roll, but don't really want it to go forward. 'Sidewalking' was all sequencers, the chorus was done once then punched in on a sampler.' The ensuing sense of liberation was exciting and with it the Mary Chain had not just revitalised their art, but found a different base on which to build.

The 1989 album, *Automatic*, embraced these new possibilities. The sound showed neither the scrawl of *Psychocandy* nor the severity of *Darklands*, but the synthesised rhythms and loud, as opposed to ravaged, guitars, brought another perspective to the Mary Chain palate. Their ability to conjure melodies redolent of pop's pubescent era nonetheless remained intact, and 'Halfway To Crazy', with its nod to 'Love Is Strange', conjures images of a psychotic Bobby Vee. 'Coast To Coast', 'Gimmie Hell' and 'Blues From A Gun' are the crucial inclusions in what remains a largely overlooked collection. Despite adopting some of clubland's beat, the Reid's avowed love of rock 'n' roll was perceived as out of step in the realignment apparent elsewhere in 1989. This misconstrued view would, of course, be later cast aside.

CHAPTER 21
'WE DIDN'T HAVE ANY SCHEME TO BE BIGGER THAN ELVIS.'

Although popular perceptions would suggest otherwise, it is over simplistic to view 80s Glasgow pop in terms of polarisation. Most groups were neither 'either on the bus or off it', to quote Ken Kesey's Merry Pranksters, but somewhere in the middle. Pastels' guitarist Brian Superstar shared a flat with Elliott Davies, who in turn looked to Postcard's collective ethos during the formative days at Precious. Orange Juice covered Al Green's 'L.O.V.E' as their debut Polydor single, and although the world still awaits Wet Wet Wet's reciprocal 'Blue Boy', a notion of entrenchment is misleading. It should not be a surprise to find acts drawing elements from both.

'I was influenced by things like Joy Division, and Gang of Four, the Fall, I was a huge fan of the Fall,' states Justin Curry, vocalist/guitarist with del Amitri. 'There were all these other seminal things, the first albums by the Damned and the Clash, but we never wanted to sound like that. We always wanted the guitars to be clean and undistorted.' Too young to be part of the Night Moves or Postcard crowds, del Amitri joined several aspiring acts at another Glasgow venue. 'Our little scene revolved around the Cafe Vaudeville. A lot of young bands played there; it held maybe 40 people and you made your stage on the floor. You'd get £10 before the gig and go round to Canarvan Link PA Hire, carry the gear back, and play. We weren't looking for deals or anything - we all considered ourselves terribly arty - we were just trying to get an audience for what we did.'

Although Pop Gun and Sophisticated Boom Boom were among the other fledgling acts featured, del Amitri became the enclave's virtual houseband, maintaining a longstanding residency when the cafe became the Warzika Club. This in turn helped focus the group's musical path and in 1981 they made their first, albeit tentative, recording. 'John Dingwall of Stand And Deliver got in touch,' Curry recounts. 'He was doing a flexi-disc with the Bluebells and wanted us to be on it as well. Our manager at that time, Jackie Gribbon, had recorded tracks for a single which never came out and so we gave him 'What She Calls It'.' Coupled to the Bluebells' tremolo-drenched 'Happy Birthday', 'What She Calls It' captures a hint of del Amitri's early affection for twisting melody. The group was still viewed as something informal, although interest in other contemporaries helped alter this innocent outlook. 'I remember going to see the Pop Gun and the Casuals at Joannas,' states Curry. 'I was quite impressed by the Casuals and they, through various incarnations, became Lloyd Cole And The Commotions.'

Derby-born Lloyd Cole arrived in Glasgow to take up a course at the city's university. It was here he met guitarist Blair Cowan, who became an integral part of his musical development, and the future Commotions; Neil Clark (guitar), Lawrence Donegan (bass) and Stephen Irvine (drums). This able unit gave sympathetic support to the singer's brylcreemed beatnik pose, but although the quintet existed on the fringe of the Postcard posse, and were courted by the fledgling Precious Organisation, they remained stoically independent.

Del Amitri's first hard-vinyl release appeared in 1983 on No Strings, a new label set up by promoter - and Mary Chain abrogator - Nick Low.

Del Amitri

'Nick made £2,000 on this New Order concert at Tiffany's and he asked us if we'd like to make a record,' says Currie. 'Naturally we said yes.' The resultant single coupled 'Sense Sickness' with 'The Difference Is', both of which offered a winsome, implicitly acoustic perspective. Postcard was an obvious reference point, but Curry's lyricism gave the set its individuality. 'They were the first songs we'd written since Ian (Harvie) joined the band,' he relates. 'We got some good reviews but it didn't seem to do any good. We were still playing dodgy gigs around Scotland.' Indeed, unlike several geographical peers, del Amitri travailed a sometimes unappealing circuit, ranging from the far-flung highlands down to the Borders. There were thus many pitfalls to encounter. 'I remember playing the 3Js in Galashiels,' states Justin. 'The only people there were eight or nine bikers who were continuously playing 'Albatross' on the jukebox. We started our first number and the song was still blaring out. We stopped and asked the barman to turn it off, but he refused. There was something like 100 credits on the jukebox and there was no way he was going to turn it off. We did our entire set with 'Albatross' going on through it.'

The No Strings' roster did not end with del Amitri, and when Low asked Currie for suggestions, the latter offered Cafe Vaudeville acolytes Pop Gun. The group, now dubbed the Suede Crocodiles, recorded 'Stop The Rain'/'Pleasant Dreamer', before being showcased at Glasgow's Mayfair alongside Lloyd Cole and del Amitri. 'At that point Lloyd was thinking about doing an independent single,' Currie recalls, 'but they wanted a lot of money to record it and it didn't work out.' Having eschewed advances from the local moguls, Cole took his group to Polydor, where *Rattlesnakes* unveiled a talent guilty of literary pretensions, yet one imbued with an engaging grip of song construction. One can only admire a composition which refers to both Arthur Lee and Norman Mailer ('Are You Ready To Be Heartbroken'), while 'Perfect Skin' rang with the de rigour spark of the Byrds and Velvet Underground and the studied phrasing of Television's Tom Verlaine. 'We used to have this grandiose idea of ourselves as the new Staples Singers,' Cole recounted in 1986, 'but it only takes a couple of weeks to know there's something missing. When we recorded (those songs) we realised we were better at that kind of thing.'

'The Commotions were the first band I knew to get a publishing and recording deal,' Currie relates, 'and that, in turn, encouraged us.' Del Amitri meanwhile continued an independent path, and by 1984 were promoting their own gigs, many of which took on the air of an event. 'It could be very twee and self-consciously unpretentious,' the singer admits. 'At the Warzika we'd sometimes give out set lists, or else ask the audience to shout out songs and we'd play them in the order they chose. We never tried to be a cool band, our contemporaries were groups like the Wee Cherubs. We didn't have any schemes to be bigger than Elvis.'

The Wee Cherubs brand of minimalism was captured on a charming 1984 single, 'Dreaming'. The group later evolved into the Bachelor Pad, a name suggestive of the swinging 60s, and a period which the newformed act would draw upon. 'Girl Of Your Dreams' and 'Sha La La' surfaced on flexi-discs given away free with the ubiquitous *Simply Thrilled* fanzine, while a double a-side single, 'Albums Of Jack'/'Jack And Julian', enforced the unit's love of nonsense words and squeezy music. Their album, *Tales Of Hofmann*, is a minor gem, although its titular allusion to a chemical godfather was only one of several mooted. 'We thought of 'Dear Mother, Love Albert' and 'Johann Sebastian Bachelor Pad',' states vocalist Tommy Cherry. 'Then there was 'Bigger Than Christ's' and 'Fuck Off We're Mad',' he adds, rather mischievously.

Despite their own light-heartedness, del Amitri found themselves the subject of increased attention, some of which was distinctly negative. 'We always were an unfashionable group, almost deliberately,' Justin declares. 'Because of the people we were and the music we made we knew we couldn't compete with the Hipsways. What we did was often wilfully wacky and, in a way, was the kind of thing the Housemartins took to a logical conclusion.' It was thus events, not just out of the group's control, but also out of Glasgow, which pushed their career onward. 'Out of the blue we got a John Peel Roadshow,' Currie recalls, 'and then a few weeks later Peel 'phoned our flat and said he'd like to do a session. That was a real break.' Del Amitri - Justin Curry, Iain Harvie, Paul Tyagi and Bryan Tolland - joined Chrysalis soon after the set was aired.

The label fostered a jejune image, partly in response to the quartet's self-confessed blithe style, and a struggle for credibility ensued. 'One of our covers featured our heads sticking out of boxes of vegetables. It was funny, but an awful lot of people didn't get the joke and thought we were trying to be like the independent Monkees.' This particular view was indeed unfortunate, as the group's debut album showed their continued grasp of deceptively pithy melodies. Like Friends Again before them, del Amitri offered a summery, windblown pop, evocative in places of the Go-Betweens, but tinged with melancholia. There are moments when these pieces gel to perfection, particularly 'Former Owner', while elements of a wider frame of reference surface on the intermittently rumbustious 'Sticks And Stones, Girl'. 'It was fresh-faced, lyrical and there was a great deal of sensitive adolescence in there,' states Currie about that first set. 'It was very easy to get compared to Aztec Camera or Everything But The Girl. These are fair comparisons, but they limited us.'

Despite the optimism with which they entered the relationship, del Amitri quickly found the politics at Chrysalis a problem. 'The idea that music is only credible on an indie label is nonsense - the Sex Pistols were always on a major company - but we signed to Chrysalis in this 'it had to be independent' atmosphere. They had this 'pretend-indie', Big Star, which like other similar ventures, was supposed to marry the integrity of a small label with the muscle of a major. It doesn't work. You end up having all the pressures of a major - you must have hits - but groups on this separate outlet didn't get any help with promotion and were ignored by the others within the structure. You were expected to do everything yourself and I think we really learned from that experience.' The group fought long and hard to secure the producer they desired, Hugh Johns, and had to argue to have singles released. When the second of those, 'Hammering Heart', barely sold 1,000 copies, it was clear an immutable impasse had been reached. Del Amitri left a largely indifferent Chrysalis in 1986.

The quartet's one-time contemporaries were meanwhile enjoying contrasting fortunes. The Crocodiles in demise, lead vocalist Kevin McDermott began a solo career with a mini-album *Suffocation Blues*, released on No Strings in conjunction with Rough Trade. The artist's subsequent path has proved somewhat chequered, although it is not without lighter moments. When one track was deleted from a handful of copies of a subsequent pressing, those 'short-changed' were rewarded when Kevin sang the missing song live in their own front room. That one winner lived in Florida proved no hindrance.

His subsequent group - the Kevin McDermott Orchestra - became a highly popular live act as tours supporting Rod Stewart, Simple Minds and Sting attested. Their acclaimed debut album, *Mother Nature's Kitchen*, was released in 1989, but the quartet was one of the casualties during a putsch at Island Records. Undeterred, they completed *Bedazzled* on Glasgow studio Barclay 2's own outlet, 13, and the result was both an artistic and commercial success.

Sophisticated Boom Boom had barely emerged from cafe society before shedding one member and re-emerging as His Latest Flame. The 'new' act was an altogether more serious proposition - it's forerunner, however appealing, was ill-focused - and their sole album, *In Your Neighbourhood*, shows a confident group forging an AOR pop path, with jangly guitars and sculpted songs. It's highlight was 'American Blue' which, as group member Trisha Reid explains, 'was written while Reagan was in power. It's about America's gung ho attitude to anyone who doesn't agree with them or any government, elected democratically, that they don't want.'

As an all-woman quartet, His Latest Flame understandably resented lazy references to, for example, the Bangles. 'Nobody compares REM and U2 on the grounds they're both all-guys,' Trisha told *TLN* during a promotional interview, but pleasure that the album had been completed proved short-lived. The group was dropped by their label within weeks of its release and split up soon afterwards.

Parallels can thus be drawn with Strawberry Switchblade. Formed in 1981 as a mixed-gender quartet, the group was later reduced to a duo of Jill Bryson and Rose McDowall. Both were friends of Orange Juice drummer Stephen Daly, which explains their use of a name at that point allied to a song and projected fanzine. 'All our friends were in groups,' Jill later recounted, explaining why the act was formed and, like many contemporaries, she looked to punk as a touchstone. 'They all went on to do creative things,' she told *Smash Hits*. 'Simple Minds and Orange Juice used (it) to free them of inhibitions.'

The pair's songs reached, and impressed, Zoo label entrepreneurs David Balfe and Bill Drummond who then tried to secure a recording deal on their behalf. "Trees And Flowers' was recorded as a demo,' Jill explained, 'but we eventually decided to put it out as a single. It was star-studded - Roddy Frame played guitar, we used the Madness rhythm section - and it got a lot of publicity.' The cast aside, this enchanting debut, issued on the unlikely-dubbed 'the 92 Happy Customers Label', captured the duo's grasp of pure pop melody. When combined with the sense of melancholia pervading all their work, it created a delicate, yet poignant, tapestry.

Drummond subsequently took up an A&R position at WEA, where he set up the Korova label with Balfe, who now managed Strawberry Switchblade. Bryson and McDowall were signed to a deal in 1984, the same year they scored a Top 5 hit with 'Since Yesterday'. This was another wonderful pop single, but the duo's skills as crafted songwriters was engulfed by column inches on their image, an explosion of polka dots, lace and ribbons. 'We'd collect everything in the house that was red, clack and gold, share it out and stick it all over ourselves,' Rose explained to a *Smash Hits* audience and this 'novelty' aspect became the act's hookline, rather than their music. A follow-up release, 'Let Her Go' barely scraped the Top 60, yet it remains one of the pair's finest creations, a sumptuous melange of sound and implicit tragedy.

Strawberry Switchblade continued in similar vein, and if the techno-pop of computerised drumming is occasionally distracting, the material is uniformly excellent. Few albums, in any sphere, are as consistent; dazzling pop songs simply follow one another, a fact which repeated concentration on visual distractions tragically obscured.

The duo's version of Dolly Parton's 'Jolene' followed in September 1985. Its merits notwithstanding, this was an ill-advised idea, and seemed to deny the group's own songwriting talent. 'You're under a lot of pressure once the record company gets a hold of you,' Jill told Q in 1992. 'We lost direction and turned into something we didn't set out to be,' Rose added, and the pair split up in 1986. McDowall later sang with, among others, Psychic TV, but although Bryson was briefly signed to Creation, no solo releases surfaced.

Lloyd Cole And The Commotions had meanwhile continued apace, although their second album, *Easy Pieces*, proved over-causal, adding nothing to its predecessor while relying on its charm. This 1985 set was succeeded by *Mainstream*, and here the group reasserted the promise of *Rattlesnakes*. Cole's lyrics were now less reliant on word-play and once superfluous images were honed to greater effect. Musically, the group was more mature, although by doing so they left behind the impish frisson of early recordings. 'It's too easy just to be a cult figure,' Cole declared to *TLN*. '(That's why) the title *Mainstream* was meant to be tongue in cheek. It's a dirty word in pop, but if a writer or artist was working in the mainstream of modern culture, that would be a compliment.'

The singer broke from the Commotions in 1989 and, having moved to New York, began an understated solo career. 'You get to a point where the impetus to keep the group on just isn't enough,' he stated. 'The desire for a bit of freedom just becomes greater. It was always in my plans to stop the Commotions at some point.'

If Cole had found a professional niche, del Amitri were still striving for theirs. Cut adrift from Chrysalis, they sought a different avenue to achieve a firmer footing. At the behest of their American-born manager, they looked to the USA. 'A fan in New York wrote offering us $2,000 if we came over and played,' states Currie. 'We had no money, we had nothing to do and thought "what have we got to lose?"' The gig was not a commercial success; the eventual fee was enough to cover the PA cost, but a precedent had been set. 'We set up this elaborate tour which depended on fans putting on gigs for us, staying with their parents and so on. We hired a van, wiring the money back as we got paid for each appearance. It was very close to the bone.

'During a gig in a record store in Los Angeles we announced to the crowd that we didn't have enough money to get to the next concert, 3,000 miles away in Milwaukee. They spontaneously began throwing dollar bills onstage, one girl gave us $40 for a signed t-shirt, and we got enough to get us through the tour. That really inspired us. We were a fairly unpopular band in Britain yet here were people shaking our hands and saying that the reason they were taking five days off work to put on a gig was because they loved our music. We went home feeling elated. It was nothing to do with the music business, it was grass roots support.'

Although galvanised by the US experience, the group was now hopelessly in debt and, as Currie relates, they became a part-time band again. 'We all got jobs. Ian drove a van for Billy's Fruit & Veg, I was a waiter in a restaurant in Gibson Street and the band was put on the back burner. We got on with having real lives, meeting new people and just hanging around. There was no pressure on us. We weren't aiming for another deal and were quite happy to languish in obscurity.'

Although continuing to write and rehearse, del Amitri withdrew from live appearances for two years. Curry did appear as part of an ad hoc country band with Ali McKenzie from the Cuban Heels, Trisha Reid and various others who, in Justin's words, 'had nothing better to do. We played a lot of country songs that Trisha knew, like Hank Williams, although we did a couple of Steve Earle things that Iain and I were into.' Such songs, several of which were new to Currie, helped focus the more traditional means of songwriting he and Harvie were pursuing. Many voiced surprise at the robust direction del Amitri unveiled when a set of new demos began circulating. For Currie, however, it was a natural progression. 'The songs were changing, I was beginning to write on my own or just with Iain, rather than the whole group. The guitar player and drummer left; we asked Mick Slaven, a famous Glasgow guitarist, to join us and from there we developed a real rock 'n' roll style. We unashamedly became the band we'd always dreamed we'd be.' Nonetheless, given the changes which had occurred, the singer toyed with changing the group's name when a deal with A&M beckoned. Pride in past achievements convinced him this would be wrong.

Del Amitri rejoined the major label marketplace with a sound ripe for its demands. The awkward juxtaposition of art and commerce, the downfall of Orange Juice, was no longer applicable, although the group's new outlet did enjoy a reputation for long-term patience rather than short-term gain. A second album, *Waking Hours*, released in 1990, captured the quartet's distillation of country, blues and rock, although a persistent air of ironic melancholia still tinged the proceedings. Del Amitri's patience was finally awarded when 'Nothing Ever Happens' reached the UK Top 20. 'When we put that out there was a real climate of 'this is now the 90s and everything's going to change,"' Currie recounts. 'It was blatantly obvious that nothing would change.' Yet, despite an air of estranged loneliness, 'Nothing Ever Happens' was not composed with negative intentions. 'It wasn't designed to be miserable, it was meant to be optimistic. We weren't just saying "everything's terrible", we were saying "everything's terrible and we should change it."'

Del Amitri's commercial ascendancy continued with *Change Everything* and its introductory single, 'Always The Last To Know'. The latter's Top 10 place in 1992 confirmed a newfound status as 'major attractions' and Curry understandably takes pride in this achievement. Their survival depended on an age-old rock ethos - bringing music to the people - and a similar in-concert workload was successful for Simple Minds, Nazareth and a host of other workaholics. The most obvious contrast to this approach is that of the Blue Nile.

Robert Bell, Paul Joseph Moore and Paul Buchanan met in 1980 while at Glasgow University. Graduates, respectively, of electronics, maths and English, the trio discovered a mutual admiration for, not just music, but specifically that

Paul Buchanan of Blue Nile

which combined the passionate and cerebral. The trio took their thumb-nail sketches to Castle Sound, the studio sited in rural Pencaitland some 15 miles east of Edinburgh. Owner/engineer Calum Malcolm had worked with bands from Postcard and Pop Aural, but he struck up an immediate affinity with this as-yet unnamed group. The three-piece eschewed demos, and thus Malcolm passed one of the finished songs, 'I Love This Life' to RSO Records, with whom he enjoyed connections through his own former act, the Headboys. 'All the business was conducted from a 'phonebox on the street corner,' Robert Bell relates, but the label duly licensed the song and the fledgling unit found itself with a career and an enigmatic name, the Blue Nile. Those discovering 'I Love This Life' in retrospect are surprised by the urgency it transmits, one quite unlike the group's later lassitude. 'I'm still proud of that single,' Bell adds, 'even if it does seem slightly different from later releases. It was a package of all our ideas and emotions, but we've slowed down a lot since then.'

RSO folded within weeks of its release. 'That made us a little wary of the record business,' confessed Bell, 'and we decided to keep working on our own, begging, stealing or borrowing studio time.' Castle Sound provided a highly sympathetic haven, although the results were largely for the trio's own indulgence. By coincidence, the Glasgow-based Linn Products, purveyors of quality hi-fi goods, was comparing digital and analogue sound. They experimented in cutting records and, having prototyped a splicing machine, contacted the studio about likely tapes to work with. 'One of our songs was on there,' Bell recounts, and on hearing it, Linn offered the Blue Nile a recording deal, despite the fact that the firm did not have a label. 'We hummed and hawed for a year because we didn't have a career in mind,' Bell remembers. 'We still had day jobs,' Paul Buchanan wryly recounted in 1989. 'Linn weren't a record company and we weren't a band.'

Buoyed by a marketing deal with Virgin, Linn funded the group's debut album *A Walk Across The Rooftops*. Few outside its tiny coterie knew of the Blue Nile's existence and thus the outside world was largely unprepared for this exquisite 1984 set. The collection was musically unlike its peers and the picaresque, urban soundscapes on offer were both delightful and haunting. Each of the songs was meticulously pieced together, yet the notion of space and, indeed, of being the outsider, was enhanced by arrangements which remained scrupulously open-ended. There were two exceptions; 'Tinseltown In The Rain' and 'Stay' showed a commercial edge and became, in turn, singles, but compositions such as 'Easter Parade' and 'From Rags To Riches' allowed the Blue Nile oeuvre to flourish more freely. An element of New Age abstraction prevails on the latter song - its keyboard pulse recalls Terry Riley - but the group's ambitiously textured sound was uniquely offset by Buchanan's wearied, elegiac vocals. 'I couldn't sing as well as anyone else in their particular style,' he states. 'What I wanted to represent was the feeling of a person rather than the technique of a singer.' His 2 am tone proved ideal for the collective sense of alienation and became the most immediate reference between the group and their prospective audience.

Despite the acclaim which greeted their debut, the Blue Nile did not countenance a tour and simply continued their crafted ways. Yet having emerged from their studio cocoon, the group was now subject to pressure and the clamour for a follow-up grew. They trio refused to rush. 'We are very intense about our approach to work,' explains Robert Bell. 'Because we're not seen in the public eye, people mistake that for lethargy. We express our commitment by spending long periods of our lives in circumstances that aren't really pleasurable, rather than have our faces up on a wall.' It was five years before a second Blue Nile LP was issued. 'We wanted to make an album as good as we could and held out 'til we did that,' he adds. 'We didn't have the same preparation as we had for the first one, so we stopped and started over a period of about two years.'

'People generally acknowledge that the second album is a problem,' Paul Moore continues. 'That situation was more alarming in our case. The first record was made in total privacy in circumstances under our control. Only once it was finished did we enter the fray of the record business.'

A more-rounded, warmer set than its angular predecessor, *Hats* was another artistic triumph. It again comprised seven songs, each of which sculpted haunting vignettes based on now-accustomed reference points; cities, people and lights. '*Hats* is a synonym for people in all their faded glory,' explains Paul Buchanan. 'A hat gives them a character and comes to represent the individual.' The album's images were indeed finely struck - the *New York Times* compared 'Downtown Lights' to seeing Manhattan for the first time - an analogy which brought the group great satisfaction. 'If you make a New Yorker express something like that, you've really achieved something,' adds Bell.

Each side closes with a tender portrait. 'Let's Go Out Tonight' is ostensibly simple, the request and yearning clearly unambiguous. This allows Buchanan room to vocalise in truly heartfelt fashion and the effect is that of aching vulnerability, suggesting an affair's end rather than its consummation. 'Saturday Night' is meanwhile a perennial pop infatuation; that of the weekend, and Robert Bell articulates how the Blue Nile felt a similar longing. 'After the various trials and tribulations we experienced between our albums and also recording *Hats*, the simple aspects of being alive reasserted themselves to us. We expressed this on 'Saturday Night'.' The result was a moment of undiluted optimism, a quintessential closure to an unequivocally beautiful set.

Hats not only signalled Blue Nile's re-emergence, it provided the basis to their first live tour. Concerts in Glasgow and Edinburgh were almost pious, and the group had clearly derived self-confidence from a previous spell supporting singer Rickie Lee Jones. 'We met in Scotland,' explains Bell. 'She was on a brief holiday, but decided she wanted to do a little work and telephoned the studio. We were in at the time, she knew our first album, and we became friends.' Chart albums, touring, guest appearances – members can be heard on former Band-leader Robbie Robertson's 1992 set, *Storeyville*, – the Blue Nile now behave like a regular rock 'n' roll crew. Yet despite promises to the contrary, a third album is, to date, far from completion.

CHAPTER 22
HAMISH MACALPINE

Where del Amitri and the Blue Nile forged careers in an unconventional manner, other contemporaries proved more traditional. Deacon Blue offered a style blending soul with pre-punk Americana, studded with the veneer of sophistication. Yet the resultant sound and image - the mature, pensive Scot - became prone to cliché.

Former schoolteacher Ricky Ross was in his 20s before founding his first group, the Glasgow-based Woza, in 1982. A year stalking the city's clubs ensued, but the Dundee-born singer dissolved the line-up when no real progress was forthcoming. Instead Ross began honing his songwriting skills and, having completed an album-length tape, sent the results to several London-based publishers. Reaction was not unfavourable and a deal with ATV was struck with the proviso he put a band together to develop his compositions. Several members passed through its ranks before James Prime (keyboards), Graeme Kelling (guitar), Ewan Vernal (bass) and Dougie Vipond (drums) established an act, initially known as Dr. Love, but which by 1985 had assumed its Deacon Blue sobriquet. A new series of demos then attracted CBS, who signed the group the following year.

The debut *Raintown* was completed with the aid of auxiliary vocalist Lorraine McIntosh. An ex-member of Rab Noakes' backing band, Gene Pitney's Birthday, she later became an integral part of the Deacon Blue line-up, offering a punctuative counterpoint to Ross's more studied lead. Its effect was exciting or irritable, according to taste, but their rather stereotypical setting confirmed the group's position firmly within rock's orthodoxy. *Raintown*'s mid-Atlantic preoccupations were that of an act captured between Springsteen and Prefab Sprout, but although there was no denying the undoubted sincerity Ross exposed in his finely-wrought, literate lyrics, Deacon Blue were a more convincing ensemble when they relaxed. 'Born In A Storm' or 'He Looks Like Spencer Tracy Now' seem less intent on impressing.

'Dignity', complete with Waterboys' inflections, was the first of several singles culled from the album. CBS employed a plethora of marketing tactics to promote these releases, including a money-back-if-not-satisfied launch for *Raintown* itself, plus a second pressing replete with 'giveaway' 12-inch. But although minor hits did ensue, Deacon Blue's commercial breakthrough followed the release of 'Real Gone Kid', a new track issued in 1988. It showed the group's strident self-confidence yet, despite the urgency on offer, the song hinged on a nagging, wordless refrain, which remained imbedded in any prospective listener long after its melody was forgotten.

This Top 10 success followed a period of intense live activity, during which Deacon Blue emerged as one of the UK's most popular acts. Their second album, *When The World Knows Your Name*, entered its respective chart at number 1 in 1989, and a series of attendant singles - 'Wages Day', 'Love And Regret' and 'Queen Of The New Year' - were all Top 30 hits. The most interesting selection was 'Fergus Sings The Blues', its punning title a nod to Joni Mitchell and her self-quizzical composition, 'Furry Sings The Blues'. Where Mitchell pondered her encounter with singer Furry Lewis, Ross queries his blue-eyed soul credentials, a particularly pertinent question given Scotland's affection for the genre. I somehow doubt that Homesick James is indeed the singer's 'biggest influence' - although it does scan well - but his determined self-examination came replete with a riffing brass arrangement, suggesting the ultimate answer was a qualified 'yes'. 'I like the idea of singer/songwriters,' Ross told Q, 'and it stuck in my mind they were more important. These are my two influences - the desire to rock out and the desire to hold the song as of paramount importance.'

A worldwide tour culminated in June 1990 with Glasgow's Big Day, a free-concert celebration which featured many of the city's most popular attractions. Deacon Blue's multi-format output was then put into perspective by *Ooh Las Vegas*, which compiled b-sides, demos and radio sessions. Their canon had embraced songs by Hüsker Dü, Julian Cope and the Hayes/Porter team, but the last-named team provided the set's sole non-original. *Ooh Las Vegas* included 'Back Here In Beanoland', a pithy reference to parsimonious Dundee publishers DC Thompson, and three songs written for the BBC production of William McIlvanney's play, *Dreaming*. 'Take Me To The Place' was meanwhile dedicated to Glasgow photographer Oscar Marzaroli, for whom Ross also assembled a various artists' tribute, *The Tree And The Bird And The Fish And The Bell*.

The final inclusion, 'Don't Let The Teardrops Start', was written on the night of the Govan by-election, in which a 'safe' Labour majority was overturned by SNP candidate Jim Sillars. Subsequent events verified this victory as temporary, yet it represented a point at which Scottish pop and politics became irrevocably intertwined. Ross was allied with the broad church demanding self-determination and, in the 1992 post-election malaise, appeared live at Scotland United rallies.

Deacon Blue's third official album, *Fellow Hoodlums*, was a marked departure from the swagger of its predecessor. Although not quite introspective, the set is couched in an implicitly rustic perspective. The hooklines nonetheless remained intact, as evinced by 'Twist And Shout' and 'Closing Time'. But in *Fellow Hoodlums* Deacon Blue have addressed the conundrum of forging a sound less reliant on rock tapestries, and more empathic with Ross's homegrown perspectives.

Despite 'outside' interests, Ricky Ross has not seen a diminution of his performing role and he remains, unequivocally, the 'lead singer in Deacon Blue'. The position of Pat Kane, vocalist in Hue And Cry, is much less defined, his status blurred by politicking and activities as university rector, columnist and opinionist.

Formed in Coatbridge, Lanarkshire in 1983, Hue And Cry comprise Pat Kane and brother Greg. The latter sibling had acquired a greater grounding in music, playing saxophone in a Gothic punk band, Valerie And The Week Of Wonders, before joining a less-radical unit, the Winning Losers. 'I joined when they needed a singer,' Pat Kane recalls, 'but we were thrown out when we began to dominate things. We were always a wee bit out of time and into 50s styles and 60s soul where our friends were inspired by post-punk bands.' Stevie Wonder and the Average White Band would also influence the pair who then began work firstly as Unity Express, then Hue And Cry. 'The name defined the function of the band,' Pat Kane recounts, 'which was to make a big intervention but to have a critical edge. I always felt that names, conceptually, relate to the work you do and ours came during that ABC/Heaven 17 period, which combined soul music with glamour.'

The Kanes completed several demos in future-manager Alan MacNeil's studio, using dead time when no other act was booked. They made little headway, however, and a frustrated Pat Kane was tempted to join Rodeo, a duo on the fringe of a recording career. Stiff Records teamed them with Midge Ure, but when the resultant master was rejected, Kane opted to rejoin his brother. The pair then won a publishing deal with Chappell Music and worked, Brill-Building style, in the company's songwriting room. They paused only to issue a single, 'Here Comes Everybody', on Graham Wilson's Stampede label. "Here Comes Everybody' is the name of a character in 'Finnegan's Wake',' Pat explains. 'I had a serious Joyceian fix at the time and was flagging my references wildly. It got us a recording deal.' Its b-side, 'The Success Of Monetarism', aired the singer's political stance. It consisted of one minute's silence.

Hue And Cry were signed to the Circa label in 1986 and the brothers secured supporting musicians - Nigel Clark (guitar), James Finnegan (bass) and David Preston (vocals) - through a series of advertisements. *Seduced And Abandoned*, the resultant album, showed the pair's soul affectations, but it was apparently clear that such interests were part of a greater lexicon. While Greg created jazz-based melodies, his brother crooned in nightclub fashion, invoking Buddy Greco or Bobby Darin as much as Luther Vandross. 'We were always interested in songs,' states Pat Kane, 'be they Tin Pan Alley or classic balladry. It's true to say we picked up our instruments because we saw everyone else had, but what we produced was at variance with the scratchy, atonal, attitude music that was around us.'

'Labour Of Love' gave the group its first hit single and showed how, despite the music's implicit escapism, Pat Kane's lyrics were almost universally pointed. "Labour Of Love' was first written as an anti-Thatcherite rant,' he explains. 'Its release coincided with the run-up to the 1987 Election, but it showed you could be political without being explicit. It was more to do with describing a better world, rather than prescribing one.' A second album, *Remote*, cut with seasoned US jazz musicians, produced a brace of chart entries in 'Looking For Linda' and 'Violently', but by this point Pat Kane had flexed other artistic muscles. A contributor to various publications, a voice for the SNP; some argued his skills were now spread rather thinly. *Stars Crash Down* from 1991 showed a broadened scope, but by doing so the group forewent firm musical direction while several critics questioned the continued use of polemic lyrics. Pat Kane, however, is unrepentant. 'If you feel passionate about something you have to go with it. It's a disservice to your own sensibility if you repress the fact you get angry about a certain situation.'

Hue And Cry were dropped by Circa later that year during a period of intense blood-letting. They re-emerged in 1992 with *Truth And Love*, issued on their own outlet, Fidelity. As such it helps foster a communal spirit Kane would wish to find in Scottish pop. 'Maybe Scotland should strike out and have a mixed economy. Recording facilities, publishing houses, managers, circuits - they should all be protected, by state subsidies, from the vagaries of the London market. We should democratise the means of musical production. This is not to say that we should nationalise all the studios, the people who run them have done so under duress and with great initiative. But the state should help them thrive and survive.'

Pat Kane and Ricky Ross represent the erudite thinking pop star. They are not the cantankerous rebels of the post-60s Diaspora, or those nihilists attracted by the sneer of punk. They are traditionalists - politically and musically - and indeed both share a passion for Dundee singer/songwriter Michael Marra. A former member of Skeets Boliver, the city's early 70s prog-rock heroes, Marra subsequently pursued a solo career in Scotland's folk clubs. Rab Noakes introduced the fledgling writer to fellow singer Barbara Dickson, who later covered one of Marr's songs, 'Peter'. He made his recording debut in 1979 with *The Midas Touch*, but a desire to write and sing in a Scottish vernacular

Hue & Cry

met resistance from London-based quarters. 'I wrote the *Gaels Blue* album to annoy my publisher,' Michael recounted in a BBC interview. 'He was horrified by it, which I began to enjoy.' Marra later wrote music for a Billy Kay play, *They Fairly Mak Ye Work* and Johnny Byrne's television drama, *Your Cheatin' Heart*. However, he achieved greater notoriety for 'Hamish McAlpine', a paean to Dundee United's penalty-taking goalkeeper, and 'Mother Glasgow', later recorded by Hue And Cry. His own recording career prospered with *On Stolen Stationery* and a support slot on Deacon Blue's 1991 UK tour, but Marra's canvas may yet prove too idiosyncratic, his acclaim confined to peers and those his music has inspired.

Marra's fellow Dundonians, Gary and Kit Clark, followed a similar path. As aspiring songwriters, the brothers left their hometown during the early 80s armed with the impression that London would welcome their talent. 'We has this idea that there would be all these A&R men leaning on bars waiting for new bands,' the former sibling recounted to *Cut*. 'When we got there we realised you could create a buzz from wherever you were.' The pair nonetheless stayed in the capital for three years, but returned home to found a new act, Spencer Tracy, with Ged Grimes. When the deceased actor's estate voiced objections, the trio took a different name from a Frank Sinatra film; Danny Wilson.

The group made its recording debut in 1987 with 'Mary's Prayer', a sweet and delicate song, which scraped the singles' chart when first released, only to reach the Top 3 slot when reissued the following year. Their attendant album, *Meet Danny Wilson*, offered a sumptuous amalgamation of cocktail jazz, Latin pop, ballads and soul, all of which confirmed the trio's unrestrained ambition. The set even featured Lester Bowie's Brass Fantasia, a radical Afro-American ensemble which the Wilsons contacted while recording in Copenhagen. 'We were in a club talking about them,' Cary Clark explained in 1988, 'and there was this poster on a pillar with 'Appearing Next Week' on it.'

Two more albums, *Beebop Moptop* and *Sweet Danny Wilson* followed, but despite offering the same late-night sophistication of that first collection, Danny Wilson was unable to secure a commercial niche. Yet there was no denying the trio's mature perspectives and when Gary Clark voiced a desire to be the 'Burt Bacharach of the 90s', few viewed this as mere pretension. However, it was equally clear that the group could no longer support three distinct songwriting talents. 'We got to the stage where we were all writing material,' Kit Clark told *TLN*, 'and there was no way we could release it all. We considered making Danny Wilson an umbrella for various projects, but Virgin weren't keen, so we decided to split up and get out of the deal.' The break was, indeed, amicable, and both his former colleagues were featured on sessions for Gary Clark's solo debut.

If Danny Wilson imploded because it could no longer function as a collective, the Bathers, Big Dish and Painted Word represented the aspirations of three individuals. Chris Thompson continued to use the first appellation, despite sundering his contract with Go Discs. He financed a second collection, which was latterly issued by Island as *Sweet Deceit*. In the meantime the singer had teamed with two ex-Commotions, Neil Clark and Stephen Irvine, and having flirted with several new names - ICT, and the Navigators among them - the trio became known as Bloomsday. However, Island decided to drop their option and when Clark opted out, Thompson revived the Bathers' name.

The original Painted Word included Alan McLusker Thompson, Mushie Weston, Robbie Ross and Nigel Hurst, and the quartet's brand of baroque pop was initially caught on 'Independence Day', a single issued on U2's Mother label. The Glasgow group was then courted successfully by Elektra, but on the day they were due to sign - the tale, possibly apocryphal, has them pen poised and ready to open celebratory champagne - the London office was closed by its US-based HQ and the deal was abandoned.

Other labels did step in, but the group gradually shed members until the act was synonymous with McLusker Thompson. One early participant was Dougie Vipond, later of Deacon Blue, and this well-travelled musician also surfaced in the Big Dish. Originally an Airdrie-based attraction centred on vocalist/guitarist Stephen Lindsay, this particular act featured another Deacon Blue acolyte, Raymond Docherty. But where Vipond eventually sided with Ricky Ross, the latter opted to stay with Lindsay. Brian McFee completed the Big Dish line-up featured on *The Swimmer*, a 1986 collection noted for dulcet melodies and classily-hewn pop. Similar qualities appeared on *Creeping Up On Jesus*, but it was three years before another set, *Satellites*, appeared. Restrained by commercial indifference and an admirable refusal to compromise, Lindsay decided to drop the Big Dish name. 'You get tired of banging your head against a brick wall,' he announced to *TLN* in 1991. 'There comes a time when you have to move on.'

A record industry in recession reacted in customary fashion when, during the late 80s, major companies slashed their rosters. This groupquake was certainly unsettling, although as a larger percentage of Scottish acts had been signed, then the profile of those dropped would be inevitably higher. Nonetheless record label lassitude still irked; the promising River Detectives were cut by WEA while Hearts And Minds, led by the much-feted Davy Scott, almost withered on CBS intransigence. Despite a strong local following, this respected songsmith could not secure a contract and having changed the group's name to the Pearlfishers, issued an EP, *Sacred*, on his own My Dark Star label. A self-confident album followed in 1992.

An early member of Love And Money, John Palmer subsequently appeared in Rab Noakes' Gene Pitney's Birthday, alongside Lorraine McIntosh. He enjoyed a brief tenure with Deacon Blue, some of whose early work he claimed credit for arranging, before founding the Right Stuff. This particular group was signed by Arista, but the label dropped them only weeks before their sole album, *Wa Wa*, was issued. Reviews were morbidly negative, and the band duly split up, although most members, bar Palmer, reappeared as part of the Ocean. The Right Stuff's tale is a metaphor for attitudes prevailing in late 80s corporate rock, which demands a tenacity of del Amitri proportions to allow an act to prosper on its terms.

CHAPTER 23
YOU'LL NEVER BE THAT YOUNG AGAIN

Creation, the Jesus And Mary Chain and Splash One - each helped refocus an independent sector which had seemed bereft of collective momentum. Buoyed by this inspiration, a new generation of cottage bands emerged and whereas the Pastels remained central to Glasgow's dissentient culture, the pivotal act in Edinburgh was the Shop Assistants.

Both groups were linked by more than common purpose, but it was the former's messianic altruism which inspired the point of contact. 'Around 1983 I got a tape of songs from David Keegan,' Stephen Pastel explains. 'I really liked them, and as he didn't have a band at the time, we put one together with several friends.' Dubbed Buba And The Shop Assistants, this one-off collective was set up to record 'Something To Do', which appeared on Pastel's own label, Villa 21. The single, however was not released until 1985, by which time Keegan had not only moved from Newtonmore to Edinburgh, he was fronting a quite different act which nonetheless retained the 'Shop Assistants' suffix.

He became embroiled in the city's 'alternative' music scene through contact with members of Rote Kapelle. 'Initially we were a trio,' explains vocalist Andrew Tully, 'but we got to know other people because we all shared the same practice rooms. David sometimes played drums with us and Alex Taylor joined after we'd advertised for a female lead singer. Then they left to form the Shop Assistants.' Although the chronology sounds clear-cut, this was a particularly incestuous period. 'Everyone played in everyone else's band,' Tully adds, and the notion of delineation would become increasingly confused.

David and Alex pursued their new venture with bassist Sarah Kneale who in turn introduced drummer Laura McPhail. The latter bluffed her way into the group - she had never touched a kit before - which in part explains the arrival of second percussionist, Ann Donald. The pair's rudimentary yet intuitive skills complemented one another and, using parts borrowed from Rote Kapelle, the group began gigging around the city. Their debut EP was

The Shop Assistants

released in 1985 and by contrasting the tenderness of 'It's Up To You' with the high-octane thrill of 'All Day Long' and 'All That Ever Mattered', the quintet revealed a charming dexterity. The set was rightly hailed as a classic and the Shop Assistants joined the Pastels at the forefront of what was, somewhat derogatorily, described as 'shambling'. The term was coined to encompass groups within the indie sector whose fumbling technique was combined with naive introspection. In common with all categorisations, it was an easy, convenient option, and one which failed to address each acts' individual merits or fallibilities.

The EP was issued on a Bristol-based outlet which reflected something of the vacuum existing in Scotland at that time. Although Bob Last re-established Fast as the Scottish arm of the Cartel distribution network, he had become increasingly sceptical of that role. 'Although we'd decided to stop releasing records,' he states, 'we continued our commitment in case others turned out something of interest. Distribution was always going to be a particular problem in Scotland which has a relatively small market within a large area. Added to that was the extra cost of getting the records up here in the first place.' By the mid-80s Last had severed his ties with the company which, as Fast Forward, came under the stewardship of Sandy McLean. Yet the need for a new, strong outlet persisted, which in turn inspired the founding of 53rd & 3rd. 'I had stayed good friends with David,' recounts Stephen Pastel, 'and there were lots of groups emerging who shared our interests and influences. We wanted to make it possible for them to make records too.' Aware of the pivotal role both Pastel and Keegan enjoyed, McLean offered them both a partnership. 'He asked if we'd like to run a label. I said I could have some input - suggest some groups and work with others - and so we began. It was named after the Ramones' song; they're David's favourite band.'

That particular interest was apparent on the label's debut single, the Shop Assistants' 'Safety Net'. It continued the group's affair with abraded pop although the enchanting coupling, 'Somewhere In China', suggested a more delicate perspective. It was this dissimilarity which made the quintet so enthralling.

Although the new label was a triumvirate, Stephen Pastel instigated its core signings. He had become acquainted with a troupe of musicians, based in the Lanarkshire town of Bellshill, each of whom shared a passion for pop's mercurial characters. 'Jonathan Richman was a major influence,' states Duglas Stewart, founder of the BMX Bandits. 'He's not really a perfect singer, his records have flaws, but he sang about personal, everyday things that weren't glamorous or rockstar-ish.' Yet while Stewart admired Richman's ingenue talents, he was equally drawn to such disparate acts as Brian Wilson, Cole Porter and Throbbing Gristle. Schoolfriend Norman Blake shared his passion for music, and together the pair began writing songs. 'Our enthusiasm rubbed off on each other,' Duglas adds. 'I had ideas in my head, and knew how I wanted them to sound, but was hopeless at playing guitar. Norman did that sort of thing for me.'

The next inevitable step was performing but, as in Edinburgh, there was no clear-cut demarcation between different groups. 'We were asked to support a punk band at a local hotel,' Duglas explains about the debut of the Pretty Flowers, which he co-founded in 1983, with Blake. Sean Dickson (keyboards) and Frances McKee (vocals) completing the founding line-up. Percussionist Hugh McLaughlin joined at a later date. Yet although the Flowers were active for two years, each of the group, bar Stewart and McKee, was also committed to a concurrent venture, the Faith Healers. This may have undermined both projects, but the notion of co-operation was an essential requirement in Bellshill throughout the decade.

The Flowers' demise paved the way for Stewart's next enterprise. 'I was left with all these songs which I felt were the best I'd written,' he explains, 'and I wanted to give them, as a thank-you, to people whose music I loved.' Those receiving the ensuing demo-tape included Dan Treacy and Stephen Pastel, the latter of whom loved the cassette and a new group, hurriedly dubbed the BMX Bandits, was formed. 'I thought we were going to split up in a week's time,' explains Duglas about the act's throwaway name, but it became a permanent fixture with the release of 'E102'/'Sad?'. This charming debut - issued on 53rd & 3rd in May 1986 - captured Stewart's jejune talents, but its aural amateurism doesn't disguise a wry perceptiveness. "E102' is a food additive,' he relates, 'and the song was about not being artificial. If you hate it it's because you hate us and not some manufactured image. Too many people tend to dehumanise themselves in rock and behave embarrassingly. We wanted to be real people, saying real things about real life.

'The song itself was seen as ridiculously jovial, but I wrote it because I'd just been having a hard time in love and its happiness was meant to be ironic.'

Despite its members' past track record, the BMX Bandits did not then collapse, although there came the inevitable, and numerous, changes. The founding line-up - Stewart, Dickson, Billy Wood (vocals), Jim McCulloch (guitar) and Willie McArdle (drums), was trimmed to a quartet for the group's second release, 'What A Wonderful World'. While McArdle and Dickson dropped out, guitarist Joe McAlinden, late of Groovy Little Numbers, stepped in. The direction, of course, remained that of Duglas, who determinedly followed a highly idiosyncratic path. 'A lot of new groups appeared at Splash One, including us, but because our music is so personal we also used to play in people's houses and flats.' The BMX Bandits were thus perceived as the consummate 'anorak' act, where an unrequited schoolboy crush seemed the sole motivation for singing. Stewart offers an alternative explanation. 'Some groups embraced it as the latest thing and then moved on, but others like us

The BMX Bandits

were sick of the macho, rock 'n' roll posturing typical in so many lyrics. If we'd had a hit, we'd have been remembered as a Toy Dolls. We didn't, and that left us with our self-respect.'

Paradoxically, it was an offshoot of the Bandits which confronted that particular dilemma. In keeping with the contemporaneous spirit, Sean Dickson had formed a group of his own while still working alongside Stewart. The Soup Dragons - Dickson (vocals/guitar), Ian Whitehall (guitar), Sushil Dade (bass), Ross Sinclair (drums) and Jackie (tambourine) - provided an outlet for the founder's own ambitions and they were quickly immortalised on 'If You Were The Only Girl In The World', a flexi-disc included in Dade's fanzine *Pure Popcorn*. By this point another Bandit acolyte, Jim McCulloch, had replaced Whitehall. The emergent quintet shared several gigs with the Shop Assistants, who in turn introduced them to the Subway Organization, the label which had issued 'All Fall Down'. A four-track EP, *The Sun Is In The Sky*, was recorded, but the Dragons suddenly disowned the set and cancelled its release, although copies were eventually leaked. With 'Jackie' now in absentia, the group's official debut, 'Whole Wide World', was issued in May 1986. Chided for aping the Buzzcocks, the single did enjoy considerable commercial success. Dickson and McCulloch promptly 'left' the BMX Bandits and the Dragons' ascension was confirmed on signing with ex-Wham! manager Jazz Summers.

The band then formed their own label, Raw TV Products. Its first release, 'Hang 10', retained an infatuation with the Buzzcocks, although a sudden flirtation with pop-art was implicit on its sleeve. The single featured

The Vaselines

McCulloch's speedy guitar and Dickson's adenoidal whine, and successive releases - 'Head Gone Astray', 'Can't Take Now More' and 'Soft As Your Face' - followed in a similar vein.

The Dragons were signed to Sire in 1988, but in a subsequent effort to jettison early influences, the group showed they had little idea how to replace them. Their debut album, *This Is Our Art*, rattled through punk, garage, pop and metal styles without any coherent direction and patently failed to match its assumptive title. Within weeks Dickson was dismissing the set as a platform for 60s' infatuations he no longer felt, but a whiff of insincerity hung around the whole proceedings. Sire dropped the group when a concurrent single, 'Kingdom Chairs', failed to chart, and the Soup Dragons duly slipped out of the limelight, pondering their next move.

'When Sean's records came out we thought, "We can do that too,"' states Norman Blake, who joined the BMX Bandits on drums, voice and recorder. However, it was with another sideline project that he made his recording debut. Jim Lambie (vibes), Raymond McGinley (bass) and Francis McDonald (drums) joined Blake and fellow-Bandit Joe McAlinden in a short-lived act dubbed the Boy Hairdressers after the first, unpublished novel by 60s' icon Joe Orton. 'We made a record and split up three months later,' Norman relates, and it is unquestionably true that the group would be an afterthought had it not cut a single. Released on 53rd & 3rd, 'Golden Shower' was an intriguing vision of 60s Americana, although its restless tune and winsome harmonies invoked the Cyrkle rather than the Byrds. Such trappings were deceptive - the spray in question was urinative - but the quintet's mildly coy approach left sufficient ambiguity intact.

McAlinden and Blake remained part of the BMX Bandits throughout this period alongside Gordon Keen, who took over from the Soup-bound Jim McCulloch, and Hairdesser McDonald. At this point, however, the latter was also a member of the Groovy Little Numbers, which McAlinden had opted to resurrect with co-founder Catherine Steven. Gerard Love (bass) completed the group's basic line-up, which was later buoyed by a highly-adventurous brass section of John McRorie (alto sax), Colette Walsh (tenor sax), Kevin McCarthy (baritone) and two trumpeters - Mairi Cameron and James Wood.

This particular facet of McAlinden's vision was not apparent on his group's lone single, which also appeared on the ubiquitous 53rd & 3rd. 'You Make My Head Explode' was a punchy, Beatlesque celebration, indicative of the guitarist's firm grasp of both melody and arrangement. His nonet meanwhile offered a much wider palate for such aspirations, and although economic demands hampered the scope of what the ensemble achieved, it was, unquestionably, Bellshill's most ambitious musical project to date. Yet if the Boy Hairdessers and Groovy Little Numbers helped develop penchants implicit to the BMX Bandits; it took the Vaselines to turn them into lust.

The Pastels

Formed as a duo in 1987, the Vaselines comprised Frances McKee (ex-Pretty Flowers) and guitarist/vocalist Eugene Kelly. The idea for a group was nurtured while the pair worked on a fanzine. 'It would have been called 'Pure Fucking Crap' had we bothered to leave the pub long enough to write it,' Kelly told *Cut* magazine, although such laxity did not prevent their two excellent singles for 53rd & 3rd. The first was 'Son Of A Gun', an exciting song aching to leave its Bobby Fuller Four-styled strictures and embrace the grunge-rock Eugene's guitar barely holds in check. His dispassionate voice is offset by Frances' innocuous delivery, although its virginal qualities were put into question by the flip-side, 'Rory Ride Me Raw'. 'Rory's the name of my bicycle, so that's that answered,' she helpfully stated when the single was released, although few believed that particular explanation.

The follow-up, 'Dying For It', exploited the abrasive elements of its predecessor. However, this second, superb 45, is better recalled for 'Molly's Lips', an innocent, almost folksy performance, hinged by a remarkably memorable hookline. Its place in the Vaselines' canon might well have remained an obscure secret, but Stephen Pastel's commitment to interlocution ensured a different fate.

Stephen's relentless enthusiasm was crucial to the path through which Scotland's West Coast indie pop evolved. Many contemporaries published fanzines, but most dropped the pastime when recording began. Throughout the Pastels' career, its guiding hand has continued to write, either through his early enterprise, *Juniper Berry Berry*, or its successor, *Pastelism*. 'I like writing about music too,' he explains, 'and wanted to do something a bit wilder than the others I'd seen. I worked on *Juniper Berry Berry* with Jill from Strawberry Switchblade and her boyfriend Peter - we made a few enemies with that. We gave advice on how to fail job interviews, how to annoy the Bluebells and debated the appeal of Bauhaus; not the art movement, the group.

'Fanzines give great scope to try anything. Calvin Johnson from Beat Happening is a massive fan of Lee Hazelwood and we commissioned a piece from him for *Pastelism*.'

Beat Happening, a US minimalist trio based in Olympia, Washington, shared many of the Pastels' idiosyncrasies. This transatlantic rapport was enhanced when the former group cut *Crashing Through* for 53rd & 3rd. It was through this attachment that the label's other releases surfaced in Washington. The Vaselines' singles certainly appealed to one of Johnson's acquaintances, Kurt Cobain, later lead singer of Nirvana. His group not only covered 'Molly's Lips', turning it into an invective noise, but featured several Kelly/McKee songs in concert. Most of these were drawn from *Dum-Dum*, the Vaselines' sole LP, on which the founding duo was joined by James Seenan (bass) and Charles Kelly (drums), refugees from another act, Seccession. The album was thus weighted in favour of Eugene's rabblehouse preferences and most of the tracks were splattered with distorted, twisted guitars. Matters carnal were still examined, but despite its demonstrably 70s' rock feel - Mott the Hoople meets the Ramones - the set's best moments came when the balance between the founding pair was more evenly struck. Yet while 'Let's Get Ugly', 'Bitch' and 'No Hope' inherit the warped perceptions of 'Son Of A Gun', there's no denying the plangent thrill of 'Lovecraft'; sitar, tabla and all. *Dum-Dum* is a quite remarkable collection, arguably the finest set released by 53rd & 3rd.

The Pooh Sticks, Tallulah Gosh, the Househunters and Beat Poets were among the other groups signed by Messrs Pastel, Keegan and McLean, although of these, only the last-named act was Scottish. Despite releasing several singles later termed 'seminal', the label was not a conspicuous commercial success. Its founders had other, more pressing commitments, and were unable, or unwilling, to devote themselves entirely to its progress. 'I felt the shambling thing had become contrived,' Stephen Pastel explains in answer to his eventual withdrawal. 'I liked other things too, like Sonic Youth,' he adds, implying that policy had become restrictive. This desire to explore a more polished sound surfaced in his own group which, paradoxically, did not record for 53rd, but was instead signed to an English-based independent, Glass. *Up For A Bit With The Pastels* opened with the orchestrated 'Ride', and while some bemoaned its smooth production, the set provided a natural extension of the previous Creation singles. Among the highlights were exquisite revamped versions of 'Baby Honey' and 'I'm Alright With You' while in 'Automatically Yours' Stephen displays an infectious joy, matched by a dexterity barely hinted at before. 'Most groups start out really strong,' he states. 'The Rolling Stones, the Velvet Underground, Jesus And Mary Chain; they each had it almost instantly. The Pastels are learning all the time.'

The group welcomed, then lost, ex-Boy Hairdresser Raymond McGinley in 1987, although Eugene Kelly, fresh from the now-defunct Vaselines, joined and remained with them until the following year. He contributed to two tracks on the Pastels' second album, *Sitting Pretty*, which continued their move away from shambling. Split between largely short songs (side 1) and lengthier pieces (side 2), the set is helped by a much rougher production than that of its predecessor, although its overall sense of aspiration is more muted. 'I like 'Nothing To Be Done', 'Ditch The Fool' and 'Baby You're Just You',' Stephen admits, 'but we ran out of steam on that LP. We made a single, 'Coming Through', which is my favourite thing by that line-up. I hoped to make an album as strong as that and I don't think *Sitting Pretty* is.' 'Nothing To Be Done' is indeed superb - the dialogue between Stephen and Aggi is endearing - while the singer's other selections capture his group at its most demanding. At 7 plus minutes, 'Ditch The Fool' is a Pastels' tour-de-force, with scraping viola, hammered cello, feedback and a relentless riff. Its creator is rightly proud of this particular achievement.

The final track, 'Swerve', contains a cameo by David Keegan, whose own group had sadly floundered. 'Safety Net' was 53rd & 3rd's best seller, and the Shop Assistants were duly lured away by the chance of a major deal. They were signed by Chrysalis/Blue Guitar in 1986, but once again business machinations would rob a band of critical momentum. John Ryan, producer of the Gap Band, was brought in to work with them, but as Alex recounted to *Cut* 'We were wrong for each other. It's not that he's a bad producer or anything, he just wanted us to sound like the Supremes.' 'He misinterpreted our ideas,' Keegan added, and thus Mayo Thompson arrived to complete the album, with Stephen Street as engineer.

Shop Assistants duly survived such traumas, although it largely confirmed their joyful noise rather than add to what the group had already achieved. 'All That Ever Mattered' and 'Somewhere In China' were reprised from previous releases, but the finest moments were those based around melancholia, notably the lovely 'Before I Wake' and 'After Dark'. Indeed there were two quite distinctive Shop Assistants - that pursuing the Ramones, that aspiring to be folk-rock - and an inability to solve this conundrum would pull the group apart.

The period during which Thompson replaced Ryan delayed the album's release. It appeared in November, a notoriously poor month to launch a new product, and four weeks after the group had completed a promotional UK tour. Drummer Ann had already left the line-up prior to the recording sessions, but the Shoppies' momentum faltered completely with the loss of Alex Taylor, who quit early in 1987. Keegan then put the project on hold, sitting in on occasions with the Vaselines just prior to their demise, while his erstwhile colleague set up Motorcycle Boy.

This new act also featured Taylor's boyfriend, Eddie Connelly, formerly of Meat Whiplash. He moved to Edinburgh from Glasgow when this latter act broke up and, through Alex, became immersed in the capital's music circuit. She passed on to him a demo tape, recorded by Jesse Garon And The Desperadoes, but although the name of the group was largely unknown, its members were not. 'If you weren't in at least two different bands there was something wrong,' states Andrew Tully, still vocalist in Rote Kapelle, but also singer with Jesse Garon. 'The Desperadoes played its first proper gig in 1985, but at that time it was seen as a secondary thing.' Indeed the two groups' personnel was initially interchangeable and because gigs were not exactly plentiful, a clash of interest seemed remote. 'It was exciting,' Tully continues. 'The Shoppies were doing well in the independent scene and, just like punk, anything seemed possible. We all went to each other's gigs - we all drank at the Green Tree in the Cowgate and if someone was on holiday, Lenny was called in.'

Lenny Helsing led the Thanes, an archetypal garage band, honed on a diet of R&B groups the Pretty Things, Outsiders and Q65. Initially known as the Green Telescope, the Thanes have surfaced on a flurry of different outlets - including another Fast Forward venture, DDT - but Helsing's devotion to primal beat remains unshakeable. 'I'd rather die than put out a 12-inch single,' he once remarked, but he was equally happy to sing, drum or play guitar whenever required.

'We promised that Rote Kapelle would be the main band,' Andrew Tully recalls, 'and nothing clashed until 86/87.' By that point he had been joined by Margarita Vazquez Ponte (vocals), Chris Henman (guitar), Ian Binns (keyboards), Malcolm Kergan (bass) and Jonathan Muir (drums). The group's 'angry buzzing noise' had been captured on 'Big Smelly Dinosaur', 'It Moves...But Does It Swing?' and 'These Animals Are Dangerous'. Andrew and Margarita (drums) concurrently led Jesse Garon, which was completed by ex-Kapelle members Kevin McMahon and Stuart Clarke (guitars) as well as vocalist Fran Schopper and bassist Angus McPake. Yet despite the initial intention, it was the latter act which prospered while its counterpart withered away.

'I heard a tape of the Desperadoes over a big sound system,' Eddie Connelly recounted in 1987. 'I thought it sounded great.' The sextet thus became the debut signing to his latest venture, a label dubbed Narodnik after a populist movement which believed Socialism could be obtained by means of a peasant revolution. Connelly was nothing if not ironic; the venture was, in part, financed by the government's Enterprise Allowance scheme.

Douglas Hart, late of the Jesus And Mary Chain, produced the session, which spawned two wonderful Jesse Garon singles, 'Splashing Along' and 'Rain Fell Down'. Lazy comparisons were inevitably drawn with the Shop Assistants, but the Desperadoes' inspirations were more widespread, their brittle pop unspoiled by fashion, alternately restrained, then debonair. Both sold well within the indie circuit, but the group maintained its capricious spirit when Margarita, Angus and Sarah Kneale formed another spin-off project; the Fizzbombs. 'It's healthy to have more than one musical outlet,' the former explained in 1987 and the new act's debut single, 'Sign On The Line' duly became Narodnik's third release. The Desperadoes, meanwhile found themselves feted from all sides. 'The Shop Assistants took us on tour with them,' remembers Andrew Tully. 'Before that we'd only played outside Edinburgh once.' The group's approach, however, remained wonderfully haphazard, and they began the tour as a quartet because two of the group had other commitments. 'We knew this was going to happen,' Tully explains, 'and if we'd had common sense or ambition we'd have rehearsed. We did some dates with Michael from Meat Whiplash and then asked David Keegan to help out. We were teaching him the songs an hour before going onstage.

'We hadn't realised this was our one chance to be famous,' Andrew adds.

The first issue of Pure Popcorn fanzine, featuring the Soup Dragons' recorded debut

'There was a buzz about - there'd been features in the *New Musical Express*, *Melody Maker*, and the like - but we just thought that's how things happened.' Indeed, on one occasion a half-page photograph appeared in *Sounds*' gig-guide, coinciding with a date in London, but only used because the paper had leftover space. 'There was a queue of around 200 people waiting before the doors opened,' Tully recalls, 'and among them were journalists and people from different record companies. We were terrified and played an absolutely terrible set.

'The following day we went to see Geoff Travis, who gave us a dressing down. It was like seeing the headmaster, standing there with hands behind our backs. He told us to go away and write 20 new songs, throw 18 away, and then bring him the other two. We were stunned - in the previous two years we'd only written 12.'

The perils of a 'showcase' gig also befell Goodbye Mr. McKenzie, a much-touted act revolving around its charismatic singer, Martin Metcalfe. '(Punk) was shit but it got me started,' he declared in 1986. 'I played in a band called the Dormant Dum Dums; we specialised in Ramones b-sides. Then we changed our name to Vitamin C.' Goodbye Mr. MacKenzie evolved when Metcalfe and 'Kelly the drummer' moved from Bathgate to Edinburgh, where they were eventually joined by guitarist Jimmy Anderson and keyboard player Rona.

Their recording debut, 'The Rattler' appeared in 1986. Produced by Wilf Smarties and released on Precious, the single became the subject of considerable national airplay until the phrase 'eating beaver' was more widely noticed. Interest in the group was nonetheless stirred, and a shuttle pregnant with A&R staff flew up to a pre-arranged MacKenzies' gig. That night they were an absolute disaster. 'That blew it for about a year,' Metcalfe admits. 'London A&R staff have this sheep syndrome and follow each others' opinion. We were about to split up because no-one was helping, but this American stepped in with finance and all of a sudden the 'phone started ringing again. We said "Go away."'

Controversy also dogged the group's follow-up, 'Face To Face', a harrowing account of multiple rape. It did provoke suspicion that the MacKenzies were deliberately courting controversy. 'Some people thought we were being outrageous to get the single banned and so get publicity,' states Metcalfe. 'But we knew beforehand that no-one was going to play it, so it wasn't a ploy.' These cumulative ructions became cautionary tales in Scottish pop folklore, but the group survived to win a contract with Capitol/EMI. Since then the MacKenzies have undergone changes in personnel, but they remain a vehicle for Metcalfe's vision - part Bowie, part Iggy, part Nick Cave.

The most interesting addition to the line-up was Big John Duncan. Since abandoning Oi, the ex-Exploited guitarist had formed the Blood Uncles with Jon Carmichael (vocals) and Colin McGuire (bass). The razor-edged 'Petrol' was succeeded by 'Libertine', but the trio failed to survive the rigours of a major label. Contemporaries the Hook 'N' Pull Gang did not even face that conundrum. Guitarist Rita Blazyca joined Alan McDade and Eileen McMullen in a group noted for scatology, venom, and a furious noise. 'Pour It Down Your Throat'/'Gasoline' is a single of naked intensity - 'music for the ugly', they defined it - but their statement complete, the trio split up.

Having failed to impress London's music cognoscenti, Jesse Garon And The Desperadoes looked to Narodnik for their next release. Connelly's venture had issued further singles by Baby Lemonade ('The Secret Goldfish') and the Vultures, but it proved an expensive luxury. 'I lose money on studio costs every time,' he admitted in a contemporary interview, 'and to be honest I don't know how much longer I'll be able to keep it up. But Creation didn't make any money until their 10th record and I've only done half that many.' Alan McGee, however, had the Living Room to cushion any losses and, without similar support, Connelly was forced to wind his label up. 'Eddie kept saying he would do another single, but he wouldn't commit himself,' Tully recalls. 'Eventually he told us he was folding Narodnik to concentrate on Motorcycle Boy.'

Former Whiplash colleagues Michael Kerr (guitar) and Paul McDermott (drums) joined Eddie, Alex and guitarist David Scott in a venture which, despite undoubted promise, failed to match its potential. A single, 'Big Rock Candy Mountain', and EP, *Trying To Be Kind*, were completed, and the quintet toured with the Mary Chain before the removal of McDermott enhanced underlying tensions. 'You And Me Against The World' then ensued, but a projected album, 'Scarlet', was the subject of numerous revisions. Eventually the line-up comprised solely of Connelly and Taylor, who began re-recording the set as dance tracks. If completed, it was never issued, and Motorcycle Boy was abandoned.

The Desperadoes continued their erratic path, although Andrew Tully concedes the momentum had faltered. 'It was February '88 before our next single came out and that nine to 10 month gap was fatal.' The sextet set up their own label, Velocity, for their next two releases, the first of which contained two unselfconsciously plaintive love songs in 'The Adam Faith Experience' and 'Laughing And Smiling'. The second set was led by 'You'll Never Be That Young Again', the music of which suggests wistful innocence, yet its knowing lyric is altogether darker. 'Who will listen to your heart if you won't find your voice,' intones Schoppler in what remains the Desperadoes' most resonant, and engrossing, recording. A cover of Blondie's 'Union City Blue' ensued, but this seemingly-incongruous move was just another part of the Garon mythology. 'We decided to do a different Blondie song at every gig,' Tully explains, 'which was fine when you were doing one every four months. 'Union City Blue' was supposed to be a free single with 'A Cabinet Of

Curiosities' (a singles' compilation), then a b-side, but it was eventually swapped around.'

The group's next single, 'Grand Hotel', was cut one-sided in an effort to save spiralling costs. As Velocity had been discontinued, the record was issued by Kevin Buckle, owner of Avalanche Records, the home of a reformed Shop Assistants. With Marguerita from Jesse Garon moonlighting on drums, David, Sarah and Laura completed two EPs for the label, *Here It Comes* and *Big E Power* which blended generic Shoppies' originals with covers drawn from the Beatles and Half Japanese. 'I'm no longer obsessed with sounding like the Ramones,' Keegan stated at the time, but although these new releases were endearing, the reunion itself proved short-lived.

The Desperadoes, however, did complete an album, although *Nixon* failed to match the enchanting elegance of previous singles. The rock-oriented sound unveiled on 'Grand Hotel' pervades much of the selection, obscuring the beautiful frailty present in the group's best work. 'Hold Me Down' and 'Eden' are absorbing, but an erstwhile sense of purpose and magic was missing.

'By that point we were having difficulty with guitarists,' Andrew Tully relates, and indeed the album features newcomer Michael Kerr, as well as debutantes John Robb and Dave Evans. 'The core of the group - myself, Fran, Marguerite and Angus - was always the same, but we couldn't get full-time commitment from others. By 1990 there was no new material, we weren't rehearsing much, and being in a band had become trying, which is not the way it started.

'The Desperadoes ended one night after playing in Liverpool. This is how groups split up; we had a blazing row over who was going to sit in the middle of the back seat. No-one spoke for hours on the way home and we knew then that it was over.'

The demise of the Desperadoes closed an era in Edinburgh's independent scene. The Thanes were the only act to survive its turmoil and, despite endless changes in personnel, this irascible unit continues to offer Lenny Helsing's vision of garage R&B. Of course at other times he's in the Offhooks or the Staircase or the Naturals - some habits never die.

CHAPTER 24
A TASTY HEIDFU

By the mid-70s folk-rock had become commonplace, and electric fiddles were no longer a novelty. The JSD Band announced their presence with *Country Of The Blind*, a tame, but promising debut. *JSD Band* and *Traveling Days* were a better measure of their skills; Chuck Fleming scraped his violin as if possessed and caught live they were a dramatic act, blending jigs with pop's simple excitement. His departure in 1974 robbed the group of its focal point, and although Iain Lyon, ex-My Dear Watson, joined in his place, the New JSD Band failed to reap the same acclaim.

John Martyn spent the decade expanding his craft. A solo act again when Beverley opted for motherhood, his *Bless The Weather/Solid Air/Inside Out* trilogy is a stunning example of a mature musician adding jazz, electronic and 'world' textures to his already abundant lexicon. 'I wanted to get away from common guitar phrasing,' Martyn stated in 1971, and his vibrant experimentation culminated in a spell in Jamaica where he worked with Burning Spear, Max Romeo and Lee Perry. A 1976 private pressing *Live At Leeds*, captured John's desire to challenge and confront, but his subsequent work has proved less consistent. *Grace And Danger*, released in 1981, chronicled the break-up of his marriage, and showed Martyn still capable of shredded-nerve emotionalism. Two years later he completed *Philentropy*, on which the singer was supported by former Pathfinder Ronnie Leahy and ex-Beatstalker Jeff Allen.

Yet despite an occasional surprise, predictability would grip folk/rock the same way it had its antecedents, and little was left to choose between the attitudes of all camps progenitors: The forms had become sanitised but if punk subverted rock's tapestries, demanding a rejection of flaccid complacency, folk was initially left untouched. By the 80s, however, several disencumbered musicians would reappraise this position. Tonight At Noon infused traditional songs with drums and synthesizers, Deaf Heights Cajun Aces brought new meaning to 'hoedown', while N'Ya Fearties suggested that a bastard mutation of rockabilly, folk and impudence could charm.

Edinburgh's We Free Kings hated the term 'folk band'. 'Celtic Thrash' was melodeon player Pam Dobson's description, while fiddle player Geoff Pagan extended the argument by proclaiming *The Clash* a folk album. Formed by lyricist/vocalist Joe Kingman and guitarist Seb Holbrock, the Kings began playing Stooges and Velvet Underground covers, but by the time their rolling personnel had been completed by Colin Blakey (reeds/whistle), Phil Bull (cello) and drummer Kenny Welsh, the group coupled 'Run Run Run' with 'Raggle Taggle Gypsies'. Comparisons with the Pogues were inevitable but, as non-musicians, the Kings were more sympathetic to punk's amateur tenet. 'We usually get a vague idea of how the songs should feel,' said Joe to *Cut*, 'rather than how they should actually sound.' Their debut release, 'The Wild Colonial Boy', was 'Single Of The Week' in Dublin's *Hot Press* magazine, and the septet subsequently toured Ireland, staying in tents.

A second single, 'Oceans', was followed by an album, *Hell On Earth And Rosy Cross*, released on DDT in 1987. This suitably ramshackle collection captured something of the group's anarchic live shows, but it was equally clear a change was needed to stop an inexorable slide into self-parodic mayhem. A period of turmoil ended in 1991 with the *Howl* EP, wherein Wee Free Kings revealed rock-based inclinations. 'I'd hate to predict our musical direction,' Kingman declared to *TLN*. 'The rest of the band would beat me up.'

We Free Kings enjoyed the patronage of Waterboy Mike Scott, a Dublin resident since 1986. 'I had known Joe for many years,' he explained. 'He was an Another Pretty Face fan and we became friends. He used to hang out with me when I was living on my own in London.' The original Waterboys - Scott, Karl Wallinger and Anthony Thistlethwaite - had completed two further albums, *A Pagan Place* and *This Is The Sea*, with the help of various temporary members. The latter set was notable for 'The Whole Of The Moon', a dramatic, impassioned song which became a Top 10 single when re-released in 1991. The group then underwent a crucial change through the departure of Wallinger and arrival of fiddler Steve Wickham, formerly of Irish group In Tua Nua, who invited Scott to live in Eire. The subsequent new direction was not solely due to this decampment, as Mike explains. 'The changes had begun before we moved. Steve's arrival altered the sound at a time I was becoming interested in different music; cajun, country, folk. Those things just happen and it certainly wasn't pre-planned.'

It was 1988 before the fourth Waterboys' album, *Fisherman's Blues*, was issued. The group was, by this point, resident in Galway, and a pastoral quality permeated the entire selection. Culled from a series of contrasting sessions, the final selection reflected Scott's newfound contentment, although its equally true that the Celtic experience had joined Christianity at the heart of his previous work. Many critics voiced disquiet about the less fervent atmosphere on offer, but there was no denying its infectious bonhomie. We Free Kings virtuoso

Colin Blakey made a cameo appearance, and remained part of the road band put together to tour in support of the albums' release.

There was, however, considerable reservation about the 1990 follow-up, *Road To Roam* where jigs, reels, love songs and ballads forged an awkward alliance crying out for cohesive direction. The loss of Wickham rattled this artistic lethargy and Scott took a stripped-down quartet on the road, where an artist renowned for a refusal to repeat sets played visceral readings of material drawn from his group's entire catalogue. A *Best Of* selection followed as this particular Waterboys drew to a close, a fact enhanced by Mike Scott's subsequent relocation to New York.

Another roots act, Swamptrash, followed We Free Kings to DDT. Their album, *It Makes No Never Mind*, was an irreverent smash and grab of cowpoke-styled originals and ferocious covers of 'Ring Of Fire' and 'Foggy Mountain Breakdown'. Adopting a 'Scritton Brothers' guise - suggestive of hillbilly incest - the sextet rampaged a path through their scurrilous repertoire and completed a second album, *Bone*, before succumbing to Edinburgh's age-old fractionation. Half of Swamptrash merged with half of the similarly-inclined Critterhill Varmints, the result emerging in 1990 as Hexology. A self-titled album appeared the following year, but this particular enterprise remains a largely studio-based concern. The remaining Varmints meanwhile became Kith And Kin, who steadfastly maintained the three units' bumpkin bluegrass tradition.

Where Swamptrash cultivated a fraternal air, the Proclaimers - twin brothers Craig and Charlie Reid - were the real thing. While the former group faked badlands accents, the siblings' deliberately Scottish pronunciation provided a unique niche. This combination lent early attention a gimmick-laden air - two Jesse Raes in jeans - although the innocent charm of the pair's early work counterbalanced such temporary trappings. 'There is a sense of ridiculousness in what we do and the way we look,' Charlie confirmed in a BBC interview, 'but it's not a big deal to us. We do songs, we play them and that's it. How you react is up to you.'

Groomed on Beatles' songs and country tunes while in their early teens, the Reids emerged from a bedroom band with the rise of 1977's punk. 'It embraced our thoughts for about three years,' said Charlie to *Cut* in 1988. 'It was all we played and listened to, unfortunately.' Two groups, the Hippy Hasslers then Black Flag, ensued, both of which appeared on an occasional basis at mining villages around the pair's hometown of Auchtermuchty. 'We weren't really thrashy,' he continued, 'it was quite tuneful, but we got into a situation, like a lot of people did in the punk and post-punk time, of writing songs about things we didn't know too much about.' By 1981 the twins had left Fife for Edinburgh, but it was another two years before the Proclaimers' notion was more fully formed. Relying solely on acoustic guitars and unabashed voices, the

Reids eschewed consistent live work in favour of honing their songs and presentation.

Restaurateur and future manager Kenny MacDonald 'discovered' the twins through a demo tape passed to him by a friend. He played the results in his brassiere - Lilligs in Victoria Street - and later caught a rare appearance by the duo at nearby Nicky Tams, the pub which occupied what once was the Place. The gig, in which the Proclaimers supported Hüsker Dü acolytes the Cateran, confirmed McDonald's affection, but it was 1987 before the Reids officially invited him to represent their interests.

An acquaintance of the twins passed one of their cassettes to the Hull-based Housemartins, who invited the Reids to contact them during a *Round Table* broadcast on Radio 1. Support slots on a national tour ensued, but it was a memorable appearance on Channel 4's *The Tube* which introduced the Proclaimers to a national audience. Here they previewed 'Letter From America', a homily to Scottish adventurism resulting, not from messianic purpose, but economic blight, a feature emphasised by the litany of place-names closing the song. A 'big-band' version, co-produced by Gerry Rafferty, was the pair's debut single on signing to Chrysalis, whereas a simpler, acoustic rendition was featured on their album, *This Is The Story*. The remaining inclusions were left similarly unadorned - the set took nine days to complete - which emphasised their Lallans dialect and unreconstructed politics. 'It's got to be as pure as it can be,' Craig told writer Mark Hagan. 'If you feel it in your gut and in your heart, what your head is telling you must be secondary. If you really feel it, then write about it.'

'Letter To America' was a number 3 hit in 1987, although its more abrasive-sounding follow-up, 'Make My Heart Fly', struggled to reach the Top 75. It was clear the warmer texture of a full band provided the twins with greater latitude. Gerry Donahue, Dave Mattacks and producer Pete Wingfield were among those fleshing the Proclaimers' sound on *Sunshine On Leith*. The punch unveiled on 'I'm Gonna Be' is indeed arresting, while elsewhere the extra musicians embellish a C&W pathos intrinsic to the duo's work. This is certainly true of the anthemic title track and a haunting version of Steve Earle's 'My Old Friend The Blues'. The brother's polemics surface on 'What Do You Do' and 'Cap In Hand', the second of which balances life's 'certainties' against one imponderable - 'I can't understand why we let someone else rule our land.'

The Proclaimers spent part of 1989 on tour, but rumours of an artistic impasse began circulating with reference to an aborted third album. 'We didn't intend spending this length of time away,' Craig stated on a 1991 radio broadcast, 'but the writing just didn't come.' The twins instead cut a version of Roger Miller's 'King Of The Road' for an Australian film, *The Crossing*. They had first devoted themselves to the 'Hands Off Hibs' campaign, a successful rebuttal to an attempt, by local rivals Hearts, to take over Hibernian Football

Club. The Reids affection for the latter side is undisguised, a factor reciprocated when *Sunshine On Leith* plays over its Easter Road terraces.

'King Of The Road' brought the Proclaimers another Top 10 hit, yet perversely reintroduced the notion of triviality. It is, however, a determination to create quality work which has absented the twins from Scottish pop during the early 90s. Their self-belief is highly laudable, and their refusal to buck to commercial demands mirrors that of another group - coincidentally also now signed to Chrysalis - Runrig.

If, in the past, Scottish pop comprised of urbanites taking its culture into the country, the late 80s witnessed a quite remarkable reversal. The notion of Gaeldom became an intrinsic part of musical perceptions and presentation; the success of Stuart Adamson's Big Country was indelibly linked to the skirl of his guitar. Runrig, however, did not simply redefine Scotland's rock with the aid of a sprig of heather; their inception and progress owed little to its traditionally-held assumptions.

The group originated on the Isle Of Skye, a place beloved by romantics, but one left largely unmoved by 60s fervency. Of course the Beatles could be heard from teenage Dansettes, but a rare Glasgow posse was more likely to be that of the Chris McClure Section - safe and predictable - rather than the impassioned Pathfinders. The cheekily-named Skyevers was the leading local attraction, but even their pop chart-inspired set was tempered by accordions and de rigeur country dance tunes. The group pursued this eclective vision on and off throughout the decade, but by 1968 they'd lost one member, Rory MacDonald, to Glasgow's School of Art. Three years later younger brother Calum travelled south to study at Jordanhill College. 'Leaving Skye was crucial,' he recalls. 'I had been writing beforehand, but Glasgow provided a focus.'

Although initially rebelling against Gaelic culture, the siblings were latterly drawn back to their heritage and Calum MacDonald found the social segregation in Glasgow alien to the pluralism of Skye. 'I don't think you can fully understand your own identity and culture, or the worth of it, unless you stand outside it. Glasgow did that for me and provided the incentive to read my own history.' This newfound self-awareness combined naturally with a continued love of music. The 'Run Rig Dance Band' made its debut in 1973 when the mother of a Glasgow-based acquaintance, Blair Douglas, required an act to play at a meeting of the Highland Society's North Uist and Bernera Association.

The fledgling group's repertoire of Scottish songs was enhanced by Thin Lizzy's version of 'Whisky In The Jar'. An excited MacDonalds/Douglas triumvirate took a similar repertoire back to Skye where they became a popular attraction, fleshing out the Scottish element with pop chestnuts drawn from Chuck Berry and Johnny And The Hurricanes. It was good-time music -

'Something to do during our student holidays,' as Calum later recalled - existing for the moment without thought of permanence. Indeed Rory later opted to stay in Skye, leaving Calum and Craig to play on an informal basis in Glasgow, although Runrig was reconvened on the island in the summer of 1974.

The mixture was as before, but the desire to present folk in a rock context was in part inspired by Fairport Convention, whose *Leige And Lief* and *Full House* married jigs and reels to electricity. 'The only way you could perform live on Skye was at the community dances,' Calum recalls. 'That meant you had to play traditional music, as well as any aspirations towards rock and pop. Fairports became the role model for us in many ways, certainly in our interpretation of Scottish dance music, and later in the way they wrote their own songs around the traditional genre.'

A fourth member, Donnie Munroe, joined the line-up that year. A former classmate in Portree of the younger MacDonald, Munroe had sung in several low-key, folk-based acts prior to taking up studies in Aberdeen. He too returned home for the lengthy holiday period and his arrival coincided with Runrig's most extensive programme to date, reaching Wick to the north and Oban in the south. The set was still comprised of cover versions - Creedence Clearwater Revival were particular favourites - yet the MacDonalds were avidly pursuing their compositional muse. 'The songwriting element existed before Runrig did,' Calum explains, 'and at that point they were still two separate strands. There was always the desire that one day we would include our own songs in the set, and were writing a lot, but we were just enjoying the early years of the band too much to bother about getting serious.'

Douglas left the line-up at this point; his replacement, Robert MacDonald (no relation), came in on accordion and while Rory vacillated between guitar and bass, the roles of Donnie and Calum - vocals and drums respectively - were, for the moment, stable. The group then moved to Dalkeith, near Edinburgh, but although they occasionally played in the capital, live Runrig appearances were still largely constrained to the Western Isles and Highlands. The 'human jukebox' element was retained until 1978, and the MacDonalds' original songs remained separate to the group until their debut album, *Play Gaelic*, was released that year. Produced by Ken Andrew and Ian McCredie, former members of Middle Of The Road, the set was given a mixed reception. While traditional Gaeldom was suspicious of this musical development, younger elements, in particular those who also looked to the radically-inclined *West Highland Free Press*, proved more enthusiastic. However, Runrig did encounter problems when material from the album became central to their set, particularly during the protracted period between its recording and eventual release. 'The reaction (on Skye) was terrible,' Donnie Munroe recounted in the group's biography, *Going Home*. 'Everybody hated it.'

In retrospect the furore seems puzzling, particularly on listening to those first tentative steps. *Play Gaelic* is almost apologetic, fearful of offence, yet it retains an appealing, albeit primitive, unpretentiousness. There's no drama, no declamatory sound, leaving an impression that opposition from within the Sgiathanaich was based on the notion of what Runrig were attempting, rather than how it sounded. 'It's still one of my favourite records,' says Calum MacDonald. 'It's naive musically, and only a few of the songs have withstood the test of time, but it holds so many memories. It was such a milestone for us that all its weaknesses can be put to one side.'

The album's release at least confirmed that Runrig's advancement of Gaelic music was not a temporary abstraction, even if gigs were tempered by those now increasingly irrelevant cover versions. Indeed the group found Lowland or 'exile' audiences more receptive to their original songs, suggesting that a sense of longing for rural culture was more potent than actually living within it. Runrig were nonetheless determined to progress – Robert MacDonald left the line-up, unwilling to turn professional – and while Blair Douglas returned to the fold, a greater emphasis on rock was signalled with the addition of guitarist Malcolm Jones. Finance, however, remained a problem, which in part explains the group's tenure on *Cuir Car* ('Turn Around'), a children's programme broadcast by Grampian Television.

Runrig

Douglas left again in 1979, the year Runrig approached an artistic crossroads. Aware of an impending impasse, they ditched their dance-band status, jettisoning cover versions in favour of original material. The quartet then began work on a second album, *The Highland Connection*, at Pencaitland's Castle Sound, the results of which were released on their own, newly-founded enterprise, Ridge Records. Launched at that year's Stornoway Mod, the set revealed a quite different act to that portrayed on its predecessor. This venom is immediately apparent on 'Gamhna Gealla', where Ross's punctuative style suggests something of Wilko Johnson from Dr. Feelgood. Elsewhere, Runrig show themselves as folk-rock, rather than folk, and their use of traditional material echoed that of Irish group Horslips, who also reclaimed the past with a music drawn from contemporary, not ethnic, styles. 'The band had progressed,' Calum confirms, 'and we knew we needed, and wanted, a harder sound.'

In 1980 Iain Bayne, formerly of New Celeste, became Runrig's drummer, leaving Calum MacDonald free to add percussive textures to what had become a brasher, yet more intricate, sound. *Recovery*, the group's third album, was produced by Robert Bell of the as-yet un-named Blue Nile, and this may account for its largely reflective atmosphere. The balance between Gaelic and English lyrics is more evenly struck as Calum drew metaphors from biblical and historical tenets ('Recovery' and 'Dust') to reflect contemporary Gaels. It was their most mature release to date and, having added Richard Cherns on keyboards, an expanded Runrig embarked on its first European tour.

Although a prototype version of 'Loch Lomond' had appeared on *Highland Connection*, the group chose to re-record the song as their debut single. A link with shortbread and cosy sentimentality has dented the appeal of a once-emotive Jacobite vignette concerning the fate of two prisoners. The one set free takes the 'high road'; the other, who will be executed, follows the 'low', and if Runrig's motives were unashamedly commercial, they have, in part, succeeded in reclaiming the song, re-presenting it within its cultural heritage.

Despite a growing approbation, Runrig's unconventional progress left them vulnerable to predators. They survived a financially punitive deal with an Edinburgh-based entrepreneur, only to fall into the clutches of Simple Records. That label's post-production manipulations and unsympathetic attitudes robbed the group of, not just an individuality, but respect. The offending tracks, 'Skye' and 'Dance Called America', were later re-recorded for *Heartland*, the album born from Runrig's determination to rid themselves of these palpable spectres. Recorded during 1985 at a variety of locations when finance allowed, the set nonetheless achieved continuity through the contribution of longstanding producer Chris Harley, and enabled the group to regain control of its career. 'We were in the doldrums for a couple of years before that,' Calum MacDonald admits, 'but these problems were a learning experience. It's the kind of thing that happens to bands - it goes with the script - but so many acts never come through. The fan base we'd developed to that point helped us stay on our feet.'

Four years had passed since the release of *Recovery*, and *Heartland* was rapturously welcomed by this enlarged audience. Although some quarters within the Gaidhealtacht expressed disquiet over a predominantly English-quotient, a contrast to the charges levelled at *Plays Gaelic*, the album combined the eloquence of its predecessor with the verve of *Highland Connection*. It was here Runrig became a rock band and, in 'O Cho Meallt', aimed a riposte at Simple Records in time-honoured style.

Richard Cherns left the group the following year. His replacement, Peter Wishart, had been a founder member of the original Big Country, but quit in sympathy when his brother Alan was axed. Yet there remains more than just a historical link between two groups aspiring to fuse roots and contemporary styles. Their origins were markedly different, yet some musical conclusions proved similar, and it remains a curious fact that as Stuart Adamson's commercial star waned, so that of Runrig ascended.

The Cutter And The Clan (1987) was the last album issued on Ridge. The following year Runrig was signed by Chrysalis, which not only confirmed the group's burgeoning popularity, but suggested they too felt confidence within a wider frame. The live *Once In A Lifetime* was the ideal précis of the previous decade, before *Searchlight* and *The Big Wheel* captured a group now truly defined as international. They trigger ardour in expatriots and provide allegories for others, yet Runrig assiduously retain their founding perspective. 'Gaelic has always been the rock on which the group has sat,' states Calum MacDonald. 'Even although 80% of our set is in the English language, Gaelic is the fulcrum of the band and will be as important in the future as it ever was in the past. I can never see a time when Runrig will put out an album without Gaelic songs.

'We never consciously decide to write in either English or Gaelic,' he continues. 'It's always a fairly natural process and comes from being open to the influence of, and speaking, two languages. Your thought processes operate in both at varying times. We've never analysed how we decide; maybe some melodies lend themselves to one or the other.'

Despite their commercial success, Runrig nonetheless remain outsiders, set apart from pop's customary foibles. They tour and record, yes, but both the group and audience are often criticised for playing on a concurrent desire for Scottish political independence - but never defining it as such - relying instead on the emotion of past wrongs and the wistful appeal of loch and moor. Calum MacDonald is dismayed at this narrow perception. 'We are not synonymous with Nationalism in any shape or form; the music is above and beyond that. I think the confusion arises because we sing about a place and cultural identity and because our music is Scottish and rooted in the Gaelic tradition. The combination of all these things leads you open to these accusations and a lot of people make that assumption.

'If anything our music is spiritual in the very wide sense and I think that is beyond something as one-dimensional as waving a flag for a political organisation.'

Critics have rounded on the saltires brought to concerts, and the conservative structure of Runrig's music. Yet those doing so fail to grasp that the group is a product of a quite different culture and what they do is daring, within its terms. And if Runrig do convey a wistful escapism - and I'm sure they would see their work in much broader terms - so too is a singer from Clydebank aping southern soul or a guitarist from Bellshill chiming Neil Young. Indeed Runrig's Scottish element is arguably more honest, yet in truth it is this parochial quality which provides problems for those unswayed by their meditations. A comparison with folk duo the Corries raises Runrig hackles, but both groups serve as conduits for aspirations an audience, rightly or wrongly, perceives the act to have. This assumption provides an immutable bond, but an onlooker failing to share that desire is inevitably suspicious of the attachment, and the music through which it passes. Runrig will always polarise opinion; as their fame grows so the strength of feeling on both sides can only intensify.

'Criticism is inevitable if you're successful,' Calum MacDonald concludes, 'you can't expect everyone to like your music. But if you feel what you're doing is of worth, and an audience appreciates it, then that's what stimulates you and that's what you put your energies towards.'

CHAPTER 25
'I MET ALL THE P-FUNK PEOPLE AND BECAME A SPACE CADET.'

If Jesse Garon or the Shop Assistants showed one perspective of Edinburgh pop, dance music exposed another. This was not the brassy soul of Glasgow's 'Wetsway' culture; a continuum from the Senate through the Average White Band, but rather one which looked to newer, more contemporary Black urban styles. Where the former groups would name-drop Marvin Gaye or Otis Redding, the latter extolled P-Funk and Bootsy Collins. 'In its original form, it was stripped down and bare, like Prince's 'Dirty Mind',' Davie Henderson of Win explains of 'Un-American Broadcasting', and such reference points in turn offered new possibilities. Having issued an affectionate reading of Sly Stone's 'Running Away' as his 'solo' debut, Paul Haig sought to follow it with a similarly buoyant album. This was not to be, as the singer relates. 'I'd been recording for Crepesule, but was also looking for a deal in Britain. Michael Duval met Chris Blackwell at a party and I became an Island artist. They suggested Alex Sadkin as a producer - I liked his Grace Jones stuff - but what seemed like a good idea changed so much during the recording.'

P-Funk keyboard player Bernie Worrell was one of several musicians Sadkin drafted in on *Rhythm Of Life*, which retained the name of Haig's collective, but not its principles. 'They wanted me as a solo pop puppet.' Yet despite moments of occasional light-heartedness; 'Adoration' toyed successfully with Human League-styled bravura, this 1983 set was curiously imbalanced, leaving Haig a stranger on his own, disappointing, album. 'We had a big argument. He seemed to want an All-Star group with me singing in the background and it became a bit of a nightmare. At one point I was playing some guitar he didn't like so he asked David Byrne to come along. He heard me play and asked Alex why on earth did he need him to do it?'

The misuse of Worrell was particularly galling given the empathy he enjoyed with another Scottish performer, Jesse Rae. Born and bred in the Borders, Rae cannot be honestly classed as part of Edinburgh's milieu, although for a short time the city housed his label and management. 'I've always been into soul music,' he states, 'I was brought up on it, but I didn't really know about it until I went to Cleveland.' Having answered a 'musicians wanted' ad. in *Melody Maker*, Rae joined the Boys, a heavy rock band based in the USA. 'It was three sets a night, six days a week; I could have been in those clubs forever. But one night our manager ran off with the truck and equipment so that seemed a good time to go.' He then moved across to the east coast where a pivotal coincidence occurred. 'When I was in Boston there were these posters for George Clinton; this guy looking wild in a pair of hot pants. He was surrounded by freaks, one with a kind of nappy on, and I thought this is unbelievable. I went down to the Sugar Shack to see them - I was the only white lad there - and back at the Holiday Inn, Bernie Worrell and I bumped into each other in the elevator and we got talking. I said, "This is it. This is the stuff I'm into. Where do you guys live?" I went down to Plainfield, New Jersey, met all the P-Funk people and became a Space Cadet.'

Jesse subsequently worked with Ruth Copeland, a singer renowned in soul circles for her 60s recordings with Clinton, before returning to Scotland in 1978, armed with several demos. Zoom was among the several labels approached, but unable to secure a deal, Rae returned to the USA. One of these songs, 'D.E.S.I.R.E.', was picked up and released on a Florida-based label, Bold, but it was another composition which proved more successful. 'I was working with Jimmy Douglas at Atlantic during 1979,' Jesse relates, 'and he told me about this group Slave. I listened to some of their stuff and liked its gritty quality, so I wrote 'Inside Out' for them but with a crossover idea in mind. They didn't want it - I respected them for that - and the song hung around in the studio for two years.

'When the Odyssey people heard it first they mimicked me, but then they thought about doing it as a single. They couldn't get the backing vocals right so I made myself sing like a lassie and put the stuff on the record. We didn't work together though. I only met them when they came to do a gig in Scotland.'

Odyssey's version of 'Inside Out' became a major UK hit, reaching number 3 in 1982. Its success coincided with a frenetic spell in the singer's career when numerous projects tumbled into place. Rae's video for 'Rusha', a bi-lingual love song issued as a single, was a prizewinner at the UCLA's International Video Music Festival where the judging panel included Francis Ford Coppola. But while appreciative of the accolade, Jesse was less than impressed with the actual award. 'They presented me the first laser video disc, but I gave it away to someone. It had some crap on it I didn't want to watch.'. 'Rusha' did become the world's first commercial video single, and while music remained of paramount importance, Rae understood the vital link between sound and visual image. 'The likes of 'Rusha' was too off-the-wall as a record; most of it is in a foreign language. Video helped draw the melody out, allowed me to experiment and take it further.' The song's cross-Cold War theme was also welcomed by the Reagan administration. 'I got an endowment of the arts - a bit paper and a grant. The US government thanked me for strengthening cultural ties with the Soviet Union.

'I even sent a tape to Andropov, but he died the day after receiving it. It was either incredible timing or the goodwill was too much for him.'

Jesse also completed a politico-rap record, 'I Feel Liberal, Alright', with the party's then-leader, David Steel. 'I wanted a Scot as Prime Minister and David is my local MP. I was recording in New York and he was in town at a dinner. I asked him to think of something he'd like to say and come down to the studio. He arrived in full evening dress. The P-Funk guys thought he was really weird.'

The singer returned to his Borders' farm in 1983. The following year he completed 'Be Yourself'/'(It's Just) The Dog In Me', an inspired mixture of offbeat funk and Jesse's unashamed brogue. He had always worn a kilt, but now Rae donned full highland dress, replete with helmet and claymore. 'As far as I'm concerned I'm 13th century,' he explains. 'I was furious when I realised how much of my heritage had been withheld from me and I wanted a way of bringing the kilt into modern music. I didn't want to be perceived as the white guy playing funk and if I was to play this music in its truest form I had to keep the character intact at all times.' Indeed Rae's garb is not only for performance, he wears it all the time, 'like the Lone Ranger.' 'Jesse always has a reason for what he does,' adds Allan Campbell, who issued 'Be Yourself' on his newly-formed label, Supreme International Editions. 'He bursts a gut for what he believes in.' The combination of sound and image was beguiling and, as Campbell relates, 'More than one record company executive flew up to Edinburgh and then took the £40 taxi down to the farm. Jesse would not go to see them. I remember Rob Dickens from WEA, sitting in front of the fire, having a lunch made by Jesse's wife.' Indeed WEA secured Rae's signature, but what they saw as a transient novelty - a tartan Tiny Tim - refused to buckle to their demands, and the ensuing ructions simply enhanced the singer's avowed mistrust of 'the English'. 'I'm not interested in selling records in London,' he states, 'I wanted to hit other places in the world, then bring the records back in as an import. In fact I wanted to sign direct to America, but I had to be signed to the country I was resident in.' Jesse even tried to sticker his records 'made in Scotland', and 'export' them south of the border. 'It wasn't a gimmick, I meant it, but WEA treated it as such. They signed me up so no-one else could get me.'

Rae's best-known single, 'Over The Sea', stalled at number 65 nationally, yet few who've seen it forget the video shot to promote it. The contrast and cuts between rural Scotland and urban New York were stunning, while the warrior figure was unashamedly procured by director Russell Mulcachy for his subsequent film, and box-office smash, *The Highlander*. Jesse acknowledges the plaudits, and is thus able to further justify his image. 'Everyone focuses on the helmet, but no-one criticises the kilt and no-one's putting down the funk. Of course there are tremendous disadvantages, but the helmet gives an edge to get things done. It allows me to stand on top of the Brooklyn Bridge and wave a sword - no-one else would be.'

Rae's debut album, *The Thistle*, finally appeared in 1987. It contained several new versions of older songs, a wondrous medley of 'Scotland The Brave' and 'Idio-Syn-Crazy', and two strong collaborations with ex-Average White Band guitarist Onnie McIntyre, 'That Kind Of Girl' and 'Don't Give Up'. The title track was meanwhile the subject of another imaginative video, the highlight of which showed Jesse standing in front of a steam train as it roared through the Scottish countryside. Pulled behind it were open carriages on which his backing group performed. Among their number was Roger Troutman, the leader of funk group Zapp, who had produced the album. 'Roger was WEA's idea,' Rae explains, 'but I'd sooner have done it with Bernie. I wanted to bring Roger here so he would understand the difference between Scotland and England. He didn't realise it but he helped them water down the music, smoothing it out and thinning down my voice. He made multis of everything which took off the Celtic edge.

'I paid for Roger to come over and do the *Thistle* video. I met him at the airport in my tractor and trailer. There were a couple of bails in it, and a wee generator, and I stuck him in the back. He wouldn't wear the kilt though.' Troutman was then stunned to see the rest of the group, Bernie Worrell, Steve Ferrone and Michael Hampton, all in full Highland dress. 'He couldn't believe the P-Funk boys were doing this and then changed his mind. Still no kilt though - his legs couldn't take it - so we got him tartan trews.

'Totally cool Roger became totally uncool and loved it. He went down Princes Street hamming it up. We then drove 40 miles to the village green where we put on a live show for 300 kids and then put him back on the 'plane. He turned to me as he left and said "I wish I had known all this before."'

Rae's dalliance with WEA ended soon afterwards. Allan Campbell, who acted as his manager at the time, puts the era in perspective. 'If the success had been there, then the image and music would all have made sense. I know Jesse wouldn't see it in these terms, but he is the ultimate punk act. 'This is what I do, this is how I do it and this is what you get.'

If other outlets captured Edinburgh's 'shambling' scene, Campbell's Supreme International Editions showed a much wider remit, releasing 'Some Indulgence' by the Hi-Bees, a short-lived alliance between vocalist Susan Buckley and two drop-outs from Aztec Camera, Malcolm Ross (ex-Josef K/Orange Juice) and Dave Ruffy, and the debut single by the Syndicate. 'Jo

Callis produced 'Golden Key' at Bob Last's studio,' Campbell relates about the latter group's sole release for his label. 'They changed after that and wanted to get into a bigger, Mott The Hoople-type thing.' The trio signed to EMI in 1987, but two years passed before their lone album, *Keep*, was issued. Guitarist/vocalist James Stewart then broke the band up.

Supreme Editions was also the home of the Juggernauts, whose sole release was dwarfed by its title - 'Come Throw Yourself Under The Monstrous Wheels Of The Rock 'n' Roll Industry As It Approaches Destruction'. 'The Juggernauts comprised James Locke, from Rhythm Of Life, Gordon Kerr and Paul and Nigel Slevor,' states Campbell. 'It wasn't a group as such but something that evolved when I ran the Hoochie Coochie Club. They'd invent an act for the 'band night' and it would be different each week. The Cargo Cult were rockabilly; the Indian Givers were smootchier, and so on.'

Stirling-born vocalist Gordon Kerr was also the founder of Botany 500, a somnolent funk act completed by Dave Galbraith. Their single for Supreme, 'Bully Beef', revealed an already well-crafted skill, particularly in its imaginative use of a live string quartet. However, Kerr's languid talent did not fully flourish until 1989 when, having signed a deal with Virgin, he split from Galbraith, replacing his erstwhile partner with Jason Robertson (guitar) and Stevie Christie (keyboards). Threatened by a lawsuit from the US Botany 500 - the wardrobe company responsible for the sartorial elegance displayed on *Kojak* - the trio took the truncated name Botany 5 and completed the shimmering *Into The Night*.

Producer Callum Malcolm imbued the set with the aura of his best-known charges, the Blue Nile, while creating an ambience reminiscent of Talk Talk. Kerr's mellifluous voice is immediately captivating, but the textures under which it's pinned reveal a bubbling imagination. The highlight, however, is the spacious 'Satellite', a delicate composition given an untrammelled fragility through the singer's desperately deep vocal.

'Our album's for when kids come home from raves,' Kerr opined in 1991. 'No crazy, out-of-hand stuff. More artistic; slow, mellow, subdued...quiet.' Yet this somewhat saturnine aspect was at adds with Botany 5 on the road, in which dance-based mixes, lights and passion forged what one reviewer described as 'the live Hyde to the studio Jekyll.' The basic trio was then expanded to include ex-Orange Juice drummer Zeke Manyika and former Paul Weller bassist Carmel as the singer declared his dissatisfaction with the limitations of pre-recorded tapes. Botany 5's survival depends on Kerr's ability to harness such disparate ideas.

His Juggernaut companion, James Locke, joined bassist Mike Peden in another Supreme act, the Beat Freaks. 'That was me doing an anti-government rap,' says Allan Campbell, who did indeed provide the voice on the group's lone single, 'The National Anthem'. 'It was done with an honest intention,' he states, while adding, 'but it did lack artistic merit.' Indeed, interest largely focused on the flip-side, which featured 'The Best Thing In The World', a master culled from the aborted Nassau collaborations between James Brown and Sly & Robbie. 'It was a terrible mistake,' Campbell announced to the press in 1986. 'We were shocked to find it on our b-side and obviously had no idea where it came from.' It was, of course, a mischievous rouse, as Allan had obtained a good monitor mix from one of his several contacts. 'The whole idea was fun,' he explains. 'and it created a bit of a stir. But then I fell out with James Locke...which is the easiest thing in the world to do.'

'Difficult' he may be, Locke nonetheless contributed to concurrent releases by the Bathers, Hipsway and Indian Givers, the last of which was an Edinburgh trio who took their name from one of those Hoochie Coochie pseudonyms. Nigel Sleaford, Simon Fraser and Avril Jamieson completed the line-up of a group which recorded an album of intelligent dance pop, *Love Is A Lie*, before disintegrating. First Fraser, then Jamieson left, and the Givers' demise was given a whiff of scandal when the departees were served with affidavits for unpaid VAT. Sleaford reportedly sold band equipment to protect his former colleagues, and the sorry affair ended when the band's outlet, Virgin, dropped them from their roster.

'I was just drumming on all those things,' Locke stated in a 1990 interview when quizzed about his wide-ranging interests. 'I decided it was time to do something for myself.' Longtime associate Mike Peden thus joined James in a new project, rooted in a mutual love of dance music. Having written and recorded several songs with different singers, the pair secured a permanent foil in Pauline Hendry. 'I heard her tape over the telephone,' Locke related to *TLN*, 'and we flew her up (from London) that weekend. We had a few hassles to start off with,' he ominously added, 'but she was the best one.' The new group took the name the Chimes in 1987, but it was another year before their demo secured a deal with CBS.

Their debut single, '1-2-3', was produced by Soul II Soul. 'They heard our stuff,' Locke continued, 'and said they'd pick two songs to produce. I don't think '1-2-3' was necessarily a brilliant choice, but we learned a lot from them.' Although both it and a follow-up, 'Heaven', featured well in dance charts, it was the trio's reworking of the U2 anthem, 'I Still Haven't Found What I'm Looking For', which gave them a Top 5 hit in the UK and US in 1990. Their album, *The Chimes* duly followed and the set exhibited a mature, at times deceptive ease, in which Henry's expansive vocals soared over textured, shifting rhythmic pulses. There was an undeniable craft to Locke's approach, and the blend of 80s beats with 70s structure - Barry White and Earth, Wind & Fire - was attractive. But the singer's technique was clinical; Jennifer Holliday rather than Gladys Knight, and although the set boasted a cognitive grasp of melody, there was no escaping the irony that the Chimes' success had come, not only from a cover version, but that of a song already well-known.

Once again an undoubted potential began to unravel. An extensive tour was planned, then abandoned, when a follow-up single, 'True Love', barely scraped the UK Top 40. Work nonetheless progressed on a second album, but recording fell apart when Pauline Hendry left, no longer able to work with the notoriously obdurate Locke. A second Chimes album was later abandoned and while his partner confirmed the act's demise, Peden declared a desire to work in films. Such behaviour confirmed suspicion that while Glasgow groups graft their way through adversity; witness Wet Wet Wet or Love And Money, those of the capital squabble and fall apart when the least hint of recognition beckons. Edinburgh pop is littered with premature casualites - Josef K, the Rezillos, Fire Engines/Win - acts which not only collapsed, but did so when it seemed the hardest part had been achieved. It avoids that 'difficult third album' cliché and perhaps adds a dash of immediate pleasure to the city's music, but it suggests that bands on east and west coasts have markedly different attitudes.

'I'm always highly dubious of something from Glasgow that's supposed to be soul,' James Locke remarked in 1990. The infatuation with 'street', as opposed to 'classic', styles prevailing in several Edinburgh groups, suggested some kind of movement to individuals desperate to categorise a mood. This impression was enhanced by two newer acts, the Apples and Sugar Bullet, the former of which was constructed around Win refugee Ian Stoddart, ex-Syndicate member Callum McNair and 'Samantha' from Hey! Elastica, a much-hyped trashy pop band which recorded for Virgin during the early 80s. Signed to Epic in 1990, the Apples released a handful of promising singles, notably the iridescent 'Eye Wonder', but locked horns with their label over their debut album. Pre-release copies showed a group trying to harness three decades of pop, from 70s guitar to 90s rhythms, but the resultant reviews were distinctly uncomplimentary. 'Epic interfered, pointlessly making us remix,' McNair explained to *TLN*. 'It looked like we were some company-manufactured pop act, which is bullshit, and got annihilated in the press as a result.' The album was then shelved, although Callum declared that the group would continue, albeit in another guise. 'I'm writing songs and hope to come back with a whole new concept.'

Sugar Bullet - Kenny MacLeod, Shaun McCabe and Izzy Coonagh was, alongside Botany 5, one of the winning acts in the 1990 talent contest Tennent's Live!, run in conjunction with Glasgow's Ca Va Studio. Unlike their meticulous counterparts, the trio's sound is a collage of often divergent styles: hip-hop, reggae, dance and rock, drawn together in a bubbling, expressive manner. Armed with a Virgin recording deal, they spent their advance on a recording studio, effectively locking the label out of the subsequent proceedings. Two years then passed, punctuated solely by the effervescent 'World Peace' single, before the group's album, *Unrefined*, was released. 'We've supposedly had the most freedom of any band who've recorded for Virgin,' said MacLeod to *TLN*, and in a rare example of solidarity, Sugar Bullet convinced Edinburgh friends and associates, including James Locke and Mike Peden, to enhance their already fervid mix. Divided between 'Negative' and 'Positive' sides, the set showed the trio's unequivocal imagination, taking the mischievous elements of a Dee-Lite to create a kaleidoscope of samples and hooklines. If an Edinburgh dance scene did exist, then it exploded into life on *Unrequited*.

Supreme International Editions continued to operate into 1987 and 'Makin' Tracks' by the Chain Gang featured James Grant, Pat Kane, Claire Grogan and Stephen Pastel as part of a cast drawn together to raise funds for a Caterpillar work-force at that point occupying their Uddingston factory. Allan Campbells' longstanding links with Paul Haig and Josef K meanwhile inspired the release of two archive sets, both of which included material from the maligned *Sorry For Laughing* sessions. However, the label was quietly set aside as its founder became increasingly involved with *Cut*, a monthly publication launched in Edinburgh in October 1986. 'I did some writing on a freelance basis for issue one,' Allan recalls, 'then joined as an associate editor in issue two. It was the right time to start a magazine which would reflect what was happening in Scotland.' Although initially parochial, the *Cut* board quickly realised - as Fast had done before them - that the ratio between Scotland's population and size could not sustain such a costly venture and thus the paper expanded its market into the north of England. The editorial emphasis also crossed the border, and although many readers mourned the loss of a purely Scottish perspective, Campbell argues this was a highly important step. 'There were sound economic reasons for moving into England and when Neil Dalglish was editor the format became national. I think it was important to show that a Scottish publication could not only deal with Scottish matters, but could deal equally well with the modern world.' Campbell took over as editor in 1988, by which time the paper seemed to have secured its niche. Founded as a broadsheet, *Cut* had been trimmed down to magazine format and in the process become more penetrative and more visual. 'We began introducing more political articles which gave it a greater edge,' Allan suggests. 'The editorial mix, and design, were later reflected in things like *Vox*. We had some good journalists; Alastair MacKay, who I think is the best music writer in Scotland, Stephen Daly from Orange Juice, who is now contributing editor to Andy Warhol's Interview, and an excellent production team. Tony Wilson declared it 'the best magazine in Britain' on *The Other Side Of Midnight*.'

However, despite its adventurism, *Cut* was plagued by internal problems. Publisher Bill Sinclair was based in London while the editorial offices remained in Edinburgh, and it seems he was being increasingly pressurised by his partners in the parent company, Complete Print International, to take the title south. A

1986 issue of Cut magazine featuring Lloyd Cole

deal struck with New Statesman Distribution proved disastrous and many viewed Campbells' departure in 1989 as the final straw. 'We fought so many battles to keep it going,' he states, 'and I just couldn't see the situation improving.' Sinclair assumed the editor's mantle while Alastair MacKay ran the Scottish office but a public row between the publisher and columnist Pat Kane over the inclusion of illustrator Grant Morrison's 'New Adventures Of Hitler' comic strip damaged the magazine's credibility. A new distribution arrangement with COMAG ensued, but internecine strife ultimately doomed this excellent paper. The final *Cut* appeared in September 1989, despite Sinclair's avowed wish to relaunch it from Scotland.

By that point the fledgling *TLN* had taken up its role as conduit for Scottish rock and pop. This free, bi-monthly magazine had evolved from the 'Tennants Special White Pages', a feature for up-and-coming bands run in *Cut* but sponsored by the Younger's Brewing Group. Keen to expand their exploitation of rock, the company launched *TLN* - Tennants Lager News - in February 1989, and its adroit combination of news, features and corporate blandishments quickly proved popular.

Both publications helped bring a cohesive sense of identity to what was loosely defined as the Scottish scene. They not only provided a slightly different perspective to what had become national or even international acts, but provided space for both emergent talent and longstanding musicians denied exposure elsewhere, yet which were fundamental to Celtic pop's environment.

Now divorced from WEA, Jesse Rae found himself increasingly marginalised. He continued to wed ambitious videos to his recordings, a practice which took on renewed urgency given that his preferred musicians lived and worked in the USA. Jesse thus relied on programmed tapes when appearing live, which in turn increased attention on his highland garb. Financing such different projects became a problem; the singer even approached the Scottish Development Association for funding. 'They wanted to undertake a feasibility study,' he proclaims. 'How many £1,000s would that cost? They could use that money to release a couple of records, or sign a couple of bands.'

Rae wrote 'Body Blasting' when the (William) Wallace Statue was cleaned and, inspired by a one-off contribution to a television show celebrating Robert Burns, recorded several contrasting interpretations of the bard's work. 'I did 'Tam O'Shanter' as a slow funk,' he explains, 'and 'Sic A Wife As Willie Had' wild and *avant garde*.' Jesse then embarked on a tortuous relationship with the Scottish Rugby Union over an anthem for the 1991 World Cup. 'I wanted rugby to be our national game,' he states. 'The players are our last warriors.' Rae duly composed 'Jacob's Pillow' - a reference to the Stone of Destiny - and directed one of his now-customary, effective videos, which intercut training sessions, international footage and dream sequences. 'I knew John Jeffries,' he continues, referring to one of Scotlands most popular players, 'and he was very supportive; all the Borders' guys were.' Jesse did, however, fall out with the game's administrators and the completed film became the subject of legal wrangles. Rae meanwhile had struck up a fascinating partnership with Adrian Sherwood And The On-U Sound System, whose world music-cum-dub brigandry is the perfect foil for the singer's unconventional approach. Recordings undertaken with Tackhead should display another facet of Jesse Rae's many talents.

Paul Haig was another musician who's career stumbled rather than soared. A second album for Island, recorded with former Associate Alan Rankine, was canned. The only tangible result of the sessions was a single coupling 'The Only Truth', a track which featured New Order in support, with a version of Suicide's 'Ghost Rider'. The singer then reverted to Crepescule and having issued a handful of low-key singles, compiled *The Warp Of Pure Fun* from different sources. 'That was recorded all over the place,' he states. 'We used some of the Island tracks, some of it was done in Edinburgh, and we pieced things together until we had an album.' Haig's interest in dance grooves nonetheless remained intact, and although the set betrays its fragmentary origins, it showed a greater degree of purpose than its flawed predecessor.

Paul later enjoyed a brief collaboration with Rankine's former partner, Billy McKenzie, and the two singers composed songs for each other's forthcoming albums. Haig's next set, *Chain*, appeared in 1989, although its release was marred by insuperable delays. 'I put up all the money and recorded it myself,' Paul explains. 'Circa liked it and signed me up, but then a year and a half passed before it came out. I was really hacked off about that because it seemed really dated by then.' Its blend of Euro-beat and funk did seem passe, although in retrospect when those anachronistic elements faded, the set provided an introduction to Haig's next release. Advance reports suggested that *Right On Line* would provide the perfect summation of the artist's love of dance music, embracing house rhythms, samples and honeyed melodies. New York cutting crew Mantronix oversaw 'Flight X', Chicago's L'il Louis took charge of 'My Kind', while the irrepressible Locke and Peden also made significant contributions as Paul re-asserted the 'collective' overview previously apparent on *Rhythm Of Life*. 'I was making dance records in 1983,' he stated when the set was finished, 'but I can't expect everyone to know that. The new stuff may seem like a radical departure, but to me it's a logical progression.' The Chimes' input was particularly apparent on 'I Believe In You', released as a preview single in 1990. The album itself, however, was never issued, as Haig recounts. 'I got a new manager who decided he wanted to change everything. He held the album back to build things up again so it would come out with an impact. By that time Circa were losing interest and did not want to spend money on promoting it.'

The cancellation of *Right On Line* derailed the singer's career although the following year he re-emerged with *Cinematique Volume 1*. 'I'd always planned to release a soundtrack-type album,' he explains. 'Circa didn't see it as a commercial venture, but this other company was interested.' The atmospheric set comprises masters compiled over the years, and affirms Haig's inventive grasp.

His sometime partner, Alan Rankine, pursued an equally unconventional path. He too recorded for Crepescule, although *The Day The World Became Her Age* (1986) and *The Big Picture Sucks* (1989) were punctuated by his major label recording, 'She Loves Me Not', which appeared on Virgin. The suave approach to danceable pop, apparent on the Associates circa *Sulk*, prevails on most of Rankine's work. However, bereft of MacKenzie's effulgent voice, it lacks an immediate, characteristic quality. Dividing his time between Edinburgh and Brussels, he also produced several different acts, notably the Delmontes, but during an end-of-year interview in 1991 Alan declared he was 'not impressed with anything I've seen recently in Britain. I'm not looking for a new record deal,' he added. 'I don't really like them.'

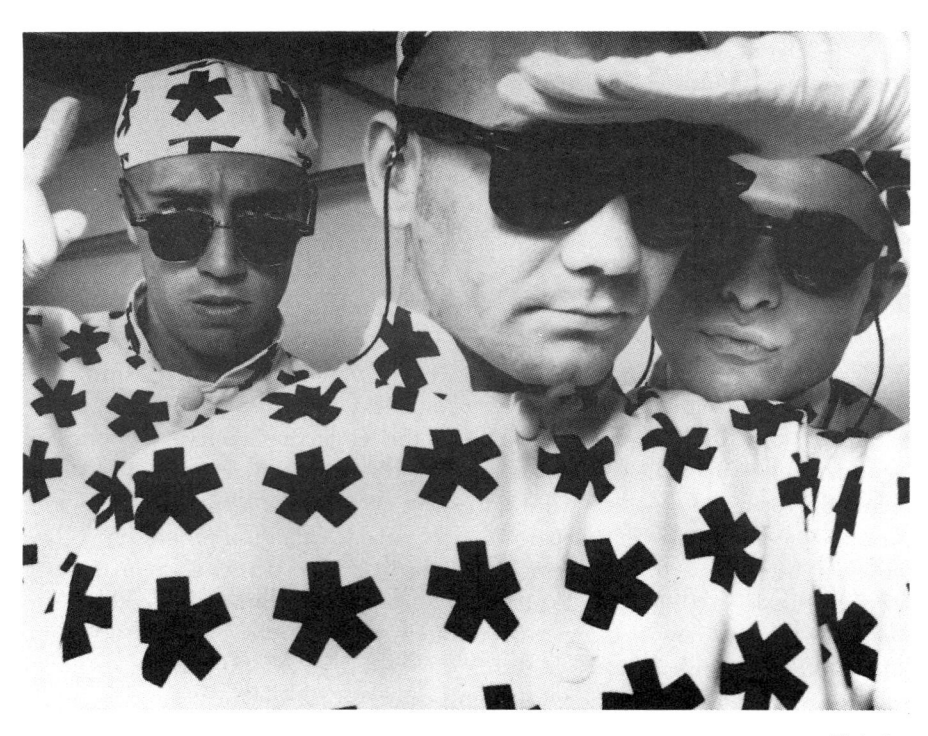

Finitribe

If Rankine and Haig offered a European view of dance, and Jesse Rae a funk-based US-styled alternative, Finitribe pursued a quite radical perspective. Formed as a sextet in 1984, the group quickly asserted its independence by founding their Finiflex label and completing the tentative 'Curling And Stretching'. Two years later they acquired their first sampler, and the last vestiges of orthodoxy were cast off in a wild, abandoned sound; part intuition, part roguery. Theatrical live shows, which involved props, paint, fire and masks, inspired comparisons with Test Department, but the Finis angrily rejected such remarks. 'We want to make things a bit unpredictable and interesting,' vocalist Chris Connelly stated in 1986, and thus the group's next release contained 'DeTestimony', a virulent anthem later embraced by Balearic and house acolytes. This in turn helped reinforce the group's new aspirations, but such rebellious attitudes were not held in isolation.

Contemporaries Ege Bam Yasi were longstanding performance artists, famed for paper mache phalluses, and as such they welcomed the surreal possibilities offered by techno and electro styles. Many individuals would pass through their ranks until, by 1990, the group had been reduced to one, the eccentric Mr Egg. Dance denizens the New York Pig Funkers completed a 1986 EP, *Hothouse*, while the Dog-Faced Hermans was another anarchic crew to evolve from Edinburgh's underbelly. Yet if Finitribe and Ege Bam Yasi looked to contemporary piracy, this rabblehouse act took equal measure from the Pop Group, Captain Beefheart and James Blood Ulmer. Their debut single, 'Unbend', appeared on the group's own label, Demon Radge, and its collision of wild voices and ugly rhythms proved highly exciting. The quartet - Colin, Andy, Marian and Wilf - was part of the Edinburgh Musicians' Collective and answered the charge of sounding extreme by stating 'it depends on what you call extreme.' Two exhilarating albums followed; *Humans Fly* and *Everyday Timebomb*, before the Hermans left their Leith enclave for Amsterdam, where they continue to forge an uncompromising vision.

Finitribe also looked beyond the UK for approbation and in 1987 began an ill-fated period with the Chicago-based WaxTrax company, home of Ministry and Front 242. Two singles ensued, but the brief relationship was not only fraught, it also exposed factionalism within the Scottish act which culminated in Chris Connelly's departure for the USA. He later became an integral part of WaxTrax collective the Revolting Cocks, as well as pursuing the solo career introduced on *Whiplash Boychild* (1991).

A trimmed-down Finitribe - Davy Miller (vocals/percussion), Philip Pinsky (bass) and John Vick (keyboards/sampling) - re-emerged in 1989 with *Noise, Lust And Fun*, a magnificent slab of cut and paste technology. Yet whereas the Chicago experience is heard in the album's brutal basslines, the trio's sense of fun is equally vital to the set's lasting qualities. 'We didn't quite know what was going on,' Vick stated to *TLN*, 'it was basically quite an unsteady period for us.' That element of uncertainty and chance provides the album's edge and shows a group developing from unfocused subversion into one with a grasp of art terrorism.

'Animal Farm' celebrated the trio's newfound confidence. Built around the 'Old MacDonald' nursery rhyme, this furious single was a savage riposte to the purveyors of Big Mac and came complete with a controversial 'Fuck Off MacDonald's' poster campaign. The ensuing ruckus obscured the sheer thrill contained within the record, the group's first for celebrated indie outlet, One Little Indian. The exceptional *Grossing 10K* ensued, and it was now clear that Finitribe were indeed serious contenders. 'We're far more knowledgeable about this album,' Vick declared upon its release, and indeed the results were startling. Their early self-indulgence had been replaced, not by conformity, but by a greater sense of communication, and the trio's cartoon humour proved equally important in the set's parodic attack on corporate thinking. Why else should they pose in bowler hats and suits, dosh stuffed into breast pockets, parading their pentagonal-star logo on guitars and brazen bow ties?

'The fact that we've never been a part of any clique in Edinburgh, let alone nationwide, should work to our long-term advantage,' Davy Miller declared to *TLN*. '(However) it's probably true to say that it's been to our short-term disadvantage.' Yet by 1992 the Tribe had not only built a digital studio and workshop, they were voicing plans to resurrect the Finiflex label and add video/photographic facilities to their Leith-based complex. Their third album, *An Unexpected Groovy Treat*, was released to critical acclaim, and its soundscape collage of dancefloor beat showed a group which had fully come of age. Their fierce independence has been crucial, not just to their music but, despite the ructions of 1987, to survival itself. They are the exception in the tale of 80s' Edinburgh woe; of missed opportunity, in-fighting and sheer bad luck, and as such deserve applause.

CHAPTER 26
'I AM THE LONE RANGER'S ONLY FRIEND. THE MARTIANS HAVE LANDED.'

'I think white rock is in a slump,' Bobby Gillespie declared in 1989. 'The most exciting things around seem to be happening in black dance music.' The advent of new sounds from urban America - rap, hip-hop, house - reinforced suspicions that those working in both mainstream and 'indie' sectors had lost the ability to either enthral or confront. Remixing, scratching and sampling had become the skills of misanthropes still bent on challenging convention, and this deconstruction in turn awakened untold areas of progression. The influence of new psychedelics, in particular MDMA or Ecstasy, enhanced its visionary elements. A rock fraternity weaned on tales of 60s hedonism took to raves and house parties as the 80s equivalent of happenings at London's UFO club or San Francisco's Avalon Ballroom. 'That whole period was a catharsis,' recalls Creation's Alan McGee. 'I'd discovered acid house through going to clubs and this really opened up my imagination. We made the label better by signing different kinds of bands and incorporating groove into our releases.' McGee's enthusiasm matched that of Gillespie, who'd become enthralled by the rave scene he discovered at Brighton's Zap Club and Shoom. This in turn introduced a new perspective on Primal Scream's own progress.

DJ Andy Weatherall had become acquainted with the group, and was zealously playlisting *Primal Scream*. 'Andy thought it was the best rock 'n' roll record he'd heard in years,' Gillespie recalls, 'and was really angry because the album had been slagged by everyone. He came to this gig we did in Exeter, then reviewed it in *New Musical Express* under the name Audrey Witherspoon. The headings were all lyrics from songs and other stuff we were into, and for him to say he really liked us was great encouragement.' Although the rock and dance cultures seemed poles apart, Weatherall and Primal Scream quickly found a common point of reference. "Don't Believe A Word'/Thin Lizzy,' states

Gillespie. 'It was like; "Are you into Lizzy, man?" because we're all massive fans. He said, "Yeah. I got Phil Lynott's autograph three days before he died." At first we thought this unreal but Andrew's theory is that it wasn't that weird and that it wasn't coincidence that we met.'

It is Innes who is generally credited with suggesting that Weatherall should remix a track from *Primal Scream*. Although a novice in the studio, he took the closing coda from 'I'm Losing More Than I Ever Had' and began tearing it down. Retaining the original guitars, congas and brass, he plundered portions of Edie Brickell's 'I Am What I Am' and sampled two of Peter Fonda's declamatory lines from Roger Corman's biker film *The Wild Angels*. The result was 1990's 'Loaded', described variously as 'a work of genius', 'the zenith of club rock' or 'a deep, dub fantasy'. Superlatives aside, it was indeed a pivotal release and, as Bobby explained to *Melody Maker*, 'It taught us about rhythm and space. The sampler opened up a whole world of psychedelic possibilities.' 'It was the first time the Primals gelled on record,' adds McGee and, more crucially, it opened up countless possibilities for the group's future direction. 'Where Primal Scream had been restricted before, now we started experimenting,' says Gillespie. 'Everyone was wide open.'

Primal Scream

The group's next single, 'Come Together', showed an even greater debt to black music. Several mixes were eventually aired, but that of Terry Farley, with percussive pulses, pumping brass and a gospel choir, became the official a-side. The song's attractive melody line was itself underpinned by a 4-note quote from Them/Lulu's 'Here Comes The Night', but it was clear that Bobby's affection for the Rolling Stones still provided inspiration. 'I saw it as a modern-day 'Street Fighting Man,' he stated in 1992, referring to a radical Weatherall remix, which teased out the constituent parts and sampled from a speech by Jesse Jackson. 'It's like 'if only the world could be as one', yet you know it won't happen.' This particular interpretation dispensed with Gillespie's vocal altogether and helped confer the notion that Primal Scream had become a broad palate, a means for diverse interests and experimental desires.

It seems more than chance that the group became embroiled in 80s dance culture following a wholesale move to England. Parallels can thus be drawn with the Shamen, but if this latter act also dissolved guitar-based whimsy into shimmering club-funk, their particular path did not take a Damascus-like conversion, but was simply a part of a natural evolution.

Formed in Aberdeen, the Shamen evolved out of Alone Again Or, a trio led by Derek and Keith McKenzie (vocals and drums respectively) and bolstered by Colin Angus (bass/keyboards). Despite deriving their name from fabled west coast act Love, Alone Again Or was squarely a synthesised pop band, and two singles, 'Drum The Beat (In My Soul)' and 'Dream Come True' combine limpid sound with ineffectual ambition. 'It was too fey more my liking,' Angus retorted when quizzed over the reasons for a subsequent re-evaluation. 'We seemed to have lost sight of our original objectives, which was dance music with a psychedelic flavour.' The seeds of future developments nonetheless lurked within the mix and the instrumental flip-sides, in particular 'Smarter Than The Average Bear', revealed the trio's interest in sequencing and programming. However, these sessions were equally important for the relationship struck with producer Wilf Smarties.

'Dream Come True' was released on Polydor in March 1985 - its predecessor had appeared on the group's own All-One label - but Alone Again Or not only escaped successfully from the relevant contract, but also secured a cash settlement in compensation. This in turn was used to finance a new venture, dubbed by Angus the Shamen in deference to the priest-like figures of ancient spiritualism. This sense of mysticism appealed to a group about to embrace psychotropic rock, and having found Smarties' extensive 60s' collection a considerable source of enlightenment, welcomed a shared love for state-of-the-art gadgetry. 'Wilf introduced us to the delights of studio technology,' reveals Angus, who wanted the new venture to be 'Something more authentic, and something I had more control over.' The revitalised group emerged as an unlikely cross between the Electric Prunes and Afrika

Bambaataa, although initially the emphasis was squarely on the former.

A keyboard player, Alison Morrison, joined the unit in 1985, although she was later replaced by Peter Stephenson. Having donated two early recordings to *Skipping Kitten* fanzine, the Shamen unleashed their debut EP, *They Might Be Right. . . But They Certainly Aren't Wrong*, in March the following year. Although its ethereal voices and shuddering guitars were firmly within indie-rock parameters, the marked use of beat-box percussion revealed a nascent dance-floor edge, particularly on 'Happy Days'. 'That track was quite hi-tech,' Angus later recalled, 'but the overall impression was still one of retro-psychedelia.'

A second Shamen single, 'Young Till Yesterday', was released on Moksha, a name derived from a collection of essays by Aldous Huxley which referred to his hallucinogenic experiences. Group manager Charles Cosh administered the label and the ensuing sense of independence allowed the quartet the chance to develop unfettered. That said, their debut album, *Drop*, marked time as the Shamen shed a traditionalist skin in favour of a bigger, more cosmopolitan sound. An attendant single, 'Something About You', revealed a greater emphasis on rhythm. Whereas its coupling, 'Grim Reaper Of Love', was drawn from 60s harmony group the Turtles, its once-frivolous title given a quite different perspective when Angus used it as a metaphor for AIDS.

In September 1987 the Shamen unleashed their most radical release in 'Christopher Mayhew Says'. Inspired by the titular Labour MP who, in 1955, agreed to ingest mescaline and then describe its effects on television, the group sampled portions of his pronouncements before unleashing a torrent of cascading tempos and searing guitar. 'We made the crossover decision at this point,' Angus recalls. 'Keith was really into drum technology and the hip-hop influence came together on that single.' The exuberant performance was a considerable influence on Jesus Jones and EMF, but its rock-dance fusion proved too radical for Derek MacKenzie, who abandoned the group for a university course. He was replaced by Willie Sinott, also known as Will Sin.

'Will was from Coatbridge,' Colin recalls, 'and had been in Edith And The Ladies, a seriously cult group influenced, by all accounts, by PiL and the Sensational Alex Harvey Band.' Sinott, like Angus, worked as a psychiatric nurse at Aberdeen's Cornhill Hospital and the pair had been introduced several months earlier by fellow carer Mickey Mann who, as Mr Mann, became a long-serving engineer with the Shamen. 'Will shared a cottage with Mickey not far from where I lived,' said Colin, 'and I'd seen him play on a video. I wanted to switch to guitar and bring in another bassist. Will was supposed to take up a post the following day, teaching English in Spain, but I told him we would be supporting Jesus And Mary Chain in Italy, so he didn't need much persuasion.' Sinott's arrival not only accelerated a musical path already undertaken, the newcomer also helped bolster the pursuit of personal enlightenment Angus had embarked upon. He empathised with the group's political edge, the polemics of which, 'Shitting On Britain' apart, were often shrouded in deceptively dispassionate vocals.

It was thus the sinuous Shamen melodies which attracted the marketing department at McEwan's brewery, who seized on the group as likely participants in their televised 'pop video' campaign. Angus mischievously offered them 'Happy Days', a vitriolic assault on the Thatcher government and, pausing only to admire the tune and write a cheque, the grateful conglomerate readied the relevant commercial. Unfortunately, the *Glasgow Evening Times* had not only noted the song's lyric, but also the group's proselytisations on behalf of the psychedelic experience. One day prior to the advertisement's first screening, the paper published a hysterical tirade and the entire campaign was hurriedly scrapped. 'The journalist contrived this lurid expose by taking stuff she'd heard third-hand through the grapevine, adding clippings from the music press, then making it more explicit.' The Shamen did keep their fee - 'It was banked, then spent, before McEwan's pulled the plug,' - although Angus is still disappointed his subversive plan was thwarted. 'It would have been shown for two weeks before anyone had sussed out the lyric. I was reluctant to get into something that promoted alcohol, but I did it to make a political point in the full hope I'd get away with it.' The group's next two singles, 'Knature Of A Girl' and 'Jesus Loves Amerika', revealed a sound in which dance elements outstripped 60s ephemera. Colin's ire still prevailed, censorship and religious fundamentalism were, in turn, addressed, and the latter sampled evangelical preachers within its wicked, riff-laden programmes. It was at this point that the final piece of the jigsaw slotted into place. 'Charles Cosh had been sending us tapes of early acid house releases,' states Colin. 'They were different, intense; you could hear its roots, but there was an energy there that wasn't contained in the music which had influenced it. We wanted to get involved and by early '88 the whole band had moved to London.' Angus and Sinott became more and more involved in the so-called Second Summer Of Love, but house proved the final straw for MacKenzie and Stephenson, who viewed the new developments as 'disco'. 'Keith was arrested for squatting,' Angus recalls, 'and understandably didn't want to do it anymore. He and Pete split back to Aberdeen. We'd already recorded the album as a quartet, but with their departure Will and I decided to go back and rework all the tracks, remix them and sequence up a lot of stuff.'

The Shamen's house debut, 'Transcendental', was issued in November 1988. It allowed the now-trimmed line-up to experiment with Chicago housemaster Bam Bam, in the UK to promote a new dance label, Desire. 'We were looking for a mixer to help us get to grips with house,' Angus recalls. 'Bam Bam was an early acid producer but his background in rock helped us connect. 'Transcendental' featured South American shamen sampled at a ceremony and was a fundamental crossover record.' The group's second album, *In Gorbachev We Trust*, followed two months later, but despite extensive redecoration, the set still showed traces of 'indie-sike' preoccupations, most notably in 'Adam Strange' and 'Raspberry Infundibulum'. Both are enchanting, but it is clear the group could no longer dwell in this particular milieu. A vicious deconsecration of the Monkees' 'Sweet Young Thing' was its final farewell as the duo embarked on a quite different entactogenic path.

'Synergy', the opening track, was the cornerstone of their subsequent development. The concept of creating something new from the interaction of two or more elements was critical to the Shamen's thinking, and the title was applied to a club the group ran at London's Town & Country Two, as well as a subsequent roadshow. 'The first tour was a 4-hour show, modelled in lighting and design on the clubs we were going to,' Colin explains. 'There were strobe lights, slide projections, films; lots and lots of smoke - it was a total stroboscopic throb. DJ Nick Hawks spun tracks before our set, which was all live, sequenced and mixed by Mr Mann, then Nick returned for an hour after we'd finished. It was a giant leap from our previous tour - I think it was the first time anyone had taken a dance club on the road - but we went for it, albeit with trepidation.'

'You And Me And Everything' - 'a self-conscious move back towards pop,' - and *Phorward* chronicled this particular period. '*Phorward* marked the start of another phase,' notes Angus. 'It was all done at Wilf's Planet on a shoestring budget, but it generated enough funds to make the next leap.' Having signed to One Little Indian, the Shamen completed 'Omega Amigo', a deceptively sinewy blend of house and ambient styles. The idea for its follow-up, meanwhile, came to Angus on the group's now-natural environment - the dancefloor. 'I could hear the lyrics and chorus,' he relates, 'and somehow I managed to remember them.' However, although the song boasted a pervasive 'move any mountain' hookline, Angus opted for the unique term, 'Pro-Gen'. 'I like to make up neologisms,' he explains. 'I took 'pro', meaning 'for', and added 'gen' for 'generation' - youth and change - or 'general knowledge'. It was a very positive title.' The track was welcomed in clubland, and it even grazed the national Top 50. But the group did not enjoy a bona-fide hit until 1991 when 'Hyperreal', boosted by soul singer Plavka's upfront vocal, reached the Top 30. By this point the Shamen were consciously sculpting singles, as Will Sin explained to *Melody Maker*. 'We knew we needed to develop certain aspects of what we were doing and so we started aiming at making our 7-inch singles pop songs, rather than just taking snatches from longer mixes.' An attendant album, *En-Tact*, confirmed the group's grasp of the dance genres they had so assiduously embraced, but it was the continued interest in 'Pro-Gen' which spurred the group's subsequent commercial breakthrough.

'The track was a popular import in America,' Angus recalls, 'and Frankie

The Shamen

Bones and Joey Beltram remixed it for the New York label, Focus. We took it back and effectively re-recorded the track, incorporating a couple of the elements of the Bones and Beltram mixes. This is a typical Shamen thing; putting something back into our own work to make it into something new.' This parthenogenesis is one facet separating traditional rock and pop from the flourishing remix culture, and begs the question is a track ever complete? 'I do like to think that a piece of music should have an extra longevity through the remix,' Angus confirms. 'This may only apply to the dance field which is constantly changing and diversifying and it's only possible to keep something relevant by reinventing it. House had brought a new definition of a track - where does it end? We all have the same super-sync packages, the same samplers, and it's easy for artists to interface with each other's work, and reconstruct each other's tracks. It's a fast-moving, interactive medium.'

Crude parallels can be drawn with the classic Tin Pan Alley songsmith, seated at a piano, providing tunes for other artists to interpret and perform. There is an immutable interest in how a third party views the initial creation. 'I think it's fundamentally creative to give a track out,' states Angus. 'Wherever possible we go along to meet and work with the people, to see how they use technology, what tricks they do, and then add them to our repertoire. We have a good idea of an individual's style, and to make a record happen as a dance

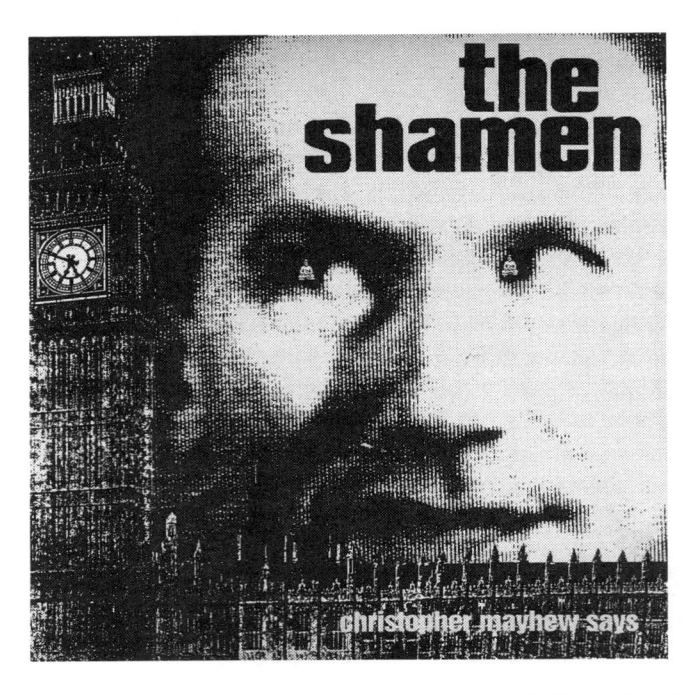

The Shamen's 'Christopher Mayhew Says'

track you have to get across to rave, garage, acid, techno and hip-hop fields. None are ever gratuitous, you have to contrive a mix for every sector.'

Having completed work on the 'new' 'Pro-Gen', now retitled 'Move Any Mountain - Progen 91', the Shamen flew out to Tenerife to shoot the accompanying video. 'We spent five glorious days on location,' Angus recalls. 'We knew the mixes we'd done were good and were convinced it would be a hit. We'd finished the video and the last time I saw Will he was about to get the ferry to Gomera. I had been intending to follow him over and check the beaches there but I got marooned on Tenerife.

'I got a call from Thompson's insurance people. At first they weren't going to tell me what was wrong and it was only when I explained that Will was not only a friend but my business partner that I was informed of the circumstances.'

On the afternoon of 22 May, Sinott took a swim in what was described as a hazardous spot off the coast of Gomera. Will was a fairly strong swimmer, but the current proved too treacherous and he drowned.

'I couldn't decide what to do,' says Colin, 'but as time went on I realised that the Shamen had been working in a state of positivity and commitment. I had to carry on: the name 'Shamen' meant a lot to Will - he knew what it meant - and there had to be a band called that.'

'Move Any Mountain' was issued two months after Sinott's death and within weeks this rhythmic single had reached the British Top 5. 'I made sure it was alright with Will's family,' says Angus, alluding to the quandary of whether to release the track or not. 'The whole experience was tempered by tragic events, but it was good to see the record achieve what Will and I thought was its destiny. I'm just sorry he wasn't around to see it.'

The single's success helped the group secure a deal with Epic in the USA, where several previous releases were hits on the specialist dance charts, 'Move Any Mountain' reached *Billboard*'s national Top 40. *Progeny*, a mini-album made up of 19 remixes, followed and the title was used to envelop the group's new in-concert extravaganza. 'The name was changed partly in deference to Will's memory. That tour was my first live work without him and it was an odd feeling. When we did two dates in Livingstone I was especially unable to fully enjoy what was going on around me. Everything was tempered by Sin's absence.'

Cockney rapper Mr. C - Richard West - had become a full member of the group. A DJ, his discs had interspersed live Shamen raves, and he had already recorded with them, notably on 'Move Any Mountain'. Jhelisa Anderson, formerly of Soul Family Sensation, completed the realigned trio which spent much of 1992 completing a new set, *Boss Drum*. The venturesome set culminates with 'Re-Evolution', a hypnotic blend of blissful sound and psychoactive lecturer Terrence McKenna's mesmeric narration. The combination confirms the transcendentalism inherent in what one writer described as the Shamen's 'cyber-pagan philosophy'. This quest for knowledge is an integral part of their approach to music, and contrasts the simpler, sybaritic pleasures of Primal Scream.

A subliminal reading of 'Slip Inside This House', originally recorded by the 13th Floor Elevators, revealed Bobby Gillespie's continued penchant for this particular act. The song's creators ran foul of their homestate's innate conservatism and, having proselytised in favour of hallucinogenics, guiding light and guitarist Roky Erickson spent a period in a mental institution - *One Flew Over The Cuckoo's Nest*-style - rather than face a penal term. The experience was devastating, and on being discharged, the musician followed a path twining rock casualty with cause célèbre. 'We cut the original down from 11 or 12 verses to two,' says Gillespie, 'and re-arranged the lyrics. Roky's on there as well. We sampled an interview with him from KSAN in San Francisco. He sings 'I am the Lone Ranger's only friend: the Martians have landed.'

'Slip Inside This House' was completed for an affectionate 'tribute' album, which coincidentally featured the Mary Chain's exuberant reading of the intoxicating 'Reverberation'. The set features another version of the song by ZZ Top, but the Reids were non-plussed, as Jim explains. 'By the time we were approached a lot of the best songs - the ones we would have chosen - were gone. We knew ZZ Top had done it already, but did ours anyway.' The Mary Chain's contribution, however contemporary, nonetheless lay within their immediate parameters, but by combining the vision of 60s experimentation with the sound of 80s psychedelia, Primal Scream invoked the essence of both eras.

This sense of spirituality culminated in 1991 with 'Higher Than The Sun', arguably the group's finest release to date. Gillespie spoke of free jazz, of John Coltrane and Ornette Coleman, with reference to this single. Yet when underpinned by guest bassist Jah Wobble's distinctive, curving lines, the piece took on the form of ambient dub, a spaceward interpretation of reggae producers Joe Gibbs and Lee Perry. 'Higher Than The Sun' was followed by 'Don't Fight It', and taken together these tracks represented a musical culmination. Having pulled this series of recordings together as the core for the *Screamadelica* album, the group completed the selection with a handful of newer compositions echoing the past year's self-expression. The Weatherall collaborations, 'I'm Comin' Down' and 'Shine Like Stars', continued the mischievous blend of melody and sound sculptures, while a haunting instrumental, 'Inner Flight', paid tribute to the Beach Boys with a chord sequence culled from the classic *Today/Pet Sounds* era. Their collective sense of fractured somnambulism, doubtlessly inspired by post-happening exhaustion and chilled-out intoxication, contrasted the euphoria so apparent on 'Movin' On Up'. It proved an ebullient clarion-call, indebted to the percussive instincts of 'Sympathy For The Devil'. This continued affection for the Rolling Stones reached an inevitable culmination when their one-time mentor, Jimmy Miller, was brought in to mix and post-produce this track, and 'Damaged', a correspondingly wasted ballad.

While the former became a deserved hit single, the latter provided the blueprint for 'Stone My Soul' and Dennis Wilson's 'Carry Me Home', two aching performances recorded in Memphis during December 1991. The ravaged vulnerability prevailing on both songs, released on the appropriately-named *Dixie-Narco* EP, proved that once again Gillespie, Innes and Young had harnessed their considerable influences to suggest new avenues of exploration. Yet the singer maintains reservations about his performance on the Wilson song. 'I wish we hadn't done that. It's a great song, but if you're familiar with the original, you'll know how ravaged he sounds. By him it's a song of experience and I wasn't ready to sing it.'

Gillespie's reverence for rock tradition is one factor helping shape Primal Scream. He qualifies his own work with frequent reference to others. 'If you listen to all the great Stones' albums, particularly *Beggars Banquet* and *Let It Bleed*, every track has a different feel to it, a different tempo and different instrumentation. It's fantastic...but it took them a long time to get there. It came from experimentation and that's always been the thing with us. "Let's try that. Let's see what it sounds like."'

Their affair with Sire over, the Soup Dragons reactivated Raw TV Productions and re-emerged in 1989 with 'Backward Dog' and 'Crotch Deep Trash', two singles which revealed that, like Bobby Gillespie on *Primal Scream*, Sean Dickson had also rediscovered the Stooges. A second album, *Deep Trash*, was announced, then cancelled, while the release of a single, 'Mother Universe', was delayed on two occasions as its initial sketch was drastically remixed.

Paul Quinn (not of Bourgie Bourgie) had replaced Ross Sinclair before the latter track eventually appeared, for the first time, in March 1990. The group's LP, retitled *Lovegod*, was issued two months later, its content the subject of similar, dance-oriented, changes. The club floor rhythms provided the Dragons with an element of continuity missing in previous work and the set was a marked improvement on the haphazard *This Is Our Art*. However, it was an attendant single which brought commercial success when their version of the Jagger/Richard song, 'I'm Free', gravitated from the group's live show into the studio.

The final track on *Out Of Our Heads*, this unassuming composition lacked the élan of 'Satisfaction' or 'Paint It Black', yet it has become a familiar part of the Rolling Stones' canon. Its limp structure was ideal for the often-fey Dragons who hitched the song to an engaging pulsebeat and brought in Junior Reid from Black Uhuru to toast over its middle eight. The result was an infectious Top 5 hit, but where Primal Scream's eclectic vision was born of a collective purpose, and welcomed as such, the Soup Dragons still struggled to rid themselves of an opportunist tag.

The reissued 'Mother Universe' provided another hit single as the quartet ignored home-based jibes and courted popularity in Europe, Australia and the USA. A 1991 release, 'Electric Blues', showed them again stepping sideways and the ensuing album, *Hotwired*, captured a group still haunted by 70s ghosts, notably Marc Bolan, which were then fused to simplistic grooves. The Soup Dragons' quest for credibility continues.

The Jesus And Mary Chain were perceptively silent during this end-of-decade turbulence. The *Rollercoaster* EP crept out in 1990, but apart from the welcome novelty of hearing Jim and William tackle Leonard Cohen ('Tower Of Song'), the set offered little they had not already achieved. The brothers were conscious of what was happening around them, but steadfastly refused to compromise their unique vision and direction. 'Whether we get it right or whether we don't, we do it,' Jim declares. 'Maybe 'Sidewalking' was an attempt at hip-hop rhythms; maybe it failed, but at least it was our attempt. It would be the easiest thing in the world to get someone else in but it wouldn't be the Mary Chain.'

'If you're going to call something your record, you want to do it your way,' adds William. 'That doesn't mean you actually have to play the part. Rather than being musicians I think we're producers. If I couldn't play a guitar part I'd get someone in and tell them what to do - "Get this sound." But I'd still call it my record because I made it up.'

The Mary Chain thus represent the antithesis of the remix culture; creating music with a finite end and purpose. While the rave culture ebbed and flowed elsewhere, the brothers were absorbed in building a recording studio, the Drugstore, and creating their fourth album. The results were previewed by 'Reverence', which wrapped slabs of reappraised feedback around a wicked, feverish rhythm. The single was hailed as an explosive rebirth, but in truth what the Mary Chain had achieved was a vibrant synthesis of what they'd already created. The concurrent excitement came from the fact that the group had recovered their erstwhile sense of danger, and once again suggested they were spinning out of control.

Distortion, melody, and the accustomed iconography abounded on the resultant set, *Honey's Dead*, which fulfilled all the promise in 'Reverence'. It is quintessential Mary Chain, and in being so makes a bolder statement than those contemporaries seeking solace in temporary diversions. The Reid's perverse blend of pop's heritage and white noise abandon has created a canon with recognisable reference points but which, as a whole, is supremely unique. Aspirants have come and gone; the Mary Chain remains a glorious racket.

The Jesus & Mary Chain

Chapter 27
Rimbaud And Me

If part of Scotland's reputation rests on stellar voices, its post-punk direction has been equally shaped by a continued affair with guitars. Although there are few Clapton-styled virtuosos, the thrill contained within that magic box - whether strewn with feedback or delicately picked - was an integral part of the process. Thus the emergence of Texas drew considerable interest, not just because of vocalist Sharleen Spiteri, but thanks to the talent of elfin guitarist Ally McErlaine. 'Neither had been in bands before,' recounts Texas' founder Johnny McElhone, 'and Ally had only ever played in his house.' A mutual friend had introduced the ex-Hipsway bassist to the aspiring singer and having secured former Friends Again/Love And Money drummer Stuart Kerr, the new quartet began forging a musical direction quite different to that of McElhone's previous groups. 'I couldn't believe how good Sharleen's voice was,' he admits. 'It was fresh and we all drew excitement from that.'

The name 'Texas' was derived from *Paris, Texas*, the acclaimed Wim Wenders' film for which Ry Cooder supplied the desolate, luminous soundtrack. Echoes of his eerie slide work abound in McErlaine's style, although Spiteri's committed vocals provided a sense of contrast. *Southside*, their 1989 debut, opened with the vibrant 'I Don't Want A Lover', a UK Top 10 when issued as a single, and a similar bottlenecked allure was recast elsewhere on the set. This rootsiness was criticised as somehow too complete, that Texas had simply recreated southern US mores, rather than offer something new. Given that Scottish rock has always aped transatlantic styles, this seemed unduly harsh, although few had exposed a debt so openly. It is also true that many qualms were implicitly based on *Southside's* commercial success - sales were in excess of two million copies - rather than its musical achievements.

Texas then undertook a punishing tour schedule, with appearances in the USA, Europe and Japan, and it was two years before a second set, *Mother's Finest*, was issued. This 1991 release introduced new drummer Richard Hynd, formerly of Slide, while Eddie Campbell, who had 'assisted' on *Southside*, had become a full-time member. His Nicky Hopkins-styled piano fills confirmed a

Rolling Stones' feel to the proceedings, and the group benefited greatly from the looser framework on offer. 'We were influenced by the Stones and the Doors,' McElhone confirms and 'This Will All Be Mine' certainly shows traces of the latter's 'My Wild Love'. The bedraggled close of both 'Walk The Dust' and 'Why Believe In You' echo the narcolepsy of *Beggars Banquet* or *Let It Bleed*, and it is clear Texas relish their newfound freedom. McErlaine's plangent steel guitar remains an integral part of the sound; it is particularly striking on 'Alone With You', but herein his wunderkind talent is equally effective on electric. 'It will take three albums to capture how we sound live,' states McElhone, 'and get that spontaneous feel.'

Texas are part of a Glasgow-based management stable which seems to thrive on monosyllabic clients, including the aforementioned Slide and Gun. The last-named emerged from a metal circuit which spawned several acts whose progress owed nothing to dalliances elsewhere, be they Postcard, Fast or Precious. The Crows, Pallas, Thee Almighty, Heavy Pettin', Lyin' Rampant, Glasgow - such groups were part of an exclusive sub-culture, the progress of which seemed largely removed from other contemporary trappings. By the late 80s thrash and melody had blurred metal's once clear-cut edges, a move which helped shape Gun's direction. The group toured assiduously to promote *Taking On The World* and their commitment was rewarded with support slots behind Simple Minds and the Rolling Stones.

In 1991 guitarist Alex Dickson, formerly of Heavy Pettin', took the place of founder member Steve Stafford, and the realigned group found chart success with the powerful *Gallus*. Stafford meanwhile formed Baby with ex-Texas drummer Stuart Kerr, and their Bellshill base indicated that musicians could thrive there and not be a part of the BMX Bandit cabal. This is certainly true of Saidflorence, whose blend of funk and waif ideology was first aired on a self-financed 7-inch single, 'Stuff Your Quiet Life'. The quartet then secured, in order, a management deal with Bruce Findlay and a recording contract with Epic, and have become one of several bands tipped 'most-likely-to' who emanate from the town.

Never in that exalted position, the BMX Bandits were even denied a place on the *New Musical Express*' *C-86* cassette of shambling bands, despite the inclusion of others, notably Primal Scream, who were appalled by the association. 'We weren't hip enough,' declares a smiling Duglas Stewart, well aware of the condescending attitude with which his group was often viewed. 'We didn't care. We knew they'd hate us anyway and that gave us freedom to do whatever we wanted. Anorak-pop did die and of course we got ignored for a while, but we sat tight and progressed naturally. We've never tried to hide our past and we aren't frightened of the future.'

By 1988 the Bandits' line-up comprised Stewart, Gordon Keen (guitar), Francis McDonald (drums) plus the nomadic Norman Blake and Joe

McAlinden. Blake had briefly passed through the Pastels, who were themselves undergoing changes. 'We dissolved,' Stephen Pastel explains. 'We'd been together too long and attained a certain level that we couldn't go beyond. The energy had drained. Brian, Aggie and I talked about it for a long time - with three it worked where it couldn't with five. There's no nice way to break up; we just disappeared and hoped the others didn't notice.'

The Pastels also 'borrowed' BMX Bandit McDonald, and the drummer was simultaneously involved in Norman Blake's next project, inaugurated with fellow Boy Hairdresser Raymond McGinley. 'We did demos on a portastudio,' Norman explains, 'two of which, 'Primary Education' and 'Speeder', ended up on the back of our first single.' They then added bassist Gerald Love and having repaired to Pet Sounds' studio, completed enough songs for an album. 'We borrowed money, rehearsed for a week, then put down every song we had,' Blake continues. 'We just wanted to do something - we knew it would be rough - but it was all our different ideas.' The session was undertaken with the full intention of releasing the results and when McDonald opted to remain with the Bandits, Brendan O'Hare became the new group's drummer. Having wisely demurred from calling themselves 'Teenage Fanny', the quartet opted instead for Teenage Fanclub, and began touting the finished master. 'It was like a jigsaw puzzle,' states Blake. 'We gave a tape to Stephen Pastel who sent it to Gerard Cosloy.' The US-based Cosloy ran the Matador label, but had won his reputation at another indie, Homestead, where he signed Sonic Youth and Dinosaur, later Dinosaur Jr. 'He wanted to bring it out, so we had an American deal first,' adds Norman, 'and we still hadn't played a gig.'

In Britain the set, dubbed *A Catholic Education*, was released on Fire subsidiary, Paperhouse. Two of its ten tracks, 'Heavy Metal' and the title song, appear in different guises, confirming the group was so new it had not yet settled on individual arrangements. Although patchy, its melange of Neil Young, Big Star and grunge was undeniably enticing. In 'Everything Flows', which was issued as a single, the Fanclub created something the equal of their mentors. Yes it is derivative, but those who preyed on that fact missed the point entirely. The group was another Bellshill fun package and only later events took them out of that axis.

In 1990 Teenage Fanclub played at that year's New York Music Seminar, where they met performer/producer Don Fleming. 'We got on well,' explains Blake, 'and went into a studio for something to do.' The result was a tongue-in-cheek version of 'The Ballad Of John & Yoko', but with its lyrics impishly amended. A one-sided single was pressed up, but then deliberately deleted the day it was released. However the US sojourn proved pivotal in the group's subsequent progress. 'There was quite a lot of interest in us in America,' Norman relates. 'Matador was hip - they had Urge Overkill and Superchunk - and *Village Voice* described our appearance at CBGB's as 'the gig of the

Teenage Fanclub

seminar'. Twelve major US labels wanted to sign us, none were interested here.

'We were unhappy with Fire,' he continues. 'We wanted them to spend more money but they couldn't afford it. I mentioned this to Bobby Gillespie who said Alan McGee would love to have us on Creation.' At the same time Geffen led the US pack and thus the Fanclub signed with both - Creation for the UK, Geffen elsewhere - but not before recording a second album.

Co-produced by Fleming, with strings and brass by Joe McAlinden, *Bandwagonesque* was a dazzling compendium of the Fanclub métiers. Yes, there are traces of Big Star, a relatively obscure ensemble with which every commentator was suddenly au fait, but as Norman states, 'So what? It's a compliment when people compare us, but we're just another band in a line of bands in an evolutionary process. In 3,000 years time who's going to care if something was recorded in 1957 or 1987.'

Bandwagonesque is an engrossing melange of dizzy melodies, longhair guitar and a lazy, carefree unpretentiousness. The assortment includes the delightful 'December' and 'Guiding Star', as well as the ingenuous 'The Concept', but the set's cumulative charm is the secret of its attraction. Teenage Fanclub sound like favoured younger brothers let loose in a record collection and only the churlish could fail to enjoy the audacious results. Indeed their impudence was made more evident with *The King*, a companion mini-album made up of rough-cut jams, rehearsals and irreverent readings of Pink Floyd's 'Interstellar Overdrive' and Madonna's 'Like A Virgin'. 'It was fun to do,' states Blake. 'It's just some mad thing you'd find at the back of the rack along with the 'proper' album.'

Teenage Fanclub entered 1992 as international heroes, yet they remained inexorably linked with their Bellshill compatriots. The word 'seminal' appeared alongside the BMX Bandits' name, in particular when aspiring archivists found that all the Fannies - bar McGinlay - had featured in the former group's late 80s line-up. 'People came up to me and said "you must be sad about Norman leaving",' Douglas Stewart relates, 'but they've missed the point. He virtually never plays with us live, but he's still as much a member as anyone else because he co-writes songs. We're not four people - here are the BMX Bandits. One night there might be seven onstage, the next only five, but we're what a group should be like. We get together to make records and have fun. I don't have to live up to people's preconceptions; if Norman has pressures doing his own thing, the Bandits can be therapeutic.'

In 1990 the group completed its debut album. 'I sent a tape of 'Whirlpool' to 25 different labels,' Duglas explains. 'but only one replied. I decided to put it out myself and took out Princes Trust-type loans to raise money to press it up.' Dubbed *C-86* by an ironic Stewart, the resultant set was enchanting. While continuing the singer's willowy quest for perfection, the more rumbustious 'Right Across The Street' would have slotted on to *A Catholic Education*. Yet where 'Rimbaud And Me' was a bossa nova, the title track suggested a folknik hoedown, and such performances forged a cheeky riposte to those pigeon-holing a band always much more than mere amateurs. 'I wanted to call all the tracks after the different groups on the *C-86* tape,' Stewart relates, 'but the rest persuaded me I was being ridiculous.'

The album's progress was suddenly halted by the collapse of Rough Trade which left Duglas, and others, in debt. Nightshift, which had assumed Fast Forward's distribution role, was also hit by the crippling insolvency now striking the independent sector. The company's head, Brian Guthrie, brother of Cocteau Twin Robin, assaulted in print what he perceived as chronic mismanagement. 'Not only am I not getting the money owed to me as a creditor, I've lost my stock,' he declared to *TLN*. The loss allegedly included master tapes by Lowlife, an indie-goth act centred on Will Heggie, formerly of the Cocteau Twins, who quit after the latter's debut, *Garlands*. Several months would pass before Nightshift resumed trading, although by that point it was solely a label.

Interest in the Bandits continued to flourish despite this impasse, even from unlikely sources. 'There's a group in Tokyo called the Japanese BMX Bandits. They do cover versions of our songs, or even songs we'd done covers of. Here we were, roped into the joke thing, but at the other end of the world was a group judging us by our songs alone, which is what I want people to do.' Stewart has since made several trips to Tokyo and it was an oriental label, Vinyl Japan, albeit one with a London office, which signed the Bandits in 1991.

By that point the group had coalesced around Stewart, Keen, McDonald, Blake, Joe McAlinden and Eugene Kelly, with string player John McCuster as a sideline auxiliary. This line-up was featured on *Star Wars*, the Bandits' second album. Despite its largely cohesive sound, it still captured Stewart's unique preoccupations. The title track is a gem, with its call-to-arms chorus and Brian Wilson melody, a feature also apparent on the lovely 'Extraordinary'. Quirky, funny, melancholic - such adjectives tell part of the BMX Bandits' story, which continues apace on Creation.

The same label secured Superstar, a band formed by Joe McAlinden in 1991. Raymond Prior (bass) and Neil Grant (drums) - formerly of the Hucksters - joined guitarist Mark Hughes in a line-up in which everyone sings, a prerequisite for a group whose work shows traces of the Beach Boys and Raspberries. Having completed a 6-track demo tape, the group rushed the results to Alan McGee, who issued it as *Greatest Hits Volume 1*. The set confirms McAlinden's grasp of pop hooklines, and his skilled arrangements. Where 'Barfly' flirts with the cut and run of *Bandwagonesque*, 'The Reason Why' and 'Let's Get Lost' affirm the quartet's independence, with strong melodies and an audacious panache. The latter features the former Groovy Numbers brass section, and the same trio appear on 'Taste'/'After Taste', the set's closing, ambitious, medley.

The latest group to emerge from this incestuous bubble was Captain America, formed by Eugene Kelly and Gordon Keen in 1991. James Keenan (ex-Vaselines) joined on bass and while Fanclub drummer Brendan O'Hare was in the early line-up, Andy Bollen took his place when commitments began to clash. Indeed the new group was propelled to early prominence in the wake of Nirvana's success. Kurt Cobain maintained an affection for Kelly's work, and not only took Captain America on tour, but sported their logo-emblazoned t-shirt throughout the fervid media circus. Two singles for Paperhouse, 'Captain America' and 'Flame On', tangled Sub-Pop label-styled rasp and early 70s couldn't-care-less joi de vivre as Eugene sought to establish a group different from both the Vaselines and Teenage Fanclub, with whom they were idly compared. Progress, however, was fraught with peril. First Seenan and Bollen were fired, an unusual step in this usually-rolling informality. Raymond Boyle (bass) and an 'on-loan' Francis McDonald completed the rejigged pack, which was then attacked by corporate paranoia. The C&A chain objected to the Captain America logo featured on 'Flame On', and the sleeve was hurriedly withdrawn. Then Marvel Comics took exception to the group's name itself - which was taken from their patriotic character - and the quartet thus opted to call themselves Eugenius.

Their debut album, *Oomalama*, appeared to mixed reviews. It has borne the brunt of a Bellshill backlash, but there is much to admire in the set's wild blend of shuddering riffs, Crazy Horse stramash and Kelly's sloppy choruses. The set does lack light and shade, but where it works, as on 'Breakfast' or the pugnacious title song, the effect is exhilarating. Having fulfilled their contract with Paperhouse, Eugenius welcomed newcomer Roy Lawrence and switched to Creation, albeit through its subsidiary outlet, August. This particular label is run by Dave Barker, formerly at Glass Records, whom Kelly knew from his spell in the Pastels. The latter group has joined them there, ending what had proved a largely unfocused portion of their convoluted history. They did continue to record, a version of Dan Johnson's 'Speeding Motorcycle' came out as a single, while their collaboration with US primitivist Jad Fair, appeared in 1991. 'Jad and I communicated a lot,' Stephen Pastel explains, 'and we went to Amsterdam to see his group, Half Japanese. We got on well and I asked him back to Glasgow. We recorded the album together in Teenage Fanclub's studio.'

Stephen and Aggi also pursued their love of speedway to the extent of sponsoring Berwick Bandits' rider David Walsh. He wears the Pastels' name with pride and, when he wins, their 'Speedway Star' is played in celebration. Melody Dog, a duo comprising Katriona Mitchell and Pat Crook, also came under the Pastel's umbrella. Stephen co-produced their fragile single, 'Futuristic Lover', for Calvin Johnson's K Label, while an eponymous 3-track EP followed

Superstar

in 1992. It includes an enchanting version of Primal Scream's 'Movin' On Up'.

Katriona also became part of a revamped Pastels, which lost Brian Superstar, but gained ex-Shop Assistant David Keegan, while Francis MacDonald and Raymond McGinley play a part whenever the need arises. The deal with August should rekindle a much-deserved profile for Stephen Pastel; Scottish indie-pop would have been quite different - and less fascinating - without him. As for the equally oracular Duglas Stewart, his précis of his group's achievements runs thus: 'The BMX Bandits haven't had the commercial success of some of the people who've been involved with us, but I like to think that we are partly responsible for some of the good things that have happened.'

Bellshill was not, of course, an exclusive haven for Greater Glasgow idiosyncrasies. Who can fail to be charmed by Hugh Reed And The Velvet Underpants, led by the rascally Hugh O'Hagan. 'I wanted to prove just how easy it was to put a band together,' he explains. 'Two weeks later we were onstage doing Velvet's covers, songs that people knew but tongue-in-cheek, like 'Pale Blue Ys' and a Glasgow version of 'Waiting For My Man'.' Yet if humour plays an integral part of O'Hagan's work, it isn't that of slapstick pantomime, but part of Scotland's self-effacing irony. This is ideally captured on 'Six To Wan'. 'That's a song about the different things that happens to someone after he sees his team getting gubbed 6-0. He gets slapped around by six fans of the opposite persuasion, six policemen arrest him - he ends up in Barlinnie Prison. It's a romantic love story.'

Part of O'Hagan's premise is a determination to sing in Scottish vernacular. 'I think it's important to be honest,' he explains. 'The worst thing is conformity, and why should I sing in a mid-Atlantic accent when I come from Maryhill?' He is also a tireless champion of Alex Harvey whose legacy he aims to keep alive. Yet it's an allegiance to Lou Reed which is most readily perceptible, one captured in Hugh's 1992 release, 'A Walk On The Clydeside'. 'Lou Reed sings songs about New York street life,' he states, 'and there's an empathy because Glasgow's that kind of a city.' Beat Poets' guitarist Tom Rafferty has proved equally aware of that psyche, titling one of his instrumental group's releases 'Glasgow, Howard, Missouri'. 'There are seven Glasgows in the USA. Each of these is presumably as important to its inhabitants as our Glasgow is to us, although it is a different Glasgow and a different view. There is a Glasgow, Barren, Kentucky,' he adds, 'but that was just too perfect.'

Rafferty was a former member of the Primevals, one of the city's first post-punk garage bands. They issued a handful of records locally, but were unable to strike a longer-term deal until an offer came from a surprise source. 'New Rose in Paris phoned us up,' recounts guitarist Micky Rooney. 'They had thought we were the New York Primevals - John Felice from the Real Kids had a band with that name - but when they heard us they liked us and followed it up.' The French label's roster included the Cramps, Panther Burns and Johnny Thunders, an ideal haven for the Scots' own inclinations. Three albums followed, after which the group veered through different outlets, without ever quite fulfilling an undoubted potential, their junk aesthetic affectionate rather than alarming.

The name Trash Can Sinatras suggests an act of similar garage propensities, yet this Kilmarnock quintet owe an affinity to early Aztec Camera. *Cake* captures their melodic purpose, yet they look to the USA for commercial solace. The group's careful, measured work deserves further recognition.

Care was anathema to the Stretchheads - Fat Bastard (vocals), Dr. Technology (guitars), Mofungo Diggs (bass) and Richie Dempsey (drums). This notoriously scabrous thrashpunk quartet was signed to Moksha in 1988 by Shamen manager Charles Cosh, and the first result of this arrangement was the wicked *Bros Are Pish* EP. An album, *Five Fingers, Four Fingers, A Thumb, A Facelift And A New Identity*, allowed a freer rein to their warped vision, which the group took to Blast First; a label renowned for dissident noise. *Eyeball Origami Aftermath* and *Pish In Your Sleazebag* were each filled with braying vocals, furious tempos and instruments goaded into febrile insanity. The latter full-length set crossed Chou Pahrot with the Birthday Party, then accelerated the result. Such warped inclusions as 'Mao Tse Tung's Meat Challenge' and 'Incontinent Of Sex' gave full rein to the Stretchheads' canon of ordure, mayhem and iconoclasm.

The Stretchheads

Mr Jason replaced Dempsey in 1990 and the latter subsequently resurfaced in Fenn, a much-touted trio completed by Mike Sutherland (voice) and Ian Baird (bass). Described by journalist Fiona Shepherd as 'an explosive distillation of Ride, Swervedriver and Fugazi', they proved that Glasgow indies need be neither precious nor eccentric.

A recluse throughout the 12-month spell since leaving Primal Scream, Jim Beattie reappeared with Spirea X in June 1990. There was an immediate buzz about the group, fawning reviews were commonplace and a *Snub-TV* slot suggested that stardom was merely a hairsbreadth away. 'The hype came too soon,' Beattie suggests, 'and it caught me unawares. I went along because it was really exciting, but we simply weren't ready for it.' Within weeks of their television debut, word filtered that the group was no more, although this had been spread by parties with whom the guitarist had severed connections. 'Our ex-manager kept the name going by telling everyone we'd split up,' Jim states. 'Record companies got in touch with me to see if it was true.'

Having purged his group of elements he no longer trusted, Beattie was now supported by keyboard player and partner Judith Boyle and drummer Andrew Kerr. Interest in his group continued, although there was a touch of wariness on both sides. 'London Records said they didn't want to ruin potentially classic songwriting,' says Jim, still puzzled. 'I took that as a compliment. However, they gave us £700 and we used that to record 'Chlorine Dream'.' This chimerian composition captured the elegiac charm of the Byrds, a group Spirea X astutely echoed. Its gorgeous swell attracted Ivo Lawrence at 4AD. He was in Scotland to meet singer Louise Rutkowski, formerly of Sunset Gun, and latterly of label collective This Mortal Coil. 'Everyone at 4AD loved the demo,' Beattie recalls, 'and so we signed with them.'

'Chlorine Dream' became the group's first single, and having issued a follow-up, 'Speed Reaction', Spirea X then began an album. 'I learned several lessons at Rockfield,' Jim explains, 'but we still made the mistake of recording right away. Half of it reminds me of the first Primal Scream LP fiasco, half doesn't, but if you're ever totally satisfied with something, then it's time to stop because you've achieved your goal.' Despite Beattie's reservations, *Fireblade Skies* is an inspired achievement, and if the ghost of 60s 12-string/harmony pop surrounds the entire proceedings, Spirea X develop areas usually ignored. They are not, for example, the McGuinn heard on 'Mr. Tambourine Man', but rather the ethereal swell present on 'Artificial Energy'. 'All my songs are heavily referenced,' states Beattie. 'I can't rip someone off, but they do show the elements I've been influenced by which are usually the less obvious things.' The set's highlights include 'Fire And Light', a beautiful composition buoyed by shimmering voices and an opaque splendour, and 'Signed DC', the singer's

Spirea X

inventive recreation of one of Love's most memorable songs. 'I'd had their first album for years,' Jim recounts, 'in fact Elliot Davis gave me a copy - he's a fanatical Love fan. We didn't plan to do it, we were just doing backing tracks and it came up, but we could see all its underlying things and its subtlety.' Spirea X not only complete a version as relevant as the original, they do so by emphasising its folk-based root. Where Love wail, Beattie is melancholic, yet the emotion portrayed by both remains the same.

Fireblade Skies was the natural culmination of Primal Scream's 'Gentle Tuesday' or 'Love You'. If the break between Beattie and Bobby Gillespie freed the latter from perceived restrictions, then his former colleague was similarly liberated. Their split produced two excellent acts, and whereas one has grabbed the headlines, the less-feted Spirea X remains an equally enticing prospect.

EPILOGUE

As I begin to wind this travelogue down, The Bluebells have reached the top of the charts with a re-released 'Young At Heart'. The Shamen were recently at number 1 with the irascible 'Ebeneezer Goode'. There is an unequivocal irony in the fact that a group whose motivator is a Scot, should enjoy such a commercial accolade with a song drawing its appeal from 'strike-a-light-guv' cockney patois. That the Shamen join a zig-zag line embracing 'Lazy Sunday' or Chas And Dave is, historically, less surprising - Lonnie Donegan abandoned his messianic path on recording 'My Old Man's A Dustman', replete with Bow Bells' rhyming slang.

Such releases suggest that in 30 plus years we are no nearer defining exactly what Scottish pop is. It is true that such acts do rarely embrace Anglicised mores - in fairness, the Shamen's rapper, Mr C, is London-born - and Postcard's Alan Horne suggests that Celtic affection for Americana is in part due to a Scottish reluctance to look to England. 'What had they to offer,' he declares, 'to compare with soul music or the Byrds or the Velvet Underground? Glasgow people in particular love Style, and America had much more of that.' The quest then becomes contradictory; certain acts achieved success by setting aside its natural progress - for example Frankie Miller's 'Darlin'' - some, such as Simple Minds, consider 'Scottish-ness' irrelevant in the first place. Others have absorbed so many global references that they fail to repeat in the USA the commercial acclaim they enjoy in Britain. Wet Wet Wet are hidebound by the Cliff Richard factor; America already boasts countless acts capable of doing what they do. This in turn is why devotees celebrate a Fire Engines, an Orange Juice, a BMX Bandits, a Pastels, a Jesus And Mary Chain - yes, they too have reference points but these have been developed to create something unique.

When Hugh O'Hagan says he hopes to keep alive the music of Alex Harvey, he does not aspire to recreate 'Vambo', but rather follow his mentor's example and take an unambiguously Scottish perspective out of a parochial arena. It is a dangerous game - the Proclaimers and Jesse Rae are tarred as novelties - but, despite critical misgivings in their home country, Runrig have achieved the aim of equating commercial success with cultural integrity. Preconceptions might well deny them an audience in England, the rest of the world affords them a more than generous welcome.

This book is drawing to its end as Scottish rock enjoys another of its periodical pauses. A generation of Bellshill bandits have bidden farewell to fraternal cloisters and embraced deals with Creation Records, its own status changed irrevocably by a worldwide deal stuck with Sony. Perspex White Out, Carol Laula, the Naturals and the Lost Soul Band are but four names touted to lead the next wave of indie-styled concepts, while Wolfstone and Ironhorse may yet secure a niche within the Gaelic rock idiom prised open by Runrig and Capercaillie. But if Scotland boasts the infrastructure - bands, venues, agencies, promoters, managers - and the will to succeed, it paradoxically lacks strong record labels. The diverse demands of dance culture have been met to some extent by two Glasgow-based outlets, Lizard and Soma, the former of which released the Nightcrawlers' 'Living Inside A Dream'. This came before the group, or rather guiding-light John Reid, was signed by Island offshoot, 4th And Broadway. Soma is owned by Slam DJs Stuart Macmillan, Dave Clark and Orde Meikle, who in turn mixed 'Fallen' for Dove, a trio headed by Jim McKinven, ex-Altered Images. 1,000 copies were pressed on Soma before Andy Weatherall signed the group to his Boys Own label.

Nightshift survived the Rough Trade trauma and it remains the home of Lowlife. Their 'San Antorium' appeared in 1991 to largely positive reviews. Avalanche has not only reissued material from 53rd and 3rd, its roster also includes the Joyriders, Riverhead and material licensed from New Zealand's Snapper label. Bruce Findlay returned to the independent fray with Bruces and Barky! Barky's 'Valentina', but how permanent this venture will be is open to question. The lack of a coherent distribution network is one mitigating factor and many indie releases are thus simply demos, available to the public, but issued to attract a better deal. Until someone, somewhere makes funds available to keep and build acts, rather than serve as a transient outlet, the Scottish jigsaw will remain incomplete. Yet despite its disadvantages; in particular the condescending attitude of an imperialist-minded culture south of its border, Scottish rock has railed against consequent ghettoisation to produce a body of music disproportionate to its small population. Slange je va.

DISCOGRAPHY

The following is not trainspotter complete, nor does it purport to be a 'recommended listening'. It is, instead, a guide to aid those seeking records noted in the text. This has been done with an eye on availability, rather than first pressings, to allow the diligent easier access to almost 40 years of Scottish music, and in some cases, an insight to those inspiring it.

Chapter I

Precious little Scottish pop was recorded in the 50s, but the following give a flavour of the sound it aspired to. The 'cool' style of saxophonist Stan Getz is compiled on *Early Getz* (Prestige, 1980) while *Paris 1954/LA 1953* (Vogue, 1987) captures the emergent Gerry Mulligan.

There are several Louis Prima sets, but *Jump, Jive & Wail* (Charly, 1986) is as good as any. *The Very Best Of Bill Haley And The Comets* (Music Club, 1992), containing 'Rock Around The Clock' and 'Two Hound Dogs', is all the passing fan requires. *40 Greatest Hits* (MGM, 1978) is a welcome précis of Hank Williams' extensive catalogue.

Trad Party (Eclipse, c. 60s) provides a representative glimpse of the Clyde Valley Stompers, while many of Ken Colyer's 50s recordings have been collected on *The Decca Years Volumes 1-3* (Lake 1985-1987). If you must - 23 tracks by Tommy Steele And The Steelemen surface on *The Rock 'n' Roll Years* (See For Miles, 1987).

Lonnie Donegan's first excursions as a group leader appear on *Skiffle* (reissued Decca Rock Echoes, 1984), while *Puttin' On The Styles* (Sequel, 1992) offers a composite view of his best-known work. Those wishing to explore his influences are directed to *Leadbelly - The Library Of Congress Recordings Volumes 1-3* (Rounder, 1991), *20 Of The Best: The Carter Family* (RCA, 1984) and *Lonnie Johnson - Stepping On The Blues* (CBS Roots 'n' Blues, 1990).

The Very Best Of Karl Denver (Decca, 1986) is self-explanatory, but those seeking Lord Rockingham's number 1 single, 'Hoots Mon' (Decca, 1958) and Jackie Dennis' 'La Dee Dah' (Decca, 1958) are referred to the original pressings.

Johnny Kidd's 'Shakin' All Over' has surfaced in many guises, but it appears on *The Complete Johnny Kidd And The Pirates* (EMI, 1992) surrounded by every other track this pivotal figure recorded. Meanwhile *Shout* (Bear Family, 1988) compiles all the Isley Brothers' RCA masters, including the full version of the gospel-tinged title track.

For an overview of the music shaping 60s (and subsequent) Scottish pop, try *The Complete Stax/Volt Singles 1959-1968* (Atlantic, 1991) and *Hitsville USA: The Motown Singles Collection 1959-1971* (Motown, 1992).

Chapter 2

Recordings by Bobby Patrick's Big Six were scattered over various labels, which has precluded repackaging. They did share an album with Kingsize Taylor, *Twistime In The Star Club, Hamburg* (Dutch Ariola, 1964), while subsequent releases included 'Shake It Easy Baby'/'Wildwood Days', 'Monkey Time'/'Sweet Talk Me Baby' and an EP, *Teenbeat Vol. 3* (all Decca, 1964). As the Big Six they completed 'Coming Home Baby'/'Starlight Melody' (Polydor, 1965).

Isobel Bond did not record officially during the Star Club era. Her late-period singles included 'When A Man Loves A Woman' (Major Minor, 1968) and 'Don't Forget About Me'/'You'll Never Get The Chance Again' (Major Minor, 1969). The McKinleys' were more fortunate, but their releases - 'Someone Cares For Me'/'A Million Miles Away', 'When He Comes Along'/'Then I'll Know It's Love' (both Columbia, 1964), 'Sweet And Tender Romance'/'That Lonely Feeling' and 'Give Him My Love'/'Once More' (both Columbia, 1965) still await re-release.

Two of Tony Sheridan's 1964 albums, *Just A Little Bit Of Tony Sheridan* and *Meet The Beat*, were reissued by Polydor, as was *Alex Harvey And His Soul Band* (all 1986). *The Blues* (Polydor, 1965), was not. A various artists' set, *Beat City* (Polydor, 1964), includes the otherwise unavailable 'Reelin' And Rockin''. The single, 'Ain't That Just Too Bad'/'My Kind Of Love' (Polydor, 1965), completes Harvey's recordings for the label; the former song can be found on *Rare Tracks* (Polydor, 1977). His last releases from this period were 'Agent 00 Soul'/'Go Away Baby' (Island, 1965) and 'Work Song'/'I Can Do Without Your Love' (Island, 1966).

The Boston Dexters' canon comprises of 'I've Got Something To Tell You'/'I Believe To My Soul' and 'Try Hard'/'No More Tears' (both

Columbia, 1965). Prior to this they cut three limited issue singles - 'Matchbox'/'La Bamba', 'Ain't Gonna Change Me'/'What Kind Of Girl Are You' and 'You've Been Talking About Me'/'I've Got Troubles Of My Own' (all Contemporary Recordings, 1964).

Ray Charles' original version of the first-named flip-side appears on *The Birth Of Soul* (Atlantic, 1991). Muddy Waters' 'I Just Wanna Make Love To You' surfaces on, among others, *Rollin' Stone* (Charly, 1990), while the Coasters' 'Framed' is compiled on *20 Great Originals* (Atlantic, 1978).

The Athenians releases were as follows - 'Little Queenie'/'You Tell Me' (Edinburgh Students' Charities Appeal, 1964), 'I Got Love If You Want It'/'I'm A Lover Not A Fighter' (Waverley, 1964) and 'Thinking Of Our Love'/'Mercy Mercy' (Waverley, 1965). Their version of 'Louie Louie' appeared, alongside the Avengers' 'I Don't Want To Spoil The Party', on Edinburgh Students Charities' Appeal EP, 1965, and an off-beat reading of 'The Teddy Bears' Picnic' accompanied Paul Revere's 'Steppin' Out' on a second Edinburgh Students' Charities Appeal EP, in 1966.

Chapter 3

The first three singles by Dean Ford And The Gaylords - 'Twenty Miles'/'What's The Matter With Me', 'Mr. Heartbreak's Here Instead'/'I Won't' (both Columbia 1964) and 'The Name Game'/'That Lonely Feeling' (Columbia, 1965) - show 60s Scottish pop in its benign form. The last-named flip was the same song cut by the McKinleys.

'I'm In Love With You'/'Always On My Mind', 'Hey Good Looking'/'Come On Come On' (both Columbia, 1964) and 'I Don't Care'/'That Broken Heart Is Mine' (Columbia, 1965) is the entire output by the Golden Crusaders.

Curiously, the Poets' 'Now We're Thru' (Decca, 1964) is not currently compiled, but 'That's The Way It's Got To Be' surfaces on *The Rubble Collection Volume Three* (Bam Caruso, 1992) alongside 'I Love Her Still', the flip of the group's third 45. The a-side, 'I Am So Blue' is on *The Rubble Collection Volume Four* (Bam Caruso, 1992), as is 'I'll Cry With The Moon', the coupling of their second single.

Lulu's catalogue is less tortuous. Her debut album, *Something To Shout About*, has been re-released (Decca, 1989), while the singer's best-known performances are collected on *The World Of Lulu* (Decca, 1969).

The Exciters 'There You Go' is compiled on *Run Mascara Run* (Sequel, 1992).

Sadly, no one yet has found space for two of the era's more exceptional singles; the Blues Council's 'Baby Don't Look Down'/'What Will I Do' (Parlophone, 1965) and the Luvvers' 'House On The Hill'/'Most Unlovely' (Parlophone, 1966).

Chapter 4

'Tango' (Fontana, 1965) was the lone offering by a footsore Mark Five. The Isley Brothers' original can be found on *Let's Go* (Stateside, 1986).

The Poor Souls' singles, 'When My Baby Cries'/'My Baby's Not There' (Decca, 1965) and 'Love Me'/'Please Don't Change Your Mind' (Alp, 1966), are as mesmerising as ever. Composer Lesley Duncan's original version of the first a-side was released simultaneously on Columbia.

Alp's pop releases included the following - 'Friday Night'/'Lonely Boy' (the Red Hawkes), 'It's Gonna Be Morning'/'I Wanna Hear You Say Yeah' (the HiFis) and 'Bad News Feeling'/'What Can I Do' (the Vikings). Each was issued in 1966.

Scotland's 'independent' singles included the Misfits 'Hanging Around'/'You Won't See Me' (Aberdeen Student Charities, 1966) and 'I'm A Hog For You Baby'/'I Can Never See You' (Norco, 1964) by Johnny And The Copycats. Phil And The Flintstones' energetic 'Love Potion No. 9'/'Honey Don't' was issued on...what else?...Bedrock (1964).

A glimpse of Radio Scotland is captured on *A Sound Memorial To Radio Scotland* (Scotia, 1967). Unfortunately, the music on offer is played by the label's supperclub combos, rather than the original artists. There is, however, a curtailed 'McLauglin's Ceilidh'. Soundbites from the station, as well as a more detailed history, can be found in *The Offshore Radio Files: Number 2: Radio Scotland* (MRP Books).

Chapter 5

The sole Buzz a-side, 'You're Holding Me Down', appears on *Freak Beat Fantoms* (Bam Caruso, 1989). The Boots releases - 'The Animal In Me'/'Even The Bad Times Are Good' (CBS, 1967) - remain uncompiled.

The Drifters 'Please Stay' (Atlantic, 1961) is both on a single and contemporaneous album (*Save The Last Dance For Me*). Tony Clarke's 'The Entertainer' (Chess, 1966) also appears on Soul (PRT/Chess, 1982). Del Shannon's 'Kelly' was another intrinsic part of Scottish teen lore. It is compiled on *Runaway Hits* (Edsel, 1983).

Tam White's late 60s pop/soul releases followed the sculpted path of a Long John Baldry. His singles included 'Amy'/'Building My World', 'Girl Watcher'/'Waiting Till The Night Comes Round Again' (both Decca, 1967) and 'That Old Sweet Roll' (Deram, 1969). *Tam White* (Middle Earth, 1970) is longhair hip, but the 70s saw the singer fall into showbiz clutches in the wake of a television slot on *New Faces*. He enjoyed a minor hit with the Mickie Most produced 'What In The World's Come Over You' (Rak, 1975), but subsequently retired. White returned to the fray as a jazz/blues singer during the 80s, ghosted 'Big Jazza's' voice in Johnny Byrne's acclaimed television drama, 'Tutti Frutti', and took thespian roles in 'Wreck On The Highway' and 'Taggart'.

The sole album by Writing On The Wall has been reissued in Germany, complete with a non-LP track, 'Child On A Crossing'. (*Power Of The Picts*, Repertoire, 1992). Their last recording, 'Buffalo' appears on *Professor Jordan's Magic Sound Show* (Bam Caruso, 1988). *Instinct* (Decca, 1970) by Human Beast meanwhile retains its cult collectors' status.

Chapter 6

The Poets' recordings for the Immediate label are compiled on *The Immediate Anthology* (Line, 1991). 'Wooden Spoon' and 'In Your Tower' can be heard on *The Rubble Collection Volume Six* (Bam Caruso, 1992). 'Dawn', one of the demos George Gallagher recorded with the Pathfinders, appears on *Freak Beat Fantoms* (Bam Caruso, 1989). In 1992 the vocalist surfaced leading the exceptional Blues Poets.

Sol Byron and the Impacts' single is constrained to the original pressing - 'Pride And Joy'/'Thou Shalt Not Steal' (Flamingo, 1964). The Gaylords' 'He's A Good Face (But He's Down And Out)' surfaces on *60s Back Beat* (See For Miles, 1985).

Of course, not every group pursued messianic paths. The Chris McClure Section always had an eye on supper-club respectability. (Chris McClure - 'The Dying Swan'/'Land Of The Golden Tree' (Decca, 1996). The singer later became an 'all-round entertainer' as 'Christian'.

The Beatstalkers: 'Everybody's Talking 'Bout My Baby'/'Mr Disappointed' (Decca, 1965), 'Left Right Left'/'You Better Get A Better Hold On', 'A Love Like Yours'/'Base Line' (both Decca, 1966), 'My One Chance To Make It'/'Ain't No Soul (In These Rock'n'Roll Shoes)', 'Silver Tree Top School For Boys'/'Sugar Chocolate Machine' (both CBS, 1967), 'Rain Coloured Roses'/'Everything Is You', 'Little Boy'/'When I'm Five' (both CBS, 1968). Of the group's early repertoire, the Tams' 'Hey Girl' is on *Atlanta Soul*

Connection (Charly 1983) and 'Daddy Loves Baby' closes Don Covay's *Mercy* (Edsel, 1982).

Alex Harvey: 'Sunday Song'/'Horizon' and 'Maybe Someday'/'Curtains For My Baby' (both Decca, 1967).

Studio Six: 'When I See My Baby'/'Don't Tell Lies' (Polydor, 1966), 'Bless My Soul (I've Been And Gone And Done It)'/'People Say', 'Times Were When'/'I Can't Sleep' and 'Strawberry Window'/'Falling Leaves' (all Polydor, 1967).

If you only have one Scottish single, make it 'Road To Nowhere'/'Illusions' (Apple, 1969) by (White) Trash. Carole King's original version is, amazingly, still in catalogue on the reverse of 'It Might As Well Rain Until September' (Old Gold, 1983). 'Golden Slumbers/Carry That Weight'/'Trash Can' (Apple, 1969) is this fabulous group's only other release.

Chapter 7

The World Of Ewan MacColl And Peggy Seeger (Decca, 1970) is one of many McColl albums. This features 'First Time Ever I Saw Your Face'. *Black And White* (Cooking Vinyl, 1990), a more recent resume, includes 'Dirty Old Town'. *Ramblin' Jack Elliott* (Big Beat/Fantasy, 1990) collects two of the singer's early 60s albums and includes his idiosyncratic reading of 'I Belong To Glasgow'. Woody Guthrie's canon is extensive - *The Library Of Congress Recordings* (Rounder, 1988) is authoritative; *The Very Best Of Woody Guthrie* (Music Club, 1992) more concise.

Hamish Imlach (Transatlantic, 'TRASAM', 1977) provides a glimpse of the singer's extensive catalogue. There are two excellent Davey Graham compilations currently available - *Folk Blues And All Points In Between* (See For Miles, 1985) and *Guitar Player....Plus* (See For Miles, 1992). The latter includes the artist's original version of 'Anji'. Another influential contemporary, Owen Hand, can be heard on *I Loved A Lass* (Transatlantic, 1966).

Donovan's folknik period can be found on *Colours* (PRT, 1987). A wider resume, including unissued material, is available on *Troubadour: The Definitive Collection 1964-1976* (Epic/Legacy, 1992).

The Gardener - Essential Bert Jansch 1965-1971 (Demon, 1992) contains the best of this innovative artist's early recordings. His peerless debut, *Bert Jansch*, has been reissued (Demon/Transatlantic, 1988). *LA Turnaround* (Charisma, 1974) and *Santa Barbara Honeymoon* (Charisma, 1975) exemplify his 70s' work.

John Martyn's releases have been the subject of two compilations; *So Far So Good* (Island, 1977) and *The Electric John Martyn* (Island, 1982). On *Couldn't Love You More* (Permanent, 1992) he makes the fatal error of re-recording several of his best-known songs. It didn't work for Little Richard.

Martyn's pivotal releases remain *Stormbringer* (Island, 1970), *Bless The Weather* (Island, 1971), *Solid Air, Inside Out* (both Island, 1973), *Live At Leeds* (reissued Cacophony, 1987) and *Grace And Danger* (Island, 1980). *The Tumbler* (Island, 1968) is the stronger of his pure-folk selections.

The ghosts of Al Stewart's past. 'The Elf' appears on *The Great British Psychedelic Trip Volume 3* (See For Miles, 1987); *Volume Four* (See For Miles, 1987) offers 'Turn To Earth'. *Bedsitter Images* (CBS, 1967) and *Love Chronicles* (CBS, 1968) capture his shift from folk to rock.

The patriarch - *Jackson C. Frank* (Columbia, 1965); reissued as *Blues Run The Game* (B&C, 1987).

There are two excellent Incredible String Band compilations *Relics Of The Incredible String Band* (Elektra, 1971) and *Seasons They Change* (Island, 1976). The US version of the former is more extensive. *The Incredible String Band* (Elektra, 1966, *5000 Spirits Or The Layers Of The Onion* (reissued Elektra, 1992) and *The Hangman's Beautiful Daughter* (reissued Elektra, 1992) are the essential original albums. The contrast between Mike Heron's *Smiling Men With Bad Reputations* (Island, 1971) and Robin Williamson's *Myrrh* (reissued Edsel/Demon, 1992) show why the group would no longer function. *Songs And Music 1977* (Awareness, 1986) collects moments from the latter's subsequent work.

'Jazz Bo's Holiday' by Robin and Clive can be heard on *The Edinburgh Folk Festival 1965* (Decca, 1965). It was produced by Nat Joseph, founder of Transatlantic Records, who's wish to sign the ISB was thwarted by Joe Boyd.

Chapter 8

The birth of Scottish progressive rock -

Clouds - *Scrapbook* (Island, 1969) *Up Above Our Heads* (US Deram, 1969) and *Watercolour Days* (Island, 1971), NSU - *Turn On Or Turn Me Down* (Stable, 1969), Tear Gas - *Piggy Go Getter* (Famous, 1970) and *Tear Gas* (Regal Zonophone, 1971), Northwind *Sister Brother Lover* (Regal Zonophone, 1971). The last-named act included Brian Young, who later established the CaVa Recording Studio.

Although two Beggars Opera's sets have been re-released - *Waters Of Change* and *Pathfinder* (Line, 1992); their first and last albums - *Act One* (Vertigo, 1970) and *Get Your Dog Off Me* (Vertigo, 1973) - have escaped repacking.

Compilations conveniently précis the Marmalade career. *The Best Of The Marmalade* (CBS, 1969) combines their 'sike-pop' output with early hits, *Ob La*

Di (Embassy, 1973), concentrates on late 60s' chart entries, while *The World Of The Marmalade* (Decca, 1976) places 'Reflections Of My Life' alongside several wonderful Hughie Nicholson songs. *There's A Lot Of It About* (CBS, 1968) and *Songs* (Decca, 1971) are the pick of their 'original' collections. Only the most committed should seek out the group's post-1972 work; their 1976 hit, 'Falling Apart At The Seams', is the title of a late-period set. (See For Miles, 1990).

Junior Campbell enjoyed hits with 'Hallelujah Freedom' (Deram, 1972) and 'Sweet Illusion' (Deram, 1973). He recorded a solo album, *Second Time Around* (Deram, 1974) and later composed the theme tune to the children's television series, *Thomas The Tank Engine*. His former colleague completed *Dean Ford* (EMI, 1975).

Blue (RSO, 1973) captures the eponymous group at their peak. *Life In The Navy* (RSO, 1974) is much less convincing, while *Another Night Time Flight* (Rocket, 1977) and *Fool's Party* (Rocket, 1978) are lachrymose. The third title does, however, include 'Gonna Capture Your Heart', the group's sole chart entry.

'I'm Never Gonna Leave You'/'I'll Hold On' (Decca, 1966) and 'Climb Every Mountain'/'I Wanna Make You Understand' (Parlophone, 1966) showcase the short-lived Frankie And Johnny pairing. Lulu's late-60s catalogue meanwhile veered from the ridiculous 'Boom Bang-A-Bang' (Columbia, 1969) to the partially sublime 'To Sir With Love' (Columbia, 1967) and 'Oh Me Oh My (I'm A Fool For You Baby')' (Atco, 1969).) *New Routes* and *Melody Fair* (both Atco, 1970) showcase the southern soul experiment. Aretha Franklin's rendition of 'Oh Me Oh My' is tucked away on the flip of 'Rock Steady' (Atlantic, 1971), while Al Green brought it all back home with his version of 'To Sir With Love' (Hi, 1979).

The a-side of the House Of Lords' 45, 'In The Land Of Dreams'/'Ain't Gonna Wait Forever', appears on *5000 Seconds Over Toyland* (Bam Caruso, 1991) while *Deram Dayze* (Decal, 1987) contains both sides of Societie's sublime 45; ('Bird Has Flown'/'Breaking Down'). Original pressings are required for Cody's 'I Believe In You' (Polydor, 1970) and the Stoics' 'Earth, Fire, Air And Water'/'Search For The Sea' (RCA, 1968).

Around Grapefruit (Stateside, 1968) encapsulates songwriter George Alexander's talent; *Deep Water* (RCA, 1969) doesn't. The Easybeats' 'Friday On My Mind' is found on *Absolute Anthology* (Albert Productions, 1980). Their second album, *Vigil*, (reissued Repertoire, 1991) boasts support from My Dear Watson, whose own records are as follows - 'The Shame Just Drained' (Parlophone, 1967), 'Stop! Stop! They're I'll Be'/'Make This Day Last' (Parlophone, 1967) and 'Have You Seen Your Saviour'/'White Line Road' (DJM, 1970).

Chapter 9

The Senate's 'Can't Stop' is contained on *The R&B Scene* (See For Miles, 1985); their album, *The Senate Sock It To You One More Time* has been revived by Line (1992). *Garnet Mimms Live* (United Artists, 1967) awaits repackaging. Connoisseurs of freakbeat avidly seek the Primitives' 'L'Incidente'/'Johnny No' (Piper Club, 1968).

'Gypsy'/'Tic Toc' (Go, 1966) and 'Timothy' (Spot, 1967) are the two singles by the Scots Of St. James; 'Little Girl' (United Artists, 1968) the sole effort by ex-vocalist Jimmy Oakey. Hopscotch recorded two 45s, 'Look At The Lights Go Up' (United Artists, 1968) and 'Long Black Veil'/'Easy To Find' (United Artists, 1969), before splintering into Forevermore. The latter group completed *Paint It Yourself* (1970) and *Words On Black Plastic* (1971), before imploding.

The Dundee Horns were members of James Litherland's Brotherhood, which was led by a Scots-born guitarist, formerly of Colosseum. This act changed its name prior to issuing the eponymous *Mogul Thrash* (RCA, 1971).

The Dream Police - 'Living Is Easy', the flip of their debut single, appears on *The Rubble Collection Volume Three* (Bam Caruso, 1992). 'Our Song'/'Much Too Much' (Decca, 1970) and 'I've Got No Choice'/'What's The Cure For Happiness' (Decca, 1971) are their other releases.

The Average White Band - *Show Your Hand* (reissued Fame, 1983) and *AWB* aka The White Album (reissued Fame, 1986), catch the group at a creative peak. *The Best Of The Average White Band* (1984) is an useful introduction to their work, while *Feel No Fret* (reissued RCA, 1981) is the pick of the group's later-period. *Benny And Us* (Atlantic, 1977) benefits from a collective ease; *Person To Person* (Atlantic, 1977) reveals the sextet's live power.

Chapter 10

Edinburgh's Bread Love And Dreams recorded three albums, *Bread, Love And Dreams* (Decca, 1969), *The Strange Tale Of Captain Shannon......* (Decca, 1970) and *Amaryllis* (Decca, 1971). Rab Noakes' best work can be heard on *Do You See The Lights* (Decca, 1970), *Rab Noakes* (A&M, 1972) and *Red Pump Special* (Warners, 1974). *Thro' The Years* (Decca, 1969) was the collaboration between Archie Fisher and Barbara Dickson which showcased several Noakes' compositions.

The Very Best Of Gallagher & Lyle (A&M, 1992) contains all the duo's popular tracks. Their recordings with the Tulsans have escaped anthologising.

Blood And Glory (Demon, 1988) complies the cream of Gerry Rafferty's work for the Transatlantic label, as a member of the Humblebums and solo. *First Collection Of Merrie Melodies* (Transatlantic, 1968) is the Harvey/Connolly version of the former group.

Right Down The Line - The Best Of Gerry Rafferty (EMI, 1989) collects the singer's best-known 70s and 80s recordings, including the inevitable 'Baker Street', while *The Best Of Stealers Wheel - Gerry Rafferty And Joe Egan* (A&M, 1978) is self-explanatory. *Out Of Nowhere* (Ariola, 1979) and *Map* (Ariola 1981) are Egan's solo albums.

Nothing But The Best (RCA, 1980) is a representative sample of Five Hand Reel and includes moving renditions of 'Carrickfergus' and 'Both Sides Of The Forth'. Try *Handful Of Earth* (Topic, 1978) and *A Different Kind Of Love Song* (Celtic Music, 1984) for contrasting versions of former member Dick Gaughan.

Chapter 11

The Bay City Rollers Collection (Arista, 1992) may seem like the ideal start, but this set is seriously flawed. The omission of, for example, 'Keep On Dancing', shows its mid-Atlantic origins. Look out their singles instead, notably 'Saturday Night' (1973), 'Bye Bye Baby' (1975) and 'It's A Game' (1977). Crass perhaps, but unapologetically adolescent. They also compare favourably with the originals - the Four Seasons' 'Bye Bye Baby' can be heard on *25th Anniversary Collection* (Sequel, 1990) while 'It's A Game' is on *The Machine That Cried*, String Driven Thing's second album (reissued Repertoire, 1992).

Les McKeown pursued an intermittent solo career, principally in Japan, while slipping in and out of various reformed incarnations. Legal proceedings ensued and at the time of writing, Wood, Faulkner, Alan Longmuir and 'Kass' lead an act known only as *The Bay City Rollers* - no abbreviations are permitted. Tam Paton, meanwhile, served one year of a three year jail sentence for committing indecent acts with males under the age of consent. Since his release in May 1983, the group's former manager has avoided popular music.

Ex-protégés Bilbo Baggins also cut a ruffian-styled version of 'Saturday Night' (Bell, 1973). Play it to current Polydor MD, Jimmy Devlin, a one-time member of the group. Meanwhile Middle Of The Road can still clear a room. Try 'Chirpy Chirpy Cheep Cheep' and 'Tweedle Dee Tweedle Dum' (both RCA, 1971).

The Best Of Pilot (C5, 1989) provides the ideal overview of this act's crafted pop. Billy Lyall's album, *Solo Casting* (EMI, 1976) shows a maturation of the style, but the artist later dropped out of active recording. He succumbed to AIDS in 1991.

Slik (Bell, 1976) combines this act's best-known numbers, plus the requisite filler. A subsequent flop, 'The Kid's A Punk' (Bell, 1976) was curiously prophetic, but while Midge Ure demurred on the chance to join the Sex Pistols, he did form the Rich Kids with the latter's former bassist, Glen Matlock. This power-pop ensemble broke up after a year, since when Ure became associated with numerous groups, notably Visage and Ultravox, and subsequently became the 'silent' partner in Band Aid's 'Do They Know It's Christmas' (Mercury, 1984). His solo hits have included 'No Regrets' (Chrysalis, 1982) and the chart-topping 'If I Was' (Chrysalis, 1985). An attendant album, *The Gift* (Chrysalis, 1985), was a major commercial success. *If I Was - The Best Of Midge Ure And Ultravox* (Chrysalis. 1993) is a useful compendium.

Chapter 12

There is a Stone The Crows compilation - *Stone The Crows* (Thunderbolt, 1989) - but the original albums are required for a fuller picture. *Stone The Crows* (Polydor, 1970), *Ode To John Law* (Polydor, 1970), *Teenage Licks* (Polydor, 1971), *Ontinuous Performance* (Polydor, 1972). *Queen Of The Night* (Polydor, 1973) is Maggie Bell's strongest solo offering in a disappointingly low-key solo career. *Suicide Sal* (Polydor, 1975), 'Hold Me' (Swan Song, 1981 - with B.A. Robertson) and the theme to television's *Taggert* do not compensate.

Cartoone (Atlantic, 1969) still attracts Jimmy Page aficionados, despite his subdued contribution.

Jimmy Dewar's best work with Robin Trower is contained on *Twice Removed From Yesterday* (Chrysalis, 1973), *Bridge Of Sighs* (Chrysalis, 1974) and *For Earth Below* (Chrysalis, 1975). *Once In A Blue Moon* (Chrysalis, 1973), *High Life* (Chrysalis, 1974) and *The Rock* (Chrysalis, 1975) capture the very best of Frankie Miller. 'Darlin'' appears on *Falling In Love* (Chrysalis, 1979), *Dancing In The Rain* (Vertigo, 1986) contains his collaborations with Jeff Barry, while 'Caledonia' (REL, 1992) was the Scottish hit of 1992. *The Best Of Frankie Miller* (Chrysalis, 1993) provides a composite compendium of this lengthy catalogue.

Cado Belle can be heard on *Cado Belle* (Anchor, 1976). Maggie Reilly now sings with Mike Oldfield, most audibly so on 'Moonlight Shadow' (Virgin, 1983). Fellow zealots of Scottish 70s sophistication included Cafe Jacques: *Round The Back* (CBS, 1977) and *Cafe Jacques International* (CBS, 1979).) Their early line-up included Gordon Hastie, formerly of the Images, while ex-drummer Mike Ogeltree went on to Simple Minds and Fiction Factory.

Taken together, *Anthology: Nazareth* (Raw Power, 1988) and *Greatest Hits:*

Nazareth (Castle Classic, 1989), provide an adequate overview of the Dunfermline group's oeuvre. Their biggest seller, *Razamanaz*, was reissued on NEMS (1980), while two other popular selections, *Hair Of The Dog* and *Rampant* have been packaged on one CD (That's Original, 1988). And they're still around...new guitarist Billy Rankin joined McCafferty, Agnew and Sweet for *No Jive* (Mainstream, 1992).

Alex Harvey's 'lost' period is chronicled on two strange releases - *Alex Harvey Sings Songs From Hair* (Pye, 1968) and *The Joker Is Wild*. *Roman Wall Blues* (Fontana, 1969) is much less problematical, while the singer is also featured on *Rock Workshop* (CBS, 1970).

The SAHB catalogue has been mercilessly repackaged although, as we go to press, efforts are being made to rectify this. With this in mind, the following dates and labels are for original pressings - *Framed* (Vertigo, 1972), *Next* (Vertigo, 1973), *The Impossible Dream* (Vertigo, 1974), *Tomorrow Belongs To Me* (Vertigo, 1975), *Live* (Vertigo 1975), *The Penthouse Tapes* (Vertigo, 1975). These are all essential. Less so are *Stories* (Mountain, 1976) and *Rock Drill* (Mountain, 1977). *All Sensations* (Phonogram/Vertigo, 1992) is as good a compilation as any; *BBC Radio 1 In Concert* (Windsong, 1992) is a priceless glimpse of the unit's early live power, replete with Sly Stone's 'Dance To The Music'.

Of his post-SAHB work, *Alex Harvey Presents The Loch Ness Monster* (K-Tel, 1977) is priceless. *The Mafia Stole My Guitar* has been reissued (Demon, 1992) while *The Soldier On The Wall* (Rock Supply, 1983), is a querulous posthumous release.

Fourplay (Mountain, 1977) is the sole recording by SAHB (Without Alex). The four members began working together again in 1992.

Chapter 13

Punk's antecedents.

The best of Roxy Music is found on *Roxy Music* (reissued EG, 1987) and *For Your Pleasure* (reissued EG, 1983). The New York Dolls output is compiled on *New York Dolls* (Phonogram, 1977). Although *Singles: The UA Years* (Liberty, 1989) offers a wider view of the Dr. Feelgood career, *Down By The Jetty* (reissued Edsel, 1982) is their most incisive studio set.

There are two excellent Ramones' compilations - *Ramones Mania* (Sire, 1988) and *All The Stuff And More (Volume One)* (Sire, 1990). R.I.P (Danceteria, 1990) offers material by Richard Hell from all points in his career. *Blank Generation* (reissued Sire, 1990) is his definitive single statement. *Kiss This* (Virgin, 1992) meanwhile rekindles the Sex Pistols' flame.

Scotland's early pioneers - The Drive 'Jerkin'/'Push 'n' Shove' (NRG, 1977) and the Exile *Don't Tax Me* EP (Boring Records, 1977).

The Sensible label's output comprised of The Rezillos' 'Can't Stand My Baby'/'I Wanna Be Your Man' (1977) and Neon's *Bottles* EP (1978).

Zoom's early releases were as follows - 'Robot Love'/'For Adolfs Only' and 'Tarzan Of The King's Road'/'Ain't No Surf In Portobello' (the Valves, both 1977), PVC 2's 'Put You In The Picture'/'Pain'/'Deranged, Demented And Free' (1977) and the Zones 'Stuck On You'/'No Angels' (1978). The last-named group was then signed by Arista, where they competed *Under Influence* (1979). The Valves later recorded a more representative 45 - 'It Don't Mean Nothing At All'/'Linda Vindaloo' (Albion, 1979).

Other Zoom singles include 'Some Other Guy'/'Rock 'n' Roll Ain't Dead' by The Questions and 'Love Is Blind'/'Nightshift'. The former group was later adopted by Paul Weller and signed to his label. 'Price You Pay', 'Tear Soup' (Respond, 1983) and 'Tuesday Sunshine' (Respond, 1984) broached the Top 75. Nightshift resurfaced on Harvest. ('Dance In The Moonlight', 1980).

'Saints And Sinners'/'Dead Vandals' (Chiswick, 1977) was the lone 45 by Johnny And The Self Abusers. 'Gimmie Your Heart'/'Party Clothes' (Stiff One Off, 1978) marked the debut of the Subs, née Subhumans; 'Smok Walk'/'Downtown' (Housewife's Choice 1977) that of the Cuban Heels. 'Little Girl'/'Fast Living Friend' (Greville, 1980) was the latter act's follow-up. The Jolt's punk career began inauspiciously with 'You're Cold' (Polydor, 1977), but the trio found a power-pop niche with *The Jolt* (Polydor, 1978).

The Exploited - Wattie Buchan, Big John Duncan, Gary McCormick and Dru Stix - completed *Punks Not Dead* (reissued Link, 1989) and *Troops Of Tomorrow* (reissued Link, 1989). Yobbish, angry, but thankfully free of the right-wing verbiage Oi is often attached to. US hardcore owes them a considerable debt. The above line-up splintered prior to *Let's Start A War...Said Maggie One Day* (Combat, 1983). McCormick later resurfaced in Zulu Syndicate and Big John formed the Blood Uncles, while Stix, née Glen Campbell - struggling with a drug habit - took to armed robbery and was jailed for seven years. Wattie, brother Willie, Gogs and Smegs make up the group's 90s' line-up - try *Totally Exploited* (Castle, 1987) for an authoritative overview.

Can't Stand The Rezillos (Sire, 1978) and *Mission Accomplished...But The Beat Goes On* (Sire, 1979) complete the album catalogue of this kaleidoscopic act. The Skids began their career with 'Charles'/'Reasons'/'Test Tube Babies' (No Bad, 1978). 'Sweet Suburbia'/'Open Sound' (Virgin, 1978) and the *Wide Open* EP (Virgin, 1978), preceded *Scared To Dance* (Virgin, 1979).

Chapter 14

Simple Minds first three albums - *Life In A Day*, *Reel To Real Cacophony* and *Empires And Dance* - were reissued by Virgin (1982). Those wishing a précis of their content should look to *Celebration* (reissued Virgin, 1982). *Sons And Fascination/Sisters Feeling Call* have again been combined (Virgin 1987). The Euro-rock inspiring the group can be sampled on Kraftwerk's *The Mix* (EMI, 1991) and more obscurely, *Neu* (United Artists, 1972).

Days In Europa (Virgin, 1979), *The Absolute Game* (Virgin, 1980) and *Joy* (Virgin, 1981) complete the Skids' 'official' releases. *Dunfermline* (Virgin, 1987) is a composite 'best of'; *Radio 1 Live In Concert* (Windsong, 1992) captures them in full performance flow.

The career of Another Pretty Face begs a definitive package. In its absence - 'All The Boys Love Carrie'/'That's Not Enough' (New Pleasures, 1979), 'Whatever Happened To The West'/'Goodbye 1970s' (Virgin, 1980), 'Heaven Gets Closer Everyday'/'Only Heroes Live Forever' (Chicken Jazz, 1980), 'Soul To Soul'/'A Woman's Place'/'God On The Screen' (Chicken Jazz, 1981), *I'm Sorry That I Beat You, I'm Sorry That I Screamed, But For A Moment There I Really Lost Control* EP (Chicken Jazz, 1981).

These are dovetailed, in recording terms, by DNV's 'Death In Venice'/'Mafia'/'Goodbye 1970s' (New Pleasures, 1979) and 'Out Of Control'/'This Could Be Hell' (Ensign, 1982) by Funhouse.

Scott's 'new' career was fully unveiled on *The Waterboys* (Ensign, 1983). Ex-APF colleague John Caldwell later surfaced in Shame with Ally Palmer, formerly of TV21. Their *Going Down The River* EP was issued on a Canadian label, Shake The Record (1986).

The Associates showed an impudence on their debut single, 'Boys Keep Swinging'/'Mona Property Girl' (Double Hip, 1980). Their album debut, *The Affectionate Punch* (Fiction, 1980) was remixed and reissued two years later. *Fourth Drawer Down* (reissued Beggars Banquet, 1982) compiles the five experimental a-sides for Situation Two, as well as several flip-sides. *Sulk* (WEA, 1982) is the MacKenzie/Rankine's last album together. *Popera* (WEA, 1990) is drawn from this and subsequent MacKenzie-led albums.

The singer's off-duty work included 39 Lyon Street ('Kites'/'A Girl Named Property', RSO, 1981), Orbidoig ('Nocturnal Operation'/'Down Periscopes', Situation 2, 1981 and MacKenzie Sings Orbidoig ('Ice Cream Factory', Double Hip, 1982).

Chapter 15

More antecedents –

The Slits' formative ramshackle ethos is represented better on *The Peel Sessions* (Strange Fruit, 1989), or *Retrospective* (Rough Trade, 1980) rather than the more coherent *Cut* (Island, 1979), their official debut. *A Retrospective: 1977-1981* (Rough Trade, 1984) is an engrossing introduction to the Subway Sect, but this seminal group is only fitfully represented on record.

The Pop Group are heard to best effect on *Y* and the attendant, towering single, 'She Is Beyond Good And Evil' (both Radar, 1979). *For How Much Longer Do We Tolerate Mass Murder* is equally uncompromising; *We Are Time* compiles out-takes and live material (both Rough Trade, 1980). For Scottish adventurism, plus humour, try *Chou Parot* (Scotia, 1978).

The Byrds (CBS Legacy, 1990) is a boxed-set anthology of this influential act's work. Sadly, the Velvet Underground has not been afforded something as comprehensive. *The Velvet Underground And Nico*, *White Light White Heat* and *The Velvet Underground* (all reissued Verve, 1985) are essential; *1969* (Mercury, 1974) and *VU* (Verve-Polygram, 1985) only marginally less so.

The Postcard label –

Orange Juice – 'Falling And Laughing'/'Moscow Olympics, Moscow', 'Blue Boy'/'Lovesick', 'Simply Thrilled Honey'/'Breakfast Time' (all 1980), 'Poor Old Soul'/'Poor Old Soul' (1981).

Material recorded for a 1981 album, tentatively entitled *Upwards And Onwards*, was issued by a reactivated Postcard as *Ostrich Churchyard* (1992). Recorded at Glasgow's Hellfire Club by ex-Simple Minds' soundperson David Henderson, nine of its songs would surface on *You Can't Hide Your Love Forever*, one more on *Rip It Up* (both Polydor, 1982). These original, fragile versions are, however, far superior, buoyed by a tender vulnerability.

Josef K – 'Radio Drill Time'/'Crazy To Exist', 'It's Kinda Funny'/'Final Request' (both 1980), 'Sorry For Laughing'/'Revelation', 'Chance Meeting'/'Picture' and *The Only Fun In Town* (all 1981). A mixture of previously issued masters and material from the scrapped *Sorry For Laughing* were compiled on *Young And Stupid*/*Endless Soul* and the *Heaven Sent* EP (both Supreme International Editions), (1987). In 1992 former members Malcolm Ross and Davie Weddell were joined by drummer Paul Mallinen in the Magic Clan.

Go-Betweens – 'I Need Two Heads'/'Stop Before You Say It' (1980).

Related releases bookending the above include Josef K's debut ('Chance Meeting'/'Romance') (Absolute, 1979) and their final release ('The Missionary'/'The Angle'/'Second Angle') (Crepescule, 1982).

The 'Urban Development' cassette was issued on Pungent; the Fun Four single – 'Singing In The Showers'/'By Products'/'Elevator Crash' – appeared on NMC Records (1979), while the Go-Betweens' 'Lee Remick'/'Karen' was originally released by Able Records (1979).

Chapter 16

Early broadsides from Fast - the Mekons, 2.3, Human League, Gang Of Four and Scars - are compiled on *Fast Product: The First Year* (EMI, 1982). Space was sadly unavailable for the Dead Kennedys' debut - 'California Uber Alles'/'Man With The Dogs' (Fast Product, 1979).

Author! Author! (Pre, 1981) was the sole Scars album.

Earcom 1, *Earcom 2* and *Earcom 3* (Fast Product, 1978) chart the label's innovative 'magazine' project. *Earcom 1* featured the Prats ('Inverness', 'Bored' and 'Prats 2') and the Flowers ('Criminal Waste' and 'After Dark'). Joy Division and DAF are among the acts showcased on subsequent volumes.

The Prats subsequently surfaced on Rough Trade with *1990s Pop EP* (1980) and 'General Davis'/'Alliance' (1981).

The Flowers - Hillary Morrison, Simon Best (née Bloomfield), Andy Copeland and Fraser Sutherland - cut 'Confessions'/'(Life) After Dark' (Pop Aural, 1979) and 'Ballad Of Miss Demeanor'/'Food'/'Tear Along' (Pop Aural, 1980).

Restricted Code - 'From The Top'/'First Night On' and 'Love To Meet You'/'Monkey Monkey Monkey' (both Pop Aural, 1981).

Boots For Dancing recorded 'Boots For Dancing'/'Parachute'/'Girls And Guitar Trouble' (Pop Aural, 1980) and 'Rain Song'/'Hesitate' (Pop Aural, 1981), prior to forming their own label, Re-Bop-X for 'Ooh Bop Sh'bam'/'Money Is Thin On The Ground' (1982). Shake meanwhile managed the *Culture Shock* EP (Sire, 1979) and 'Invasion Of The Gamma Men'/'Night By Night' (Sire, 1980). The Job Bobnik EP, *Woah Yeah!*, is on Pop Aural (1981).

TV 21's output comprised of 'Playing With Fire'/'Shattered By It All', 'Ambition'/'Ticking Away'/'This Is Zero' (both Powbeat, 1980) and *A Thin Red Line* (Deram, 1982). The Revillos' oeuvre is captured to perfection on *Rev-Up* (Snatzo, 1980) and *Attack* (Superville, 1983). Fay Fife and sundry Revettes support William Mysterious/Alastair Donaldson on his solo 45, 'Security Of Noise'/'Alright' (Mezzanine, 1982). Several ex-Revettes joined one ex-Rezillo (Ally Patterson) in country act So You Think You're A Cowboy?

The Contortions' *Buy* (Ze, 1979) and *Off White* by James White And The Blacks (Ze, 1979) offer the ideal insight into renegade punk saxophonist James White/Chance. Portions of both albums are compiled on *Second Chance*

(Ze/PVC, 1980). Every release by the compulsive Fire Engines appears on *Fond* (Creation, 1992), although 'Big Gold Dream' is edited from the original single (Pop Aural, 1981). The set also includes two performances from a 1981 John Peel session, 'Dischord', and 'We Don't Need This Fascist Groove Thang'.

Releases on Cuba Libre - a name derived from an essay by black activist Amiri Baraka - included *Skin 'Em Up* (1981) and *Celts And Cobras* (1982) by the Shakin' Pyramids. *Work Our Way To Heaven* (1981) was the sole album by label gurus the Cuban Heels. Their previous 45 - 'Little Girl'/'Fast Living Friend' (Greville, 1980). James King's solo 45, 'Back From The Dead'/'My Reward'/'As Tears Go By' (Cuba Libre, 1981) preceded the Lone Wolves debut 'I Tried'/'So Alone' (Cuba Libre, 1981).

Metropak - 'You're A Rebel' and 'Here's Looking At You' (both Barclay Towers, 1980). Positive Noise - *Heart Of Darkness* (Statik, 1981). Another popular indie release - The Freeze *In Colour* EP (A1, 1979) which includes the then crowd-pleasing 'Paranoia'.

Chapter 17

Alan Campbell's Rational label issued, among others, 'Tous Les Soirs'/'Gaga Infectious Smile' and 'Don't Cry Your Tears'/'So It's Not To Be' (1981) by the Delmontes, and the Visitors' 'Compatibility'/'Poet's End' (1981). The latter act previously cut an EP, *Electric Heat* (Deep Cuts, 1979) and 'Empty Rooms'/'Orcadian Visitors', (Departure, 1980). Paul Haig's Rhythm Of Life completed two singles, 'Soon'/'Summertime' and 'Uncle Sam'/'Portrait Of Heart' (both Rhythm Of Life, 1981).

New Gold Dream (Virgin, 1982) is hailed by most commentators as Simple Minds' finest set. *Sparkle In The Rain* (Virgin, 1984), *Once Upon A Time* (Virgin, 1985) and *Street Fighting Years* (Virgin, 1989) each have their aficionados. *Glittering Prize* (Virgin, 1992) provides the resume of their 80s' work.

Former drummer Brian McGee reappeared on *Building Beauty* (Virgin, 1983) by Glasgow's Endgames. His replacement, Kenny Hyslop was central in two subsequent acts; Set The Tone (*Siftin' Air Affair*, Island, 1983) and the One O'Clock Gang (The One O'Clock Gang, Arista, 1985), while third drumstool occupant, Mike Ogletree, found temporary success as a member of Fiction Factory; Top 10 hit - 'Feels Like Heaven' (CBS, 1985); first album *Throw The Warped Wheel Out* (CBS, 1986). In 1992 McGee joined ex-Minds' bassist Derek Forbes in a new group, the Flys.

Fairport Convention's reading of 'She Moved Through The Fair' can be heard on *What We Did On Our Holidays* (Island, 1968).

The Crossing (Mercury, 1983) and *Steeltown* (Mercury, 1984) capture Big Country at their commercial peak. *Through A Big Country* (Mercury, 1990) is a representative sample of their work. Richard Jobson's solo albums include *The Ballad Of Etiquette* (Cocteau, 1981), *The Right Man* (Crepescule, 1986) and *16 Years Of Alcohol* (Crepescule, 1987). *Badman* (Parlophone, 1988) was a rock-oriented selection, released following the break-up of the Armoury Show - sole album *Waiting For The Floods* (Parlophone, 1985).

The Silencers - *A Letter To St. Paul* (RCA, 1987), *A Blues For Buddah* (RCA, 1989), *Dance To The Holy Man* (RCA, 1991).

Chapter 18

The Best Of Altered Images (Connisseur Collector, 1993) provides an overview of Altered Images' career. 'Love Bomb' (London, 1987) was Clare Grogan's lone solo single. The former singer opted for largely thespian ambitions when a projected album, *Trash Mad*, (1988) was shelved. She did front the short-lived Universal Love School with ex-Images guitarist Steve Lironi, whose first group completed an eponymous album; *Berlin Blondes* (EMI, 1980).

Sisters (Sire, 1984) is the only Bluebells album issued while the group was extant. *Aware Of All* (reissued Vinyl Japan, 1992) was the spin-off project by the McCluskey Brothers. The siblings regenerated their career with *Favourite Colours* (Kingfisher, 1992) while, *Second*, a follow-up Bluebells' album shelved on their collapse, has been exhumed from the vaults (Vinyl Japan, 1992). *Collection: The Lovin' Spoonful* (Castle Collector Series, 1988), is a useful introduction to a group providing an indelible influence on Robert Hodgkins.

Late-period Bluebell Neil Baldwin joined Doppelganger with Fiona Morrison ('Misty Eyed', Hollywood, 1986). The group, which also included Jason Robertson, later of Botany 5 and Witness, then took the name A Girl Called Johnny. Debut single - 'Precious (Hello It Isn't Me) (10, 1987).

Aztec Camera provided Postcard's swan-song with 'Just Like Gold'/'We Could Send Letters' and 'Mattress Of Wire'/'Lost Outside The Tunnel' (both 1981). *High Land High Rain* (Rough Trade, 1983), *Knife* (Warners, 1984), *Love* (Warners, 1987), *Stray* (Warners, 1990) show Frame's expansive, maturing talent.

Win's flawed, yet subversive, muse is caught on *...Uuh Tears Baby (A Trash Icon)* (London/Swamplands, 1987) and *Freaky Trigger* (Virgin, 1988). *Dali's Surprise* (Creation, 1992), is Russell Burn's album under the non de guerre Piefinger; Davey Henderson meanwhile forged the Nectarine Number Nine.

'The Angels Know'/'I Don't Care If You Live Or Die' (Swamplands, 1985) was the last single by James King And The Lone Wolves. Prior to this, following their exit from Cuba Libre, the group cut a 5-track 12-inch, *Texas Lullaby* (Thrush, 1983). The singer then formed Fun Patrol - 'The Right To Be Wrong' (Thrush, 1987). 'You Supply The Rose' (Swamplands, 1985) was the lone single by Orange Juice offshoot, Memphis.

The OJs themselves completed a mercurial career with *Texas Fever* and *The Orange Juice* (both Polydor, 1984). *In A Nutshell* (Polydor, 1985) was a flawed anthology; *The Esteemed Orange Juice...The Very Best Of* (Polydor, 1992) is much superior.

Edwyn Collins continues to create engrossing records. *Hope And Despair* (Demon, 1989) and *Hellbent On Compromise* (Demon, 1990) balance wit, self-deprecation and the ability to enthral. His earlier collaboration with Paul Quinn, 'Pale Blue Eyes', was released on Swamplands (1986). Quinn was a founder member of the Jazzateers (as was Graham Skinner) but when the latter quit - he later surfaced in Hipsway - the group took the name Bourgie Bourgie (*Bourgie Bourgie*, MCA, 1984). The band reclaimed their 'Jazzateers' name on Quinn's departure (*Jazzateers*, Rough Trade, 1984).

The singer was briefly associated with Assembly, a collective led by Vince Clarke, later of Erasure. The pair recorded 'One Day' (Mute, 1985). In 1992 he resurfaced on the reactivated Postcard label with *The Phantoms And The Archetypes*. Backed by the Independent Group - Bobby Bluebell, Blair Cowan, Campbell Owens, James Kirk - and produced by Edwyn Collins, Quinn sways through original songs and surprising cover versions, including Leon Russells' 'Superstar' and Jim Diamond's 'I Should Have Known Better'.

Alan Horne may yet repackage Postcard's past; he may not, but this quotable individual remains as acerbic as ever. 'I live in the Postcard encampment of Satellite City', he proclaimed in a 1992 BBC interview. 'I have no burgeoining desire to feature in next week's hit parade of hell - no intention of becoming television digestible. It's a utopian cottage industry, a virus movement, made up of the disenchanted and the disenfranchised. I'm in the business of creating my own world and within that my own value system. It may seem like so much pretentious shite to you, but it means something to me.'

Chapter 19

Something To Believe In (Red River, 1986) compiles every APB single recorded between 1981 and 1985. *Cure For The Blues* (Red River, 1986) is a cohesive introduction to their music.

The pride of Dingwall - The Tools - 'Gotta Make Some Money'/'TV Eyes' (Oily Records, 1979). Unrecorded - 'Alness' (Alness, what a mess.)

Trapped And Unwrapped (Mercury, 1984) is the sole album by Friends Again. Former vocalist Chris Thompson then founded the Bathers - *Unusual Places To Die* (Go Discs, 1987) and *Sweet Deceit* (Island, 1990). Hipsway completed two albums; *Hipsway* (Mercury, 1986) and *Scratch The Surface* (Mercury, 1989).

Love And Money's albums are as follows - *All You Need Is Love And Money* (Mercury, 1986), *Strange Kind Of Love* (Mercury, 1988), *Dogs In The Traffic* (Mercury, 1991).

Sunset Gun completed *In An Ideal World* (CBS, 1985) before splitting. Louise Rutkowski later recorded with This Mortal Coil, while Ross Campbell formed Wyoming with Shug Brankin, ex-of Sugar Sugar; (*Wyoming*, CBS, 1987). The Wake released a low-key single, 'On Our Honeymoon'/'Give Up' (Scan, 1982) before cutting two albums - *Harmony* (Factory, 1983) and *Here Comes Everybody* (Factory, 1985). The same label later scooped another Scottish act, the Wendys (*Gobbledegook*, Factory, 1991).

The Wets - *Popped In Souled Out* (Phonogram, 1987), *The Memphis Sessions* (Phonogram, 1988), *Holding Back The River* (Phonogram, 1989), *High On The Happy Side* (1991). For a glimpse of what they aspired to in working with Willie Mitchell try Al Green's *Al* (Beechwood, 1992), *The Love Chimes* Syl Johnson (Hi, 1988), *Ann Peebles' Greatest Hits* (Hi, 1990) and *The Wright Stuff*, O.V. Wright (Hi, 1987). In 1990 the group recorded *Cloak And Dagger* (Phonogram), a selection of favourite cover versions, under the pseudonym Maggie Pie And The Imposters. A low-key in concert set, *Live* (Precious), was issued the following year.

Chapter 20

Background listening -

The Stooges - *The Stooges* (Elektra, 1969) and *Fun House* (Elektra, 1970). *23 Great Recordings By Jonathan Richman And The Modern Lovers* (Essential, 1990) showcases the precocious Richman vision. 'Surfin' USA' appears on *Surfin' Safari/Surfin' USA* (repackaged Capitol, 1990). Creators the Beach Boys arguably peaked on *Today/Summer Days And Summer Nights* (repackaged Capitol, 1990) and *Pet Sounds* (reissued Capitol, 1990).

Television Personalities - 'Where's Bill Grundy Now' and 'Part Time Punks' can be found on the EP *Where's Bill Grundy Now?* (originally issued on King's Road, 1978). 'I Know Where Syd Barrett Lives' is on *And Don't The Kids Just Love It* (reissued Fire, 1990). The superb 'Someone To Spend My Life

With' first appeared on *The Painted Word* (reissued Fire, 1991).

Psychocandy (blanco y negro, 1985), *Darklands* (blanco y negro, 1987), *Automatic* (blanco y negro, 1989) and *Honey's Dead* (blanco y negro, 1992) are the original Jesus And Mary Chain albums to date. There are two fascinating, and useful, compilations; *Barbed Wire Kisses (B-sides And More)* (blanco y negro, 1988) and *Sound Of Speed* (WEA Japan, 1992).

Douglas Hart resurfaced in the Acid Angels ('Speed Speed Ecstasy', Product Inc., 1988).

Suck On The Pastels (Creation, 1988) collects material from the group's Rough Trade and Creation releases, as well as two BBC sessions. *Truck Load Of Trouble* (Paperhouse, 1993) provides an even more comprehensive overview. *Songs For Children*, meanwhile, has been repressed with two early demos; (Overground, 1990). *Up For A Bit With The Pastels* (reissued Paperhouse, 1991) and *Sittin' Pretty* (Chapter 22, 1989) are the group's original albums, while *Jad Fair And The Pastels* (Paperhouse, 1991) and *This Could Be The Night* (Paperhouse 1992) marks their collaboration with Jad Fair.

H2O debuted with 'Hollywood Dream'/'Children' (Spock, 1981) before scoring a Top 20 hit with 'Dream To Sleep' (RCA, 1983). The Laughing Apple released the following - *The Ha Ha He He EP*, 'Participate!'/'Wouldn't You' (both Autonomy, 1981) and 'Precious Feeling'/'Celebration' (Essential, 1982).

Biff Bang Pow! have completed six albums to date, plus an EP and sundry singles. The best is collected on the effective *L'Amour, Demure, Stenhousemuir - A Compilation 1984-1991* (Creation, 1991). Track 2 - 'Someone To Spend My Life With'.

Creation Soup Volumes 1-6 (Creation, 1991) cover the label's early releases, from The Legend's '73 In 83' to Blow-Up's 'When You Smile'. Missing - Jesus And Mary Chain's 'Upside Down'/'Vegetable Man' (Creation, 1984).

How Does It Feel To Feel (Edsel, 1982) is a best-of selection by 60s pop-art exponents, the Creation. It included 'Biff Bang Pow' - the group and song obviously impressed the young McGee.

Sonic Flower Groove (Elevation, 1987) is Primal Scream wrapped in LA/Paisley-patterned sequins. *Primal Scream* (Creation, 1989) crosses Alex Chilton with Iggy Pop and the Flamin' Groovies. Red Crayola's 'Hurricane Fighter Plane' is, for reference, on *Parable Of The Arable Land* (Decal, 1988).

Chapter 21

Although 'What She Calls It' and 'Sense Sickness'/'The Difference Is' (No Strings, 1983) showcases fledgling origins, *del Amitri* (Chrysalis, 1985) captures the group's winsome talent more fully. *Waking Hours* (A&M, 1989) shows their switch to traditionalism, while *Change Everything* (A&M, 1992) indicates a consummate ease with crafted rock.

Rattlesnakes (Polydor, 1984) is the most cohesive set by Lloyd Cole And The Commotions, *Mainstream* (Polydor, 1987) their final flourish. *1984-1989* (Polydor, 1989) is a worthwhile compilation.

The Wee Cherubs' singles include 'Dreaming'/'Waiting For My Man' (Bogateen, 1984). Successors the Bachelor Pad are best caught on 'Albums Of Jack' (Warholasound, 1987), the live EP *Frying Tonight* (Egg, 1988) and their sole album (so far), *Tales Of Hofmann* (Imaginary, 1989). The Suede Crocodiles were immortalised on 'Stop The Rain'/'Pleasant Dreamer' (No Strings, 1983). Ex-vocalist Kevin McDermott solo - *Suffocation Blues* (No Strings/Rough Trade, 1986); with the Kevin McDermott Orchestra - *Mother Nature's Kitchen* (Island, 1989) and *Bedazzled* (13, 1991).

A repressing of Strawberry Switchblade's debut, 'Trees And Flowers'/'Go Away' was included with early copies of the pair's sole album, *Strawberry Switchblade* (Korova, 1985). All the pair's other singles feature on this fabulous record, 'Jolene' (Korova, 1985) apart. Dolly Parton's original of the last-named song appears on *The Collection* (Castle, 1993).

'I Love This Life'/'The Second Act' (RSO, 1982) is Blue Nile's spikey - in their terms - debut. *A Walk Across The Rooftops* (Linn, 1984) and *Hats* (Linn, 1989) are as enigmatic as they were upon release. A single culled from the latter set, 'Headlights On The Parade', is backed by a haunting version of 'Easter Parade', recorded with Rickie Lee Jones. Calum Malcolm was a member of Badger ('Biding My Time', MCA, 1975) before that group evolved into the Headboys - *Headboys* (RSO, 1980).

Chapter 22

Deacon Blue - *Raintown* (CBS, 1988), *When The World Knows Your Name* (CBS, 1989), *Fellow Hoodlums* (CBS, 1991). *Ooh Las Vegas* (CBS, 1990) sweeps up various b-sides and outside projects. Joni Mitchell's 'Furry Sings The Blues' is found on *Hejira* (reissued WEA, 1987).

Hue And Cry - *Seduced And Abandoned* (Circa, 1986), *Remote* (Circa, 1988), *Bitter Suite* (Circa, 1989), *Stars Crash Down* (1990), *Truth And Love* (Fidelity, 1992).

Michael Marra - *The Midas Touch* (Polydor, 1979), *Gael's Blue* (reissued Eclectic, 1992) and *On Stolen Stationery* (Eclectic, 1991).

Big Dish - *The Swimmer* (Virgin, 1986), *Creeping Up On Jesus* (Virgin, 1988), *Satelites* (East/West, 1991).

Danny Wilson - *Meet Danny Wilson* (Virgin, 1987), *Be Bop Mop Top*

(Virgin, 1989), *Sweet Danny Wilson* (Virgin, 1990).

Having recorded 'Independence Day' for U2's Mother label, the Painted Word survived the Elektra trauma to record *Lovelife* (RCA, 1989). His Latest Flame debuted with 'Stop The Tide' (Go Discs, 1986) before completing *In The Neighbourhood* (London, 1989).

The River Detectives' first album - *Saturday Night, Sunday Morning* (WEA, 1989); their second is *Elvis Has Left The Building* (Vital, 1992). Witness recorded *House Called Love* (A&M, 1991) and the Right Stuff completed *Wa Wa* (Arista, 1990). *The Pearlfishers* is on My Dark Star (1992).

Chapter 23

'Something To Do'/'Dreaming Backwards' (Villa, 1985) is the sole release by Buba And The Shop Assistants. 'All Day Long' (Subway, 1985) captures the formative group now shorn of its prefix. 'Safety Net' appeared on 53rd & 3rd (1986), which in turn was succeeded by *Shop Assistants* (Blue Guitar, 1986). The reformed line-up issued two EPs; *Here It Comes* and *Big E Power* (Avalanche, 1990).

Motorcycle Boy completed 'Big Rock Candy Mountain' (Rough Trade, 1987), *Trying To Be Kind* (Blue Guitar, 1988) and 'You And Me Against The Wind' (Blue Guitar, 1989) before splitting.

Rote Kopelle can be heard on *Big Smelly Dinosaur* (In Tape EP, 1985), 'These Animals Are Dangerous' (In Tape, 1986) and *It Moves...But Does It Swing* (In Tape EP, 1987). Five of the songs recorded for Narodnik by Jesse Garon And The Desperadoes are collected on *Billy The Whizz* (Narodnik, 1987). The 12-track *A Cabinet Of Curiosities* (Velocity, 1988) chronicles the next stage, although three songs are remakes from the earlier period. *Nixon* (Avalanche, 1989) shows the group drawing to a close.

The Fizzbombs 'Sign On The Line'/'The Word That' (Narodnik, 1987), was followed by the *Surfin' Winter* EP (1988) which included a version of Neil Diamond's 'Cherry Cherry'. A further song, 'You Worry Me', was coupled to Jesse Garon's 'Hank Williams Is Dead' for a give-away flexi-disc. Baby Lemonade cut a solitary 45 - 'The Secret Goldfish' (Narodnik, 1986) - with Douglas Hart as producer, but their 'Postcards For Flossy' appeared on another 'zine-based floppy.

Good Feeling (53rd & 3rd, 1988) is a various artist's selection collected from within and outside the label by Stephen Pastel. *Fun While It Lasted - The Compilation* (Avalanche, 1990) provides an introduction to 53rd releases by the BMX Bandits, Boy Haidressers, Vaselines and Groovy Little Numbers, but the label deserves a more thorough reappraisal.

The Vaselines entire output has been collected on *All The Stuff And More* (Avalanche, 1992). Nirvana's versions of 'Molly's Lips' and 'Son Of A Gun' appear on *Incesticide* (Geffen, 1992).

A portion of the Soup Dragon's early work appears on the expanded US version of *Hang Ten* (Sire, 1987). *This Is Our Art* (Sire, 1988) remains hopelessly unfocused.

The Hook'n'Pull Gang are immortalised on 'Pour It Down Yer Throat'/'Gasoline' (Bitch Hog, 1987). The Blood Uncles' *Petrol* (Drastic Plastic, 1986) was followed by *Libertine* (Virgin, 1987). Goodbye Mr. Mackenzie issued 'The Rattler' (Precious Organization, 1986) and 'Face To Face' (Mack, 1987) before striking a major deal. *Good Deeds And Dirty Rags* (Capitol, 1989), *Hammer And Tongs* (EMI, 1990) and a compilation, *Fish Heads And Tails* (EMI, 1991) have ensued.

The Thanes have recorded on a multitude of labels. Try *Thanes Of Cawdor* and *Hubble Bubble* (both DDT, 1988). The Green Telescope completed two singles, 'Two By Two' (Imaginary, 1985) and 'Face In The Crowd'/'Thoughts Of A Madman' (Wump, 1986).

Blues 'N' Trouble's melange of Otis Rush, Sonny Boy Williamson and Texan guitar bands can be found to varying effect on *Blues 'N' Trouble* (Ammunition Communication, 1985), *No Minor Keys* (Ammunition Communication, 1986), *Hat Trick* (Blue Horizon, 1987), *Live* (Cacophony, 1988), *With Friends Like These* (Un-American Activities, 1989), *Down In The Suffle* (Tramp, 1991). *Poor Moon* was issued on the group's own label, Barkin' Mad (1993).

Chapter 24

The JSD Band canon is found on *Country Of The Blind* (Regal Zonophone, 1971), *The JSD Band* (Fly, 1972) and *Travelling Days* (1973). Tonight At Noon can be heard on *Tonight At Noon* (Stretch, 1988) and *Down To The Devils* (Lismore, 1988).

N'ya Fearties' album *A Tasty Heidfu* (L.Y.T. ,1986) is riotous; the entertaining, but less impish, Deaf Heights Cajun Aces are captured on *Les Frames D'Enfer* (Temple, 1987) and, as Deaf Heights, by *Set Me Free* (Re-Dem, 1991).

Hell On Earth And Rosy Cross (DDT, 1987) marks the album debut by Wee Free Kings; previous singles were compiled on the 12-inch version of 'Death Of A Wild Colonial Boy' (DDT, 1987). Their *Howl* EP appeared in 1991.

It Makes No Never Mind (DDT, 1987) and *Bone* (1990) are the albums by Swamptrash. Kith And Kin recorded *Kith And Kin* (Kith And Kin, 1991), while Hexology completed *Hexology* (Nightshift, 1991). *Mothers* (Iona, 1992) by the Humpff Family maintains Scotland's psychobilly tradition.

Mike Scott implied a Celtic wanderlust on *A Pagan Place* (Ensign, 1984) and *This Is The Sea* (Ensign, 1985), but this interest came to sonic fruition on *Fisherman's Blues* (Ensign, 1988) and *Room To Roam* (Ensign, 1990). *The Best Of The Waterboys* (Ensign, 1991) is adequate, but the singer's complex canon deserves a fuller retrospective.

This Is The Story (Chrysalis, 1987) and *Sunshine On Leith* (Chrysalis, 1988) are the Proclaimers' albums to date. A lengthy hiatus followed their *King Of The Road* EP (Chrysalis, 1990).

The twins' shared a passion for country music with the Liberties, an Edinburgh duo - Alison MacFarlane and Richie Henderson - formerly known as the Dan Blocker Experience. The Liberties cut a promising album, *Distracted* (Chrysalis, 1991), showcasing a US-style of music for which Scotland continues to boast affection.

The Cateran weren't folk - originally from Inverness, they owed a debut to US hardcore act Hüsker Dü. Singles - 'Little Circles' (DDT, 1986), 'Last Big Lie' (DDT, 1987); EP - *Black Album*; LP - *Bite Deeper* (both Imaginary, 1988). Part of the group evolved into the Joyriders.

Runrig - *Runrig Play Gaelic - The First Recordings* (reissued Lismor, 1990), *The Highland Connection* (Ridge, 1978), *Recovery* (Ridge, 1981), *Heartland* (Ridge, 1985), *The Cutter And The Clan* (reissued Chrysalis, 1988), *One In A Lifetime* (Chrysalis, 1988), *Searchlight* (Chrysalis, 1989), *The Big Wheel* (Chrysalis, 1991).

Former member Blair Douglas has completed two solo albums - *Celtology* (Red Burn Records, 1984) and *Beneath The Beret* (Macmeanmna, 1990), the latter of which was produced by Chris Harley. For a sample of the Corries try *Spotlight On The Corries* (Phillips, 1977) and *The Compact Collection* (Lismor, 1988). Both contain versions of the late Roy Williamson's anthemic composition, 'Flower Of Scotland'.

Fairport Convention's definitive English folk-rock canon is found on *Liege & Lief* (Island, 1969) and *Full House* (Island, 1970). *The History Of Fairport Convention* (Island, 1974) provides a useful overview of the group's several phases. Horslips boast a lengthy catalogue - try *The Best Of Horslips* (reissued I&B, 1989) or *Horslips' Story - Straight From The Horse's Mouth* (Homespun, 1989) for a glimpse of 70s Celtic rock from an Irish perspective. Christy Moore's folk-rock indulgences are captured on several Moving Hearts' albums, including *Moving Hearts* (WEA, 1982) and *Live Hearts* (WEA, 1984).

Several Gaelic-based acts have followed in Runrig's wake, notably Capercaillie, whose canon includes *Cascade* (SRT, 1984), *Crosswinds* (Green Linnet, 1987), *The Blood Is Strong* (Celtic Music, 1989), *Sidewaulk* (Green Linnet, 1989) and *Get Out* (1992). The Inverness-based Wolfstone can be heard on *Unleashed* (reissued Iona, 1992) and *The Chase* (Iona, 1992).

Chapter 25

Rhythm Of Life (Island, 1983) and *The Warp Of Pure Fun* (Crepescule, 1985) show a measure of Paul Haig's talent, but while the first is marred by an overbearing production, the second suffers from its piecemeal origins. Paradoxically, *European Sun Collection 1982-1987* (Crepescule, 1987) is more satisfactory, despite gathering rare singles and unissued cuts. *Chain* (Circa, 1989) is dancefloor pop, *Cinematique Volume 1* (Les Tempes Modernes, 1991) is more cerebral.

Ex-Associate and occasional collaborator Alan Rankine has completed *The World Begins To Look Her Age* (Attitude, 1986), *She Loves Me Not* (Virgin, 1987) and *The Big Picture Sucks* (Crepescule, 1989).

The Thistle (WEA, 1987) is a compromised introduction to Jesse Rae. Odyssey's 'Inside Out' appears on *Greatest Hits* (Stylus, 1987).

The Hi-Bees 'Some Indulgence', the Juggernauts' 'Come Throw Yourself Under The Monstrous Wheels Of The Rock 'n' Roll Industry As It Approached Destruction' and the Beat Freaks 'The National Anthem' provide an insight into the late-period Supreme International Editions label (all 1986). *Keep* by the Syndicate (EMI, 1989) and Botany 5's *Into The Night* (Virgin, 1991) show how two former acts have progressed. The latter group's Talking Heads' inflections were caught on their previous 45 'Bully Beef' (Supreme International Editions, 1987).

Love Is A Lie (Virgin, 1989) by the Indian Givers, *The Chimes* (CBS, 1990) and Sugar Bullet's *Unrefined* (Virgin, 1991) meanwhile offer contrasting visions of Edinburgh's 'dance' culture. Hey! Elastica's *In On The Off Beat* (Virgin, 1984) show how inchoate it once was.

'Unbend' (Demon Radge, 1987) is the declamatory debut by the Dog-Faced Hermans. Two subsequent albums, *Humans Fly* and *Every Day Timebomb* have been put together on one CD (Konkurrel, 1991). *Mental Block For All Ages* (Konkurrel, 1992) continues their enchanting melange.

Finitribe's first four years were captured on several singles, notably 'Curling And Stretching' (Finiflex, 1984) and 'Let The Tribe Grow (DeTestimony)' (Cathexis, 1986). Their spell at WaxTrax spawned a version of Can's 'I Want More' (WaxTrax, 1987), but the bulk of the group was unhappy with their experience there. Vocalist Chris Connelly begged to differ, remaining with the Chicago-based label as a member of Ministry and the Revolting Cocks. *Whiplash Boychild* (reissued Devotion, 1992) is his solo debut; *Phenobarb Bambalam* (Devotion, 1992) the follow-up.

Finitribe meanwhile completed 'Fun Noise And Lust' (Finiflex, 1988), before signing to the One Little Indian label for 'Animal Farm', *Grossing 10K* (both 1989) and *An Unexpected Groovy Treat* (1992).

Egy Bam Yasi releases include 'Circumstances' (Survival, 1986), the *Acid*

Indigestion EP (1991) and 'Highlow' (Groove Kissing, 1991). The New York Pig Funkers were immortalised on the *Hothouse* EP (Pasta, 1987).

Chapter 26

Screamadelica (Creation, 1991) is the zenith of rave rock; the subsequent *Dixie Narco* EP (Creation, 1992) shows Primal Scream taking their accumulated totems to a logical conclusion. One such influence was the 13th Floor Elevators whose first two albums, *Psychedelic Sounds* and *Easter Everywhere* have been combined on one CD (Decal, 1990). 'Reverberation' was originally on the first-named set, 'Slip Inside This House' the second. 'Sympathy For The Devil' is available on several Rolling Stones albums; notably *Beggar's Banquet* (reissued Decca, 1984) and *Singles Collection: The London Years* (London, 1989).

There have been four Shamen LPs – *Drop* (One Big Guitar, 1987), *In Gorbachev We Trust* (Demon, 1989), *En-Tact* (One Little Indian, 1990) and *Boss Drum* (One Little Indian, 1992). *Strange Day Dreams* (Moksha/Materiali Sonori, 1988) collects oddments from the group's psychedelic era. The Alone Again Or releases – 'Drum The Beat (In My Soul)' (All One, 1984) and 'Dream Come True' (Polydor, 1985) – are uncompiled.

The original 'Sweet Young Thing' is on *Meet The Monkees* (reissued Rhino, 1985). The Turtles' 'Grim Reaper Of Love' enhances *Wooden Head* (reissued Rhino, 1984). Kim Fowley's 'California Hayride', a tune used to introduce the live Primal Scream spectacular, is on *Outrageous* (Imperial, 1969).

The Soup Dragon's version of 'I'm Free' (Raw TV Products, 1989) temporarily revitalised a flagging career. *Lovegod* (Raw TV Products, 1990) and *Hotwired* (Big Life, 1992) showed them courting commercial approbation yet still failing to gain critical acceptance. The Rolling Stones' 'I'm Free' also surfaces on the above *Singles Collection*.

Chapter 27

Texas have completed two albums, *Southside* (Mercury, 1989) and *Mother Heaven* (Mercury, 1991). Ry Cooder's *Paris, Texas* is on WEA (1985). Gun's releases include *Taking On The World* (A&M, 1989) and *Gallus* (A&M, 1992). *Down So Long* (Phonogram, 1989) is the debut album by Slide.

Glasgow's GR management stable does not have a monopoly of monosyllabic names – Edinburgh's Slice spawned singer Mick Robertson, (*Bulletproof Boy*, Circa, 1991) – while having left Marillion, vocalist Fish returned to Scotland and settled on the outskirts of Haddington in East Lothian. Two albums, *Vigil In The Wilderness Of Mirrors* (EMI, 1990) and *Internal Exile* (Polydor, 1991), have ensued, and the singer now enjoys the support of ex-Pilot mainstay, Davie Paton.

Horse, fronted by its eponymous, androgynous lead singer, completed a powerful debut album, *The Same Sky* (Capitol, 1990). Group member Angel McAlinden was half of Horse's previous act, Astrakhan, which issued a flexi-single, 'And She Smiled', and a hard-disc, 'Power Of Touch'.

The first BMX Bandits album had been repackaged, with additional material, as *C86 Plus* (Vinyl Japan, 1992). Indeed, a mini-plethora of Bandito discs have surfaced of late; not only did the group's second set appear (*Star Wars*, Vinyl Japan, 1992), a mischievous mini-album, *Gordon Keen And His BMX Bandits* (Sunflower, 1992) also surfaced. It includes another TV Personalities' cover, 'Girl At The Bus Stop', Badfinger's 'Come And Get It' and the Clydesmen's 'Kylie's Got A Crush On Us'.

A Totally Groovy Live Experience (Avalanche, 1990) catches a rabblehouse BMX gig and includes a version of the Dead Kennedy's 'Nazi Punks Fuck Off'. Their relationship with Creation was launched with 'Serious Drugs' (1992), while attendant publicity announced that Eugene Kelly and Gordon Keen would no longer feature in the live line-up. Drummer Francis McDonald meanwhile founded yet another offshoot, the Radio Sweethearts. Gerry Love (Teenage Fanclub), Brian Taylor/Superstar (ex-Pastels) and John McClusker of the Battlefield Band are also members.

Note - The BMX version of 'Someone To Share My Life With' appeared on Clawfist, 1990.

Teenage Fanclub - *A Catholic Education* (Paperhouse, 1990), *The King* (Creation, 1991) and *Bandwagonesque* (Creation, 1991). Early demos, 'Primary Education' and 'Speeder', are on the flip of 'Everything Flows' (Paperhouse, 1990). The group's version of Alex Chilton's 'Free Again' was coupled to one of Beat Happening's 'Bad Seeds' (K, 1992).

The composer's original version of the former song appears on *Stuff* (New Rose, 1986), while his recordings with Big Star are currently collected as follows - *No.1 Record/Radio City* (Big Beat, 1987), *Sister Lovers* and *Big Star Live* (both Creation, 1992).

Greatest Hits Volume 1 (Creation, 1992) is Superstar's debut; the Captain America name surfaced on 'Captain America', 'Flame On' and a give-away 45 'I Won't Try' (all Paperhouse, 1992). Redubbed Eugenius, the group completed *Oomalama* (Paperhouse, 1992). For a glimpse of the Hucksters, try *Seventh Sense* (Rocket 1988).

'Futuristic Lover'/'Tomorrow's World'/'Sun Drenched Beach In Acapulco' (K, 1991) and 'Cassie'/'Movin' On Up'/'Light Shade' (Seminal Twang, 1992) are the singles, so far, by Melody Dog.

Nightshift releases include *Skinnydipping* by the Matter Babys (1990), but albums by Lowlife fill its catalogue, including *Rain* (1985), *Permanent Sleep* (1986), *Diminuendo* (1987) and *Godhead* (1989). Try *From A Scream To A Whisper - A Retrospective 1985-1989* (1991) for a representative sample.

The Beat Poets distinctive growl can be found on 'Glasgow, Howard, Missouri', (53rd & 3rd, 1987) and *Totally Radio* (53rd & 3rd, 1988). The Primevals' releases include *Sound Hole* (New Rose, 1985), *Live A Little* (New Rose, 1988) and *Neon Oven: Live At The Rex, Paris* (DDT, 1989).

The Trash Can Sinatras - *Cake* (Go Discs, 1990). Hugh Reed 'Six To Wan' (Ball, 1990), 'Walk On The Clydeside' (Ball, 1992).

One-sided and wrapped in a brown paper bag, *Bros Are Pish* (Moksha EP, 1988) introduced the Stretchheads to an unsuspecting world. *Five Fingers, Four Thingies, A Thumb, A Facelift And A New Identity* (Moksha, 1989) and *Piss In Your Sleazebag* (Blast First, 1990) continue their ferocious attack. *Barbed Anal Exciter* (Blast First, 1992) is a posthumous mini-album.

Fireblade Skies (4AD, 1991) captures Spirea X in all their dazzling glory. Sadly, the group and label have since parted company. Love's first version of 'Signed DC' appears on *Love* (reissued Edsel, 1987); an impassioned re-reading is compiled on *Out There* (Big Beat, 1988).

BIBLIOGRAPHY

Banks, Iain: *Espedair Street*; Macmillan, London, 1987.
Barnes, Richard: *Mods!*; Eel Pie; London; 1979.
Blazwick, Iwona (editor): *An Endless Adventure...An Endless Passion...And Endless Banquet - A Situationist Scrapbook*; Verso/ICA; London; 1989.
Bockris, Victor/Malanga, Gerard: *Up-Tight - The Velvet Underground Story*; Omnibus, London, 1983.
Bos, Victor: *The Race Is The Prize*; Virgin, London, 1984.
Davis, Sharon: *Motown: The History*; Guinness, London, 1988.
DiLello, Richard: *The Longest Cocktail Party*, Charisma, London, 1972.
George, Nelson: *Where Did Our Love Go - The Rise And Fall Of The Motown Sound*; St. Martin's Press, New York, 1985.
Green, Jonathan: *Days In The Life - Voices From The English Underground 1961-1971*; Heinemann, London, 1988.
Gray, Alasdair: 1982 *Janine*; Jonathan Cape, London, 1984.
Guralnick, Peter: *Sweet Soul Music - Rhythm & Blues And The Southern Dream Of Freedom*; Virgin, London, 1986.
Haynes, Jim: *Thanks For Coming!*; Faber & Faber, London, 1984.
Henderson, Hamish: *Alias MacAlias - Writings On Songs, Folk And Literature*; Polygon, Edinburgh, 1992.
Imlach, Hamish/McVicar, Ewan: *Cod Liver Oil And The Orange Juice - Reminiscences Of A Fat Folk Singer*; Mainstream, Edinburgh, 1992.
Jackson, Alan: *Salutations - Collected Poems 1960-1989*; Polygon, Edinburgh, 1990.
Kane, Patrick: *Tinsel Show - Pop, Politics And Scotland*; Polygon, Edinburgh, 1992.
Legge, Gordon: *The Shoe*, Polygon, Edinburgh, 1992.
Lulu: *Lulu: Her Biography*; Granada, London, 1985.
MacDiarmid, Hugh: *Lucky Poet - A Self Study In Literature And Political Ideas*; Methuen, London, 1943. Jonathan Cape, London, 1972.
McLuhan, Marshall/Fiore, Quentin: *The Medium Is The Message*; Bantam, New York, 1967.
McMillan, Joyce: *The Traverse Theatre Story*; Methuen Drama, London, 1988.

Mairowitz, David (editor): *Some Of It*; Knullar, London, 1969.
Miles, Barry: *Ginsberg - A Biography*; Simon And Schuster, New York, 1989.
Morgan, Ted: *Literary Outlaw - The Life And Times Of William Burroughs*; The Bodley Head, London, 1991.
Morton, Tom: *Going Home - The Runrig Story*; Mainstream, Edinburgh, 1991.
Purser, John: *Scotland's Music*; Mainstream, Edinburgh, 1991.
Robertson, John: *The Jesus And Mary Chain - A Musical Biography: Omnibus*; London, 1988.
Rogan, Johnny: *Timeless Flight - The Definitive Biography Of The Byrds*; Scorpion/Dark Star, London, 1981. Revised & Updated Edition; Square One, London, 1990.
Starmakers And Svengalis - The History Of British Pop Management; Queen Anne Press, London, 1988.
Savage, Jon: *England's Dreaming - The Sex Pistols And Punk Rock*; Faber & Faber, London, 1991.
Scott, Andrew Murray: *Alexander Trocchi - The Making Of A Monster*; Polygon, Edinburgh, 1991.
Sweeting, Adam: *Simple Minds*; Sidgwick & Jackson, London, 1988.
Thompson, Dave: *Glittering Prize*, Omnibus, London, 1986.
Trocchi, Alexander: *Young Adam*; Olympia Press, Paris, 1954. Heinemann, London, 1961.
Cain's Book; Grove Press, New York, 1961. John Calder, London, 1963.
Invisible Insurrection Of A Millions Minds - A Trocchi Reader, (ed. Andrew Murray Scott), Polygon, Edinburgh, 1991.
Wilkie, Jim: *Blue Suede Brogans*; Mainstream, Edinburgh, 1991.

Magazines and Publications

During the 60s Scotland boasted two stellar publications, *Beat News* and *242 Monthly*. These encapsulate the hopes and dreams of that generation's next-door pop.

In the 70s fanzines provided an accurate barometer of grass roots preoccupations. The best included *Ripped & Torn*, *Jungleland* and *The Next Big Thing*, the last-named of which still makes an occasional appearance.

Cut and paste publications proliferated during the 80s and if interest naturally focuses on Stephen Pastel's 'Juniper Berry Berry' and 'Pastelism' or Bobby Bluebell's 'Ten Commandments', 'Simply Thrilled', with its various flexi-discs, best captures Scotland's indie aspirations; *Tear It Up* contains early etchings by future *Glasgow Herald* columnist David Belcher and writer/producer/broadcaster Stuart Cosgrove.

Cut and *TLN* meanwhile took a mainstream overview and if both shed a Scotland-only editorial, early issues chronicle the commercially fertile mid-to-late 80s. The latter survives amid the less certain early 90s, although INXS are as likely to be cover stars as Eugenius.

INDEX

Adams, Derroll, 95
Adamson, Stuart, 7, 164, 203, 239, 323, 327
Agnew, Pete, 31, 49-50, 116, 142
Alex Harvey Soul Band, 23, 25, 27-28, 114, 372
Alone Again Or, 345, 397
Alp Records, 58
Altered Images, 231, 243-246, 250, 258, 388, 406
Angus, Colin, 345
Another Pretty Face, 203-206, 320, 384, 406
APB, 256, 390
Apple Records, 89, 90, 111, 124, 272, 273, 335, 376, 391
Apples, 335
Armoury Show, 241, 388
Arrows, 74
Associates, 166, 206-208, 235, 336, 340, 384
Athenians, 32, 36, 135, 373
Avalanche Records, 318
Avengers, 36, 373
Average White Band, 119-120, 122-123, 136, 256, 263, 265, 297, 329, 379, 406
Aztec Camera, 219, 228, 230-231, 246, 249, 251-252, 258, 286, 332, 365, 388
Baby Lemonade, 317, 393
Bachelor Pad, 286, 392
Backstabbers, 212
Bain, Jimmy, 66
Barber, Chris, 17
Barclay Towers, 226, 232, 256, 387
Barky! Barky, 370
Barnes, Ricky, 16-17, 19-21, 25-26, 27-28, 105, 131, 401

Barrett, Syd, 270, 272, 274-275, 391
Barrowlands Ballroom, 87, 237
Barry, Jeff, 140, 381
Bathers, 258, 301, 334, 390
Bay City Rollers, 131-133, 380
Beach Boys, 33, 276, 281, 352, 361, 390
Beachcombers, 65, 136
Beat Freaks, 333, 396
Beat Happening, 311, 398
Beat News, 37, 42, 44, 51, 78, 403
Beat Poets, 312, 364, 399
Beatles, 8, 11, 27, 31, 36, 39, 41, 49-50, 52, 55, 60, 62, 67-68, 77, 79, 89, 107, 109, 123, 138, 204, 224, 264, 318, 321, 323
Beatstalkers, 75-80, 84-85, 90, 102, 124, 375
Beattie, Jim, 273, 277, 366
Beck, Jeff, 144
Beggars Opera, 103, 377
Behan, Dominic, 249
Bell, Freddie, And The Bell Boys, 21, 145
Bell, Maggie, 104, 137, 142, 381
Bell, Robert, 290, 292-293, 326
Berlin Blondes, 245, 388
Berns, Bert, 42
Berserk Crocodiles, 119
Best, Simon, 224, 386
Biff Bang Pow!, 273, 391
Big Country, 240-243, 323, 327, 388
Big Dish, 301, 393
Big Star, 279, 287, 358, 360, 398
Bilbo Baggins, 136, 380
Black, Clint, 140
Blake, Norman, 305, 309, 357-358
Blood Uncles, 316, 383, 394

Blue Nile, 290-295, 326, 333, 392
Blue Workshop, 117
Bluebell, Bobby, 246, 389, 403
Bluebells, 231, 243, 246-250, 283-284, 311, 369, 388
Blues 'n' Trouble, 394
Blues Council, 46, 52, 131, 374
BMX Bandits, 305-309, 357, 360-361, 364, 369, 394, 398
Bo Weevils, 103
Bond, Isabel, 27, 87, 104
Bonici, Albert, 11, 50, 60, 102
Boots For Dancing, 225, 228, 386
Boston Dexters, 33-35, 50, 64-66, 80, 131, 372
Botany 5, 333, 335, 388, 396, 500
Bourgie Bourgie, 254, 353, 389
Bovell, Dennis, 209, 251
Bowie, David, 85, 206-207
Boy Hairdressers, 309
Boyd, Joe, 95, 99, 130, 377
Boyle, Mark, 63
Bread, Love And Dreams, 124, 379
Brinsley Schwarz, 138
Brown, James, 53, 225, 256, 334
Bruce's Record Shop, 72
Buba and the Shop Assistants, 303, 393
Buchanan, Paul, 290, 292, 293, 406
Bungalow Bar, 159, 217, 228, 230, 246, 273
Bungys, 32-33, 52, 66, 72
Burchill, Charlie, 159, 202, 235
Burn, Russell, 223, 253, 255, 388
Burroughs, William, 62, 402
Buzz, 65, 71, 95, 113, 300, 316, 366, 374
Buzzcocks, 211, 220, 222, 268, 308
Byrds, 68, 112, 211, 228, 248, 272, 276, 285, 309, 366, 369, 385, 402
Byron, Sol, 75, 113, 375
Ca Va Studios, 265, 335, 377
Cado Belle, 143, 381
Cafe Jacques, 381
Cafe Vaudeville, 283, 285
Caldwell, John, 203-204, 384
Callis, Jo, 156, 218, 224, 227
Campbell, Allan, 84, 232, 331-333
Campbell, Junior, 39, 81, 107, 118, 378
Capercaillie, 370, 396
Captain America, 362, 399

Carter, John, 33
Cartoone, 137, 381
Castle Sound Studios, 214, 227, 292, 326
Casuals, 284
Cateran, 322, 395
Charles, Ray, 23, 33-35, 46, 71, 104, 139, 373
Cherry, Tommy, 286
Chicken Jazz, 206, 384
Chilton, Alex, 279, 391, 398
Chimes, 277, 334-335, 339, 390, 396
Chiswick Records, 160, 164, 383
Chou Pahrot, 209, 365
City Lynx, 232
Clan Balls, 57-58
Clark, Gary, 300
Clash, 155, 211, 230, 248, 261, 283, 313, 320, 362
Cleminson, Zal, 103, 144, 149
Clinton, George, 330
Clive's Incredible Folk Club, 93
Clouds, 109, 111, 143, 160, 164, 377
Clyde Valley Jazz Band, 20
Clyde Valley Stompers, 16, 30, 371
Cobain, Kurt, 311, 362
Cocteau Twins, 361
Cody, 108, 142, 378
Cole, Lloyd, and the Commotions, 284, 289, 392
Collins, Edwyn, 211, 216, 222, 230, 246, 252, 254, 389
Colyer, Ken, 17
Connelly, Chris, 341, 396
Connelly, Eddie, 278, 313-314
Connolly, Billy, 125
Contortions, 386
Cordell, Denny, 78
Costello, Elvis, 248, 251
Coutts, Donnie, 49-50, 52, 54, 114
Cramps, 160, 227, 279, 365
Creation Records, 7, 370
Critterhill Varmints, 321
Cuba Libre, 232, 253, 387, 389
Cuban Heels, 161, 232, 272, 290, 383, 387
Cunningham, Tom, 261, 264-265
Curry, Justin, 283, 286
DAF, 201, 221, 386
Daly, Stephen, 212, 230, 232, 253, 270, 288,

336
Danny Wilson, 300, 393
Davis, Elliot, 261, 266, 368
Deacon Blue, 8, 295-297, 300-301, 392
Dead Kennedys, 386
Deaf Heights Cajun Aces, 319, 394
Dean, James, 14, 32
Deep Purple, 54, 103, 140
del Amitri, 283-287, 289-290, 295, 302, 392
Del-Jacks, 45-46, 75
Delmontes, 222, 233-235, 340, 387, 406
Dennis, Jackie, 18, 22, 134, 372
Dennistoun Palais, 75, 77, 87, 104
Denver, Karl, 19, 22, 371
Destroy All Men, 227
Dewar, Jimmy, 41, 75, 104, 138, 142, 381
Dickson, Barbara, 124, 298, 379
Dickson, Sean, 306, 308, 353
Dirty Reds, 223
DNV, 203-204, 206, 384
Dog-Faced Hermans, 341, 396
Donegan, Lonnie, 7, 15, 17-18, 46, 92, 125, 369, 371, 406
Donovan, 7, 95-99, 376
Doris, Jimmy, 105, 139
Douglas, Blair, 323, 325, 395
Dowd, Tom, 260-261
Doyle, Jill, 92
Dr. Feelgood, 158, 326, 382
Dream Police, 115, 117-119, 123, 379
Drive, 80, 90, 158, 382
Duncan, John, 162, 316, 383
Dundee Horns, 117, 142, 379
Dylan, Bob, 91-92, 204, 249, 273
Earcom, 220-221, 386
Easybeats, 58, 111, 378
Egan, Joe, 125-126, 380
Ege Bam Yasi, 341
Eire Apparent, 139
Elevation Records, 278-280, 391
Elliott, Ramblin' Jack, 91, 95, 376
Endgames, 235, 387
Epstein, Brian, 50, 67, 101, 131
Erickson, Roky, 352
Eugenius, 362, 399, 403
Exile, 61, 63, 95, 158, 325, 383, 398
Exploited, 162, 212, 220, 311, 383
Fair, Jad, 362, 391

Fairport Convention, 129, 238, 324, 387, 395
Farina, Richard, 62
Fast Forward, 305, 314, 361
Fast Product, 218, 221, 386
Fehilly, Bill, 117, 143, 146, 151
Fiction Factory, 381, 387
Fife, Fay, 156, 163, 386
Fifth Column, 125
53rd & 3rd, 305-306, 309, 311-313, 370, 393-394, 399
Findlay, Bruce, 32, 66, 72, 160-161, 239, 357, 370
Fingerprintz, 239
Finitribe, 340-342, 396-397, 406
Fire Engines, 222-224, 229, 235, 254-256, 278, 335, 369, 386
Fish, 296, 394, 398
Five Hand Reel, 129, 380
Fizzbombs, 314, 393
Fleming, Don, 358
Flowers, 18, 129, 221-223, 225, 273, 288, 306, 311, 386, 392
Ford, Dean, and the Gaylords, 32, 39, 45, 81, 124, 373
Forevermore, 117, 119, 248, 379
Foster, Joe, 275
Frame, Roddy, 219, 228, 251, 258, 288, 406
Frank, Jackson C., 99, 377
Frankie and Johnny, 104, 378
Freeze, 387
Friends Again, 257-260, 286, 356, 390
Fun Four, 212-213, 385
Funhouse, 206, 384
Gallagher, Benny, 45, 124, 128
Gallagher, George, 26, 31, 42, 45, 50, 75, 81, 86-87, 89, 375, 406
Gallagher and Lyle, 124-125, 128
Gang Of Four, 220, 283, 386
Garon, Jesse, And The Desperados, 313-314, 317-318, 329, 393
Gateway Exchange, 233
Gaughan, Dick, 129, 380
Giant Moth, 88
Gillespie, Bobby, 272-273, 276-278, 343, 352-353, 360, 368
Glen, Chris, 103, 149
Go-Betweens, 216, 272, 286, 385

Golden Crusaders, 40, 114, 373
Goodbye Mr. MacKenzie, 316, 394
Gorrie, Alan, 7, 53, 113, 115, 117, 119-120, 123
Graham, Davey, 92, 97, 376
Grant, James, 256, 260, 264, 267, 336
Grapefruit, 111, 378
Green, Al, 261-262, 283, 378, 390
Green Telescope, 314, 394
Grimes, Jimmy, 28, 30
Grogan, Claire, 243, 253, 336
Groovy Little Numbers, 306, 309, 394
Gun, 260, 262, 282-285, 311-312, 357, 366, 390, 394, 398
Guthrie, Woody, 30, 91, 93, 97, 124, 249, 376
H2O, 272, 391
Haig, Paul, 212, 216, 227, 233, 329, 336, 339, 387, 396
Hair, 14, 19, 75, 88, 140, 143, 146, 155, 164, 265, 382
Haley, Bill, 14, 16, 17, 21, 371
Half Japanese, 318, 362
Hart, Douglas, 274, 278, 314, 391, 393
Harvey, Alex, 7-8, 19-21, 23, 25-28, 41, 46, 74-75, 90, 114, 131, 138, 145-147, 150-152, 161, 346, 364, 369, 372, 376, 382, 406
Harvey, Leslie, 30, 46, 87, 93, 104, 143
Hastie, Gordon, 36, 381
Haynes, Jim, 62, 72, 92, 401
Headboys, 292, 392
Hearts And Minds, 301
Hell, Richard, 155, 223, 382
Helsing, Lenny, 313, 318
Henderson, Davey, 222, 224, 253, 388
Henderson, Hamish, 91, 249, 401
Henry, Stuart, 55
Heron, Mike, 92-93, 99, 130, 377
Hexology, 321, 395
Hey! Elastica, 335, 396
Hi-Bees, 332, 396
Hi-Fis, 60
Hipple People, 36, 131
Hipsway, 258-260, 334, 389-390
His Latest Flame, 287, 393
Hook 'n' Pull Gang, 317, 394
Hopscotch, 115-117, 379
Horne, Alan, 7, 211, 218, 222-223, 227, 243, 246, 248, 252, 369, 389
Horse, 362, 395, 398
Horsley, Sebastian, 233
Horslips, 326, 395
House Of Lords, 111, 378
Houston, Cisco, 91, 93
Hudson, Johnny, 49, 52
Hue And Cry, 297-300, 392
Human Beast, 73, 375
Human League, 220-221, 226, 386
Humblebums, 125, 379
Humpff Family, 395
Images, 36, 50, 98, 138, 231, 240, 243-246, 250, 258, 282, 289, 293, 370, 377, 381, 388, 406
Imlach, Hamish, 92-93, 376, 401
Incredible String Band, 88, 93-95, 99-100, 124, 129, 377, 406
Indian Givers, 333-334, 396
Innes, Andrew, 271-274, 279
Isley Brothers, 23, 52, 68, 120, 372, 374
Jackson, Alan, 72, 209, 401
Jansch, Bert, 8, 92, 95-97, 99, 124, 376
Jasmine Minks, 273
Jazzateers, 254, 258, 389
Jesus And Mary Chain, 268, 274-276, 303, 312, 314, 346, 354-355, 369, 391, 402
Jobson, Ricky, 164
Johnny and the Self Abusers, 159, 211, 383
Johnson, Calvin, 311, 362
Jolt, 158, 160, 383
Jones, Rickie Lee, 293, 392
Johnny And The Copycats, 60, 111, 374, 406
Josef K, 212-214, 216, 223, 227-228, 231-233, 235, 252, 335-336, 385, 406
Joyriders, 370, 395
JSD Band, 319, 394
Juggernauts, 333, 396
Jungleland, 158, 203, 403
Juniper Berry Berry, 311, 403
Jury, 67-68, 131, 246
Kane, Pat, 297-298, 336, 338
Kansas City Counts, 20-21, 23
Kansas City Skiffle Group, 20
Katz, Gary, 264
Keegan, David, 303, 313-314, 364
Keen, Gordon, 309, 357, 362, 398

Kelly, Eugene, 311-312, 361-362, 398
Kerr, Bobby, 30, 104
Kerr, Gordon, 333
Kerr, Jim, 7, 159, 199, 202, 237, 240, 406
Kidd, Johnny, 4, 23, 372
King, Bobby, 221-222
King, James, 252-253, 389
Kingman, Joe, 320
Kinning Park Ramblers, 30, 104
Kirk, James, 211, 253, 389
Kith And Kin, 321, 395
Kutner, Beverley, 99
La Cave, 24, 26, 138
Laula, Carol, 370
Last, Bob, 7, 218, 222-223, 232, 253, 305, 333
Laughing Apple, 271-273, 391
Les Cousins, 95-96, 98
Les Disques De Crepescule, 228, 241, 339-340, 388, 396
Lewis, Ken, 33
Liberties, 395
Ligertwood, Alex, 75, 113, 122
Linder, 220
Locke, James, 224, 233, 333-336
Lomax, Alan, 91
Lord Rockingham's Eleven, 22, 372
Loser, Jimmy, 159-160, 212
Lost Soul Band, 370
Lothian, Andy, 30, 50, 52, 57-58, 102
Love And Money, 260-261, 264, 266, 301, 335, 356, 390
Lovin' Spoonful, 68, 249, 388
Low, Nick, 274, 284
Lowlife, 361, 370, 399
Lulu, 40-43, 45, 61, 105-106, 124, 137, 139, 142, 345, 373, 378, 401
Luvvers, 40-42, 124, 374
Lyall, Billy, 132, 135, 380
MacColl, Ewan, 91, 93, 97, 376
MacDonald, Calum, 323, 325-328
MacDonald, Francis, 364
MacLean, Norrie, 115
Mair, Alan, 75, 84, 151, 204
Malcolm, Calum, 292, 392
Manyika, Zeke, 231, 333
Mark Five, 52, 58, 78, 116, 374
Marmalade, 82-84, 86, 88, 106-109, 111, 113, 118, 377-378, 406
Marra, Michael, 298, 300, 392
Martin, Bill, 35, 79, 107, 133, 136
Martin, Dougie, 52, 54, 60
Martyn, John, 4, 8, 93, 98, 263, 319, 376
McAlinden, Joe, 306, 309, 360-361
McCafferty, Dan, 52, 116, 140
McClure, Chris, 323, 375
McCluskeys, 249
McDermott, Kevin, 287, 392
McElhone, Gerry, 246
McElhone, Johnny, 243, 258, 356, 406
McGee, Alan, 7, 271, 278-279, 317, 343, 360-361
McGinnis, John, 46, 75, 142
McGowan, George, 16-17, 22-23, 28, 30
McGuinness Flint, 124
McIntosh, Robbie, 117, 119
McKee, Frances, 306, 311
McKenna, Hugh, 149
McKenna, Ted, 118, 143, 149, 151
McKenzie, Billy, 339
McKeown, Les, 133-134, 380
McKinleys, 33, 372-373
McLaughlin, Jack, 56-57
McLean, Sandy, 305, 406
McLuhan, Marshall, 220, 401
Meat Whiplash, 278, 313-314
Meehan, Tony (DJ), 53, 56-58
Meehan, Tony (Shadows), 88-89
Mekons, 218, 220, 386
Melody Dog, 362, 399
Meridians, 32, 76, 86
Metcalfe, Martin, 316
Metropak, 232-233, 387
Middle Earth (club), 70, 72, 99
Middle Earth (label), 70-71, 375
Middle Of The Road, 134, 324, 380
Milarky, John, 159, 161, 232
Miller, Davy, 341-342
Miller, Frankie, 45, 75-76, 105, 138-139, 263, 369, 381
Miller, Jimmy, 353
Mimms, Garnet, 42, 52, 67, 114, 379
Misfits, 60, 374
Mitchell, Joni, 140, 296, 392
Mitchell, Willie, 262, 390
Mogul Thrash, 119, 379

Moksha, 346, 365, 397, 399
Moonrakers, 38, 65, 136
Moore, Paul Joseph, 290
Morley, Paul, 213, 223, 228, 253, 270
Morrison, Hillary, 218, 222-224, 253, 386
Motorcycle Boy, 313, 317, 393
Mr. Smiths, 66-67
Mulvey, Andi, 81, 103
Munroe, Donnie, 324
My Dear Watson, 111-112, 378, 406
Mysterious, William, 156, 162, 204, 227, 386
N'Ya Fearties, 319, 394
Narodnik, 314, 317, 393
Naturals, 318, 370
Nazareth, 31, 116-118, 140-142, 145, 151, 290, 381
New York Pig Funkers, 341, 397
Next Big Thing, 159, 403
Nicholson, Hughie, 108, 115, 144, 378
Nightshift (group), 161, 383, 399
Nightshift (label), 361, 370, 394
Nirvana, 311, 362, 394
Nixon, Malcolm, 30, 88
No Strings, 284-285, 287, 392
Noakes, Rab, 124, 126, 128-129, 295, 298, 301, 379
Norco Records, 60, 373
NSU, 111, 377
Nu-Sonics, 21
O'Rahilly, Ronan, 55
Oakley, Jimmy, 115
Odyssey, 330, 396
Oldham, Andrew Loog, 42, 103, 273
One O'Clock Gang, 387
1-2-3, 67, 70, 73, 109, 334
Orange Juice, 210-214, 216-217, 223, 228, 230-231, 243, 246, 250-253, 255-257, 270, 276, 283, 288, 290, 332, 336, 369, 385, 389, 401
Orbidoig, 207, 384
Osborne, John, 14
Painted Word, 301, 391, 393
Palmer, Clive, 92
Pastel, Stephen, 268, 270, 274, 276, 303, 305-306, 311-312, 336, 358, 362, 364, 394, 403, 406
Pastelism, 311, 403
Pastels, 233, 268-270, 273, 276, 279, 283, 303, 305, 310-312, 358, 362, 364, 369, 391, 406
Paterson, Bill, 19-20
Pathfinders, 86-90, 103, 107-108, 124, 323, 375, 406
Paton, Davie, 132, 135, 398
Paton, Tam, 131, 380
Patrick, Bill, 16, 18, 25, 46, 87, 151
Patrick, Bobby, 25-26, 104, 372
Patterson, Linnie, 9, 32, 66-68, 103
Pearlfishers, 301, 393
Peden, Mike, 333-334, 336
Pellow, Marti, 261
Pentangle, 97
Perspex White Out, 370
Phil and the Flintstones, 60, 374
Pilot, 135, 380
Planet Pop, 227
Plastic Meringue, 68
Poets, 26, 31, 38, 42-43, 45, 50, 74-75, 77, 80-81, 85-88, 90, 108, 124, 144, 312, 364, 373, 375, 399, 406
Poor Souls, 52-54, 60-61, 131, 374
Pop Aural, 221-222, 224, 232, 235, 292, 386-387
Pop Group, 35, 105, 124, 135, 209, 212, 251, 341, 381, 385
Pop Gun, 283-285
Positive Noise, 232, 387
Postcard Records, 212, 228
Prats, 221, 386
Precious Organization, 263, 394
Premiers, 32, 67
Presley, Elvis, 7, 14, 32, 67
Pretty Flowers, 306
Prima, Louis, 16, 25, 371
Primal Scream, 273-274, 276-280, 343-345, 352-354, 357, 364, 366, 368, 391, 397, 406
Primevals, 364, 399
Primitives, 114, 379
Proclaimers, 233, 321-323, 369, 395
Pure Popcorn, 308, 315
PVC 2, 383
Questions, 8, 14, 161, 383
Quinn, Paul, 254, 353, 389
Quintones, 75, 86
Radio Caroline, 55
Radio Scotland, 55-58, 78, 374

Rae, Jesse, 329, 338-339, 341, 369, 396
Rafferty, Gerry, 8, 125, 127, 322, 379-380
Rafferty, Tom, 364
Ramones, 159, 162, 261, 268, 305, 312-313, 316, 318, 382
Rankine, Alan, 206, 208, 339-340, 396
Rational Records, 233
Red Hawkes, 52, 58, 116, 374
Reed, Hugh, 364, 399
Reid, Charlie, 321
Reid, Craig, 321-323
Reid, Trisha, 287, 290
Reid, William, 7, 268, 275, 278
Renbourn, John, 97
Restricted Code, 386
Revillos, 226-227, 386
Revolving Paint Dream, 273
Reynolds, Eugene, 7, 156, 160, 227
Rezillos, 156-158, 160, 162-164, 218, 222, 224, 226, 228, 335, 383
Richard, Cliff, 22, 248, 369
Richman, Jonathan, 305, 390
Right Stuff, 302, 393
Ripped And Torn, 158, 403
River Detectives, 301, 393
Rock Workshop, 143, 382
Rockatomic, 227
Rodeo, 297
Rodgers, Jimmie, 18, 30
Rolling Stones, 8, 28, 42, 76, 119, 143, 155, 226, 268, 312, 345, 352-353, 357, 397
Rooney, Micky, 364
Ross, Malcolm, 212, 214, 230-231, 252, 332, 385
Rote Kapelle, 303, 313-314
Rough Trade, 214, 216, 218, 231, 233, 261, 270-271, 287, 361, 370, 385-386, 388-389, 391-393
Roxy Music, 158, 161, 382
Runrig, 323-328, 369-370, 395, 402
Rutkowski, Louise, 366, 390
Sabres, 32, 74, 76, 85
Scaffold, 63, 209
Scars, 221-222, 225, 233, 386, 406
Scots Of St. James, 113, 115-116, 379
Scott, Mike, 203, 320-321, 395
Scott, Tommy, 35, 79, 88
Secret Goldfish, 317, 393

Senate, 74-75, 113-114, 329, 379
Sensational Alex Harvey Band, 145-147, 346, 406
Sensible Records, 158, 160, 383
Set The Tone, 130, 387
Sex Pistols, 155, 158-159, 286, 381-382, 402
Shadettes, 31, 50-52, 61, 116, 142
Shake, 26, 224, 372, 384, 386
Shakin' Pyramids, 232, 387
Shame, 111, 281, 378, 384
Shamen, 345-352, 365, 369, 397
Sheridan, Tony, 27, 111, 372
Sherwood, Adrian, 339
Shields, Tommy T.V., 55
Shop Assistants, 303-305, 308, 313-314, 318, 329, 393
Showbeat Monthly, 56, 75
Silencers, 241, 388
Simon, Paul, 60, 98
Simple Minds, 66, 161-162, 199-203, 233, 235-239, 241, 243, 258, 287-288, 290, 357, 369, 381, 384, 387, 402
Sinott, Will, 346-347, 351
Siouxsie and the Banshees, 221, 243
Situationists, 64, 220
Skeets Boliver, 298
Skids, 164-166, 202-203, 235, 240-241, 383-384
Skin, 73, 165, 224, 232, 258-259, 281, 285, 346, 387
Slice, 105, 279, 398
Slik, 136, 161, 380
Slits, 155, 209, 211, 222, 385
Smarties, Wilf, 223, 256, 316, 345
Societie, 111, 378
Sock 'Em J.B., 75
Soft Machine, 64, 84
Soma, 370
Sonic Youth, 279, 312, 358
Sophisticated Boom Boom, 283, 287
Soup Dragons, 308-309, 315, 353-354
Spirea X, 366, 368, 399, 414
Splash One, 279, 303, 306
Stampede, 297
Stand And Deliver, 283
Stax, 23, 50, 54, 66, 86, 103, 120, 211-212, 372
Stealer's Wheel, 126, 128, 406

Steele, Tommy, 21-22, 371
Stewart, Al, 98, 377
Stewart, Duglas, 305, 357, 360, 364
Stiff Records, 297
Stoics, 105-106, 139, 378
Stone The Crows, 138, 142, 381
Stooges, 275, 280, 320, 353, 390
Strawberry Switchblade (fanzine), 212
Strawberry Switchblade (group), 288, 311, 392
Stretchheads, 365, 399, 406
Stuart, Hamish, 115, 117, 119, 123
Studio Six, 88, 376
Sub Club, 260
Subs (Subhumans), 160, 383
Subway Sect, 209, 211, 222, 385
Suede Crocodiles, 285, 392
Sugar Bullet, 335-336, 396
Suicide, 134, 143, 148, 282, 339, 381
Sunset Gun, 262, 366, 390
Superstar, 270, 283, 361, 363-364, 389, 398-399, 406
Superstar, Brian, 270, 283, 364, 398
Supreme International Editions, 331-332, 336, 385, 396
Swamptrash, 321, 395
Syndicate, 53, 332, 383, 396
Talkovers, 222
Tamla Motown, 23, 50, 66, 79, 85-86, 103, 116, 120, 122
Taylor, Alex, 303, 313
Tear Gas, 103, 119, 143-145, 166, 377
Teenage Fanclub, 4, 358-360, 362, 398, 406
Television, 22, 26, 41, 55, 98, 140, 155, 162, 202, 241, 270-271, 285, 300, 325, 338, 346, 366, 375, 378, 381, 389, 391
Television Personalities, 270-271, 391
Ten Commandments, 246, 403
Texas, 251, 253, 356-357, 389, 398
Thanes, 313-314, 318, 394
The Burns Howff, 105, 117, 137, 144
The Combination, 72-73, 85, 93, 113, 139, 143, 145-146, 202, 233, 237, 331, 351
The Crown Bar, 92
The Doune Castle, 159, 257
The Flamingo, 28, 42, 74, 87, 375
The Fringe, 62, 284, 297
The Gamp, 32, 50, 66, 72
The Howff Club, 92
The Living Room, 272, 275, 317
The Paperback, 62-63, 92
The Picasso, 86
The Place, 21, 32-35, 50-51, 55, 66, 70, 72, 81, 119, 136-137, 165-166, 224, 235, 272, 279, 296, 305, 311, 319, 322, 339, 357, 369
The Pontiac, 35
The Scene Club, 46, 75
The Scotch Hoose, 95
The Traverse, 63, 218, 401
The Troubador, 93
13th Floor Elevators, 223, 230, 352, 397
39 Lyon Street, 207-208, 384
Thompson, Chris, 257, 301, 390
Thompson, Mayo, 279, 313
Three's A Crowd, 66-67, 73, 111
TLN, 8, 252, 287, 289, 300-301, 320, 334-336, 338, 341-342, 361, 403
Tobin, Eddie, 102, 119, 135, 144, 146, 151
Tonight At Noon, 319, 394
Tools, 256, 390
Top Storey, 50, 65, 72, 132
Top Ten Club (Dundee), 52, 58
Top Ten Club (Hamburg), 26-27
Toussaint, Allen, 263
Trash, 89-90, 108, 134, 155, 226, 254, 353, 365, 376, 388, 399
Trash Can Sinatras, 365, 399
Travers, Harry, 257-258
Travis, Geoff, 214, 218, 261, 271, 316
Treacy, Dan, 270, 272, 306
Trocchi, Alexander, 402
Troutman, Roger, 332
Trower, Robin, 138, 381
Tully, Andrew, 303, 313-314, 317-318
Tulsans, 124, 379
TV 21, 226, 386
TV Art, 212
U2, 241, 287, 301, 334, 393
Urban Development, 230, 385
Ure, Midge, 136, 161, 297, 381
Valves, 161, 163, 233, 383
Vaselines, 308-309, 311-313, 362, 394
Velvet Underground, 159, 211, 216, 275, 285, 312, 320, 369, 385, 401
Vick, John, 341
Vikings, 53-54, 60-61, 113-115, 117, 374

Visitors, 233, 238, 387
Waldman, Brian, 34, 70
Waldman, Paul, 32
Waterboys, 206, 295, 320-321, 384, 395
Watson, Fraser, 74, 80, 85-86, 88, 119
Waverley Records, 32, 35-36, 60, 373
Weatherall, Andy, 343, 370
Wee Cherubs, 285-286, 392
Wee Free Kings, 320, 394
Wet Wet Wet, 8, 117, 261-263, 265-266, 283, 335, 369
Wexler, Jerry, 105, 120, 142
White, James, 223, 386
White, Tam, 33, 65, 71, 375

White Riot Tour, 211, 222
White Trash, 89-90, 108, 376
Williamson, Robin, 92, 377
Wilson, Dennis, 353
Win, 57, 253-255, 258, 316, 329, 335, 388
Witness, 54, 259, 335, 388, 393
Wolfstone, 370, 396
Worrell, Bernie, 329-330, 332
Writing On The Wall, 9, 68-70, 72, 375
Zappa, Frank, 101
Zones, 161, 202-203, 235, 383
Zoom Records, 160-162, 199, 201, 204, 206, 330, 383

Photographic Acknowledgements

Pictorial Press Ltd: pages 15, 94, 100, 106, 118, 122, 128, 147, 172, 173, 177, 178, 179, 180, 181 bottom, 184 top, 188, 189, 192, 193, 198. Christopher Patrick O'Dell: page 81. Donald Milne: page 87. Lynda Morrison: page 176. Carl Heidiken: page 182 bottom. Harry Popadopoulos: page 182 top. Terry Lott: pages 184 bottom, 244. A&M Records pages 187 top, 284. Alistair Indge: pages 190 bottom, 308. Lawrie Evans: page 205. Robert Sharp: page 213. Kevin Low: page 219. Hilary Morrison: page 225. Robin Gillanders: page 234. Jacki Morton: pages 237, 291. Karen Parker: page 269. Peter Ross: page 340. Kevin Westenberg: page 344. Andy Catlin: page 355. Steve Gullick: page 359. Stefan Karra: page 363. Bleddyn Butcher: page 365. Schoerner: page 367.

Additional Material courtesy of:
Johnny Stewart (Johnny And the Copycats, My Dear Watson etc), Johnny McElhone (Altered Images), George Gallagher, Sandy McLean, Stewart Cruickshank, Harry Papadopoulos, Stephen Pastel (Pastels) and Alex Ogg.

All other material supplied by Brian Hogg